ENGENDERING THE STAGE
IN THE AGE OF SHAKESPEARE AND BEYOND

Engendering the Stage in the Age of Shakespeare and Beyond

EDITED BY
PETER COCKETT AND MELINDA GOUGH

UNIVERSITY OF TORONTO PRESS
Toronto Buffalo London

© University of Toronto Press 2025
Toronto Buffalo London
utppublishing.com
Printed in Canada

ISBN 978-1-4875-4191-0 (cloth)   ISBN 978-1-4875-4193-4 (EPUB)
                                   ISBN 978-1-4875-4192-7 (PDF)

Library and Archives Canada Cataloguing in Publication

Title: Engendering the stage in the age of Shakespeare and beyond /
    edited by Peter Cockett and Melinda Gough.
Names: Cockett, Peter, editor. | Gough, Melinda J., 1967– editor
Description: Includes bibliographical references and index.
Identifiers: Canadiana (print) 20250200155 | Canadiana (ebook)
    20250200244 | ISBN 9781487541910 (cloth) | ISBN 9781487541927 (PDF) |
    ISBN 9781487541934 (EPUB)
Subjects: LCSH: Theater – Europe – History. | LCSH: Theater and society –
    Europe – History. | LCSH: Actresses – Europe – History. | LCSH: Gay
    actors – Europe – History. | LCSH: European drama – History and
    criticism.
Classification: LCC PN2570 .E54 2025 | DDC 792.094 – dc23

Cover design: Val Cooke; John Beadle
Cover image: E.M. Parry, *Beyond the Globe*, 2022. Digital Collage.

We wish to acknowledge the land on which the University of Toronto
Press operates. This land is the traditional territory of the Wendat, the
Anishnaabeg, the Haudenosaunee, the Métis, and the Mississaugas of the
Credit First Nation.

This book has been published with the help of a grant from the Federation
for the Humanities and Social Sciences, through the Awards to Scholarly
Publications Program, using funds provided by the Social Sciences and
Humanities Research Council of Canada.

University of Toronto Press acknowledges the financial support of the
Government of Canada, the Canada Council for the Arts, and the Ontario
Arts Council, an agency of the Government of Ontario, for its publishing
activities.

Canada Council
for the Arts

Conseil des Arts
du Canada

ONTARIO ARTS COUNCIL
CONSEIL DES ARTS DE L'ONTARIO
an Ontario government agency
un organisme du gouvernement de l'Ontario

Funded by the
Government
of Canada

Financé par le
gouvernement
du Canada

Canada

MIX
Paper | Supporting
responsible forestry
FSC® C103567

Contents

Illustrations

Artwork by E.M. Parry appears on pages 58, 202, 218, and 219.

Illustrations for chapter 16 begin on page 283.

Acknowledgments

The co-editors acknowledge that the work behind this book has been instigated and completed on the land of the Mississaugas of the Credit, the Haudenosaunee Confederacy, the Anishinaabe, and other nations, acknowledged and unacknowledged, recorded and unrecorded. Haudenosaunee society is matriarchal; hereditary leaders are elected by the clan mothers; and clan affiliation is passed down from mothers to their children. The Anishinaabe have specific words to describe a multiplicity of gender identities. The cultures from which early modern theatre emerged officially acknowledged only two. We hope this book can offer pathways to repairing some of the harms caused by the imposition of this binary understanding of gender on this land and its peoples.[1]

We are deeply grateful for the enriching collaborations we have enjoyed with scholars and artists whose work is featured and referenced in this volume. Without the support of the Stratford Festival, and especially Artistic Director Antoni Cimolino, none of this would have been possible.

In addition to the artists and scholars who are our co-contributors in this book, we would like to thank all other participants in the Engendering the Stage workshop at the Stratford Festival Laboratory, including Logan Brideau, Pamela Allen Brown, Megan Caines, Mariah Campos, Barbara Fuchs, Mark Harapiak, Daren E. Herbert, Zoe Hudson, Erin Julian, Elizabeth Cruz Petersen, Stephen Purcell, Genny Sermonia, and Danielle Wade. We also thank Erin Julian for her work with interview transcriptions.

Much additional thanks is owed to Keira Loughran for her commitment to the work from its outset through to its conclusion. We are so grateful that we had you by our side to help us navigate the complexities of integrating academic practice with the professional structures of the festival. The operation of the week's workshop was kept running smoothly by the gracious work and presence of stage manager Renate Hansen.

Our 2018 workshop was made possible through the financial support of the Social Sciences and Humanities Research Council, and through additional funds from the Stratford Festival and from McMaster University via the Faculty of Humanities, the Socrates Project, and the Taylor family. At McMaster, Grace Pollock in the Faculty of Humanities provided invaluable guidance on funding applications. We are grateful to the Arts Research Board at McMaster for funding supporting the development of this publication.

The journey from grant writing through to the workshop and this book's publication has been a long and arduous one. Along the way, the insight and enthusiasm of our fellow performance as research scholar, Kim Solga, has been an invaluable motivator.

At the University of Toronto Press, many thanks to Suzanne Rancourt, Mackenzie Gould, Carolyn Zapf, Janice Evans, and Aditi Parikh.

To our immediate family members, Catherine, Jonathan, Ella, Tish, Sophia, Charlie, Jeffrey, Cecilia, and Henry, who have been with us every step of the way whether they liked it or not, we cannot thank you enough for your continuing love, support, and encouragement.

And to our parents who helped us find our way to fulfilling work we value, much love and gratitude.

NOTE

1 Two-Spirit artist Awanigiizhik Bruce (Anishinaabe, Turtle Mountain Reservation, @awanigiizhik.art) identifies sixteen distinct terms describing genders within the Ojibwe language. Language affirming a range and multiplicity of genders is prevalent in Indigenous cultures across Turtle Island, and each culture has their own way of naming them. Harlen Pruden identifies 130 terms indicating different genders, each of which is nation specific (https://bestendeavours.ca/two-spirit). Kai Pyle's "Naming and Claiming: Recovering Ojibwe and Plains Cree Two-Spirit Language" reveals how the binary gender system of colonial writers constrains their ability to comprehend the multiplicity of gender identities they encountered on these lands and furthers the ongoing work to recover the language that supports that complexity within Ojibwe culture.

Abbreviations

2SLGBTQ+	Two-Spirit, Lesbian, Gay, Bisexual, Trans, Queer, Plus …
admin	administrative
AFAB	assigned female at birth
AMAB	assigned male at birth
BA	Bachelor of Arts
BFA	Bachelor of Fine Arts
bi	bisexual
c.	circa
cis	cisgender
EDI	Equity, Diversity, and Inclusion
fol., fols	folio, folios
GNC	gender-nonconforming
IBPOC	Indigenous, Black, and People of Colour
Ind.	Induction
l., ll.	line, lines
n	note
OED	Oxford English Dictionary
pan	pansexual
PaR	performance as research
Q	Quarto
REED	Records of Early English Drama
RSC	Royal Shakespeare Company
SD	stage direction(s)
SKCS	Surrey and Kent Commission for Sewers
TLN	through-line numbering
transmasc	transmasculine
UK	United Kingdom

PART ONE

Setting the Stage

Introduction

PETER COCKETT AND MELINDA GOUGH

The really helpful thing [about] thinking with performance is that performance [is] very future oriented ... One of the things Keira [Loughran] said very early in our session is that, if a particular performance fails, that's okay because you learn things to bring to the next one; I think that's a really helpful way for academics to think about our work too. I think there's always this pressure to have a conclusion, at a really basic level, a conclusion to whatever essay or book that you're writing, and those are the parts that are hardest for me to write because ... it is a closing down. But that's always the goal of the genres that we write in, to get to that conclusion. And I wonder if there's a way we can think about our work more in this future-oriented way in which the ending is an opening towards other things that you could try at another point in time. So it feels more processual and less that I'm producing a product.

– Ellen Welch, scholar and workshop participant[1]

The week-long process was gloriously messy, inconclusive, exhausting, and expansive.

– Emma Frankland, workshop guest artist and leader[2]

We dipped our toes in, but we realized it was an ocean.

– Denise Oucharek, Stratford company actor and workshop participant[3]

This book is not a publication of findings nor a simple collection of essays presented at a conference. It is not a book that aims to draw conclusions. It is the continuation of a process.

The volume is inspired by a small yet catalytic moment in theatre research: a five-day workshop at the Stratford Festival Laboratory entitled "Engendering the Stage." This workshop drew together scholars, students, and professional theatre practitioners with an aim of stimulating more equitable approaches to gender within commercial and educational theatre settings as well as within academic early theatre history. Together, academics and practitioners explored how the training and skills of early modern European actresses and English boy players helped shape how gender was performed on early modern stages. The workshop fostered significant interactions between scholars, students, the festival's company actors, and Two-Spirit, trans, and non-binary guest artists working outside, or on the edges, of classical theatre communities in Canada and the United Kingdom.

The workshop had its flaws in conception and realization, but as trans theatre artist Emma Frankland notes in the passage quoted above, there was value in the messiness and inconclusiveness. In this volume, we foreground that messiness: the exciting incompleteness of the work, the informative errors of conception, as well as the many insights arising from participants' shared willingness to "get into the sandbox and play."[4] Such insights include observations, reflections, and provocations by scholars, students, and professional theatre practitioners who hold deep investments in gender equity in their respective workplaces and sites of learning. Incorporating guest artist and actor commentary, a poem, a zine, scholarly essays and reflections, a new play-text, and three specially commissioned visual art pieces, the book adapts to print form the open and exploratory spirit of the workshop itself by embracing the emphasis on trans-disciplinary, provisional knowledge creation and dissemination that is central to performance as research (PaR) methodologies. Rethinking the lens through which we approach archival records of early modern performance and bringing new research in theatre history together with contemporary performance practice via PaR, our contributors look to the past to imagine new horizons for gender equity within early modern theatre studies, on contemporary stages, and beyond.

The Plan

The workshop proved more provocative and far-reaching, intellectually but also emotionally, than we had imagined in the planning stages. The original conception for the week's work grew out of our previous experience working together on the 2015 conference "Performance as Research in Early Modern Theatre Studies: *The Three Ladies of London* in Context."[5] For Engendering the Stage, we wanted to integrate scholars and artists in a more sustained way, with a focus on the research value of scholars participating alongside performers in workshop activities and rehearsal processes. Our collaboration with the Stratford Festival provided the opportunity to conduct PaR with professionally trained rather than student actors. Our planned workshop aimed to provide a learning opportunity for academics, students, and artists through mutual intellectual and embodied engagement with selected historical sources.

Working in the context of settler Canada, we knew meaningful research on gender in performance beyond a cis-centric frame demanded Two-Spirit, trans, and non-binary participants (and not just a token one or two).[6] We argued strongly in our grant application for the use of research funds to hire these artists as key research collaborators alongside Stratford company artists and invited academics. Prior to the workshop gathering, scholars, drawing from their own areas of expertise, submitted initial papers and shared primary resources on the performance of gender in early modern Europe. The company actors at Stratford were available to us for five hours a day, but their contracts, we realized quite late in the planning process, did not include time to read these shared materials. In collaboration with Callan Davies, we created three short educational videos designed to capture core ideas from the scholars' papers in an open and accessible format. Our first video, *Beyond the Globe*, directly addressed the myth of the "all-male" stage that is foundational to patriarchal theatre histories that take as their focus the professional stages of London and organize their evidence and arguments around the figure of William Shakespeare. This video drew on feminist theatre histories and introduced extensive evidence of female and genderqueer participation in the making and performance of early modern theatre across Europe. The second video, *Stepping Beyond Binaries*, provided historical evidence regarding the gendered expectations for social and physical comportment placed on the upper classes of early modern Europe. The final video, *Disruptive Boys*, invited participants to imagine the boy players of the professional London stage as queer, subversive, and seductive disruptors of the gender binary. In addition to the videos, we devised two physical workshops for actors and scholars to encourage embodied engagement with this research: the first was on the pragmatics of carrying and drawing a sword, while the second was inspired by the comportment manuals' advice on the appropriate gait (walking style) for gentlemen and gentlewomen.

The week's schedule was organized around rehearsal of four scenes selected from Dekker and Middleton's *The Roaring Girl*, Fletcher and Massinger's *Love's Cure*, Beaumont and Fletcher's *The Maid's Tragedy*, and Juan Ruiz de Alarcón's *The Lieutenant Nun* (*La Comedia famosa de la monja alférez*).[7] Each scene featured a sword-wielding assigned female at birth (AFAB) character and included at least one character whose gender as rendered in the play-text resonates outside a patriarchal cisgender heteronormative frame. Each day's schedule was divided into an initial presentation of research videos, followed by open discussion, a workshop activity, scene work in four smaller groups, and a concluding debrief.

The scenes were all cast in advance of the workshop in collaboration with the Stratford Festival Laboratory's Associate Producer Keira Loughran. The plan was to present rough performances of the scenes to the Stratford Festival's artistic director, other members of the company, and a select group of volunteers from the local community later in the week, with an aim of amplifying the impact of provisional research both within the festival and in a more public-facing way. The plan also budgeted for brief consultation with our Two-Spirit, trans, and non-binary artists in advance of the workshop to discuss their casting and our approach to the week's work. In practice, this allotted time – for rehearsal and for consultation with guest artists – proved grossly insufficient.

The Pivot

The flaws in this planned process seem so obvious to us now, and may to you as readers, but they were not fully apparent to us in 2018 prior to the start of our week's work. Our sincere hope was for an equitable exchange between scholars, company actors, and guest artists, but we did not adequately anticipate the full weight and complexity of the systemic inequities standing in the way of our objectives. In practice, we faced a multiplicity of social and institutional assumptions and biases to unpack before the research could effectively begin. At the start of the second day, the guest artists asked for greater time for discussion as a large group regarding gender (in)equity. While we had built in some flex within our packed research schedule, it was not enough. This request meant that our best laid plans would, to some degree, have to be abandoned, or at least drastically reorganized, but our commitment to gender equity meant this discussion took priority. Productively, therefore, we abandoned key aspects of our planned process on the second day to make time and space for leadership by Two-Spirit, trans, and non-binary guest artists. We say "productively" because tools for holding space introduced by these leaders proved essential to navigating significant tensions in the days that followed and opened up the PaR process to many of the musings and insights in this volume. We did return to many originally planned activities, but as Emma Frankland puts it, the guest artists "derailed the expectations of the workshop in a really glorious way," and their "knowledge and presence encouraged the room to further deconstruct … assumptions of gender and think differently."[8]

The principle of respecting pronouns had been introduced powerfully in the welcome session on the first day, but for many this principle takes practice, and on the morning of the second day, the guest artists let the group know that they were sometimes being misidentified and that this misgendering was causing harm. Respecting pronouns is now common practice in our classrooms and research circles, and it may be in yours too, but it was far less common in 2018. The guest artists drew on their deep experience working in queer and trans spaces and introduced techniques for gently reminding participants when they used the wrong pronoun. The primary method introduced was a simple, surprisingly effective technique known as "Oops … Ouch." When someone uses the wrong pronoun, anyone in the room is free to say "Oops" to flag the error. It might be the person speaking, it might be the person who was misgendered, or it might be someone else in the conversation or within hearing of the conversation. Then anyone else can respond with "Ouch." The choice of words is key here: "Oops" suggests a slip, an error, rather than imputing de facto choice or intent, and "Ouch" acknowledges that harm has been caused. Misgendering is a potentially (re)traumatizing experience, and choosing language that acknowledges the harm without escalating the mistake is a generous act, one that allows space for cisgender participants to learn the importance of respect. Once the error has been flagged and the harm recognized, the group commits to carry on the conversation without pausing for lengthy apologies, explanations, or justifications that might risk increasing harm (for example, by centring the person who was responsible for the initial misgendering). The group can move forward with the confidence that a mistake has been corrected, the harm felt, acknowledged, and understood, and in the trust that the person making the error has been "called in" to learn the accurate pronoun and use it in future. This technique proved powerfully effective in the workshop; it was a key foundation for the growing sense of trust that emerged across our group by the end of the week, as scholar participants Zoe Hudson and Stephen Purcell have noted.[9]

From the outset, we were committed to conducting research *with* trans and Two-Spirit practitioners rather than merely *about* them. The intervention of the guest artists on the second day called us in to enacting this principle more meaningfully in practice. Their leadership raised the emotional and intellectual stakes in the room. It drove home how researching early modern gender-nonconforming characters, many of whom are subjected to harm even within scenes that depict resistance, is far from a dispassionate intellectual process; rather, such research can require deep emotional labour, especially, but not exclusively, for Two-Spirit, trans, non-binary, gender-nonconforming, and queer people. Their generosity opened space for all participants to reflect on the role of gender oppression in their lives, including in the practice of studying and performing early modern texts. From this point on, each day began with a "check-in" and "check-out," where participants were free to articulate how they were feeling about the work. These additional techniques drawn from the guest artists' experience in social justice circles have their own conventions. Everyone assembles, preferably in a circle, and each member of the group is given the opportunity to speak about whatever is important to them. No one is obliged to speak, but everyone has a moment to raise any concerns or offer insights to the group. As Stratford company actor Denise Oucharek commented, giving everyone time to speak to their feelings runs the risk of becoming "indulgent at times, but when you reveal yourself to other people – this was the scholars, the actors, everyone all together – when you allow yourself to be vulnerable and share a bit of your own humanity with other people, then the work, when it comes time to work again, is very different."[10] Our "PaRchivist," Callan Davies, speaks eloquently about this technique's impact in his blog post describing the third day of the workshop, writing that checking in and checking out

> helped create a room in which openness and warmth have felt like default views. This method has been instrumental in creating an open and protected space that enables generosity and allows for vulnerability for everybody in the room, while keeping us all in constant dialogue. Our opening check-ins then move into open, fluid discussions about the research at hand, the scholarship underpinning and responding to the performance workshops, and the impetus for the afternoon's work.
>
> This way of "working" might seem like an addendum or "warm-up" to the performance workshopping, but as almost everybody has remarked, it's in fact integral to the explorative nature of the *play* that "practice as research/PaR" or workshopping generally is about: this is the process; this is the learning. Here's a call for more spaces, more default personal and work environments, that are able to bring together personal state of mind, openness, and dialogue as the fundamental basis for what we do and how we do it.[11]

Many of the week's most challenging and potentially transformative conversations happened during these moments of reflection. Participants' heightened emotional engagement with the work intensified the learning, increasing emphasis on listening, hearing, and reflexivity in ways that continue to register across this volume.[12]

Integrating lived experience of Two-Spirit and other gender-nonconforming artists laid bare further significant systemic roadblocks standing in the way of meaningful collaboration. At our check-in on the third day, Carmen Alvis (Métis, Two-Spirit) took the opportunity to share her reluctance to participate when initially invited to attend the workshop. While she was interested in the subject, she hesitated to commit to working at an institution – the Stratford Festival – that was expressly designed to impose colonial culture on this land. Early modern texts and performances have been used and continue to be used as a tool of colonialism, a means to justify past and ongoing violence against her peoples. Carmen's sharing of these insights, together with Kitoko Mai's spoken word poem "Let Shakespeare Die" (included in Mai's co-authored chapter 16 of this volume), profoundly framed our work going forward, challenging the very assumptions of our undertaking and making everything we were doing strange, in the Brechtian sense. These interventions highlighted the intersections of gender with issues of race, colonialism, and Indigeneity.

The guest artists also requested some work be completed in affinity groups.[13] The value of setting aside time for gender-nonconforming participants to discuss and debrief was immediately apparent to us: they needed dedicated space to collaborate in a context where they did not have to explain aspects of their identities. Additionally, however, the guest artists requested that, for the check-outs at the end of the day, we should separate into two groups: scholars and artists. Acceding to this request was more challenging for us as it stood in contradiction to our planned mechanisms for breaking down sectoral barriers between the academy and the theatre profession (one of our key initial goals). With the benefit of hindsight, the logic of their request is now clear.

The unpacking of cultural assumptions and biases needed for more equitable engagement in the research was not restricted to the issue of gender alone. The workshop process also worked through the sometimes implicit, sometime explicit assumption that scholars would provide the intellect and actors the affect, as well as an ongoing association of scholars with theatre critics and histories of extractive attitudes towards artists on the part of academics. Beginning the work without unpacking these assumptions and biases meant lack of clarity about the terms on which we were all engaging. Although we had conceived the workshop as a collaboration of equals with scholars and artists bringing different sets of skills and knowledges to explore the same subject, different parties entered the room with unacknowledged assumptions and expectations about the relationship between scholars and actors. Reflecting on the final day, scholar participant Elizabeth Cruz Peterson worried we had fallen into an extractive model of scholarship: "The actors were like tools for us ('I'd like to see you do this' and 'Can that happen?'). Even when I asked, 'What do you think of this?' I wonder if they were thinking …

'Well, what do you want me to think of this?' What stake did they have in this process?"[14] Erin Julian, one of the workshop's graduate research assistants, shared similar concerns, noting "there were a few moments where the actors were asking, 'What are we doing for you?' – I'd like to see us thinking about what we're doing for them."[15] By contrast, Stratford company actor Denise Oucharek was enthused and empowered by the process and felt the presence of the scholars in the room was a great benefit. In our post-workshop interview, she says:

> We have scholars here, you guys! This is great! If we don't understand, *they do!* You know, we're not in a rehearsal hall trying to make it work, *we've got them!* They're here! That to me was the most exciting part about the work. I didn't have that stress about getting it right or understanding the text and spending all that time to understand it.[16]

But even Oucharek's enjoyment of the process as expressed here seems to be founded on a belief that scholars know the right way to interpret classical play-texts. This assumption is not one that any of the assembled scholars professed but one that was projected onto them due to common cultural assumptions.

That said, Oucharek was a greatly influential presence at the workshop because she understood that we had come to the workshop to "get into the sandbox and play," with actors and scholars engaging in the same experimental, "messy" exploration of our subject. Oucharek also pointed out that the actors assembled for the workshop came with different skills, different levels of familiarity with early modern drama, and different expectations about rehearsal. Not all rehearsal rooms are experimental or exploratory. In many instances, directors come with a plan for the final performance and then work to have the actors execute their plan. Rehearsal rooms have traditionally been hierarchical, not collaborative, and in many cases remain so. Our workshop was also part of a series in the Stratford Lab, and previous leaders that season had designed workshops to provide specific training. All these factors led to differing expectations among various subgroups of participants.

Time was a limiting factor here too, and time, of course, is money. If we had been able to secure funding for three weeks instead of one, we would have been able to set aside time to address and unpack assumptions about the workshop process collectively prior to enjoying a period of risk and play and then working on developing more polished performances. Perhaps even better, we could have engaged in some of the increasingly open explorations of the texts we had initially envisaged, with the actors switching roles to reveal additional performance possibilities.

The possibilities expanded exponentially as the workshop progressed, but the time available to us remained constant; as Oucharek puts it in the epigraph to this chapter, "We dipped our toes in, but we realized it was an ocean."[17]

The vulnerability of actors in the moment of performance was an additional complicating factor for our plan. Such vulnerability is always present, even in the rehearsal room. We insisted that scholars join in with our workshop exercises to give them access to embodied learning but also so they would experience this vulnerability first hand. This strategy opened up deeper understandings of what is risked by performers, as Melinda Gough observes in "Performing Gender 'from the Ground Up,'" chapter 10 of this volume, but it perhaps did not go far enough. Our plan to share scene work with the festival's artistic director and volunteers from the local community on the fourth day added a professional pressure that interfered with the free exploration of our subject matter. The risks of public performance, while an expected aspect of actors' lives, are still risks, and experimental risk-taking is harder in public. Within the institution of the Stratford Festival, performing in front of artistic directors and members of the local public is a high-stakes matter for company actors, even when the "product" being shared is expressly experimental and provisional. Prioritizing company actors' willingness to freely explore and experiment, we decided to cancel our planned performances of the scenes on day four. This modification disconnected the research from key decision-makers at Stratford, reducing the potential impact of the research on programming and casting, but it also took pressure off our scene work, allowing for more risk-taking and open play. This choice also facilitated deeper reckoning with methodological questions of process and/versus product in early theatre studies and in research more broadly – as Ellen Welch notes in comments quoted at the beginning of this introduction and, at greater length, in chapter 4.

Pressure of different kinds was also felt by the scholars, especially for those precariously employed but not exclusively so. We maintain that the workshop process itself is a substantial piece of PaR scholarship, but that position is not supported in all institutions. Our academic colleagues from the United Kingdom in particular were under intense pressure to document the outcomes of their research, including public impact, in ways that would be legible to funding bodies (currently this requirement is not something demanded by the government funding body that supported this workshop in Canada, at least not to the same degree).[18] The pressure to deliver scholarly outputs and prove impact from PaR is also disproportionate for graduate students, precariously employed early career researchers, scholars of colour, and even established (female) scholars working under intensified neoliberal funding schemes. The imperative to prove worth in empirically measurable ways (like published articles) makes PaR work risky, and this risk is experienced inequitably by racialized scholars, scholars from different countries, and scholars at different levels of employment and in different career stages.

People (Not) in the Room

Research projects are deeply and inevitably defined by the people in the literal and metaphorical room, as well as by the institutions that both enable and constrain such rooms. The complex combination of guest artists, scholars, and actors in the rehearsal room for our PaR workshop continues to frame the ongoing research in this book. Our workshop group included eleven actors from the Stratford company, none of whom identified as trans; four guest artists (one of whom doubled as a student research assistant) who identified as Two-Spirit, trans, nonbinary, and/or gender-nonconforming; and nine scholars who provided research papers in advance, four scholar observers, and three facilitators (ourselves and Keira Loughran, the Stratford Festival's associate artistic director and lab coordinator), all of whom were cisgender. Our book harnesses collaborative exchanges between these diverse artists and scholars; it also includes additional contributors whose areas of expertise, including lived experience, provide important perspectives that were under-represented in the original workshop. As noted earlier in this introduction, academic institutions carry restrictions on time and resources, as well as habitual processes and systemic structures that wield their own biases. While deep in the process of conceiving and writing the grant that would help fund the workshop, we largely deferred to the familiar when inviting scholar participants. This option meant that, although we succeeded in recruiting a group of strong feminist peers at various career stages whose research was relevant to the project, we were left with an overall imbalance between the artist group that contained Two-Spirit, trans, and gender-nonconforming participants and a group of predominantly white scholar participants, none of whom, to our knowledge, identified as trans or non-binary. In our planning, we did not take sufficient care to seek out scholars with lived experience of Indigeneity and gender nonconformity who would bring crucial insight to the table.

The work of artists, actors, and scholars assembled for the workshop relied on behind the scenes labour by women, similar to the feminized labour often rendered invisible in traditional scholarship on early modern theatre history. Such contributions included work by the Stratford

Lab's stage manager, Renata Hansen, staff in the Stratford Festival's costumes department, and two additional paid student research assistants from McMaster University. It also included a childminder paid to ensure the safety of company actor Logan Brideau (fourteen years of age at the time).[19] This behind the scenes work is a powerful example of how female labour, usually rendered invisible, is often indispensable to theatre practice. Not only did the childminder ensure the safety and comfort of Brideau, for whom the risks of playing Evadne, a sexual(ized) adult woman in *The Maid's Tragedy*, were particularly obvious, but her presence was also crucial for ensuring the safety of the adult actors who performed alongside him: an important consideration given the marked revival of public hysteria around protecting children from trans and queer people, together with homophobic conflations of queerness with grooming, paedophilia, and child abuse.[20]

Barriers standing in the way of our desire for equity in representation were also apparent in the process for hiring gender-nonconforming guest artists. We had hoped to include transmasculine actors, for example, but struggled to find individuals who were available for our planned dates and felt themselves to be expert enough to tackle early modern texts in the company of Stratford actors. This difficulty was due in part to the hiring practices of classical theatre companies and the consequential lack of opportunity for training and experience available to gender-nonconforming actors in general and AFAB trans performers in particular. We did eventually find a transmasculine actor who was interested and available, whom we hoped to cast specifically in the role of Guzmán in *The Lieutenant Nun*. The selected scene, however, involves other characters trying to force Guzmán into a dress – a plot line that the actor in question believed would be too triggering and harmful to him. In many ways, early modern texts reveal the complexities and fluidities of gender, but these plays also include a great deal of gender-based violence. The harm potentially provoked by stepping into artistic explorations of this oppression can be a significant barrier to participation, and finding trans and non-binary artists interested in exploring early modern performance, and providing safety for them in doing so, takes time and care as discussed above.

Our efforts towards more equitable representation within the artist group working on the project, limited as they were, involved significant labour on our part and that of our co-organizer, Keira Loughran, and ultimately we were confronted by restrictions on time and resources, as well as by academic and artistic cultures that have excluded and continue to exclude Two-Spirit, trans, and non-binary researchers and performers. As previously noted, our scenes all featured sword-wielding "women," characters assigned female at birth (AFAB) but who within the action of the play are associated with forms of violence gendered as masculine within their societies. The absence of transmasculine perspectives for the workshop's exploration of these scenes was a serious problem, one that has continued to influence the ongoing development of our research in the creation of this book. To partially address this gap within the volume, we have included chapters by two AFAB trans or gender-nonconforming scholar-artists who were not present for the workshop itself but whose research-creation practices align closely with methodologies and topics central to our PaR project. SL Grange's performative explorations of queer history through and with contemporary drag king culture serve as a touchstone for several contributor chapters that discuss *The Roaring Girl*, and we are grateful for the opportunity to publish Grange's script *A Note to Moll Frith*, performed originally in January 2020 at Shakespeare's Globe. The volume also features three artworks commissioned from costume and set designer E.M. Parry. These pieces were created through an ongoing iterative collaboration with Parry that has pushed our research in new directions. These works of art are accompanied by in-depth interviews that document the process behind the pieces, demonstrating Parry's deep knowledge of early modern drama and trans studies and drawing on their theatre design expertise and their experience as a drag king, scholar, and multidisciplinary artist.

Present Pressures and Opportunities: Why This Research Now?

Contributors to this volume, extending insights set in motion at the workshop, bring to light rich evidence of previously overlooked feminist, queer, and trans histories, tracing "ghost[s] of trans embodiment" within early modern play-texts.[21] They also show how PaR experimentation by and with women, trans, and Two-Spirit artists can open new possibilities for mobilizing such histories in classrooms, play editions, performance repertoires, and beyond. Such engagement with archival records uncovers and develops a recognized and recognizable history that is important to marginalized communities, including communities of women, trans, and gender-nonconforming students, scholars, artists, and audiences: the very people whose pasts are so often rendered invisible in the stories we tell about Shakespeare's era, as well as in contemporary productions of plays from this period.[22]

Present day transphobic commentary, playing into moral panic surrounding access to health care and gender recognition for trans adults and especially youth, asserts that transness is a fad or trend from which women and children must be protected. "Some anti-trans campaigners,"

Kit Heyam notes, "have taken these connotations of newness to their logical extreme, denying all possibility of trans history on the basis of our supposed absence from 'the historical record' and arguing that to even suggest our historical existence is 'anachronistic.' Underlying these claims is a sense that historicity provides legitimacy: that the newfangledness of trans identities means policymakers and the general public do not need to, and indeed should not, take them seriously."[23] Dismissing transness while simultaneously exaggerating its power, anti-trans rhetoric frames trans identity as "something that has come out of nowhere to threaten an existing way of life, and against which women and children – groups positioned, often without their say, as vulnerable victims in this hastily constructed fight – must be protected at all costs."[24] Recent laws targeting the transgender community and the so-called gender critical movement that is behind them purport to be protecting women when they criminalize trans identity and trans life, yet this movement's "fundamentalist interpretation of gender and the obsession with the gender binary hurts all people who do not conform to traditional gender stereotypes, not just transgender people, by imposing strict norms on human expression and experience through the use of shame and stigma."[25] In the face of such harms, ceding the historical past, including the theatrical past, to cis-sexism – the assumption, either explicit or implicit, that "because trans people are a minority, cisgenderness is the default, or 'unmarked,' state of all human beings"[26] – is not a viable option. Nor is allowing feminist, queer, and trans histories and liberation struggles to be pitted against one another.[27] Instead, the work of Engendering the Stage, including this volume, seeks to enrich what we know – and the kinds of questions we ask – about the many genders of Shakespeare's era.

This research requires a paradigm shift away from the myth of the all-male stage that powerfully persists in common perceptions of early modern theatre. On the commercial stages of early modern London, boy players who had taken female parts sometimes remained famous for their femininity as adults, both on and off stage.[28] In professional acting companies on the continent, meanwhile, women starred in a range of gendered roles – including, in Spain, that of the *mujer varonil* or manly woman.[29] How such developments in gendered casting cross-pollinated across national traditions and how play-texts on both sides of the channel register these and other circulating effects of gender variance in performance remains largely unexplored, however, thanks in part to the founding methodologies of theatre history.

Natasha Korda has analysed how scholars in the first decades of the twentieth century "solidified the 'all-male stage' as the basis for theater history by defining female performance as its 'other.'"[30] In an effort to establish Elizabethan theatre history as a legitimate discipline, Korda shows, researchers including E.K. Chambers, Thornton Shirley Graves, and Hardin Craig leaned into the cultural capital of Shakespeare and other male playwrights from his era. Taking the professional troupes that performed regularly in purpose-built London playhouses as theatre history's proper object of study, these scholars dismissed, as unprofessional amateurism, questions about women's allegedly irregular theatrical and performance activities on other stages. Thus limiting the borders of their discipline, they sought to legitimize their own research in the eyes of the academy by adopting a pseudoscientific positivism rooted in empiricism as defined against the more speculative, allegedly less rigorous methods required to find and trace "irregular" theatrical activities – such as those involving women – not limited to one place (the London playhouses) and one set of performers (the liveried troupes who performed there).[31] In this way, "even though women's theatrical activity flourished outside the commercial playing companies that performed in London in the sixteenth and seventeenth centuries … the male players of the London playhouse companies became representative of English theatre per se."[32]

By the 1990s, Korda notes, such foundational assumptions about what counts as theatre and performance had begun to shift thanks to interdisciplinary frameworks introduced by performance studies and women's studies. Activities beyond Shakespeare's direct orbit, including instances of cultural production by women that had been selectively ignored, became legitimate objects of study. Sustained work on the Records of Early English Drama project (still ongoing) has identified ample documentation, often hiding in plain sight, demonstrating extensive female performance of many types and in many different locations: in the streets, in domestic settings, and at court, for example. Women ranging from queens to commoners also supported theatrical activity behind the scenes as named patrons, playhouse owners, moneylenders, audience members, gatherers, dressers, craftswomen, and more.[33]

Many of the working women whose skills with luxury textiles and accessories London playing companies relied on for costuming had arrived in England from France and the Low Countries, Korda shows.[34] In fact, women who crossed national borders are everywhere in the archives relevant to theatre-making and performance across early modern Europe. Beginning in the 1570s, for example, mixed-gender troupes were performing professionally in and among various locations including France, Poland, Germany, Spain, and England.[35] Meanwhile, English girls took speaking parts in convent dramas on the continent; French women performed in salons as well as publicly; French princesses took speaking roles on stage alongside female companions and carried such practices with them when they moved elsewhere, thanks to dynastic marriages; and mixed-gender Italian troupes set up in Spain, where women had long performed professionally, and female managers (*autoras*) would go on to own and run theatre companies.[36] Attention to these and other transnational networks of mobility and exchange productively challenges isolationist models that rely on "construct[ions of] a metonymic relationship between the commercial stage in a given country's capital city and the nation" – a relationship that in English theatre history especially "often serves to marginalize the foreign and the feminine."[37]

Engendering the Stage, the workshop and this book, attends to synergies across national, linguistic, and geographic divisions to help us to rethink gender on the early modern stage more broadly. How can this revisionist, transnational history be marshalled to help create and hold space within classical theatre today, not only for women performers but also for performers of other historically marginalized genders? Initial attempts to rethink how gendered practices in different performance locations overlapped with and impacted one another have pointed to moments of direct contact, such as boy actors and royal women appearing together on the English masque stage or moments of temporal and geographical overlap between continental mixed-gender troupes and English companies at home and abroad.[38] Attending to celebrity as well as shared structures and scenarios – what in a different context Louise Clubb calls "theatergrams" – can yield further insights regarding circulating networks in the gendering of early modern performance across national theatrical traditions.[39] In this regard, Rachel Poulsen's concept of the "actress effect," which involves "a conjuring of the idea and practice of the Italian diva-actress through the charisma and technique of the English boy actor," has been especially fruitful for feminist theatre history.[40] As taken up by scholars such as Julie Campbell, Sophie Tomlinson, and Pamela Allen Brown, Poulsen's concept suggests how thinking about networks of rivalry and influence across various European performance traditions helps to surface some of the complex, multilayered, heterogeneous ways that gender manifested on the early modern stage, including in the performance of roles scripted as female on stages, like Shakespeare's, that allegedly excluded women.[41]

We say "allegedly" because, as recent work in the field of early modern trans studies suggests, the assumption that no women performed on the early modern stage is not only patriarchal but is also cis-sexist. Early theatre historians who established the all-male English stage assumed that London's boy actors, even the ones most famous for their femininity, were male. Feminist theatre history has tended to cede this position, looking for "real" women's theatrical activity elsewhere. Scholars influenced by queer and trans theory have troubled the easy elision of distinctions between boy and adult male players. Early modern audiences, such scholars argue, viewed the boy player as a figure whose gender did "not signify in any stable or monolithic fashion."[42] For playgoers in early modern London, this argument runs, the engendering of boy players would have been queerly indeterminate or non-binary – even, potentially, when these players graduated from their apprentice positions to take on adult male roles.[43]

How might these players have experienced their own genders? They may have identified as non-binary, to use a contemporary term, but other possibilities exist including (binary) trans ones. Indeed, Emma Frankland, centring her experience as a trans woman performer, asserts that "there will certainly have been trans women on stage who were read as cisgender women or as cisgender men performing as female impersonators. For example, I am certain that in modern terminology, for example, some of the 'boy players' who specialised in female roles in Elizabethan England would have identified as trans."[44] As Frankland notes, "coming out" in community with other trans people can be liberating, but when that is not a safe option, for example, in the case of

> a young trans woman in Elizabethan England (acknowledging again that it is undoubtedly a misnomer to use modern parlance with reference to the past), perhaps another answer would have been to join a theatre company and be granted the permission and legal space to dress and perform as a woman – something that could have offered a way to explore gender and help feelings of dysphoria. It has been frequently claimed that, in Elizabethan England (as in many other countries), women were not permitted to perform on stage, resulting in a theatre ecology where for the most part actors were people who had been assigned male at birth (AMAB). Of course … it is reductive to say "women did not perform" as I question whether some of these AMAB actors were in fact trans women. Similarly, it is unthinkable that there were not some examples of AFAB actors who were read as men (or boys) who would also have found their way on stage. Trans history is full of people who quietly transgressed the rules and got away with it.[45]

Here, Frankland tackles head-on the reductive cisnormativity behind the all-male stage myth. As Heyam explains, "historical methodology – the way we're accustomed to doing and thinking about history academically – tends to demand a much higher standard of evidence to 'prove' that someone in the past can be called trans than it does to 'prove' that they can be called cis … This pervasive cisnormativity means that the cis perspective is – just like the male perspective, as Simone de Beauvoir argued – positioned as objective truth. This means historians tend to interpret people from the past as, effectively, cis until proven otherwise."[46] Once we recognize this bias, we can (re)turn to the records of early (transnational) theatre history with what Sandra Harding has called, from a feminist perspective, "strong objectivity": a method of inquiry that in our context takes as its starting place the situated knowledges of not only women but also queer and trans practitioners and researchers.[47]

Archives-based early theatre research that seeks to move beyond the patriarchal cis-centric all-male stage myth is now buttressed by a wealth of scholarship in early modern trans studies published in the years following our 2018 workshop, including but not limited to Simone Chess, Will Fisher, and Colby Gordon's groundbreaking 2019 *Early Modern Trans Studies* special journal volume. In 2022, REED researchers reassessing Cambridgeshire records of performance reported having identified "instances of potentially queer gender performance and dress" (examples that they thought might serve as "case studies for REED to explore tagging criteria for gender in its online editions").[48] Engendering the Stage's UK-based team, meanwhile, has undertaken extensive research in archives across England aimed at uncovering further evidence of performance by women, children, and gender-nonconforming people in Shakespeare's time.[49] Such reassessments of early theatre records can also be productively taken up beyond a focus on England. Discussing "mixed-gender" professional troupes on the continent, scholars have tended to presume that this mix involves (cis) men and (cis) women. If we approach this performance history outside of not only an androcentric but also a cisnormative lens, however, surely trans men, trans women, and non-binary players cannot (and should not) be ruled out.

Such a heuristic of cis-spicion suggests that, not only were some boy actors "especially nonbinary," as Chess has argued, but that the gendering of so-called continental "mixed-gender" troupes was very likely more mixed than has been previously supposed.[50] Take, for example, one of the plays we selected for our workshop scene work, *The Lieutenant Nun* (*La Monja alférez*). This play's protagonist, Guzmán, is revealed in Act 1 to have been assigned female at birth. This aspect of his story resembles that of the historical figure on which the play is based: Antonio de Erauso (born Catalina de Erauso), who after escaping a Spanish convent lived in Peru and fought in Chile under the name Alonso Rodriguez de Guzmán. As Edward McLean Test and Marta Albalá Pelegrín note in the introduction to their edition of *La Monja alférez* in English translation, "throughout the play, Guzmán refuses to be recognized as a woman, making statements such as, 'I'll die before making public that I am a woman,' and 'I am not a woman.' The only staged moment of cross-dressing in *The Lieutenant Nun* is not when Guzmán is donning male attire, but the reverse, when Guzmán is asked to wear female clothes in a scene with violent overtones."[51] Simone Chess, discussing non-binary boy actors who carried femininity and gender queerness into their adult careers, suggests that English playwrights "specifically created and designated parts suited to the particular range and talents of individual actors," not only in terms of physical types but also "sexual types" in the sense of erotic appeal to audience members on the basis of physical appearance, training, roles for which they were already famous, and queer gender performance on or off stage.[52] Might continental playwrights such as Ruiz de Alarcón have done something similar when composing plays for star performers of their day?

Ellen Welch, in chapter 4 of this volume, notes that Elisabeth Dispannet, a famous seventeenth-century actor who appeared under the stage name Mademoiselle de Valliot, specialized in gender-nonconforming AFAB characters who appeared on stage in male clothing. Such roles allowed actors like Valliot to perform active parts in the love plots central to Baroque comedy. Might Isaac de Benserade have had Valliot in mind when writing his *Iphis et Iante* (1634) for the company she was a member of, at the Hôtel de Bourgogne? At around the same time, Spanish playwright Luis Vélez de Guevara crafted his early seventeenth-century play *La serrana de la Vera* (*The Mountain Girl of La Vera*), the autograph manuscript of which specifies that Gila, the play's genderqueer AFAB protagonist, should be performed by Jusepa Vaca, an acclaimed actress known for erotic intrigue and for playing emotionally and physically demanding *mujeres varoniles* roles; indeed, scholars have suggested that Vaca must have been important to, and was perhaps inseparable from, the playwright's development of Gila's character.[53] Ruiz de Alarcón, when writing his protagonist Guzmán for *The Lieutenant Nun*, may also have been influenced by the availability of famous gender-nonconforming performers. From the title page of the play's 1626 print edition (Figure 15.2), we know that Luisa de Robles starred in this role. Robles had catapulted to fame when two years previously, at a performance of Ruiz de Alarcón's *El Anticristo*, the leading actor Manuel Vallejo could not bring himself to jump into a cloud machine: Robles literally leaped in, saving the show. Commemorated in a sonnet by one of the period's well-known poets, this renowned incident made Robles famous for a physical courage typically associated with masculinity, and as Sherry Velasco notes, such associations would have carried forward in the minds of audiences who encountered Robles as Guzmán.[54] We do not have access to historical records about how performers like Valliot, Vaca, or Robles experienced their own genders. They may have been cisgender women comfortable in their assigned genders, no matter how much their embodiment of femininity on or off stage transgressed stereotypes.[55] On the other hand, the insistent transmasculine coding in such plays helps us to question previous assumptions, not only about the characters but also about the actors who played them: why should we necessarily assume these AFAB performers were cis?[56] Opening possibilities beyond patriarchal cisnormative ones means reading for binary trans possibilities, such as the identification Guzmán's character vocally asserts, but also for non-binary ones. As Heyam cautions, trans people have been and continue to be subjected to limiting diagnostic processes in order to prove their realness, with many harmful effects including the reduction of transness to forms that are "binary, stereotyped, and stable."[57] Similarly, Alexa Alice Joubin – like Jack Halberstam before her – warns against reductive imposition when approaching transness, instead proposing a "trans lens" that reads for gender variance in the transitive spaces that numerous characters inhabit in film and on stage. "Seeking to understand rather than diagnose diverse social practices," Joubin writes, "the trans lens sustains the indeterminant state of being without pinning down characters' genders or medicalizing their ambiguity."[58] Few characters in plays from Shakespeare's era insist on binary transness without ambiguity the way that Guzmán in *The Lieutenant Nun* does, but that does not mean we should continue reading them (or non-binary trans characters either, for that matter) from a "cis until proven otherwise" default perspective. Rather, our volume extends the kind of heuristic that Joubin proposes, beyond Shakespeare and beyond England, and in ways that centre PaR as a method for deconstructing patriarchal restrictions on what genders are possible in classical theatre both historically and today.

We are not the first to engage PaR in such ways. Emma Frankland and Andy Kesson, for example, undertaking extensive research and development work with actors in Before Shakespeare and other projects, make a strong case for the queer and trans stories hiding in plain sight in John Lyly's play-text for *Galatea*.[59] Barbara Fuchs, too, drawing on staged readings with actors at the Stratford Festival, points to gender fluidity as a central aspect of Leonor/Leonardo's characterization in Ana Caro's *Valor, agravio y mujer* (*The Courage to Right a Woman's Wrongs*).[60] What new possibilities for gender variance might reveal themselves once we take up a transnational lens – considering plays for "all-male" English companies *alongside* those for "mixed-gender" troupes? Natasha Korda has argued that, in early modern Europe, "the effects of gender in performance existed on a continuum and circulated between performers of different genders."[61] Approaching such circulations through a mode of inquiry that is both transnational and trans inclusive, we suggest, moves us yet further beyond the heuristic limits of diagnosis and of exceptionalities that prove the "cis" rule, in the process helping us to imagine a richer, more expansive set of stories about the multiple engenderings of early modern theatrical worlds.

PaR's (Provisional) Affordances

PaR methodologies, which embrace the embodied and processual knowledges of actors,[62] can offer particularly generative approaches for reconceiving understandings of gender, past and present. PaR is well established in UK-based early modern theatre research in projects such as Staging the Henrician Court (2010), Staging and Representing the Scottish Renaissance Court (2013), and Before Shakespeare (2016–present) and in Canada with Shakespeare and the Queen's Men (2006) and Performance as Research in Early Theatre Studies (2015).[63] Much of this work emphasizes the playfulness and experimentation of rehearsal over the finality of performance.[64] PaR is a particularly apt method for (re)making theatre history, which, like gender itself, entails fluid processes of imagining and revisioning. An insistence on imagination is especially appropriate since our object of study is theatre – a practice that is fundamentally imaginative. Inviting us to imagine possibilities, PaR helped us to playfully explore what happens when we acknowledge that the seemingly fixed boundaries of binary gender (and sexuality) are not so fixed.

Using performance as a means to conduct research in theatre history is simply logical. Archival research and textual/pictorial analysis remain cornerstones of the field, and through them, theories about past theatre practice are effectively conjured and disseminated. Bringing archival evidence, textual analysis, and scholarly interpretations into the rehearsal room through PaR experimentation, however, adds dimensions to the research process that align the methodology of research with the object of study. PaR in theatre history situates the exploration of archival evidence in the bodies of the researchers and makes it move through time and space under the observations of others in ways that are fundamental to theatre as an art form.

According to Bruce Barton's categorization of artistic research (AR), our work at the Stratford Festival might better be described as practice-based research, since its results "cannot be fully comprehended without direct access to the creative products and processes of its incorporated practices."[65] However, we have retained the descriptor "performance as research" to protect the status of artistic work by academics as research in its own right. The Engendering the Stage workshop in and of itself constitutes research, regardless of our volume's subsequent attempts to publish the embodied experience of the week's work. Melissa Trimingham asserts that PaR "is doing itself no favours by claiming that 'all practice is research.'"[66] Yet the "task of the researcher to translate" the knowledge produced by PaR "into analytical language" is logocentric and, within the context of the lands on which we work, colonial. While written analysis still holds value for us, as workers in colonial universities, we reject the idea that it is the only and necessary outcome of PaR work. Research "demands purposeful activity towards a specified end," as Trimingham suggests, but the embodied work of performance used towards that "end" constitutes a research product in and of itself and should be accorded status as such within the academy.[67] The performance workshop at Stratford was research *in the moment* of its unfolding – *and* it has remained the subject of further research, part of, in fact, an ongoing performative engagement with theatre history. Writing a book about the experience unavoidably shifts that research into an analytical, logocentric mode, but we have undertaken this volume with the desire to retain some of the affordances and impact of PaR on its pages.

Trimingham herself acknowledges that the attraction of using performance as a means of research arises from, as Mark Fleishman argues, performance's "refusal of binaries (body – mind, theory – practice, space – time, subject – object), its radical openness, its multiplicities, its unrepresentability, its destabilization of all pretentions to fixity and determination"[68] – effectively, its complex, embodied messiness, its lack of strict order. Our approach to PaR at the workshop and in this volume has been deeply influenced by the work of Christian Billing and Rob Conkie, both of whom were keynote speakers at our 2015 conference "Performance as Research in Early English Theatre Studies: *The Three Ladies of London* in Context."[69] As Billing asserts, an embodied rehearsal process adds important layers to the propositional knowledge (I know *that*) made available through traditional scholarly analysis. Theatre artists working through/with texts and archival evidence bring *procedural* knowledge (I know *how to*) and personal or experiential knowledge (I know *of*), born from their previous experience rehearsing and performing plays.[70] All three ways of knowing are present within the emergent processes of embodied rehearsal, and all three kinds of knowing are therefore not constrained to words, to thinking, or to writing but enter the realm of the physical and the affective world of feeling and embodied imagination. Performance is a powerful tool for research because "human beings learn more actively and effectively (in three-dimensional, interactive and temporally mediated situations such as those that regulate social and theatrical communication) through play, risk-taking, trust and embodied discovery than they do through didactic instruction or emulative models of skills-based instruction."[71]

Conkie's theories of PaR emphasize how rehearsal "exceeds" the public performance of plays "as a means of imaginative, affective and interpretive engagement."[72] His work encourages us to embrace the "interpretive fluidity of rehearsal process" over the "interpretive fixity of a finished production." At our Stratford workshop, this approach to PaR proved appropriate because we needed a research method that could exceed the sense of "fixity" that traditionally adheres to historical evidence. Exploring feminist, trans, and queer histories necessitates resistance to the supposed objectivity of positivist scholarship. It must, of practical necessity, rely on the study of traces of lives lived in documents that were created in a period where the power of the cis-patriarchy could be violently enforced. Furthermore, theatre histories are built on fragments and demand we embrace the ephemeral and fill out our understanding with imagination. History, like gender, is fluid and performative. Its lessons are always provisional.

Notably, one of the IBPOC artists who directed scenes at the workshop started the process with movement rather than words: a clear resistance to the logocentrism of colonial culture. When first imagining the writing of this book, we were aware that, in spite of the ways that the workshop worked towards decolonizing our thinking, we would be reverting to a less holistic and more colonial practice. Trimingham speaks of how the very "act of analysis … returns us to the Cartesian modes of thinking from which, some hoped, PAR offered an escape."[73] We accept that as inevitable to a degree, but we reject her argument that "if we want to understand and not just experience we have to think."[74] The experience of the workshop gave us insights and understandings that were situated in our bodies and hearts as well as in our brains, and we believe that embodied experiential knowledge should be valued as much as the knowledge arising from writing and reading. We know that the scholars and artists who participated in the workshop have carried the embodied experience on into their lives and work, as have we, and our hope is that this book captures and approximates some of that impact.

Negotiating this somewhat impossible intention, this book offers readers a mix of genres and formats that together honour affective, embodied, exploratory ways of sharing, learning, and knowing. Throughout, the volume's integration of workshop activity descriptions, artist and scholar reflections, and original commissioned artworks attempts an open-ended and creative design. Emphasizing process over product, we have insisted that each scholar include reflection on the workshop experience as part of their writing, even for chapters that present revised work originally circulated in advance of the workshop as prompts for embodied exploration (as is the case with contributions by Natasha Korda and Clare McManus). We have sustained our commitment to art as research, a powerful means to generate and disseminate knowledge in its own right, by incorporating a script, a zine, and E.M. Parry's three new art works. Our hope is that this design – integrating scholarship, creative work, and artist commentary – will inspire readers' own embodied explorations of gender outside a cis-patriarchal binary and influence new imaginative engagement with plays and historical records.

Simone Chess notes that trans-inclusive pedagogies require methodologies that encompass humility and flexibility with respect to language and terminology in ways that call on teachers to be "willing to make mistakes and course corrections." She notes that "the rules and norms of trans-inclusive discourse are not hardbound, and require us not to follow any one stricture but rather to stay flexible and evolving in our language and usage. Though rethinking and reworking language that feels familiar and comfortable can be challenging and awkward, by being humble and flexible, we open more conversations than we close."[75] Chess's essay is addressed specifically to academics who teach early modern women writers, but her efforts to bring trans-informed and trans-inclusive approaches to the broader canon of queer and feminist early modern texts speak to our experiences of PaR at the Stratford workshop and in our work on this volume as well.

Language became key to research at the workshop since, as noted above, the work depended on many cisgender participants learning the care involved in using pronouns. The workshop gave a tangible experience of how binaries in gendered pronouns within the English language resist and constrict our imaginations about the past, our conversations in the present, and our hopes for the future. Scholars working in Spanish and French asserted how gendered verbs and nouns made this tendency arguably even more problematic in their fields. Some of the most productive explorations in the workshop took place through movement alone, which shifted attention to embodied experiences of gender beyond their codification merely in spoken or written words. Writing a book, of course, makes such experience less accessible. For this volume, we need language that avoids assuming that historical figures who were identified as inhabiting one side of the colonial gender binary would necessarily have identified themselves that way if given other options. We also wish to avoid defining their gender for ourselves in ways that would deny the range of possible identifications pertaining to each individual.

Within the confines of the English language, the gender binary remains frustratingly and insidiously persistent. The term "cross-dressing," for example, a frequent term of reference in much scholarship to date that has focused on gender fluidity in early modern theatre, carries the binary embedded within it. Accepting that gender is a spectrum invites us to ask what exactly is being crossed. We have not found singular solutions to the complexity of these linguistic issues. We sometimes default to the terms "men" and "women" as an unfortunate necessity when trying to describe and signal this historical (and ongoing) binary. At other times, we make use of the acronyms AFAB (assigned female at birth) and AMAB (assigned male at birth) that signal a potential difference between genders assigned and genders felt, even as we acknowledge, drawing on Kit Heyam's insights, that these terms "don't fully make sense for [historical] contexts without official birth registration" and may risk reimposing a binary even as they seek to resist it.[76] We have encouraged our contributors to find their own ways to open up possibilities for gender multiplicity when approaching historical individuals and characters in plays. "Female-identified" and "male-identified," in the past tense, are terms used at moments and refer to how the characters were commonly identified *by their culture*, but these terms should not be presumed to suggest that these persons themselves would necessarily identify in this way. As Chess asserts, a level of flexibility is required around language as we learn to speak more clearly and inclusively. We humbly offer these provisional solutions that work for us, admittedly incompletely, at this moment in the development of our own understanding.

On our final day, guest artist Emma Frankland led the entire group in an exercise originally pioneered by Lois Weaver of Split Britches as part of her Public Address Systems series. As the webpage for this project states, "Public Address Systems create spaces that are hospitable and open so that alternatives can be modeled and critical questions staged."[77] The group all sat on chairs facing the same direction so that we could feel each other's presence but could not see each other directly. We then responded to the invitation to complete the following sentences: "I imagine … I wonder … I think … I feel … I wish …" There was no structure to the exercise beyond that. There was a lot of silence. Participants spoke when they felt the urge, and listened. Such explicit permission to speak and listen without the need to judge or immediately respond was healing. The exercise fostered an open atmosphere of reflection and encouraged us to look beyond the end of the workshop, to imagine other possibilities, other avenues for artistic creation, pedagogy, and research.[78]

Many of our chapters end with versions of this exercise in written form: alongside our contributors, we articulate concerns that remain current, hopes for future work, anxieties about what we have done and what it will mean in the world. In this way, the book, like our approach to PaR itself, is designed to be expressly provisional. We offer this volume only as a moment in an ongoing process. We offer it with the hope that it will provide ways for scholars and artists to pick up its concerns in the academy, in the profession, and beyond.

Sections and Chapters

We have arranged the book's chapters into pairs or triads that, in conversation with each other, continue the provisional process of our research. The first grouping, "Setting the Stage," connects this introduction with insights and reflections from our key collaborator at the Stratford Festival, Keira Loughran. Loughran's "The Meeting of Art and Academia" draws on her extensive experience as an artistic producer within Canada's theatre ecology to ask what the workshop can teach us about forging alliances between academics and theatre artists who together are working to deconstruct the traditional gender binary as represented in classical plays. Loughran considers PaR as a methodology for bringing together artists and scholars; the inclusive principle of "nothing about us without us" and its implications for the planning, execution, and outcomes of PaR; and the need for further research that connects theatre scholars and theatre artists in order to deepen understandings of the role of theatre in our contemporary world. Loughran's account of the workshop's greatest successes and failures differs productively from our own; together, these varied perspectives "set the stage" for the rest of the volume by emphasizing the challenges, and the potential, of equity-focused PaR work.

The next section, "Beyond the Globe," highlights contributions by two gender-nonconforming artists who do not easily find themselves represented in the early modern European dramatic canon. Academic institutions such as McMaster University and arts institutions like the Stratford Festival were created specifically to impose colonial ideologies on these lands. Why would people erased and excluded within this world view want to engage with a canon that is historically white, middle and upper class, and cis-centric? E.M. Parry's artwork *Beyond the Globe* moves beyond the limits of such patriarchal histories of the period and provokes readers of this volume to do the same. "Architectures of Gender," our interview with Parry, helps situate this artwork by describing evidence of women on the early modern stage, outlining how scholars, actors, and guest artists at the workshop initially responded to this evidence and sharing details of the creative/intellectual process Parry undertook in developing this commissioned work for the volume. Parry reflects on their connection to *Beyond the Globe* as a contemporary set and costume designer and flags how their piece reveals the invisible labour that supports theatre-making – usually unacknowledged and often performed by women. Parry also interrogates their own position as a white transmasculine person representing the power and presence of the early modern women who dominated the stages of Europe. The next chapter, by Two-Spirit Turtle Mountain Michif artist Carmen Alvis, raises further questions about the intersection of race, gender, and colonialism in classical theatre production, past and present. In "We Tell Our Stories. We Continue to Exist," Alvis describes how, beginning in the 1950s, colonial supremacy positioned the Stratford Festival as the exemplar of the theatre arts in Canada at a time when First Nations, Inuit, and Métis peoples participating in traditional song, dance, and language were criminalized. Acknowledging this difficult history, Alvis examines the ongoing institutional structures and working practices that make inclusion of Two-Spirit artists deeply important to reclaiming the act of storytelling on these lands and waterways. Using an analysis of Indigenization and reflecting on her Stratford scene work on *The Maid's Tragedy* 5.3, Alvis imagines the equitable engagement of Two-Spirit artists, advocating powerfully for Indigenous, Black, and culturally diverse authorship of the stories that define the arts in settler-occupied Canada.

"Energies, Evidence, Emergent Practices" groups three chapters that, in very different ways, engage traces of gender nonconformity obscured by patriarchal canons and theatre histories. In "Potential Energies in the Early Modern French Repertoire," Ellen Welch notes that plays from the first several decades of seventeenth-century France, of significant scholarly interest for their insights on early modern ideas about gender, are rarely performed today. Given the growing but still limited visibility of queer and trans actors in the French theatre, what might this forgotten repertoire offer today's theatre-makers? Welch takes Isaac de Benserade's *Iphis et Iante* (1634) as a case study for exploring both the opportunities and pitfalls of reviving early modern plays to speak to current contexts. Staging the stranger more neglected plays of the early modern era, Welch suggests, highlights the complex stakes entailed in viewing works as both archive of the past and repertoire for the present. Those stakes include significant implications not only for how we understand gender but also for the product-centred focus of scholarly research. Similarly emphasizing process over product, Callan Davies's chapter explores methodologies for archiving PaR when the performance work involved is definitively not aimed at producing a "final" output. In "The PaRchive and Scraps: Archiving Process in Practice as Research and the Work of

Theatre History," Davies extends previous approaches to PaR and performance documentation to explore how such work can be digitally preserved at the point of delivery: a form of live archiving through social media, website, and film and audio recording. Such archiving navigates ethical responsibilities to extend the research "process" beyond the rehearsal room and make it accessible to a wider public. Putting PaR into direct conversation with the documentary archive of theatre history, moreover, shows that many of the sixteenth-century materials so integral to theatre history are themselves aligned with process-based PaR. Theatre history has a narrativizing tendency to excerpt scraps from their wider contexts and treat them as whole or discrete documents, but Davies suggests that, when we set scraps alongside contemporary PaRchives, we can better attend to their incompleteness: their remaining in process both within their original historic contexts and in subsequent uses and interpretations. SL Grange's chapter, which uses emergent practice as a starting place for communing with queer ghosts, is in some ways an ideal litmus test for such theorizations of in-process incompleteness (Davies) and potential energies (Welch). "A Note to Mary Frith" was initially commissioned by Shakespeare's Globe for their winter 2020 event *Notes for the Forgotten She-Wolves*. In this chapter, Grange shares the script for this performance piece and contextualizes it in light of their larger PhD project, which explores being in love with the long-deceased Mary/Moll Frith and seeking to meet her through magic, improvisation, and other performance practices. Emergent practice, in "A Note to Mary Frith," involves gathering evidentiary "scraps" documenting Mary's "true" self (a biography and diary, a will, legal documents registering Mary's court appearances, and Middleton and Dekker's play-text), setting these fragments alongside one another in all their complexity and incompleteness, and re-embodying them, via performance, as a "living archive." In conversation with one another, this section's chapters by Grange, Davies, and Welch offer important methodological reflections, theoretical framings, and creative prompts for the sections that follow.

Together, the book's next two sections – "Skill, Power, and Swordplay" and "Stepping Beyond Binaries" – centre embodied physicality as a mode of PaR experimentation capable of opening up, in unexpected ways, what we think we know about the performance of gender in early modern plays, whether as objects of theatre history or in contemporary performance. At the Stratford Lab, gendered hierarchies in theatre training posed an initial barrier to such embodied experimentation: many actors who participated, particularly those who are cisgender women, had not been afforded prior training with stage swords. "Drawing Your Weapon" by Peter Cockett and Melinda Gough, with Carmen Alvis, Emma

Frankland, Lily McEvenue, and Denise Oucharek, outlines how the first day's fight session addressed this inequity. Led by Stratford Festival fight captain Wayne Best, the session included exercises focused on the technical and cultural expectations of simply carrying and drawing a sword and on ways actors might reveal character by performing such protocols effectively or ineffectively. This chapter describes and reflects on Best's training session, incorporating multiple actors' comments on the experience – responses that vary in relation to the artists' gender identities and previous professional experience with swordplay. In "Casting *The Roaring Girl*: Embodied Skill, History, and Lived Experience," Clare McManus builds on the workshop discussions about embodied gender and skill with swords to rethink both theatre history and textual editing. The protagonist of Middleton's *The Roaring Girl* is a virtuosic sword-wielding character who was assigned female at birth. Taking cues from the Stratford workshop and from emerging creative and scholarly work on the play's trans valences (including SL Grange's chapter in the volume's previous section), McManus reflects on guest artist Emma Frankland's scene work with *The Roaring Girl* by exploring historical parallels for Frankland's physical exploration of skill, muscularity, sweat, and bodily labour in the work of early modern performers of femininity who have been marginalized from traditional theatre history. McManus maps performance skills shared by Frankland, the English boy actress, and early modern tumblers and rope-dancers to show the extent to which such skills, rather than pertaining to one binary gender category or another, circulate in a queering commonality between distinct and diverse groups.

"Stepping Beyond Binaries" moves from skills of swordplay to skills of everyday courtly comportment, including gait and posture. In "'Mincing Steps' and 'Manly Strides': Practising Gendered Footwork on the Early Modern Stage," Natasha Korda notes that, even though scholarship on the enactment of gender in early modern theatre tends to focus on attire and voice, footwork was equally crucial to gender performance both on and off stage. Drawing on explicit and implicit stage directions, this chapter explores how in early modern England character was built, and gender was performed, through stance, gait, and other forms of theatrical foot-skill. Reflecting on our workshop's scene work on *Love's Cure, or The Martial Maid* 2.2, Korda concludes by asking how PaR might expose, rather than reinforce, the physical and emotional labour of performing binary gender coded through stance, gait, and carriage. The next chapter, "Performing Gender 'From the Ground Up,'" maps movement exercises at the workshop inspired in part by an earlier version of Korda's paper circulated to scholar participants prior to our week's work. Embodied research on the performance of gender in a context that seeks to challenge the colonial gender binary demands language for the rehearsal room that avoids the description of movement as masculine or feminine. With these ideas in mind, our movement exercises used the training techniques of Rudolf Laban to provide inclusive language through which directors and actors might explore the performativity of gender. Describing and reflecting on these exercises, this chapter integrates commentary by Emma Frankland, Lily McEvenue, André Morin, Marcus Nance, and Denise Oucharek and encourages readers to move beyond gendered clichés in order to imagine more inclusive ways to cast, direct, and perform early modern plays. This section concludes with Parry's piece *Two Shadows to One Shape*, followed by "Playing with Gender: Stance, Gender, Embodiment, and Prosthetics." The chapter situates Parry's artwork in light of their experiential, embodied knowledge as someone who works intimately with clothing as a costume designer and performer. Parry discusses how the image plays with both embodied gesture – in the form of posture, stance, countenance, spatial positioning – and prosthetic gender signifiers. They reflect on queer and trans possibilities inspired by historical evidence for early modern portraits as arising from a conglomeration of temporalities, props and prostheses, and bodily processes. This conversation also outlines how research outlined in the previous two chapters resonates with Parry's work as costume designer for Shakespeare's Globe, seeking to abandon stereotypes of gendered movement and encouraging performers to allow clothes to do the work of engendering the stage.

"Disruptive Boys" similarly seeks to disrupt received notions, this time with a concerted focus on boy players. Parry's *Boi-Actrx* diptych responds to a video we created for the workshop in which a portrait of Nathan Field, a well-known boy actress of the period, featured prominently. In these paired images, Parry provokes the volume's reader to imagine connections between players like Field and contemporary drag performance and to reflect on what it means to fashion and present oneself as male. "Disruptive Affects: Portraiture, Staging, and Drag" reflects on the wider stakes of reimagining boy players. Summarizing archival evidence presented in video form at the 2018 workshop and offering an account of the emotional discussions of PaR ethics that it generated among participants, this chapter touches on the politics of gender presentation in early modern England, the precarious status of male-identified performers playing women's roles, Nathan Field's portrait as an example of conscious self-fashioning within that context, and contemporary right-wing anti-drag and anti-trans legislation as modern day analogues to the gender policing and anxieties prevalent in early modern Puritan commentary regarding boy actresses of this era. "A Question to Be Asked: Boy Actors, Performance as Research, and Theatre History," by Roberta Barker and Lucy Munro, further investigates the performers who played female roles on the early modern English stage, interrogating archival research and practice as research as interrelatable sources for our understanding of these actors' careers. Theatre historical research now provides a basis for detailed study of the careers of boy actors such as Richard Robinson, Richard Sharpe, John Thompson, and Stephen Hammerton, and this material in turn enables us to explore variations between their repertoires, as well as the institutional and creative structures within which they worked. Examining these performers' ages and backgrounds, their training relationships with older actors, and their individual impacts upon the roles written for them, Barker and Munro work alongside Parry to show how practice as research might be fused with archival research to challenge the cis-patriarchal assumptions of previous histories and to open up space for imagining the queer possibilities of the past.

The week's work at Stratford disrupted many assumptions – about gender, about the early modern dramatic canon, about scholarship, about teaching, and about the relationship of all these things. The book's penultimate section, "Rehearsing, Teaching, Translating," seeks to further harness this disruptive energy, prompting readers to consider how the workshop's interruption of cis-patriarchal history's assumptions can feed into the work of teachers and translators. In "Calling Across from Our Difference: Teaching (Gender)-Nonconforming Characters in Early Modern English Drama," Jessica Swain describes devising and teaching an upper year undergraduate seminar on non-Shakespearean Renaissance drama inspired by projects, undertaken by SL Grange, Emma Frankland and Andy Kesson, and others, which engage plays from the early modern period to actively claim space for queer, trans, and gender-nonconforming bodies today. Swain's students studied the interconnections between gender and genre on the early modern English stage, with a focus on the sociocultural work of transgressive AFAB characters in plays such as Middleton and Dekker's *The Roaring Girl*, John Lyly's *Galatea*, and Margaret Cavendish's *The Convent of Pleasure*. This chapter shares teaching resources Swain developed and outlines some of her students' compelling intellectual discoveries. Edward McLean (Mac) Test, in "Rehearsing *The Lieutenant Nun*: Translation in Action," traces pivotal aspects of our workshop impacting his translated edition, with Marta Albalá Pelegrín, of *The Lieutenant Nun* (*La Monja alférez*). Test reflects on unexpected and surprising changes to his collaborative edition of the play that occurred because of the risk, play, and experimentation that was central to our workshop's rehearsal room. In particular, Test speaks to how working with trans actors and directors significantly shaped the (then in-process) translation and edition. These artists made it abundantly clear that trans and queer elements are already present in early modern culture, and Test describes how exploring the play-text with such realizations in mind freed him as a translator to use language that might have initially seemed too anachronistic. Swain's and Test's chapters both challenge us to consider how knowledge is generated and disseminated through process and the ongoing rehearsal of ideas, pointing to just how deeply pedagogical PaR methodologies can be.

The book's final section, "Dreaming PaR Futures," revisits questions of canons and PaRchives with an eye to more just futures. Alongside our own short "(Non)Conclusions," the book's final word – and image – goes to two student research assistants and artists at the workshop, Madeleine Krusto and Kitoko Mai. Their co-authored zine, "To Degender Is to Decolonize," builds on Mai's spoken word poem "Let Shakespeare Die," performed on our first day at the Stratford Lab and included here in written form. In "Let Shakespeare Die," Mai spoke from their position as a non-binary Black multimedia and theatre practitioner, challenging us to consider who is included in productions of early modern plays and whose experiences are and can be represented in and through classical theatre. Krusto and Mai's chapter takes this questioning a step further, asking whether inclusive, decolonial PaR theory means ridding ourselves of not only Shakespeare but also the power dynamics of the spectating (white) academic. "To Degender Is to Decolonize" interweaves drawing, poetry, and collage to imagine a future PaR that Krusto and Mai can see themselves engaging with and facilitating: one that is decolonial, fluid in gender and sexuality, community-based, accessible, collaborative, and anti-capitalist. Embracing a zine format that is itself fluid and collaborative, they propose that, when we engage with PaR through these types of frameworks, we may be able to find possibilities for decolonial, restorative justice.

NOTES

1 Ellen Welch, quoted in Engendering the Stage, "Futures for Practice, Performance, and Research."

2 Frankland, "Toward a Trans Canon."

3 Denise Oucharek, in conversation with Peter Cockett and Melinda Gough, unpublished interview, 2010.

4 Denise Oucharek, in conversation with Cockett and Gough.

5 This John Douglas Taylor Conference was organized by Peter Cockett, Jessica Dell, Melinda Gough, Erin Julian, Helen Ostovich, Jennifer Roberts-

Smith, and Chantelle Thauvette. For further details, see Performance as Research in Early English Theatre Studies.

6 "Two-Spirit" is an adjective that, according to Harlan Pruden, was coined in 1990 by and for communities of Indigenous people "as a way to identify those individuals who embody diverse (or non-normative) sexualities, genders, gender roles, and/or gender expressions ... while evoking the time before the harshness of colonization where many, not all, First Peoples had traditions and ways that were non-binary, where some Nations had 3, 4, 5, 6, or even 7+ different genders and these genders were not only accepted and honored but also had distinct roles within their respective Nations" (Pruden, "August 4, 2020 'TWO-SPIRIT' Turns 30!!"). Pruden also notes that there are "about 130 terms within our own languages that name, account and identify these other genders – each word is Nation specific" (Pruden, "Explanation of Two-Spirit Terminology").

7 Specific scenes workshopped were the following: Act 3, scene 1 from Middleton and Dekker, *The Roaring Girl*, ed. Mulholland (scene 5 in *The Roaring Girl*, ed. Kahn); Act 2, scene 2 from Fletcher and Massinger, *Love's Cure, or The Martial Maid*, ed. Pérez Díez; Act 5, scene 3 from Beaumont and Fletcher, *The Maid's Tragedy*, ed. Craik; and Act 3, lines 2420–628 from Ruiz de Alarcón, attrib., *The Lieutenant Nun*, in *The Lieutenant Nun: Annotated Translation of the Play, Historical Accounts and Documents about Antonio/Catalina de* Erauso, ed. and trans. Pelegrín and Test. We are grateful to José Pérez Díez, Albalá Pelegrín, and Edward McLean (Mac) Test, for sharing their prepublication editions for use at the workshop.

8 Frankland, "Toward a Trans Canon."

9 Hudson and Purcell, who attended the last day of the workshop following the most significant pivots in our original plan, shared that they were "struck by the levels of trust and openness that the week had established between the participants and the commitment that everyone involved brought to the work. Participants were thinking and working very deeply, rigorously examining both the texts and their own instincts and interpretations. The week had also fostered a mutually respectful dialogue between academics and practitioners" (Engendering the Stage, "Futures for Practice, Performance, and Research").

10 Oucharek, in conversation with Cockett and Gough.

11 Davies, "SF Day 3: Scenework, Walking, and Sharing." The term "PaRchive" is coined by Davies, chapter 5 of this volume.

12 It also became clear that equitable engagement on the subject of oppressions past and present requires acknowledgment of the additional emotional labour involved for those who have lived experience of such oppression. We sought ways to partially address this imbalance after the fact by writing additional grant applications to cover honoraria for all

contributors to this volume not already paid as student research assistants or salaried faculty members, but explicit provisions for such costs should be built into budgeting for future PaR projects.

13 For further discussion of the impacts that holding space for these groups had during our workshop, see Alvis, "We Tell Our Stories. We Continue to Exist," chapter 3 of this volume. For helpful working definitions of affinity spaces, see the 2022 room agreement facilitated by Emma Frankland as featured in Solga, *Women Making Shakespeare in the Twenty-First Century*, 37, and Racial Equity Tools, "Racial Equity Tools Glossary: Caucusing (Affinity Groups)."

14 Elizabeth Cruz Petersen, quoted in Engendering the Stage, "Reflections on Practice, Performance, and Research."

15 Erin Julian, quoted in Engendering the Stage, "Futures for Practice, Performance, and Research."

16 Oucharek, in conversation with Cockett and Gough.

17 As Callan Davies notes in chapter 5 of this volume, both André Morin and Marcus Nance, reflecting on the workshop in separate Fall 2019 conversations with Peter Cockett and Melinda Gough, lamented the restrictions on time (and funding) that limited what could be accomplished in our scene work. Morin stated in that interview, "In school, someone said something, just offhand, that I've remembered for a long time: 'you need about an hour of work for a minute of stage time, just to be at square one' … [T]o have people in the room who just knew, rather than me having to go home after a full day in rehearsal, look it up, go to the library: that was very exciting. But the thing that was problematic was, again, we didn't have enough time … To do performance as research decently will require an enormous investment. And it will produce probably very exciting things" (André Morin in conversation with Peter Cockett and Melinda Gough, unpublished interview, 2019). On the significant resources needed for equity-centred structural change within "the economy of the Shakespeare industry," see Solga, *Women Making Shakespeare in the Twenty-First Century*, 64–6.

18 On this issue, see Davies, chapter 5 of this volume, as well as Clarke, "The Impact Market."

19 On the Engendering the Stage website and in this volume, all photo and video images as well as references to or direct quotes from Brideau appear with parental consent in addition to the consent of the actor.

20 For further discussion of these issues, please see Parry with Cockett and Gough, "Disruptive Affects: Portraiture, Staging, and Drag," and Barker and Munro, "A Question to Be Asked," chapters 12 and 13, respectively, of this volume.

21 Adams, "'His Play Shan't Ask Your Leave to Live.'"

22 Sophie Tillotson, "From Gimmick Casting to Standard Practice," argues that the practice of women performing roles designated as male in

Shakespearean drama is now more accepted. However, Kim Solga suggests that the ongoing need for more hospitable ecologies of theatre is especially acute for queer, trans, and non-Western female-identified artists who still work primarily outside of mainstream theatre yet are ready to claim space at the centre (Solga, "Gender and the Aesthetics of Occupation").

23 Heyam, *Before We Were Trans*, 22.

24 Heyam, 22.

25 Lemkin Institute, "Statement."

26 Heyam, *Before We Were Trans*, 19.

27 On this topic, see, for example, Butler, *Who's Afraid of Gender?*

28 Chess, "Queer Residue." See also Barker and Munro, "A Question to Be Asked," chapter 13 of this volume.

29 McKendrick, *Woman and Society*; McKendrick, "Representing Their Sex."

30 Korda, "Women's Involvement," 283.

31 Korda, 282–4.

32 Gough and McManus, "Introduction," 190.

33 Korda, "Women's Involvement," 288. Engendering the Stage's archival wing also explores women's involvement in the commercial side of theatre practice, showing, for example, that women were important shareholders and managers of London playhouses such as the Fortune. See, for example, Munro, "Women's Investment."

34 Korda, "Women's Involvement," 288; see also Korda, *Labors Lost*, 93–109, 114–33.

35 Wofford and Tylus, "Introduction," 193.

36 See Gough and McManus, *Transnational Mobility*. This special section for *Renaissance Drama* includes essays on transnational convent drama (Bicks, "Repeat Performances"); travelling mixed-gender Italian troupes (Brown, "The Travelling Diva," esp. 261–6 on the Ganassa troupe's residency in Madrid); female performance in Spanish Golden Age drama (Carrión, "Legally Bound," esp. 233–4n2); and French women's theatrical activities in salons and elsewhere (Gethner and Gough, "Advent"). For discussion of theatricals by French princesses such as Henrietta Maria, who continued such practices after moving to foreign courts, see also Britland, *Drama at the Courts* and Gough, "Courtly *Comédiantes*."

37 Gough and McManus, "Introduction," 190–1.

38 As Korda notes, Mary Sullivan in 1912 raised the question of how court performances by queens and noblewomen might have influenced the "all-male" stage of Shakespeare and his contemporaries. In response, "an anonymous reviewer in *The Nation* (1913) … dismissed her suggestion as 'absolutely gratuitous and the kind of misleading surmise that unsteadies the half-informed'" (Korda, "Women's Involvement," 284).

39 Gough and McManus, "Introduction," 193–8.

40 Poulsen, "Women Performing." This paraphrase of Poulsen's concept is from Gough and McManus, "Introduction," 194.

41 Campbell, "'Merry, Nimble, Stirring Spirit[s]'"; Tomlinson, "The Actress"; Brown, *Diva's Gift*.

42 Graham, "'[N]or Bear I in This Breast,'" 112. Graham, 109, also helpfully cites Eve Kosofsky Sedgwick's elucidation of "queerness" as "the open mesh of possibilities, gaps, overlaps, dissonances and resonances, lapses and excesses of meaning when the constituent elements of anyone's gender, of anyone's sexuality aren't made (or can't be made) to signify monolithically" (Sedgwick, *Tendencies*, 8). Graham's argument draws on previous work on boy players, including Orgel, *Impersonations*; Levine, *Men in Women's Clothing*; Stallybrass, "Transvestism"; Shapiro, *Gender in Play*; and Masten, "'Reading 'Boys.'" On the period's distinction between the gender of adult men and that of boys, including boy players, see Will Fisher, "'His Majesty the Beard': Beards and Masculinity," in Fisher, *Materializing Gender*, 83–128, as well as Rycroft, *Facial Hair*.

43 Masten cautions against deploying a "developmental model of boyhood" (boys as not-yet men) in ways that close down the gendered and the erotic complexities inherent in audience engagement with the figure of the boy player (Masten, "'Readings 'Boys,'" 111). Simone Chess further emphasizes how some of these actors were "especially nonbinary, and that they did not always grow out of these trans genders" but instead staged genderqueer performances into adulthood (Chess, "Queer Residue," 242).

44 Frankland, "Trans Women on Stage."

45 Frankland, 784.

46 Heyam, *Before We Were Trans*, 20.

47 Harding, "Rethinking Standpoint Epistemology."

48 McKellips, "'Immodestly in Mans Apparrell.'"

49 See Leverhulme Trust, "Engendering the Stage: The Records of Early Modern Performance." See also A Bit Lit, "Engendering the Stage: Making Space for an Inclusive Performance History," as well as various blog posts on the Engendering the Stage in the Age of Shakespeare and Beyond website, https://engenderingthestage.humanities.mcmaster.ca/.

50 Chess, "Queer Residue," 242.

51 Pelegrín and Test, Introduction to *The Lieutenant Nun*.

52 Chess, "Queer Residue," 258. Here, Chess brings work on physicality in early modern "type" casting (Palfrey and Stern, *Shakespeare in Parts*) into conversation with the notion of "sexual types" (DiGangi, *Homoerotics*).

53 Much has been written on this topic. See the helpful summary with bibliographic references in Erdman, Introduction to *The Mountain Girl from La Vera/La Serrana de la Vera*, trans. Erdman, 25–7.

54 Petersen, *Women's Somatic Training*, 41–2; Pelegrín and Test, "Translating a Trans Ancestor: Antonio/Catalina de Erauso," 18–19; Velasco, *The Lieutenant Nun*, 40–2; Velasco, "Foreword: "Antonio/Catalina de Erauso," esp. 75–6.

55 See Heyam, who notes that a trans person is someone who does not identify with the gender they have been assigned, who moves away from it, whereas "a cis woman is someone who was assigned female at birth, and is happy to describe herself as a woman – regardless of how much she defies society's idea of what 'woman' should mean" (Heyam, *Before We Were Trans*, 2–4).

56 On trans coding in the play-text, see Edward McLean (Mac) Test, "Rehearsing *The Lieutenant* Nun," chapter 15 of this volume. Test's notes helpfully reference scholarly discussion regarding the gender of both the character within the play and the historical personage on which the character is based.

57 Heyam, *Before We Were Trans*, 11–13, 23–6.

58 Joubin, "Shakespearean Performance Through a Trans Lens," 82. Insisting on the asterisk in "trans*," Jack Halberstam, in *Trans**, similarly emphasizes the importance of resisting categorization and naming, given the ways that classification systems have arisen historically from, and continue to be imbricated with, colonial ways of knowing and governing.

59 Frankland and Kesson, "'Perhaps John Lyly Was a Trans Woman?'" See also Frankland, "Trans Women on Stage"; Lyly, *Galatea*, ed. Kesson.

60 Fuchs, "The *Courage* to Transform." See also Wofford, "Cross-Dressing and Technologies."

61 Korda, "Women's Involvement," 290.

62 Billing, *Rehearsing Shakespeare: Alternative Strategies*; Billing, "Historiography, Rehearsal Processes."

63 UK Research and Innovation, "Staging the Henrician Court"; Staging and Representing the Scottish Renaissance Court, http://stagingthescottishcourt .brunel.ac.uk/index.html; Before Shakespeare, https://beforeshakespeare .com/; Shakespeare and the Queen's Men, https://thequeensmen .ca/; Performance as Research in Early English Theatre Studies, http:// threeladiesoflondon.mcmaster.ca/.

64 Conkie, "Rehearsal: Pleasures."

65 Barton, "Introduction I: Wherefore PAR?," 5. The quotation is Barton's paraphrase of Candy, "Practice-Based Research: A Guide," 3.

66 Trimingham, "Methodology," 54.

67 Trimingham, 54–5.

68 Fleishman, "Difference," 32.

69 The Performance as Research in Early English Theatre Studies website includes revised versions of these keynote talks by Billing and Conkie.

70 Billing, "Rehearsing Shakespeare," 385–6.

71 Billing, 388.

72 Conkie, "Rehearsal: Pleasures," 411.
73 Trimingham, "Methodology," 55.
74 Trimingham, 55.
75 Chess, "Teaching Transfeminisms," 45.
76 Heyam, *Before We Were Trans*, 31; see also 5. Heyam also points out that that AMAB and AFAB are often problematically used in ways designed to constrain people to "real" genders and in ways that "separate non-binary people into another artificial binary" (31).
77 Split Britches, "Public Address Systems." Frankland adapted our activity from the "Porch Sitting" exercise shared here.
78 For discussion of some of these developments, see our "(Non)Conclusion" in this volume.

1 The Meeting of Art and Academia

KEIRA LOUGHRAN

Over the last twenty-five years, there has been a growing push in Canadian theatre, from both artists and government funding priorities, to be more inclusive of the diverse identities of today's Canadian artists and audiences. This directive has created an economic tension in the Canadian theatre ecology between support for new Canadian plays written, performed, and created, particularly by marginalized artists, and the continued production of British and American canons of plays that have historically been held as the standard of excellence in anglophone theatre in this country. As a critical mass of marginalized artists gain experience, opportunity, and voice in professional theatre, a serious reconciliation is erupting between these artists and mainstream producing companies to acknowledge, unpack, and address the impact that this historically dominant British theatre tradition and training has left on marginalized artists and on English-language theatre practice in Canada today. Universities find themselves in a similar situation, particularly with regard to gender equality and recognition of non-binary gender identification, and so the academic community, particularly within English and theatre studies, has the potential to be an ally in challenging and deconstructing the traditional gender binary perceived in the early modern and classical texts that form foundational canons for our country's largest theatres. Exploring and better understanding possibilities and implications for such an alliance was a key aim of the experiment that this article reflects on, conducted within the Stratford Festival Laboratory in 2018 in collaboration with scholars led by Peter Cockett and Melinda Gough from McMaster University. It focused on the presence and portrayal of gender in early modern texts with consideration and inclusion of a non-binary and gender-fluid lens.

In 2013, the Stratford Festival, under Artistic Director Antoni Cimolino, launched the Stratford Festival Laboratory – a space for artistic research and development within the organization with an aim to diversify the work of the festival: who was working there, how we were working, what we were working on. As the inaugural associate producer for the laboratory, it was my job to conceive programs, research and assess projects, and make recommendations for development and exploration that were aligned with this priority. With approval from the artistic director, I was then responsible for managing and overseeing those programs through all stages – planning, execution, and follow-up. Through various programs in the lab, questions pertaining to the experience of women and 2SLGBTQ+ artists at the festival and in the industry at large had been raised and discussed internally in the company around both personal experiences and onstage portrayals of gender and sexual orientation in the institution. The explosion and impact of the Weinstein allegations and ensuing #MeToo movement beginning at the end of 2017 and, much closer to home, the allegations against Artistic Director Albert Schultz and Soulpepper Theatre in Toronto in early 2018 made it all the more urgent to examine our methodologies with consideration to gender when engaging with these classical texts.

European plays from the early modern period that continue to be produced today were written within societies that propagated and normalized a binary notion of gender, particularly with regard to the roles and responsibilities in those societies of male and female persons. While the texts themselves may have originally intended to challenge or satirize these roles, colonization has imposed a gender binary on this land, and these European texts have been used by colonizers as a means to impose colonial culture on this land and entrench these binary gendered roles and responsibilities in our colonial settler psyche. As our awareness and understanding grows of a wider spectrum of gender identification both historically and across cultures – many Indigenous languages point to at least five and as many as fifteen distinct gender identities – how might our understanding of these plays change? What does it mean to allow ourselves to examine these play-texts without those assumptions and within a non-binary context? What new meanings are revealed through these texts when we approach such plays through a non-binary lens? How does an audience relate to them if they challenge, rather than reinforce, the assumptions and world view of binary gender? Can we discover new inspiration within the ambiguity and complexity of meaning that a non-binary lens often reveals? These were the questions I was eager to explore through this project.

Once all participants were in the room together, however, the nature of the project revealed itself quite quickly in ways that had eluded me, Melinda, and Peter, despite our planning. The scope and ambition of these questions was so broad and the participants (ironically) so diverse that our work together would have needed far more time to tackle this research. The project proved far more informative as an experiment in the bringing together of scholars and artists, helping us to discover the benefits and challenges of this type of collaboration and to generate important recommendations for taking this type of collaboration forward, especially when aiming to bring necessary new perspectives to these historical plays.

This chapter will reflect on and critique three aspects of our work that I found to be the most revealing through this project: performance as research (PaR) as a methodology for bringing together artists and scholars; the inclusive principle of "nothing about us without us" and its implications in the planning, execution, and benefit of the work when working with historically marginalized communities; and finally, the role that scholarship from social science and humanities departments can play to connect theatre scholars and theatre artists and deepen the impact of theatre in our contemporary world. I write from my perspective as an artist and artistic producer: my intentions (in which I stand strong), my failures (of which there are many), as well as the project's success (for which I claim little) in all its "glorious mess" (as Emma Frankland has called it).[1] Perhaps most important, it illuminated for me what we as artists and producers can do to expand and evolve theatre practice in this country, with the aim of supporting and building an inclusive and vital theatre culture for *all* Canadians.

Performance as Research

I had not heard much about performance as research as a methodology prior to Peter and Melinda approaching me with this proposal. What I understood was that it was a relatively new and evolving artistic and creative methodology within academia known for its fluidity and responsiveness to discoveries made through performance. That was exciting to me. As theatre-makers, we often don't have time or resources to put solely to research; in my experience, contemporary performance methodologies are largely underdiscussed in the professional theatre, with most mainstream companies predominantly defaulting to a hybrid of American method acting and British classical methodology, despite more recent trends of devised theatre and actor as creator being introduced in theatre training programs. Funded theatre companies, which are generally our professional employers, are primarily focused on artistic product within a free market economy rather than on studying process for the advancement of our craft and connection to our community.

Furthermore, collaborations in Canada between professional artists and theatre scholars seem quite rare; I know very little about research being conducted in my field by scholars, nor am I regularly presented with the findings of scholars, nor have scholars been very involved in rehearsal processes. Their work and conclusions, to me, often seemed drawn mostly through evaluations of final productions or analysis of play-texts rather than through meaningful engagement with process.

As a practising artist and woman of colour, however, I am constantly exploring larger artistic questions around the impact of inclusive and diverse practices in and through my work. My work becomes ongoing research in this area, my colleagues, collaborators in this work. I see the same drive in the work of many of my IBPOC and 2SLGBTQ+ colleagues. My artistic curiosity, particularly when involved in staging historic/ canonical texts, can often be best articulated through this question: How can this production artfully subvert the status quo and prompt audience reflection and transformation? In other words, how can I be a playful disruptor? This curiosity for and commitment to this role for artists in society has also defined much of my work as an associate producer at Stratford, particularly for the laboratory and its goal of diversifying the work of the company. I felt that partnerships between these historically marginalized communities and scholars could readily serve the exploration of, experimentation with, and reflection on theatre as a vehicle for social and cultural transformation and evolution. Dissemination of such research and conclusions among working theatre artists and producing companies, and the opportunity to engage scholars for support in this aim, all made PaR a very enticing proposal.

As a theatre artist, the development and use of PaR felt very natural to me: how else can theatre research have practical relevance unless it is tested and borne out in performance? The Engendering the Stage project at the lab felt like a winning combination: dedicated scholars experiencing, examining, and analysing our work in ways that could impact our professional practice and art form beyond the ephemeral existence of the run of a play itself. Our experiment revealed, however, that, while this idea may hold true, much more work needs to be considered and done by both scholars and artists, and their respective funding organizations, to ensure PaR is an effective and accountable methodology for the evolution of professional theatre practice. The exploration opened my eyes to how differently theatre artists and scholars understand the work, despite all best intentions, and how wide the gap can be in what it might mean to all stakeholders to challenge and push our art form and field. Bridging this gap, however, becomes increasingly pressing when the art form is looking to be more inclusive and reflective of diverse experiences and create a united community across increasingly disparate cultures. PaR may still serve as a useful methodology for this continued aim. But how does PaR relate to the contemporary production of theatre, outside the confines of academia? What parameters should be considered to provide focused and structured research, and how can we ensure that conclusions from the research are shared widely with other professional theatre practitioners?

Bruce Barton, a friend, colleague, and core member of the Performance as Research Working Group of the International Federation for Theatre Research (IFTR/FIRT) and director of the School of Creative and Performing Arts at the University of Calgary, clarified some of the key elements and attributes of artistic research – an umbrella term for pedagogies that include PaR – in a conversation I had with him in preparing to write this chapter.[2] In hindsight, it was a conversation I wish I had had to better prepare me for the Engendering the Stage workshop, but happening as it did after the fact, it has given me a clearer framework through which to assess our work. A key attribute of PaR is that the mode of research is carried out through practice to some degree and in some capacity, as opposed to research through observation. He also identified three key elements. First is the idea of "emergence": all researchers expect that the research will clarify itself and change from its original conception. Second, the practice is "fully embodied," which often necessitates inter/trans disciplinary approaches to the work. Finally, the research is "highly situated" in that the conclusions of the project are not easily transposable or reproduceable but rather are transferable in principle, which makes the research worthwhile.

Within this understanding of PaR, our experiment conceptually made a lot of sense. Entering into this relationship, my original hope was that PaR would be a method through which an artistic practice might be tested and evaluated, and its results disseminated, within an area much in need of study – namely the role that gender plays in the exploration of early modern texts within the context of a gender non-binary lens – without the pressure of financial payoff from box office. The research that emerged, however, was quite different from what either Peter, Melinda, or I had first conceived, and I think it is worth examining why.

While PaR can be an exciting and useful research and development methodology to push theatre practice, my experience on this project demonstrated that it requires an even higher level of communication, planning, and regular review/evaluation throughout the process. Additionally, I would recommend the following conditions be met from the outset for a focused PaR experiment that involves collaboration between academic scholars and professional theatre artists.

- Research should be focused on a single prioritized question, even if that question shifts as the research continues.
- All participants must be engaged as equal researchers and equally committed to finding greater clarity on the question and possible answers to it.
- Goals of the initiative should not centre on the codification of practice but should instead prioritize clarification of practices and impacts of changing variables.

I was encouraged to find out from Bruce that these conditions have also been identified by other PaR practitioners, who understand the need for agreement by all parties on what the project is, acknowledge the challenge posed by multiple points of entry and multiple objectives inherent within the group of researchers, and recognize the need for appropriate priming and preparation of participants.

To the first point, while I believe all participants intellectually understood we were exploring the portrayal and embodiment of gender in early modern texts, I think Peter, Melinda, and I at least all had different ideas of what that meant. While this proposal has many interesting components, the question I would have prioritized is, How might the understanding of non-binary gender impact contemporary stagings of early modern plays?; while Peter was starting more from a question, How might gender have been performed on early modern stages, and what is the impact of non-traditional casting on the audience's experience of gender today?; and Melinda was more focused on something like, How did boy actresses in England as well as female actresses at the English court and on the continent contribute to the portrayal of gender complexity in early modern plays? While these are all interesting and valid questions, they are all very different questions. These differences impacted what ultimately was too wide an array of activities for our project, the group of people assembled, and the primary resources we looked to.

To the second point, within a PaR process, all participants are ideally working from a known skill set with which they have a confident degree of expertise, while simultaneously recognizing that their expertise, alone, is insufficient to fully investigate the research question. This premise gives everyone equal capacity to contribute and to learn. All participants should have the same availability to the work, within their respective capacities, and be given priority when their expertise is most relevant to the prioritized question at hand. In our project, while the diversity of experience in the room was very exciting, the structure of the work did not support all participants being seen or supported as equal researchers, and it sometimes magnified the hierarchies that continued to exist within the room. For example, whole sections of the schedule only included the scholars, some of whom had little to no understanding of the craft of acting at a professional level and assumed a place for their expertise within the rehearsal process that was not always helpful. This assumption also severely handicapped the actors from participation in the scholarly discourse where they might have provided unique and enlightening perspectives. Furthermore, due to the structure of this lab experiment, the company actors available to us had severe limits on what they might be asked to do, as much of the work was outside the terms of the season contract under which they were working, and in this case, the majority of the actors had little to no expertise with the canon of early modern plays and could not be called experts within that work. Within this structure, it was very difficult for the actors to feel like much more than subjects in the experiment rather than equal researchers. It was the transgender, non-binary, and Two-Spirit guest artists who proved to be the most influential agents in the room, and it was through their investment and participation that the project saw the most success. I will speak more to this point in the next section, "Nothing About Us Without Us."

The third point is the one in which I feel our project saw the most success. While there were many oversights and errors in our methodology due to the lack of clarity and unity in the focus of the lead researchers, namely myself, Melinda, and Peter, our experiment did shed a lot of light on implications of our practices and the impact of changing variables for each group of participants. The assembled scholars all articulated a much greater understanding of the work of professional actors, and the workshop clearly opened up new considerations for their scholarly research on theatre that previously didn't exist. The actors gained insight into the complexities of identity with regard to gender and complicity as contemporary storytellers and in propagating gender stereotypes entrenching old narratives when staging these centuries-old plays. Perhaps most satisfying: the transgender, non-binary, and Two-Spirit guest artists have gone on to work together in new collaborations of their own devising. This development was hugely exciting to see happen and to know that our work facilitated their meeting and created a ground on which they might continue to build artistic collaborations. Emma Frankland was also engaged by the festival to lead a new exploration born of this work in the lab in 2019 that she has since written about and which, I understand, was quite exciting. I would love to see the resources of PaR within academia available and effectively shared with the not-for-profit theatre in ways more similar to other disciplines like science and medicine: where findings are shared globally and work to advance theatre practices as reflections of contemporary society and collective humanity.

Nothing About Us Without Us

Marginalized artists – women, visible minorities, 2SLGBTQ+ people – while fighting to survive within the dominant system, often discover that their struggles give them unique artistic strengths and insights. The challenge for mainstream organizations is to recognize, trust, and give platform and opportunity for these unique voices to be included. Mainstream theatre organizations often assume that the work of these artists at best has a limited niche audience and at worst is inferior and will alienate their audience. Contrarily, the assumption (and often the experience) of marginalized artists is that the inclusion of such diversity makes the work stronger – accessible to a wider audience, more transformative, more adaptive, more collaborative, more creative. We have earned our place in the mainstream, when given the opportunity. Within EDI (equity, diversity, and inclusion) work, the phrase "nothing about us without us," first used in English by South African disability activists in the late 1990s, has become a rallying cry for the marginalized and a guiding principle in developing methodology for the work over the last five years. The complexity comes in determining who, how, and when that inclusion happens and in recognizing and giving agency to those people in the artistic creation and conception of the work. To be clear, there is no "right" method for such determination to date, but rather, diverse methods are being employed to build meaningful, long-term, and sustainable inclusion and agency for these marginalized communities within the mainstream that we hope will move EDI work forward within professional theatre practice as a whole. My hope for this project was to try one such method, bringing together a diverse group of artists and scholars, and creating a safe environment of curious, passionate, and open-minded people to explore how early modern plays might intersect with a contemporary gender non-binary lens. Despite these intentions, I think our planning and conception for Engendering the Stage, however, failed to bring these EDI priorities right to the fore from the beginning, which impacted our ability to practise the "nothing about us without us" principle to full effect.

To be fair, I do not know how prioritized EDI was to this project as originally conceived by Melinda and Peter. For me, the inclusion of trans artist Emma Frankland and her experience and perspective on the presence and portrayal of gender in early modern texts, as suggested by Peter and Melinda in consultation with their collaborators Clare McManus and Lucy Munro (who had worked with Emma previously), was particularly exciting and reinforced one of my biggest motivations for including the Engendering the Stage project in the lab. We then chased the impulse to include Indigenous artists and to further research non-binary experience and perspectives in the work by inviting additional guest artists to join. Our failure, as the three lead producers on the project, was in not recognizing the significance of the shift of focus that was necessitated by their inclusion and the emergence of new research questions arising from this inclusion: What is the goal? Who should be involved? How should our time be broken down? What other resources are necessary? In not discussing and clarifying in more depth the aim, opportunity, and terms of engaging them in this research, we subsequently failed to engage these artists as equal lead collaborators on the project to inform all aspects of the work going forward. Instead, Peter, Melinda, and I focused on establishing the producing relationship between the two organizations we were working for – the Stratford Festival and McMaster University – within which many parameters were already established: the company actors were selected more by availability than suitability to the work; scholars had already been invited for a specific expertise and within an assumed methodology that was not necessarily in balance with what we would have done had the transgender artists been involved in those conversations. We focused on leveraging our resources within the structural or organizational constraints of our institutions as creative problem solving, rather than clarifying and prioritizing the goal and engaging the people who needed to be included to contribute to the further planning. I think this situation happens often within both the development of artistic projects and the development of academic research. The challenge is as follows: it is all well and good for us to say we want to explore the presence and portrayal of gender in early modern play-texts, and then to determine that we want to include the perspective on that subject of diverse artists by including those who identify as trans and non-binary, but we need to recognize that, unless they are engaged as equal contributors and leaders from the beginning, we risk these artists becoming objectified as we are asking them to come into our research essentially as *subjects* rather than *scientists*.

So what is an alternate method? Let's assume, as I believe was the case, that Melinda, Peter, and I all agree that we want to prioritize the inclusion of diverse artists, particularly those who identify as trans and non-binary. Following "nothing about us without us," we then need to find artists who self-identify as trans or non-binary AND who are interested in this same topic of research, namely, the presence and portrayal of gender in early modern texts. Within this small demographic, we managed to hire one person – Emma Frankland – who had experience and was personally invested in the early modern canon. The inevitable next question then is, Is one enough?; and the question after that is, How many is enough? Is it fair to ask Emma to hold full responsibility for how trans and non-binary people are included in an investigation of classical theatre practice going forward? We discovered an answer to this question when the first non-binary artist we invited, who was new to the festival, articulated that their participation would be contingent on not being the only trans artist in the room. This requirement was in keeping with artists from the trans, non-binary, and Indigenous communities who, on other projects, have made similar requests when asked to participate in work of this nature. We ourselves had identified Two-Spirit perspectives to be another important voice needed at the table, recognizing the sovereignty of Indigenous people on Turtle Island and how non-binary understandings of gender within many Indigenous nations might contribute vitally to the work. In the end, we were able to engage several non-binary guest artists, including Carmen Alvis, in addition to Emma Frankland. These artists brought less experience with early modern texts than Emma did, and it is difficult to say if they were as much interested in the topic as they were in being included in the work. In my experience within the lab, this attitude is common. Marginalized artists in Canada rarely have extensive experience or interest in the classical canon, let alone early modern texts outside of Shakespeare, as there is generally more support for them to create their own work, and many have experienced these texts as tools of cultural oppression. Their commitment to participate requires a generosity and opportunity to validate their experience of this work whether positive or negative. All institutional and mainstream assumptions about its value and meaning are best left at the door. It is hard to reconcile this with the value and level of "expertise" usually required for academic support, but I think it is vitally necessary to make space, time, and resources available to explore the possibility. Ironically, when collaborations do happen between traditionalists and artists from marginalized communities, I have found the discoveries of marginalized artists through the mainstream work to be some of the most artistically exciting and authentic, as these artists often have an objectivity to the work that allows them to truly enter, explore, and reveal it in new ways.

Within the rest of the assembled people, there was definitely consideration of further inclusion of diverse people with regards to gender, ethnicity, age, and sexual orientation. The lack of clarity, discussion, and understanding of the role and agency of each participant, however, undermined the intention of assembling such a diverse group.

To Melinda and Peter's credit, once we were all assembled, the trans, non-binary, and Two-Spirit guest artists were given strong agency to shape and structure the work, and we deferred to them when it came to determining our actual practice for the day. I think it happened as the clarity of our research and questions grew, and we realized that too much of our preparation had taken place without the inclusion or consultation of these artists and without acknowledgment of the shifting focus of the work. This shift included establishing structural parameters on the day – checking in and checking out, changing roles within working groups, leading exercises, and facilitating discussions. Unfortunately, this work was done *reactively*, rather than *proactively*, and often fell outside of the work the guest artists were being paid for on the face of their contract. This inequity was one of the biggest learning points for me and ties into the PaR principle of engaging all researchers as equals and Bruce's point of appropriate priming and preparation of participants. It is important that all participants are engaged on the same terms and with the same expectations. The challenge is to provide sufficient leadership while simultaneously being an equal collaborator and researcher, and acquiescing to those whose perspective and experience are of more relevance to the work at hand as it presents itself. Following "nothing about us without us," it is always useful to specifically answer the following questions as a foundational locator for what is happening:

- Who gets to decide who is in the room?
- How are each of the participants compensated?
- What are the terms under which each participant is engaged?

The answers to these questions should be transparently and proactively shared with all prospective participants, who should then have agency to respond and make changes to the proposed answers.

If we had better recognized the focus of the work necessitating the expertise of trans, non-binary, and Two-Spirit artists, for example, our engagement with them would have been much more extensive and involved from the early planning stages. There should also have been opportunity to reassess the balance of people in the room – the number of scholars and their areas of specialization, the number of trans and gender non-binary artists (including assigned female at birth [AFAB] and transmasculine artists), the expertise and diversity of the other actors involved, and so forth. For example, if we had truly recentred the work following its emergence on the impact of trans and gender non-binary perspectives in the interpretation and staging of early modern plays, it may have been useful to have researchers that collectively have expertise in non-binary gender studies, early modern theatre, contemporary theatre, and even contemporary practices for early modern works. Instead, we stayed centred in our original research and just widened the circle of our work by seeking and including more diverse perspectives and experiences of gender and by allowing our questions to remain diverse and accommodating to the expertise of the scholars already gathered; the focus of our work was diffused, which created challenges in uniting the room on equal footing.

Classical Plays in Contemporary Times

The industry and economy of staging classical repertoire can be a contentious subject to begin with among many contemporary Canadian artists, particularly IBPOC and 2SLGBTQ+ artists. Outside of the Stratford and Shaw Festivals, there is little governmental support for the development and production of plays that are not written by Canadians. Contracts with those companies, however, are some of the most lucrative theatre contracts to be had by any artist in the country. With such focus on original Canadian work in the industry, but so little money to be earned in creating it, the staging of classical plays can immediately trigger questions of how such endeavours meaningfully support diverse artists and whether they emancipate the artist or further entrench a colonial practice of theatre that Canada is only just at the beginning of reconciling.

Conversely, I would guess the majority of academic theatre scholarship is on material that is outside of the Canadian canon. Traditional scholarship on those canons may have limited use to contemporary artists, while the passion and drive of contemporary artists (particularly those from traditionally marginalized communities) may be outside the interest of traditional theatre scholars. Furthermore, expertise and scholarship in areas outside of theatre, English, or drama might provide unexpected and fruitful fodder for research in contemporary theatre practice. I also often envy the space, time, and resources afforded to academics and the impact their research can create in their respective industries. As a theatre artist who wants to be an agent in making theatre that changes the world, I actively look to build bridges and dialogue across communities, and collaborative PaR processes could be a vitally necessary avenue to do this.

At the time of writing, the world is experiencing a pandemic that has effectively shut down the live performance industry and is forcing theatre artists to question and reassess their place and function in society. What is the role of theatre in our contemporary world? How has it changed in the past and why, either in Canada or beyond? What have been the clearest measures of "success" for theatre in Canada, and are those measures aligned with the role that theatre has played previously and may play in society going forward? Finding potential collaborators to explore these questions may require further rigour but may also be a worthy avenue of pursuit for future PaR projects in theatre practice. This idea is not an indictment of the scholars who did participate in our project but rather a recognition, as the leaders of the project, that we did not clarify in advance the role of each of those scholars, or question how their contribution was balanced with others, or consider in advance who else might have been in the room to open up insights within a more focused line of questioning.

That being said, there was an amazing commitment offered by all participants to this project, even (or especially) when things got crunchy, which was an incredible accomplishment and valuable part of the process. PaR offers an exciting opportunity to grapple with these questions and find useful bridges between these two communities, but a unified focus and vision for the research will be both necessary and likely hard fought. I believe our project discovered, in true PaR fashion, this unified focus and vision in the equal commitment and curiosity Melinda, Peter, and I discovered to centre the experience and perspective of transgender, non-binary, and Two-Spirit artists. It is through the actions we took to support this focus that I think the leadership team did our best work and where the most important learning and discoveries among all participants were understood and shared. They include the following:

- The history and experience of gender-nonconforming and gender non-binary people is and often has been at play in early modern work. How we articulate, explore, and expose those stories creates rich opportunities for contemporary artists who identify anywhere along the gender spectrum.
- Deep, specific scholarly knowledge of the world in which a classical text was written is most useful in its capacity to free the artist's imagination into a more specific circumstance to confidently inhabit and take action from.
- The deeper the personal investment made by both audience and actor in embracing the ambiguity and complexity of story, the greater is the capacity of the work to deeply move artists and audiences and create emotional connections between artist and spectator.
- When PaR is used as a methodology for research among a group of scholars and professional artists, both groups must be prepared to

become fully invested as artists as well as scholars, no matter their
previous expertise. The project must be understood and conceived
with the process being an end in and of itself, turning the idea
of a linear trajectory to an ultimate end product on its head, as
traditionally framed in the mounting of a play (and the writing of
an essay!). The role and responsibility of the actor extends beyond
the interpretive craft of acting in and of itself but also is served
by an accountability to the group research, personal reflection,
communication, and critique – aspects of the profession that,
while vital in my experience, I have always practised outside of the
responsibilities on the face of my contract.

The flexibility and interdisciplinary qualities of PaR are qualities often
cherished by artists but are perhaps challenging to scholars as these
qualities play against the drive for conclusive findings so cherished by
academia. Through PaR, however, theatre has an unmatched opportunity of pursuing and examining process: to have process be the object
of reflection, to have it studied, analysed, and disseminated in hopes of
creating frameworks within which new processes and projects might be
understood, conceived, and pursued within a purely professional theatre
context. Expanding the dissemination and opportunities for impact and
reflection on this research, particularly to practising theatre profession-
als, is of specific interest to me going forward.

While there are many things I would do differently if presented with
the opportunity to engage in another PaR process like this one, I believe
there was much that was learned through this initiative, and I have hope
that the ripples of it will continue to reach out beyond the time and space
we shared together. They already have. Projects and research like Engendering the Stage can do important work to innovate, test, and disseminate best practices that are much needed in an industry that has been
rocked, particularly in Canada, by #MeToo, the Truth and Reconciliation
Commission, the evolution of gender identity and expression, and the
exposure of systemic racism experienced by IBPOC artists. Projects like
these help expand the practice of theatre artists beyond the commercial
status quo and keep artists connected and contributing to the vitality and
evolution of their craft.

Despite the challenges and shortcomings discovered of this process, I
cannot stress enough what a tremendous opportunity it provided to the
festival and how much was gained through our participation. For the
laboratory, it created a level of accountability and clarity to which the festival could be held in pursuit of these activities. It created relationships
between the festival and transgender, gender non-binary, and Two-Spirit

artists that have continued to be nurtured and developed. It created relationships between the festival and numerous universities and scholars with a passion and expertise in the early modern canons that have also continued in various forms throughout the organization. Perhaps most important, it created a necessary platform, resource, and model for pure professional research, lifting the organization from simply being the largest producing theatre company in the country, or providing professional training to actors, directors, and designers, to being a leader in the development of our art form in society through the artistic values of innovation, risk, critique, and continued creativity.

NOTES

1 Frankland, "Toward a Trans Canon."
2 Bruce Barton, personal correspondence, 4 February 2020. See also Barton, "Introduction I: Wherefore PAR?"

PART TWO

Beyond the Globe

MASQUER, ROPE-DANCER, BALIA, INNAMORATA, PRIMA DONNA,
FARSANTA, AUTORA, IMPRESARIA, MUJER VARONIL
GRACIOSA, SANTA, ANACORETA, COMEDIENNE, CONFIDENTE
LAUNDRESS, GATHERER, STRAW-DRAWER, PLAYHOUSE-OWNER,

2 Architectures of Gender

E.M. PARRY WITH PETER COCKETT AND MELINDA GOUGH

The workshop process began with the presentation of a short video introducing, in snapshot form, how English theatre history's obsession with William Shakespeare has skewed perspective on the historical records. Focused primarily on London commercial stages such as the Globe, on which Shakespeare's plays were performed and where even female roles were played by young men and boys, we have tended to think of theatre at this time as synonymous with an "all-male stage." But what histories of gender and of performance might this typical approach leave out or obscure?

Our video showcased the well-trained actresses of Paris, whose availability for performance significantly changed French Baroque theatre; the great diva actresses of Italian commedia dell'arte, whose physical and linguistic versatility attracted royal patrons across Europe; and the many women involved in Spanish Golden Age theatre: female actors, who often earned more than their male counterparts, as well as women directors, producers, and theatre owners (*autoras*). The wild popularity of actresses on the Spanish stage led to the creation of a varied group of characters known as the *mujer varonil* (literally translated as "manly woman"). These actors, many of whom wielded swords, defied conservative ideologies of women, demonstrating high levels of athleticism in their performances, riding horses, showing virtuosic skill in dancing and fencing, and creating characters empowered to pursue their own objectives. The video also provided background on *The Lieutenant Nun* (*La Monja alférez*), one of the plays explored by the actors in the workshop. This play's central character, Guzmán, originally enacted by the highly athletic Luisa de Robles, is based on the biography of Antonio de Erauso, who was assigned female at birth, escaped a convent, joined the army, fought for Spain, and was ultimately given special dispensation to live as a man.

With this view from the continent in mind, the video returned to England with fresh eyes. While women did not typically appear on the public stages of London, Mary Frith, a famous local pickpocket and subject of *The Roaring Girl*, famously did appear at the Fortune Theatre, playing a lute and singing. Furthermore, ladies of the court were central to English masques, where they appeared on stage – sometimes beside boy actors from commercial playing companies.

The notion of an "all-male" early modern stage has thus been created, and upheld, by a refusal to look "Beyond the Globe" at evidence that refutes its mythology. Such evidence suggests, instead, a rich and complex history of women and gender-nonconforming performers and characters in England as well as across Europe, all of whom contributed to the dynamic, creative economy of early modern performance.

All the scenes in the week's workshop featured characters who challenged conservative definitions of gender, and the video encouraged the actors to explore these roles with the same vigour and creativity shown by their early modern counterparts.

After the workshop, we shared the video with multidisciplinary artist, theatre designer, scholar, and drag performer E.M. Parry as a starting point for their image presented on the page before this chapter. Impacting the viewer through its combination of historical source materials, contemporary photography, costume, stance, make-up, and framing text, Parry's image stands as a self-contained example of practice as research (PaR). In a manner comparable to the workshop at Stratford, but not identical to it, Parry's art brings evidence of the past into the complexities of the present. In this way, it moves us visually and somatically to engage with the book's subject matter – women and gender on the stages of early modern Europe and beyond – as more than historical abstraction.

The following interview builds on this important artistic research by inviting the reader into the collaborative, conceptual process behind Parry's work.

Interview: E.M. (Mal) Parry with Peter Cockett and Melinda Gough

PETER: Let's talk about your process in creating this piece.

MAL: I started by gathering materials, as I often do, and by playing with ambiguous signifiers of gender. The big pannier underskirt and the breastplate (this one literally has two breasts grafted onto a masculine breastplate – it's a costume that's been adapted at some time in its history) were inspired by images of female performers in English masques that the three of us had looked at together when discussing this topic [Figure 2.1]. By happy coincidence, I had these things already in my collection of costumes, so it was easy to go to my dressing-up box and pull them out (which is an interesting privilege to have after many years of being a designer, making and acquiring props and costume pieces along the way – so they already carry some history for me, and in themselves …). I was attracted to those images, and to those items, because in different ways they demonstrate a kind of architecture of gender – they're structural garments that inscribe gender on the body, whilst also masking or concealing the body itself. They speak to ideas we discussed regarding the performance of femininity on the early modern stage. At that time, men and boy actors and assigned male people created very constructed and prosthetic performances of female identity on stage. If I'm thinking about that in terms of *women* and assigned female people performing female roles in a way that is still, potentially, very prosthetically constructed, that further invites us to think about how gender is constructed in that time, and what models of gendered behaviour people had then and have today.

We also talked about women taking up space in the world of theatre both on and off stage – it was fun and interesting to get to be assertive and to literally take up space in these physically imposing garments and to explore prosthetic female signifiers. Deliberately – and assertively – presenting as female: that's not something I do either in my day-to-day life or in my performance. I found that it felt like drag. Looking at my body in this "Beyond the Globe" image, created more recently in a later stage of transition, as compared to my body from a few years ago as represented in the images for "Two Shadows to One Shape" [chapter 11 of this volume]: that was interesting, too – to put very female gendered things on my more masculine-reading body. If you didn't know me personally, you might not quite have a sense of what might be "underneath" in this image – whether it's an assigned male or female, a cis or a trans body. In a lot of discourse around gender and transness, there's this desire or pressure to discover what's "underneath" – what's underneath the clothing and the make-up, whether somebody's had surgery or not, how somebody's "inner" sense of gender aligns with their body or their presentation, or how they're read … I'm interested in disrupting the idea that there's one, originary truth to be "uncovered." Layers of signifiers, and signifiers that don't quite align or match up, help to resist and disrupt those ideas.

Figure 2.1. Costume design for Penthesilea in *The Masque of Queens*, Inigo Jones, 1608. Pen and black ink washed with greenish grey. Wikimedia Commons.

Thinking about my physical body and what has happened to it, what I've done with it, the ways in which it's transformed, and putting that up against these much more prosthetic and very clearly constructed signifiers: it's interesting to put all of that in conversation with the wider theatrical world of early modern Europe outlined in your work. And that brings me back to the other elements in the image.

There's my body of flesh and blood and bones and hormones, and then these costume items that I'm wearing quite loosely, really: there isn't any attempt at anything very formalized, they really are just grabbed from a dressing-up box, and it's all kind of quite rough and ready. And then I've collaged it together with the stage that I'm standing on. The quite simply drawn lines of that stage, and the border as well, are taken from an image of Mary Frith in the frontispiece to *The Roaring Girl* [Figure 2.2].[1] And behind that is an image taken from a sketch by Inigo Jones.[2] That sketch is actually a technical drawing, so it's doing similar work to the costuming in that it shows its own process, the construction that goes into creating the spectacle, the illusion – of nature, of gender … It's also exciting for me as a practitioner, as somebody who designs sets and who has worked as a scenic painter, to look at this drawing. It isn't purely an image of aesthetic pleasure; it's a working plan – a tool. You can still see the marks and the numbering for the measurements and for the scaling up that would have been done to take his little drawing and recreate it at an epic scale. I love being able to see the workings of that, to relate to it as one professional to another. I enjoyed that moment of resonance, of feeling like I was having a moment of understanding, of collaboration, in fact, with a stage designer from the past. In the past, being a stage designer, somebody who designed costumes and sets, was a rare occupation and not one that's been well documented. The idea that it's a whole separate job is quite modern. So yeah. I don't have that many people to look back to, for patterns, for a sense of what they would have been doing that's similar or different to what I do now. The history of stage design is largely told as a male story too, but given how involved women have always been in material culture, and especially with clothing and sewing – and acknowledging a long tradition of actors providing or choosing their own costumes – that story of sole male auteurship needs to be complicated and revalued in terms of a more collaborative and transversal practice. One that's also messier, queerer, and more complex in terms of agency and self-fashioning too, I think – especially when we think about female characters and performers.

Figure 2.2. Mary Frith (Moll Cutpurse), after unknown artist woodcut, probably published 1780 (1611). 5 3/8 in. × 3 1/4 in. (138 mm × 82 mm). National Portrait Gallery, London.

And then for around the frame: the three of us pulled together a number of different job titles, basically, of things that women and assigned female people were doing on stage and off stage in the early modern period. There are these job titles in the image but also my body taking up space on a historical stage: as a performer, I'm mostly doing drag in queer, fringe, or underground spaces – bars, clubs, parties, cabarets, art spaces, etc. – not traditional or mainstream stages. When I work in more traditional theatre spaces, I'm mostly there as a theatre designer, but I've also worked as costume and prop maker and sourcer, wardrobe supervisor, scenic painter, I've built sets: I've done most of the off-stage jobs that have to do with the material world of theatre. So with this image, I'm allowing my body to do quite a lot of representing for people whose labour has been erased by the binary and patriarchal myth of an "all-male" theatre, both on stage and off.

MELINDA: I really love how this piece turned out. And one of the things I value about it is the way it puts pressure on notions that persist in scholarly writing about the early modern stage.

One such idea is that the "all-male" London commercial stage was its own island, if you will, having really nothing to do with what was going on in the continent. Your image takes English things like the masque, its costume and scene designs by artists like Inigo Jones, even the boards from *The Roaring Girl* frontispiece, and literally frames them in ways that make visible the material labour on and off stage by assigned female theatre-makers in England but also on the continent. The job titles in the frame, in multiple languages, represent that labour.[3] They are set in small type, but visually everything in the image is set up by them.

At the same time, your body in the image literally steps outside of that frame with the placement of your feet. And I think that's so powerful too. There's often been a tendency amongst scholars to focus on either presumed cisgender female performers from the continent or the English boy actor (or boy actress) but not to think of these histories in tandem. It is like these two strands of scholarship run on parallel tracks, but with a kind of tension between them that for me is emblematic of a frequent tension between a certain strand of feminism and a certain strand of queer and trans studies. Our project, at least from my perspective, seeks to refuse that division and to consider ways that rethinking gender in the early modern period might help us to push beyond what threatens to keep feminist, queer, and trans studies from productive alliance. So I really appreciate how your image emphasizes that it isn't only femininity as instantiated by a boy actress that's prosthetic: the gender of assigned female performers, even including presumed cisgender women in masques on the continent or in England, is in process, too.

MAL: Definitely. As somebody who works with costume and materiality a lot, I would say that the more I've worked in this period especially, the more apparent it becomes how much gender is constructed on the body in formative ways. And then the more you discover about the ways in which gender was managed and understood as a process and a discipline, the more it reveals the ways in which that is true *whatever* your relationship to your gender is.

And of course, the "all-male" stage cliché is a massive oversimplification, given what we've been discussing here and elsewhere about how gender was understood in this period. Boy actresses and assigned male people who played female roles would not necessarily have been understood or understood themselves as uncomplicatedly male. Without mapping contemporary gender categories onto the past, these disruptions of the all-male stage assumption give us an opportunity to acknowledge and make space for transfeminine and non-binary experience too.

What's interesting for me about the early modern period is not so much that it seems any more or less queer or trans than our time but that you can look at it from a distance, through different lenses, and also use it as a lens to look at ourselves and how we create and experience gender now.

When creating this image, it was fun and satisfying, personally, to get to do a bit of female drag, if you like, but also to get to take up a bit of space as a trans person *and* as an assigned female person, someone who's lived as a woman and previously identified in that way. I no longer identify *as* a woman, but I still identify *with* women, and I'm still invested in women's concerns and history. So it was exciting for me to learn more about what women and assigned female people were doing in this period and what sort of stakes they had in performance culture.

By putting myself in Mary Frith's shoes – I put my feet pretty much exactly where they go in the frontispiece image that I took those stage boards from [Figure 2.2] – and using her shadow in that image as *my* shadow, I get to draw on a famous, what we could call proto drag king performance that she made as a kind of special guest at the Fortune Theatre.[4] This was something the people who put on that production thought would be popular and exciting for the audience. It's such an interesting window into a particular moment because it's something that's known about partly because they got in trouble for it. But if one assigned female person could get on that stage, that encourages us to look for others. It shows a moment of slippage between different performance cultures and invites us to think of them as less separate and siloed than they've historically been framed. Like this idea that it was illegal for women to act in Shakespeare's time that we hear repeated so often – there was no such law. There were numerous social and cultural factors that prevented women participating as performers on the public commercial stages of England, but to take that as evidence of an exclusively male theatre culture is a massive oversimplification. We know there were women, assigned female and female-identified people doing all sorts of performing at lots of different levels of society. Because of this idea of the "all-male" stage, Frith's performance feels anomalous, but given everything else that was happening culturally in Europe at this time, we have to question that framing and the assumptions behind it.

It seems to me that if we were to look at English theatre data now, but we only studied the outputs of the National Theatre and the RSC [Royal Shakespeare Company], we might have this idea that it was probably illegal for anyone other than cis white men who went to Oxford or Cambridge to make theatre –

PETER: Old Eton boys.

MAL: Yeah. It's not quite as bad as it was, but it's still not great. But if historians of the future took the output of the National Theatre in its entire existence and then applied that to all of English theatre of the twentieth and twenty-first centuries – which is sort of what we do by taking Shakespeare as a stand-in for all early modern European theatre – so much would be missed.

PETER: I think your image really opens up that space. Your body actually frames the rest of it, and I love the juxtaposition of the left arm gesture and the right foot: it's like you're striking out.

MAL: It feels very powerful, and empowering personally, as a trans person, to have the opportunity, the privilege to take up space in this context – to historicize myself, in a way. The visibility of trans people historically is complicated and contested, and even today, we don't have that much visibility, and much of what we do have is negative, objectifying, or just not on our own terms. At the same time, I need to acknowledge, in connection with this as well as the other pieces, that slim-bodied non-disabled white people have historically taken up a lot of space and continue to do so. And certainly within Shakespeare and Shakespeare-adjacent theatre culture. So while my image disrupts some tropes, I can't simply separate it or myself from the culture that created those tropes.

MELINDA: That's such an important point: when we talk about gender equity in theatre, we have to think intersectionally. For us, and for our workshop, this was a key goal, especially given the colonial histories that inform the gender binary and the history of European theatre on the lands where the Stratford Festival and McMaster University, the hosting institutions, are situated. There's so much more to do.

NOTES

1 For additional discussion of the two different frontispiece images for *The Roaring Girl*, see Parry with Cockett and Gough, "Playing with Gender: Stance, Gesture, Embodiment, and Prosthetics," chapter 11 of this volume.

2 *Festival Designs by Inigo Jones*, 61. Strong titles this image "For the Proscenium" and connects it with *Albion's Triumph*, a royal masque performed 8 January 1632 with text by Aurelian Townshend.

3 Peter and Melinda thank scholar participants from the 2018 Stratford workshop, especially Pamela Allen Brown, Callan Davies, Clare McManus, Lucy Munro, Mac Test, and Ellen Welch, for help identifying job titles from multiple national traditions.

4 Frith's appearance on the Fortune stage is referenced in the *Consistory of London Correction Book* for November 1611 to October 1613 (London Metropolitan Archives, DL/C/310, ff 19–20); this record is transcribed and analysed in Mulholland, "Date of *The Roaring Girl*," 30–1. See also Middleton and Dekker, *The Roaring Girl*, ed. Mulholland, 12, 262–3; Middleton and Dekker, *The Roaring Girl*, ed. Panek, 147–8.

3   We Tell Our Stories. We Continue to Exist.

CARMEN ALVIS

My name is Carmen Alvis, and I'm a Two-Spirit Michif (Turtle Mountain Métis) artist sheltering in place in Tkarón:to on Mississauga-Anishnaabe, Haudenosaunee, and Wendat territories. One of the treaties in effect in this area is the Dish with One Spoon wampum covenant, an agreement between the Haudenosaunee and the Mississaugas of the Credit First Nation and other Anishinaabe nations to peaceably share the land and waterways in this area.[1] I use she/her pronouns as a rebalancing for my Two-Spirit identity. My feminine spirit has been with me, alongside my masculine one, since before western medicine assigned me male at birth. At the time that I attended the Engendering the Stage gathering in 2018, I was using they/them pronouns to encapsulate my Two-Spirit, transfeminine, and non-binary experience with the given name Cole. Recently, I began using my chosen name: Carmen with she/her pronouns.

My ancestors include Métis and Chippewa peoples from Turtle Mountain (a series of rolling hills in southern Manitoba and northern North Dakota) as well as English and Irish settlers who have occupied farmland on those hills for over a century. In the past decade, members of my extended family have been reconnecting with the Métis and Chippewa traditions within our matriarchal line, while we learn what it means to be Michif – the Métis word for our nation and language. It is lifelong work to reclaim our blood. I continue to seek my role as a Two-Spirit storyteller within my family and communities. Community member Lauren Greene (Ojibwe) shared with me the history of early colonizers targeting Two-Spirit and matriarchal leaders. The intention behind this action was to destabilize Indigenous nations as a strategy to dispossess them of their land by infiltrating a world view steeped in misogyny and transphobic christian colonialism. Another colonial project with harrowing impacts was the residential school system, in effect for over 100 years, that forcibly removed Indigenous children from their families and communities with the express intent to shame them out of speaking their language and replace their culture with a euro-christian world view. The intergenerational effects of this genocide are explored in the collection *Indian Act: Residential School Plays*, edited by Donna-Michelle St. Bernard. Playwrights Canada Press describes their publication as "a tribute and thank you to those who survived the Indian Residential School system so that future generations could be free to pursue their lives unhindered by educationally enforced lowered expectations and institutionalized abuse. Seven plays by contemporary First Nations and Metis playwrights cover the broad scope of residential school experiences, all kinds of characters, and no stereotypes, giving voice to those who could not be heard."[2]

Growing up in a little town on Treaty 7 territory, I was raised to value the written word, absorbing storytelling structures from the likes of William Shakespeare and other white, often cis-male, writers. Duchess, Alberta (population 1,085), was built along a railway, referred to as the Royal Line, that connects nearby hamlets and villages with romantic names like Patricia, Millicent, Princess, and Countess. These colonial identifiers assert a foreign culture and history onto the Plains as grain and other resources are extracted for the economic gain of the settlers with minimal accountability to the Indigenous nations of Turtle Island (North America). Later in life, I learned this area is governed by Treaty 7, "an agreement signed between First Nations and Queen Victoria," through a play by the Indigenous theatre company Making Treaty 7 and that, by being raised in this territory, I am beholden to this treaty.[3] As a child, I was introduced to Indigenous relations with these lands from a field trip to a local World Heritage Site called Head-Smashed-In Buffalo Jump. According to the United Nations Education, Scientific, and Cultural Organization (UNESCO), "Head-Smashed-In Buffalo Jump is one of the oldest, most extensive and best preserved sites that illustrate communal hunting techniques and the way of life of Plains people who, for more than five millennia, subsisted on the vast herds of bison that existed in North America."[4] The site's powerful exhibits also highlight the impact of colonialism on this land and show how the decimation of the buffalo was key to the genocide of Indigenous peoples that is still going on today. Despite the existence of treaties between Indigenous nations and settlers, my experience growing up saw these sacred agreements downplayed in favour of colonial narratives, including Shakespearean stories, along the Royal Line.

Storytelling plays a key role in the maintenance of the settler's ongoing occupation of Indigenous territories in what is called Canada. Falen Johnson (Mohawk-Tuscarora), celebrated playwright and co-host of the CBC podcast *The Secret Life of Canada*, once described ceremony to me as telling stories we already know so that we don't forget. Leaving behind our languages and traditions is something the women in my matriarchal line were compelled to do to prevent the settler government from taking their children away. Rather than "residential school," my family uses the word "convent" when we tell our story. My grandmother was raised by a survivor of this colonial project, and the intended impact of intergenerational forgetting is still felt in my family today.

Critical context for understanding the landscape of inequity within the arts on Turtle Island requires engagement with the Truth and Reconciliation Commission of Canada's 94 Calls to Action that direct us to redress the intergenerational impacts of residential schools,[5] as well as the criminalization of Indigenous dance and ceremony under the Indian Act until 1951.[6] These failed policies prevented Indigenous artists from being recognized or even considered while the foundation for the arts in Canada was being laid on stolen land. Leading up to Canada's centennial in 1967, the Canadian government invested new funding to support the creation of a uniquely Canadian artistic voice, moving away from presentations of imported work and artists from places such as Britain, France, and the United States. This moment was an opportunity for the arts in Canada to live the values of the treaties and to uphold the inherent rights of Indigenous peoples by providing leadership opportunities within the arts. There are moments like this every day, and it is up to artists, scholars, and anyone who lives, works, and plays on treaty territories to redress the impacts of ongoing colonialism.

Since its inception in the 1950s, the Stratford Festival of Canada has been telling stories that assert settler-colonial legacies responsible for the ongoing displacement and subjugation of the Indigenous peoples of Turtle Island. For decades, this well-resourced and culturally specific festival has played a key role in defining the arts in Canada; indeed, its budget far exceeds that of any Indigenous performing arts organization. Its festival stages were designed to platform imported styles of performance, complete with proscenium arches and a thrust stage, without consideration for the performance needs of Indigenous artists and stories from the land on which these buildings stand. In recent decades, the festival has moved away from exclusively hiring British actors for lead roles; they no longer require Canadian actors to use British accents; and more recently, they have attempted to cast Indigenous and culturally diverse artists within their eurocentric works. When I use the phrase "culturally diverse," I am recognizing the unique cultures of Deaf, hard of hearing, blind, mad, and disabled peoples, as well as intersections of race, class, gender, and other intentionally marginalized identities. Today, the Stratford Festival Laboratory, described as "a suite of experiments and investigations that drive our artistic and organizational evolution in an era of exciting cultural change," presents cracks in the festival's foundation.[7] It is within these fractures of a colonial theatre festival where Two-Spirit, trans, and non-binary artists can take back their sacred role of storyteller within a canon that would prefer we not exist. Shining a light into these areas to propel cultural change, beyond the festival's workshop studios and onto the mainstage, was on my mind when I attended Engendering the Stage's exploratory workshop on the performance of gender in classical theatre.

My participation was important to ensuring Two-Spirit representation in the workshop's creative process. When I was offered this engagement, I thought of the buffalo and the Royal Line, while considering how my participation might render me complicit with white supremacist storytelling. I had previously participated in a Stratford Lab focusing on Indigenous directors and enjoyed engaging with Shakespeare among other First Nations, Inuit, and Métis directors and performers. Engendering the Stage offered the opportunity to participate alongside artists with intersections of various genders. We were a small group of Two-Spirit, trans, and non-binary folx, and the prospect of learning from each of them motivated my participation despite the rocky terrain.

Kitoko Mai (they/them), an artist and scholar in their final year of undergrad at McMaster University's School of the Arts at the time, shared a poem, "Let Shakespeare Die," which names the exclusionary nature of Shakespeare from their perspective as a Black non-binary person.[8] Featuring their work on the first day suggested critical discourse on racism and colonialism within classical theatre was welcome at this gathering. Kit's poem provided a powerful map for how to centre those who continue to be marginalized when classical texts have supremacy over other modes of creation, particularly ones that may not be written down such as intergenerational song lines and other modes of ancestral storytelling.

Emma Frankland (she/her) spoke of her experience workshopping the early modern text *Galatea* by John Lyly that presences queer and trans characters in a historical context, pushing back on the contemporary and exclusionary narrative that identities beyond the gender binary are "new." Emma and collaborator Andy Kesson discuss their revival of *Galatea* in "Perhaps John Lyly Was a Trans Woman?"[9] Their article traces the alterations present in *Twelfth Night* and *As You Like It*, both updates of *Galatea*, where Shakespeare "troubles Lyly's conclusion with characters who seem to be openly homophobic in the face of potential queer desire. Orsino will not kiss Viola while she is dressed as a boy, and Phoebe is so disgusted by the revelation of her desire for another woman that she chooses to marry her stalker."[10] Emma's assertion that trans and non-binary people existed before, during, and after the publication of early modern texts points to an ongoing and intentional erasure when uncritical interpretations of Shakespeare are embedded within the fabric of the education system, weaponizing exclusionary storytelling structures to maintain colonial culture. Two-Spirit identities have existed on Turtle Island since time immemorial, and while the term "Two-Spirit" was created in 1990, Dr. Harlan Pruden, Cree scholar and editor of the *Two Spirit Journal*, confirms that "many, not all, First Peoples had traditions and ways that were non-binary, where some Nations had 3, 4, 5, 6, or even 7+ different genders and these genders were not only accepted and honored but also had distinct roles within their respective Nations."[11] The colonial project's strategy of criminalizing Indigenous languages, ceremonies, and culture, when combined with an exclusionary focus on eurocentric storytellers and their world view, enacts an agenda of cis-heteronormativity that erases the legacy of Two-Spirit, trans, and non-binary artists, thinkers, and leaders. Kit, Emma, and I interrupt the status quo's narrative that attempts to censor our existence. By telling our stories, we push back on the normalizing of gender as an immovable binary that is non-consensually branded at birth. Our participation in the gathering necessitated a broadening of the concept of gender within the exploration, a process that can discomfort when participants are called to engage with the spectrum of identity more completely.

As is often the case in settler-Canadian theatre, there was a risk of our presence being tokenized if space was not made for our contributions to disrupt the status quo. Buoyed by the presence of my peers, I leaned into the facilitation and artistic leadership skills that I have been developing, alongside those of being an actor, to recentre the focus of our discussions onto the exclusion of Indigenous, Black, and culturally diverse ways of knowing when engaging with early modern texts. It is vital to understand the impacts of ongoing colonialism on Turtle Island and how the eurocentric focus of storytelling perpetuates outright erasure or harmful appropriations of Indigenous peoples and their cultures. There were moments when we, as Two-Spirit, trans, and non-binary participants of Engendering the Stage, chose to self-advocate inside a gathering poised to prioritize characteristics of white supremacy culture such as either/or binary thinking and worship of the written word.

The facilitators Melinda Gough and Peter Cockett's patience and willingness to change made it possible to deepen the gender analysis to include ongoing impacts of colonialism within the performing arts. We advocated for ourselves and each other, leading conversations and sometimes the room. These efforts resulted in the gathering being less harmful for those with intersecting identities, albeit through unpaid emotional, artistic, and academic labour (these skills are not within an actor's contract at the festival, even though such labour is often required). As a result, time and space were carved from the larger programming for Two-Spirit, trans, and non-binary participants to gather on our own. Racial Equity Tools describes this solidarity strategy as an affinity space or caucus where colleagues can "meet separately and create a process to rejoin and work together collectively."[12] Free from the burden of representing our identities for those who do not share our experiences, we had the opportunity to recharge, to speak freely, to offer and receive support. Providing affinity spaces is an action that can be foundational, particularly for Indigenous, Black, and/or culturally diverse artists engaging with predominantly white institutions.

While disruption, discomfort, and alterations in the pursuit of equity were themes throughout the workshop, it was also enjoyable to get to perform. In a scene study from *The Maid's Tragedy* by Francis Beaumont and John Fletcher, I was cast as Aspatia, a character assigned female at birth who disguises herself as a man and encounters her betrothed, only to have him fall in love with her as a he. The experience of dressing up in "boy drag," and having the scholars in on the knowledge that my feminine spirit was being asked to conceal herself to teach her husband a lesson, affirmed my experience of gender as a spectrum. Collaborating with scene partner Marcus Nance as Amintor was excellent: he made me believe, when Aspatia presents herself as a man, that the love they have for each other transcends clothing and binary gender roles. The experience of having my feminine spirit recognized by being cast as Aspatia was significant. At various points in my life, I have been redirected by family, friends, and my communities, for their comfort, to adopt a performance of masculinity to the exclusion of my femininity. In the world of the play, Aspatia accepts the task of wielding a sword because she has decided a sword fight is how she must die. For this scene, I allowed my disdain of performative masculinity to show, in keeping with Aspatia's ambivalence towards gender. It was refreshing for my authentic reluctance with the performance of masculinity to be an asset in exploring our interpretation of Aspatia. As part of the scene study, we used they/them pronouns to describe Aspatia, even though the colonial world view of the play asserts a fixed binary. While both the character Aspatia and I as an actor were given permission to be our whole selves through the use of inclusive pronouns, the play-text as written requires Amintor not to recognize Aspatia in man's apparel. One take of our scene study had Amintor being in knowledge of Aspatia's gender spectrum. This turn became an affirmation for Aspatia's male presentation, complete with a feminine spirit. Performing the scene as characters aware of the gender spectrum highlighted for me the folly evoked by gender as a binary within Aspatia and Amintor's jilted marriage and society at large. While it was affirming to have my whole self invited into a role not originally envisioned for a person with both a feminine and a masculine spirit, ultimately this story of gender transgression leads to Aspatia's and Amintor's deaths. Such a stark outcome confirms how vital it is that Two-Spirit, trans, and non-binary representation surpass the tropes that often relegate us to victims of murder, martyrdom, or the cautionary tale. In order to engage equitably in storytelling, it is necessary to move beyond representation through casting and to ensure that those whose culture is being represented hold leadership roles when it comes to how their stories are being told.

Beyond the scene work, one of my takeaways from the gathering is the necessity for subversion and movement building. Academia and the Stratford Festival teaming up for an exploration of gender in pre-Shakespearean texts became of interest when I was invited to work alongside Two-Spirit, trans, and non-binary people of colour. I relished the opportunity to circle up, in solidarity with my peers, and share my living experience with those who hold positional power and can, through their actions, centre gender-nonconforming people in their communities and in the arts. A positive outcome of our labour during Engendering the Stage came when the Stratford Festival invited Emma Frankland back in 2019 to lead a Stratford Lab called "Toward a Trans Canon" that featured Two-Spirit, trans, and non-binary participants, including Samson Bonkeabantu Brown (he/him), Rhiannon Collett (they/them), Cassandra James (she/her), Beric Manywounds (they/them), Subira Wahogo (they/them), and myself. Emma's reflections on our time together, along with a collectively written list of recommendations for engaging Two-Spirit, trans, and non-binary artists, have been published in *HowlRound*.[13]

In June 2020, I was invited to speak on a panel at the Stratford Festival called Ndo-Mshkawgaabwimi – We Are All Standing Strong, which shared stories of endurance, resistance, and resilience from members of the Indigenous Circle at Stratford.[14] Joining my colleagues to share our experiences at the festival was both fraught and forward moving, with difficult truths being voiced alongside calls for systemic change. The event took place at a time when predominantly white institutions were rushing to post black squares on their social media platforms in support of Black Lives Matter, often before looking critically at how they uphold values of anti-Blackness within their organization and communities. In an attempt to move the festival beyond performative allyship and towards action, I voiced an expectation that, in the next five years, their current programming will make up half of their season and the other half will be led by Indigenous, Black, and culturally diverse artists telling their stories on their own terms. The vision for this call to action is in support of the 1613 treaty between the Haudenosaunee and the Dutch represented by Gaswéñdah (Two Row Wampum), an agreement to "travel side by side down the river of life. Each nation will respect the ways of each other and will not interfere with the other."[15]

While the structural impact of flashpoints like Engendering the Stage, Toward a Trans Canon, and Ndo-Mshkawgaabwimi are yet to be seen, it is my hope that the labour of artists speaking up will result in meaningful change at the Stratford Festival and beyond. Peter Cockett and Melinda Gough's commitment to systemic change sees me continuing to navigate academia. In 2021–22, I was the inaugural artist in residence in the School of the Arts at McMaster University. I experienced this placement as being one of artistic rigour alongside the beginnings of institutional change that aims to maintain Indigenous sovereignty and social justice principles at the centre. Highlights included co-creating, alongside Peter Cockett, McMaster theatre students, and Haudenosaunee poet Kahsenniyo Kick, a collective creation called *Kontatewenní:yos ne Tyonathonwí:sen* (*The Women Are Free*),[16] as well as working alongside Rhéanne Chartrand (Métis), curator of Indigenous art at McMaster Museum of Art, on the creation of a first-year course introducing essential moments in Canadian colonial history as a primer for students to learn about Indigenous sovereignty.

As settler-colonial industry found other ways to haul grain in Treaty 7 territory, the iron rail of the Royal Line was removed from the land where I grew up. Yet an indelible impression remains. It is the work of my family and me to seek our ancestral connections to this place. When I consider the treaties that make it possible for us to be on Turtle Island, I see pathways that guide us towards equity within the performing arts. Steeped in Indigenous languages and world view, these pathways require Indigenous leadership and participation in the creation, presentation, and critical analysis of performance from coast to coast to coast. To remain accountable to the sacred agreements, as potent today as when our ancestors sat in ceremony to create them, national arts organizations have a responsibility to maintain meaningful relationships with Indigenous artists, community leaders, and language keepers from the nations upon whose land they make their art. Respecting the inherent rights of Indigenous peoples becomes paramount to the success of storytelling so that settlers cannot forget how to be good, albeit uninvited, guests on stolen land. The reparations required to rebalance what has been stolen over centuries of extraction-based relationships are immense, as witnessed by the ratio of resources maintaining a cultural supremacy within the arts in

Canada. What might our stories look like were those advantages applied equitably to Indigenous, Black, and culturally diverse world views? Where might stories take us when they are told by artists bringing their ancestral protocols from the world over? How might these narratives resist complicity with ongoing colonialism? Two-Spirit, trans, and non-binary thinkers, creators, and community members are sharing the song lines of tradition, liberation, and futurism that we need now. We are telling our stories, and when everyone does their part to restore the inherent rights of Indigenous peoples, we will not only exist, we will truly be free.

NOTES

1 "Dish with One Spoon."
2 St. Bernard, ed., *Indian Act: Residential School Plays*, pressbook description.
3 Making Treaty 7 Cultural Society.
4 UNESCO, "Head-Smashed-In Buffalo Jump."
5 Truth and Reconciliation Commission of Canada, "Truth and Reconciliation Commission of Canada: Calls to Action."
6 Truth and Reconciliation Commission of Canada, "The Indian Act Said What?"
7 Stratford Festival Laboratory, "About the Lab."
8 Mai's spoken word poem "Let Shakespeare Die" was originally published on the Engendering the Stage in the Age of Shakespeare and Beyond website and is reproduced in Krusto and Mai, "To Degender Is to Decolonize," chapter 16 of this volume.
9 Frankland and Kesson, "'Perhaps John Lyly Was a Trans Woman?'"
10 Frankland and Kesson, 286–7.
11 Pruden, "August 4, 2020 'TWO-SPIRIT' Turns 30!!"
12 Racial Equity Tools, "Racial Equity Tools Glossary: Caucusing (Affinity Groups)."
13 Frankland, "Toward a Trans Canon." This piece appears in a series of five articles and conversations that grew out of explorations at the Stratford Festival Laboratory during the 2019 season, curated by ted witzel and Sadie Berlin.
14 *Ndo-Mshkawgaabwimi – We All Are Standing Strong.*
15 Onondaga Nation, "Two Row Wampum – Gaswéñdah."
16 *Kontatewenní:yos ne Tyonathonwí:sen* (*The Women Are Free*).

PART THREE

Energies, Evidence, Emergent Practices

4 Potential Energies in the Early Modern French Repertoire

ELLEN R. WELCH

There aren't *better* choices, only *different* choices. Versions of this statement punctuated the workshop I observed, as three thoughtful, energetic, talented actors (Mariah Campos, Denise Oucharek, and Danielle Wade) explored the seemingly limitless interpretations of a short scene from *The Lieutenant Nun*. Their mantra, and their experimentation, made vivid for me something that I know as a theatregoer but tend to forget in my academic work. When viewing productions, I take pleasure in the variety of interpretations performance can elicit from a script. In teaching, I emphasize the multiplicity of possible readings of a play-text to encourage students to voice their own diverse perspectives. Yet when approaching plays as a literary scholar, I view my reading practice as a collaboration with fellow critics, past and present, to move towards richer, more precise contextualizations and ever more subtle, refined analyses of a given text to bequeath to future readers – in short towards *better* choices (better, at least, within a chosen academic framework) rather than simply *different* ones.

However well-trained in postmodern theory, however committed to valorizing multiple viewpoints, many of us scholars end up, even unconsciously, tacitly endorsing a rather teleological view of research. The rhetoric of academic writing demands that we articulate how our work builds on the work of others, how it advances a discourse, how it fills a gap in collective knowledge. Above all, it demands a product. Observing the actors' experimentation, I began to wonder whether there might not be a less goal-oriented way to frame the significance of academic research. Would it be possible to imagine a mode of scholarship that fully embraced the performers' ethos of "not better, just different," which valued process over result, which captured the abundance of possibilities that emerge from reading rather than jettison all but the most refined and contextually nuanced or the most theoretically "cutting edge" interpretation?

Leading me to question – or at least be more mindful about – the unspoken aims of my scholarship is just one of the ways Engendering the Stage unsettled me. (Taking part in movement exercises, talking about emotions in a professional setting – these also threw me off balance.) In the unstructured scene work and slowed-down discussions of the workshop, my sense of the temporality of investigation also shifted. Letting go of the drive to produce "better choices" also released us from the need to define our goals with respect to the play's early modern origins – a relationship all too often represented, in both theatrical and academic contexts, as a binary choice: Do we treat a play as an archival document and read it in context for what it can tell us about the past? Or do we prioritize its relevance for the present, highlighting how it resonates with up-to-date critical vocabularies? Do we seek to employ historically accurate performance spaces and practices? Or do we strive to make the play as relevant as possible for today's audiences? Do we move towards the past or towards the future? Individual participants in the workshop might, in their own work, generally prefer to go in one or the other direction. But as a group, I think we managed to unsettle that momentum. Caught between the modernizing push and the historical pull, we mined what could be called the "potential energy" of our texts.

Designating the stored energy of an object ready to drop from a height, of a stretched elastic band about to be snapped, of a particle before it reacts with another, potential energy provides an apt analogy for investigating the particular dynamism of the early modern play-text in a performance workshop. The idea of potential energy acknowledges the power inherent in a situation that looks like stasis or directionless tension. It calls attention to the vibrancy of the moment before action or movement takes place. Finally, it emphasizes the force of relationality – since this form of energy derives from the relative position of objects in a system. (The energy stored in a book precariously balanced on the edge of a desk, for instance, depends on its distance from the floor.) These qualities were also present in our scene work in Stratford, as well as in many other recent scholarly and performance projects focused on early modern theatre. The Before Shakespeare project, for example, recognizes the vitality of the English theatre before the catalyst represented by that most canonical author launched a forward-moving narrative of national theatre history.[1] Appreciating the "earliness" of the era and the works it produced entails noticing the roads not taken, the potential paths unrealized in subsequent times.[2] In addition, by uncovering older, largely forgotten plays, such projects challenge modern interpreters to contemplate their "relative position" to the past, the exciting push-and-pull of alienation and attraction, strangeness and surprising familiarity that we might feel when working on the early modern repertoire.

Coming to this conversation as a scholar who focuses primarily on early modern French studies, I acknowledge that, in distinction to its anglophone counterpart, the French-language theatre scene has not yet had its "before" moment. Productions rarely venture into an earlier repertoire than the plays of Corneille, Molière, and Racine, the seventeenth-century triumvirate that performs an equivalent role to Shakespeare in marking the glorious beginning of a French-language theatrical tradition. Theatre-makers' approaches to this canon, moreover, gravitate towards the poles of historicization or modernization. On the one hand, troupes such as the Paris-based La Lumineuse or productions associated with the early music group Le Poème Harmonique, influenced by Eugène Green, favour a historically informed performance practice. Reviving Baroque-era acting techniques, gestural languages, even diction, they seek to create an exotic and destabilizing experience for the contemporary theatregoer who feels transported to a foreign past.[3] On the other hand, most mainstream productions opt to bring early modern plays up to date with anachronistic costumes and décor. In its most thoughtful and nuanced version, this tactic acknowledges the canonical status of the plays by representing their long histories of reception in production. As the director Daniel Mesguich states of his own method, "texts that have traversed time, the 'classics,' have this advantage to have swollen like rivers fed by streams."[4] He calls for theatre-makers to avoid "dusting off" early modern texts, since this "dust" – reception history, cultural baggage attached to classical works – allows us to perceive and consider the distance between past and present.[5]

While theatre-makers debate approaches to the French classical drama canon, scholars have been reviving interest in prior generations of playwrights, the pregnant era "before" the more familiar age: the "bloody tragedies" of the late sixteenth and early seventeenth centuries, the Rouen-produced plays that represented France's early colonial entanglements, the works of libertine dramatists such as Tristan L'Hermite and Théophile de Viau, the Baroque romps of Jean de Rotrou. Motivated perhaps partly by an anxious suspicion that all that could be said has been said about the classical canon, this wave of rediscovery has also been inspired by contemporary critical concerns with violence, imperialism, race, and gender – turning towards a more distant and unfamiliar past to speak to the current moment. For the most part, this work on the pre-classical repertoire has remained the purview of scholars rather than performers or theatre-makers.

One recent exception – with special relevance to the themes of Engendering the Stage – is the director Jean-Pierre Vincent's 2013 revival of a long-forgotten comedy from the early modern French repertoire, Isaac de Benserade's *Iphis et Iante* (1634), which had been published in a new scholarly edition by Anne Verdier in 2000.[6] Based on the tale in book IX of Ovid's *Metamorphoses*, the play stages the story of Iphis, a young shepherd born female but raised as a boy in order to placate the child's violently misogynist father. As the play begins, Iphis has been living happily as male and is about to marry the beautiful Iante. For the first time, the disjuncture between Iphis's biological sex and lived gender provokes a crisis, with Iphis caught between loving Iante and wanting to marry her, on the one hand, and feeling guilty about duping Iante, on the other. The wedding goes ahead nonetheless, and on the morning after a confusing wedding night, Iphis goes to the temple of Isis, prepared to resolve this intractable dilemma by self-sacrifice at the altar. Instead, Isis transforms Iphis into a young man, and the newly-weds live happily ever after.

As this brief plot summary makes clear, Benserade's play speaks to issues of sexuality and gender identity that have come to the forefront of contemporary social and political discourse. This contemporary resonance surely motivated Vincent's choice to produce a minor play from an obscure pocket of the Baroque archive. In fact, reviewers, who largely admired the production, overwhelmingly interpreted it as a celebration of "marriage for all."[7] This conclusion might be expected, given the timing of the performance: France legalized equal marriage in May 2013. The production invited its viewers to make this connection, casting a well-known female actor, Suzanne Aubert, in the role of Iphis and including an extended wedding-night scene performed on a bed, photos of which comprised the play's publicity campaign (see, for example, Figure 4.1). In encouraging viewers to see the play as an early modern endorsement of same-sex marriage, however, the production downplayed the significance of Iphis's metamorphosis. Vincent admitted his bemusement at the deus ex machina scene in an interview where he described the transformed Iphis as "visibly uncomfortable in his new identity. In others' eyes, he's become a monster: a girl in a mustache."[8] The implication – shared by some scholars who have worked on the play – seems to be that the marvellous dénouement provides "cover" for a theatrical depiction of a same-sex romance that would have been otherwise unacceptable to early modern audiences.[9]

Different choices, better choices? Staged and interpreted as a story of same-sex love, the play as directed by Vincent clearly resonated with a public ready to celebrate equal marriage (and perhaps pat itself on the back for having come so far since the seventeenth century). For a subset of the audience, this interpretation of the play may have offered the sense that their stories and identities had a history longer and deeper than previously imagined. These are valuable effects for a revival of a

Figure 4.1. Still image from Jean-Pierre Vincent's production of *Iphis et Iante* at the Théâtre Gérard Philipe in 2013 with Chloé Chaudoye (left) as Iante and Suzanne Aubert (right) as Iphis. Photo: Rafaël Arnaud.

historical play. Yet, emphasizing this reading of the story also means downplaying significant ambiguities in the text. The language of the play, for example, studiously avoids fixing Iphis's gender – a remarkable feat in a Romance language and an effect I attempt to replicate in this brief discussion by referring to the character as either he/him or she/her according to the pronouns used in the passages under analysis. Most of the play's characters accept Iphis's identity as masculine and refer to the character using male pronouns and adjectives. Only Iphis's mother, Télétuze, and a busybody young man from the neighbourhood, Ergaste, who is in love with Iphis, know the story of the character's birth and (at times) use feminine pronouns and grammatical agreements to speak to and about her. Iphis, meanwhile, resists identification as female. The character's own speeches skilfully evade adjectives that would require a gendered agreement in French. Her crises of conscience occur when Télétuze reminds her of her birth sex. Iphis replies to one such reminder, "J'oubliais quelque temps que j'étais une fille" (I forgot for a while that

I was a girl, 114). Iphis's gender identity is at once highly dependent on social recognition – it depends on who is talking – and intensely subjective. As Kathleen Long remarks, "gender is as much a feeling as it is a corporeal state in this play."[10]

This subjective approach to gender enables interpretations of the play as a story about a character who could be identified in today's vocabulary as transmasculine or gender non-binary. Several scholars have drawn from this vocabulary to comment on the play's fluid approach to gender. Jennifer Row, for example, offers a persuasive reading of the "queer temporality" of the play in which the apparent "mistiming" of the wedding and Iphis's transformation take part in an "eroticization of delay." By showing us that Iante loved Iphis both before and after the metamorphosis, "both as a man and as a woman," the play asks "what does love for a genderqueer or genderfluid person look like?"[11] Representations of trans and non-binary identities – and roles for performers who identify as such – are still very rare in the French cultural scene, where, as Todd Reeser observes, the state's role in enforcing sexual binarism through national ID cards and other bureaucratic apparatuses has shaped and restricted the kinds of narratives produced about trans experiences.[12] Benserade's play has much to offer in this context.

If claiming Iphis as a trans or non-binary person gets a little closer to recognizing the text's nuanced and contradictory approach to the character's gender, this choice, too, requires eliding some of the play's complexities, specifically those historically situated aesthetic and philosophical frameworks that do not sit easily with modern views of identity. The play's ambivalence towards Iphis's sex and gender derives in part from Benserade's engagement with notions of illusion typical of the theatre of the pre-Corneille/Molière/Racine period that has come to be labelled "Baroque" and in part from his creative appropriation of the idea of an unstable self, inherited from its Ovidian source. Together, these aspects of the play construct a view of gender identity that both resonates with and resists modern categories and questions, offering many potential paths to interpretation and staging.

In fact, far from a work that was somehow ahead of its time, *Iphis et Iante* emerged from a theatrical context and generic tradition in which female actors routinely donned male clothing on stage. During the Baroque period of French theatre (roughly the 1620s–40s), dozens of plays featured cross-dressing plots. Significantly, only a handful of these have a male character disguise himself as a woman.[13] Meanwhile, over sixty plays, mainly comedies, involve female characters who cross the gender binary including through attire.[14] The question of why such stories in particular should have been particularly ubiquitous has been a topic of fascination for many scholars. Derval Conroy, for example, reads it as a literary expression of anxiety about women's social role, crystalized by several high-profile historical examples in early modern French society of presumed female historical figures wearing male clothing.[15] Others stress the potential for audience "titillation" and homoeroticism in such plots.[16] Theatre historians have investigated the popular storyline in light of a sudden surge in the number of prominent actresses attached to Parisian theatre troupes in these years.[17] This type of plot does give especially dynamic roles to female characters and the actresses who play them. Moreover, unlike stories in which characters identified in the text as male dress as women, stories in which characters identified in the text as female put on male attire allow these characters to play the traditionally active role in love plots. Indeed, evidence suggests that certain actresses specialized in playing such gender-nonconforming characters. This is the case for Elisabeth Dispannet Valliot of the Hôtel de Bourgogne, who may have created the role of Iphis at that theatre.[18] In most of these plays, the female character's performance of masculinity utterly succeeds in convincing everyone around her until the moment when she reveals her "true" identity, often by unveiling physical signs of femaleness. Again and again in this subgenre, the idea that gender is completely performative and theatrical defers in the dénouement to the "truth" of an original, anatomical sex.

Benserade's play subverts some of the conventions of contemporary cross-dressing plays to unsettle the relationship between bodily truth and theatrical performance. From early in the play, Iphis's dialogue uses the Baroque language of disguise and transparency to undo the typical distinction between a true sex and a borrowed gender costume. For example, in Act 2, scene 3, the first dialogue scene for the two young lovers, Iante accuses Iphis of cooling towards her in the hours before their wedding. She senses Iphis is hiding something. Iphis reassures her that their marriage will reveal the depth of their love:

> Vous ne douterez pas, toujours (ma chère vie)
> Des transports amoureux dont mon âme est ravie,
> Et vous verrez peut-être avant la fin du jour,
> Comme Iphis est pour vous un miracle d'amour.

> You will not doubt (my dear life)
> The transports of love that still ravish my soul[19]
> And you will see perhaps before the end of the day,
> How Iphis is for you a miracle of love. (68)

Iante remains unconvinced, accusing Iphis of the false flattery used commonly by lovers, to which Iphis responds:

> Vous apprendrez aussi qu'Iphis n'est pas comme eux;
> Si je n'imite pas leurs flammes insensées,
> Mon cœur ingénument découvre ses pensées;
> Si je ne donne assez d'encens à vos appâts,
> Mon âme pour le moins ne se déguise pas.

> You will also learn that Iphis is not like them;
> If I do not imitate their foolish passions,
> My heart artlessly reveals its thoughts;
> If I do not praise your allures enough,
> My soul at least does not disguise itself. (68)

While Iante feels as though Iphis's true feelings are being concealed from her through a veil of indifference or a buffer of conventional sweet talk, Iphis speaks of a soul that is transparent and a heart that is guileless, even while alluding to some other thing remaining disguised, to be revealed at a future time. This tension between clarity and obscurity is further complicated by the way, throughout this scene, Iphis switches between first and third person. "Iphis" is a miracle; "Iphis" is not like other lovers. "Je" (I) is a feeling being with a loving heart and spirit. Iphis's rhetoric matches up with the idealizing Neoplatonism of traditional (often narrative) pastoral, positing an essential soul whose true nature is defined by love for Iante, regardless of outward appearance. While in traditional pastoral cross-dressing stories, the revelation of gender disguise permits the hero and heroine to be together, in this case the deceptive material appearance posing a temporary obstacle to the lovers' union is double: both Iphis's gender presentation (which misleads Iante and impedes the couple's emotional intimacy) and Iphis's biological sex (which makes a heterosexual marriage impossible).[20] Iphis's dialogue establishes a division, in other words, not between "natural" sex and gendered disguise, as in the case of other cross-dressing dramas, but rather between a realm of material appearances in which various biological, gestural, and vestimentary signs of gender can be hidden or performed and a loving essential self that can be articulated without reference to gender at all. In this view, all sex and gender identities – whether assigned at birth or later adopted, whether made visible through anatomical traits or clothes and gestures – belong to the realm of the unreliable surface.

As the play unfolds, other characters build on this idea that questions of gender and sex remain separate from articulations of an authentic self. The best example of this questioning occurs in Act 5 as Iante tries to make sense of her memories of her wedding night:

> Qui vît jamais au monde un prodige pareil?
> Pour moi je l'attribue aux effets de sommeil,
> Et dans l'incertitude où mon esprit se plonge,
> Un semblable incident me passe pour un songe.

> In all the world who ever saw such a wonder?
> For me, I attribute it to the effects of sleep,
> And in the uncertainty in which my mind is immersed,
> Such an incident occurs to me like a dream. (107)

Whereas in most contemporary plays with a female-identified character dressed as male, the unveiling of the character's body breaks the illusion, the (off-stage) revelation of Iphis's female form does not quite have the same effect. Entertaining the possibility that her memory of the previous night was a sort of dream, Iante fails to distinguish with any certainty what Iphis's "true" identity might be. She goes on to predict that only more confusion will follow if others learn about Iphis: "qui ne jugeant rien que par l'extérieur, / Connaissent assez mal ce que j'ai dans le cœur" (who judging nothing except by the exterior, / Know rather poorly what I have in my heart, 108). There is an irony in Iante's line that reproaches not those who accepted the outward appearance of Iphis's masculine clothing but rather those who would be scandalized by the revelation that Iphis was born a girl. Iante considers anatomical sex to be a deceptive "exterior" trait opposed to an interior, authentic self. She points to "what I have in my heart" as a surer guarantor of truth, a truth in which Iphis is an appropriate recipient of her love, regardless of outward form. This speech could be read as a reflection of a heteronormative context in which only a male body would be an acceptable object for Iante's affections. From another viewpoint, it could equally resonate with contemporary articulations of agender and transgender identity. Yet Iante's language of exterior deception versus interior certitude draws from a Baroque philosophical and aesthetic tradition that opposes the veil of worldly illusion to an inaccessible, immutable truth expressed in rather disembodied, spiritual terms. In this passage, then, the play represents gender identity as complex, changeable, and transcendent over simple binaries in ways that speak to today's discussions. Yet it also departs from these contemporary discourses in distancing questions of sex and gender from an idea of authenticity that remains central to many of today's articulations of trans and non-binary identities. Many (although of course not all) of today's narratives of trans and non-binary experiences – as well as many narratives of cisgender experiences, for that matter – presume the existence of an authentic identity in describing a journey to express, affirm, and be recognized as oneself. [21] Reflecting the legacy of post-Enlightenment, Western ideals of selfhood, this type of narrative may be uncomfortably challenged by Baroque texts that ask readers to continually question the boundary between truth and illusion, to wonder whether an "authentic" self exists at all.[22] Taking the time to appreciate this distinctly unmodern dimension of the text *together with* its sometimes-uncanny closeness to present-day ideas uncovers the rich potential of Benserade's play.

In many ways, *Iphis et Iante* demands an interpretation that lingers in the space of potentiality. Its resistance to hermeneutic closure, particularly when it comes to defining Iphis's gender identity, derives in part from its Ovidian source material, which itself probes the question of gender's place in the distinction between essence and form.[23] The ancient *Metamorphoses* assume that some kernel of self can remain constant despite the fluxes of the material world, that individuals remain in some way themselves even when transformed into cows or trees, celestial constellations, or disembodied voices. Metamorphosis for Ovid consists of "a change which preserves, an alteration which maintains identity."[24] The idea that a being might remain constant through change also suggests an uneasy linkage between the self and its physicality. Marie Louise von Glinski emphasizes Ovid's use of similes to describe his characters as almost-but-not-really something other than what they appear to be, suggesting that his figures are constantly ambiguous, "neither fish nor fowl," not quite at home in any embodied form.[25] Coming from a different perspective, philosopher and historian of science Justin Smith points towards the way in which ancient literature and myth (including the *Metamorphoses*) might challenge and expand even the most progressive current articulations of identity by stressing "the continuity human beings experience between the identity assigned to them at birth and the many other sorts of identity with which, in a narrow empirical sense, they are nonidentical."[26] This sense of being not completely at home in any physical shape yet continuous with multiple identities certainly characterizes Iphis's sentiments throughout the play.

Of course, this multiplicity or indefinability is difficult to reconcile with the dramatic imperative to achieve a satisfying ending to the plot. This issue becomes clear in the highly ambiguous dénouement to *Iphis et Iante*. Benserade dramatizes the metamorphosis scene as a classic deus ex machina, suggesting that this transformation provides the resolution and certainty about the character's gender that has been lacking throughout the play. Yet Ovidian metamorphosis, as the critics cited above suggest, is in many ways incompatible with such decisive finitude. This tension becomes clear when the goddess Isis announces the transformation and Iphis narrates its physical effects:

> Miracle! Je suis homme, une mâle vigueur
> Rend mes membres plus forts aussi bien que mon cœur,
> Mon corps devient robuste en un sexe contraire,
> Et je marche d'un pas plus grand qu'à l'ordinaire,
> Vénus, qui toute seule occupait mes regards,
> Se resserre en mes yeux pour faire place à Mars;
> Ni ma peau, ni ma voix n'est plus si délicate,
> Et c'est d'un ton plus fort que ma parole éclate;
> Mon sein que je cachais est devenu tout plat,
> Et je crois que mon teint n'a plus son vif éclat.
> Ç'en est fait, rendons grâce à la bonne Déesse
> Qui me fait ressentir l'effet de sa promesse.
>
> Miracle! I am a man, a male vigour
> Strengthens my limbs and my heart,
> My body becomes robust in a contrary sex,
> And I walk with a longer pace than usual,
> Venus, who alone occupied my gaze,
> Narrows in my vision to make space for Mars;
> Neither my skin, nor my voice is so delicate anymore,
> And it's with a louder tone that my words ring out;
> My breast that I hid has become completely flat,
> And I believe that my complexion is no longer so bright.
> It is done, let us give thanks to the good Goddess
> Who makes me feel the effect of her promise. (124)

Cataloguing physical aspects typically associated with masculinity (strong, "robust" limbs, a flat chest, toughened complexion) alongside what we might consider performative indices of maleness (a way of walking and speaking), the transformation speech constitutes a lesson on how to act the part of a man. Yet presumably, even before the moment of metamorphosis, Iphis – and the performer incarnating the role – would have already been displaying some of these masculine modes of embodiment, understood in dramatic context either as a result of education and socialization or as a strategy to pass as male. What really changes in the transformation scene? Does the performer signal some sort of bodily or behavioural change? Or does a consistent physical performance create an ironic contrast with the rhetoric of metamorphosis (as in Vincent's production)? Either choice may leave an audience confused about the significance of the goddess's actions. The play, especially in performance, suggests that transformation is not the teleological endpoint it promises to be.

Refusing to give audiences the sense of satisfying closure they might expect from conventional comedy, *Iphis et Iante* replicates in its dramatic structure the uncertainty and flux that characterize its approach to gender. In Benserade's play, the crisis over Iphis's gender, which nearly produced tragedy, comes from the insistence that there is one fixed, knowable truth about identity – that Iphis is "really" this or that at any moment in time. Accordingly, casting and staging decisions that would define Iphis according to modern categories of identity (whether binary, non-binary, or trans) necessarily reduce the ambiguity that arguably is at the centre of the play's dramatic economy. As Valerie Traub notes, all the ancient and early modern versions of this myth are characterized by a profound "hermeneutic uncertainty and epistemological opacity … particularly in regard to the presumed intelligibility of Iphis's body"; the metamorphosis with its troubling "'before and after' syntax" fails to fix the character's gender but rather raises questions: "What exactly has been transformed? On what grounds do we know a transformation has occurred? What is the basis of our certainty?"[27] In Benserade's version, the skilful manipulation of the conventions of Baroque drama foregrounds the undecidability of Iphis's identity. It is only by engaging with the unmodernizable philosophical and aesthetic dimensions of the drama that Benserade's radical take on gender identity – perhaps identity *tout court* – can come to light.

So what does this mean for theatre-makers seeking to stage a complex historical work such as *Iphis et Iante*? What are the ethical responsibilities to artists, to audiences, to texts? Modern interpreters might find solidarities with early modern texts, might discover stories that take their place in a reconstructed history for individuals and identities occluded in mainstream visions of the past. The potential to create roles, and livelihoods, for performers excluded from the mainstream, particularly when it comes to a classical repertoire (in any language tradition), is important and salutary but perhaps also entails a risk of smoothing out the knotty temporalities of the early modern, of overly domesticating the strangenesses of early works in our own contemporary terms, or of using the past to "dress up" present issues in a form of "archival drag."[28] While any production entails making decisions that foreclose some readings while emphasizing others, it remains important to ask: In claiming the past for the present, what gets left out? What other potential readings remain unexplored?

Sharing her experiences with staging another early modern Ovidian adaptation, John Lyly's *Galatea*, with the Engendering the Stage workshop, Emma Frankland clearly demonstrated the ambiguities of that play's approach to gender identity and sexuality by offering a series of impromptu performances of one scene. Emma and Denise played and replayed a dialogue in which the young heroine Phillida is ordered by her father Melebeus to dress as a boy and hide in the woods to avoid ritual sacrifice to Neptune. As they swapped roles and imagined different identities for the two characters, they brought out surprising but always convincing resonances in the text's approach to familial relations, power dynamics, and gender identities. Yet more compelling than any one version of the scene was the juxtaposition and accumulation of diverse possibilities generated through the process of experimentation. Of course, workshop performance and play are conducive to this kind of exploration in a way that the performance schedules of commercial theatre – and the format of traditional scholarship, for that matter – are not.

These reflections already occupied my mind when towards the end of our workshop, for diverse and complex reasons, the group decided to cancel a planned "performance" of the scenes under study.[29] As an academic participant rather than a performer in the scene work or facilitator of the workshop, I was not directly implicated in this choice. Yet I nonetheless felt a sense of relief at seeing that event evaporate from our agenda and along with it any need to choose one approach to share with an audience as a more finished (or "better") version of the many possible interpretations of the text we had seen over several days. I wondered and continue to wonder: what would remaining in a practice space, in a workshop mode, look like in the scholarly arena?

This question might be especially urgent for those of us studying and performing early modern theatre. Early modern plays' potential for the present resides not only in their perceived prestige value but in their "earliness" – in their reserve of potential energy and the unrealized cultural and aesthetic directions they might contain. A performance that realized these potentials might itself have the potential not only to reflect or speak to but to unsettle current ways of understanding vexed concepts such as gender. Rather than rushing towards the categories we know in the present or what we think we know about gender identities in the past, we can be unsettled by dwelling in that uncomfortable middle where nothing quite fits and yet many things could.

1 The project takes as its objective "to remember how pioneering, unusual, and shocking" theatres were before the well-known Elizabethan context

(UK Research and Innovation, "Before Shakespeare: The Beginnings of London Commercial Theatre").

2 See, for example, DeGrazia, "Hamlet Before Its Time," 375. I also draw inspiration from Cherbuliéz, "Waking Early."

3 Green, *La Parole baroque.*

4 "Les textes qui ont traversé le temps, les 'classiques,' ont cet avantage d'avoir grossi, comme, par leurs affluents, on le dit des fleuves" (Daniel Mesguich's annotations to Viala and Mesguich, *Le théâtre,* 46). All translations are mine unless otherwise specified.

5 "Ne 'dépoussiérons' donc pas (la poussière, c'est l'histoire du texte) … Jouons bien plutôt, le rapport de ce siècle au nôtre, celui du passé au présent, et celui, aussi, du présent au passé" (Viala and Mesguich, *Le théâtre,* 83). On Mesguich's approach to classical texts, see also Spriet, "Des voix venues d'ailleurs"; Fayard, "Shakespeare with a *Différance.*"

6 The production débuted at the Théâtre du Gymnase in Marseille in January 2013. There was an earlier production by Didier Doumergue with student performers from the Studiolo-IRTS de Lorraine in Metz in 2001, which received much less publicity. References to the play will be from the second modern edition, Benserade, *Iphis et Iante, comédie,* ed. Verdier with Biet and Leibacher-Ouvrard; English translations are my own. See also a re-edition of the play accompanied by short articles about the 2013 production: Benserade, *Iphis et Ianthe,* in *L'avant scène théâtre.*

7 See, for example, Darge, "Mariage pour tous"; Quirot, "Un mariage homo … en 1634."

8 "Disons que la fin du texte avec l'intervention de la déesse qui change Iphis en homme et rétablit l'hétérosexualité du mariage est une véritable farce. A mon sens, cette fin libératoire n'annule point l'audace précédente: Iphis, sitôt changée en homme, devient une sorte de petit macho. Ce nouveau jeune homme n'est visiblement pas à l'aise dans sa nouvelle identité. Aux yeux des autres, il est devenu un monstre: une fille avec une moustache" (Olivier Celik, "A contre-courant: Entretien avec Jean-Pierre Vincent," 75–6).

9 Variations on this argument appear in Leibacher-Ouvrard and Verdier, "Pièce d'hier "; Harris, "Disruptive Desires"; Dupas, "Lesbianism."

10 Long, "Illegible Bodies," 234.

11 Row, "Queer Time," 59–60, 66.

12 Reeser, "TransFrance."

13 These include Du Ryer's *Argénis et Poliarque ou Théocrine,* Desfontaines's *Euridemon,* and Rampale's *Bélinde.*

14 See Conroy, "Cultural Politics," 136; Lyons, *Theater of Disguise,* 42. Georges Forestier's census of plays produced from 1550 to 1680 counts 152 instances

of cross-dressing of which over 120 are characters identified in the text as female, dressed as male (Forestier, *L'Esthétique de l'identité,* 58, 443).

15 Conroy, "Cultural Politics," 135–6. For a historical account of female cross-dressing practices in early modern France, see Steinberg, *La confusion des sexes.*

16 Harris, *Hidden Agendas,* 170; Senelick, *The Changing Room,* 184–5.

17 Berlanstein, *Daughters of Eve,* 22; Evain, *L'Apparition des actrices,* 69; Scott, *Women and the Stage,* 123–4.

18 Scott, *Women and the Stage,* 124. On Valliot, see also Lacour, *Les premières actrices,* 112–20.

19 "Toujours" in this context can mean both "still" and "always." The word's bivalence is important in these lines.

20 The dialogue between Iante and Iphis in the wedding-night scene (Act 4, scene 1) reprises this discourse of the truth of the heart and soul versus the deception of the body.

21 On this point, see also Todd Reeser's critique of the linearity and normativity of contemporary French transpositive narratives that presume a "trans self that was there all along" through comparisons to migration and "arrival" (Reeser, "TransFrance," 7–8).

22 See, for example, Egginton, *Theater of Truth.*

23 Benserade seems to have been inspired by the Ovidian idea of metamorphosis throughout his career. Aspects of Ovid's tales found their way into his subsequent plays, *La Mort d'Achille* (1635–36) and *Cléopâtre* (1636). He published a translation, *Métamorphoses d'Ovide en rondeaux,* in 1676.

24 Solodow, *World of Ovid's* Metamorphoses, 174.

25 "While metamorphosis is presented as neatly divided by the before and after of the physical transformation, the continuity of the mind, in memory and consciousness, connects the two states. The simile captures this ambiguity of being 'neither fish nor fowl'" (Glinski, *Simile and Identity,* 155).

26 Smith, *Irrationality,* 222.

27 Traub, Introduction to *Ovidian Transversions,* ed. Traub, Badir, and McCracken, 15.

28 Román, "Archival Drag," 140. See also Schneider, *Performing Remains,* 14.

29 For additional discussion of this decision, please see Cockett and Gough, "Introduction" in this volume.

5 The PaRchive and Scraps: Archiving Process in Practice as Research and the Work of Theatre History

CALLAN DAVIES

Scrap, 1578

In 1578, the Ipswich scrivener and writer John King was paid 40 shillings, having "taken paynes for the Towne about the setting forthe of pagent{es}," alongside related sums for "workemens labors."[1] The town's record offers one example of the historical archive's recording of "process" – here, styled as "paynes" (and indicating the financial, intellectual, and physical labour involved) – in the construction of early modern performance. Unlike many types of documents often central to our enquiry about early modern performance practice, which are treated as though they arise from or out of theatrical *products*, entries such as King's payment obliquely acknowledge collaborative theatrical activity at its genesis or *process*. For us today, the phrase "setting forth" also happily carries with it a sense of unfinished journey, a beginning, an exploration.

John King's "paynes" offer a way into understanding the type of performance as research (PaR) work central to the Engendering the Stage project's residence at the Stratford Festival Laboratory in Ontario, Canada, in September 2018, as well as its recording, documentation, and dissemination. We might call these "labors" our "setting forth of PaR" or, emphasizing the reiterative nature of engaging with past processes and materials, our "setting forth *again* of PaR." This chapter will address concrete questions of how we did so, before exploring the relationship of PaR methodology to administrative records such as the sixteenth-century City of London Corporation materials and Surrey and Kent Sewer Commissions, thereby re-evaluating PaR's implications for archives past and present.

Indeed, the relationship between archives, documentation, and performance has been a central question of performance studies for at least the last thirty years. Recent experiments in and reflections on PaR work have added to both practical and theoretical consideration of how "live" discovery might be recorded and disseminated. Unlike performance events, which are a more final – if ephemeral – "product," and even unlike rehearsal, which is by definition product-orientated, the form of PaR we were exploring at the Stratford Lab was not invested in either a "final" practical product or in concrete answers to a set of predetermined questions.

Such openness can sometimes result in frustration or confusion for all parties in the room – *What are we trying to do here?*[2] – but it is in the "paynes" of PaR that we might begin to open up conceptual and practical understandings of both past and present theatrical environments: it's in the journey, the beginning, the exploration. Such an ethos is in keeping with Peter Cockett's reflections on PaR historiography: "the key thing is not the authenticity of any of the choices we made, but the way those choices reveal the theatrical company as a process rather than a fixed entity."[3] This ethos of openness also relies on what Stephen Purcell identifies as "an iterative process," moving through various stages from archival study to practical experimentation and back again.[4] Such work, as it concerns early modern theatre history, involves playing with an existing historical archive that, as I explore here, is already itself a largely iterative process – of play-texts, administrative details like King's payments, material items, archaeologies of all kinds, which from their very inception were and are partial, subject to ongoing revisions and changes. We might therefore gloss Purcell's observations and situate PaR work as participating in a longer historical chain of process, thereby making it *re*-iterative.

Such a "process" might not always provide concrete answers for some of the more materially direct questions of theatre history (*Was a balcony used here? Can doubling in this scene tell us about company structures?*) – though perhaps sometimes it may – but performance archival work can usefully be put into conceptual conversation with the material, documentary archive. In this chapter, I explore how documenting the week's research at Stratford at the point of delivery required a form of *live archiving* through social media, website, interviews, and film and audio recording. Such archiving navigates ethical responsibilities to extend the research "process" beyond the rehearsal (or in our case, workshop) room and make at least part of the conversation accessible to a wider public, thereby becoming part of the performance research and amplifying its scale. I am interested in how such documentation can help us conceive of "process" in the early modern archive and today. To that end, I demonstrate how a number of the sixteenth-century materials so integral to theatre history narratives can themselves be aligned with process-based PaR. Theatre history often excerpts scraps from their wider contexts to treat them as whole or discrete and temporally fixed documents (as, for instance, above with John King's pageant payments – taken from a repository of diverse council activity). Putting these scraps into dialogue with the PaRchive recentres attention on their incompleteness: their remaining *in process* – both within their historic contexts and in subsequent uses and interpretations. Practice as research workshops such as Engendering the Stage's offer a fresh conceptual paradigm for the scrappy work of theatre history more broadly.

Documenting: *Scrap, 2018*

In late morning on 19 September 2018, Lily McEvenue was helped into an arcing blue dress (*o' this filthy fardingale!* 2.2.57) and fitted with a sword, decked out as a "martial maid" like Francis Beaumont and John Fletcher's Clara from the play *Love's Cure* (*these are not my hips*). Ran tan tan tan, ran tan tan tan, ran tan tan. *I would love to cast myself in a role like Clara.* The next day, Emma Frankland played Moll Cutpurse, the Roaring Girl, and Daren A. Herbert played Moll Cutpurse, the Roaring Girl. On 22 September, three actors who had been working with scenes from *The Lieutenant Nun* were at what they called Ground Zero. They talked about the experience of playing different genders, and Denise Oucharek elaborated on the "power of transformation" in theatre – its capacity to teach and push boundaries – while meditating on the tricky ethics of casting in a period where many performers from historically marginalized communities remain under-represented in large institutional productions. How "literal" should casting be? How can we best channel "nothing about us without us" – a "rallying cry" Keira Loughran explores (critiquing its implementation at Stratford) in this volume?[5]

The week's workshop involved moving between briefings and check-ins, discussion, physical exercises that merged historical and contemporary experience (such as gendered notions and practices of walking), and scene work with the select group of plays that formed the workshop's core focus: *The Maid's Tragedy, Love's Cure, The Roaring Girl,* and *The Lieutenant Nun.* We were working with scraps – of history, of exercise, of conversation – as we explored gendered performance (for us now, for the texts, for the players and people from 400 years ago who formed at least part of the impetus for this workshop). Our workshop labours were recorded: in blogs, in tweets, in notepads, and by a video camera running intermittently at the sides of the room.[6] These scraps help form the "archive" that is PaR: where the historical records of Carolyn Steedman's *Dust* meet both scholarly methodology and theatre-making, where personal, professional, and practical join to produce and redistribute fragments.[7]

A more sober definition: Robin Nelson defines "practice as research" as "a research project in which practice is a key method of inquiry and where, in respect of the arts, a practice (creative writing, dance, musical score/performance, theatre/performance, visual exhibition, film or other cultural practice) is submitted as substantial evidence of a research inquiry."[8] More broadly, for Purcell, it is any "scholarly work in which performance practice constitutes a major part of the research enquiry," and he embraces criticisms of PaR as its strengths: "its indeterminacy, its open-endedness, its situatedness within the present, and its collaboration with non-academics."[9] Both Nelson and Purcell entertain the question of what exactly "constitutes the research output" and how documentation might function for researchers – particularly in a climate (in the United Kingdom at least) where recorded "evidence" of research outcomes is a compulsory product for higher education frameworks and funding bodies.[10]

Such impetus underpinned the drive to record materials at the Stratford Lab, with funding from the University of Roehampton (on top of the main funding from the Social Sciences and Humanities Research Council of Canada) specifically geared towards gathering "evidence" – in the language of the UK's Research Excellence Framework (which largely determines higher education funding) – of "impact": Does the work you are doing *change* anything other than mere academic discourse? Prove it. (And show your workings.) Such institutional demands can easily be dismissed as bureaucratic, neoliberal red tape; moreover, Paul Clarke has articulated the potentially insidious nature of "performance-making" that finds itself, through the requirements of funding and academic life, "subjugated" to the late capitalist machine of the modern university and its creeping territorialization of extramural political and theatrical activities.[11] But collecting evidence can also be a valuable exercise, and there are of course good reasons why institutions are invested in how funded collaborative research will continue to bear fruit beyond, say, a (predominantly) academic collection like this one. Indeed, Nelson makes the point that practice research may not provide ostensibly objective "hard knowledge," but gathering and articulating findings can nonetheless "inform future practices and/or practitioner research, and knowing may be shared not only within an arts community but across the academy and thence out to broader communities."[12]

Considering and collecting "impact" (or whatever term might be preferred) forces both researchers and performers to ask about the "ends of PaR," to adapt a phrase from Peggy Phelan and Jill Lane.[13] In turn, it prompts us to consider what methodologies and materials we might adopt to gauge our progress, our success, our change – and how those methodologies and materials might link the past and present. These considerations have implications for the way non-practice research works too, affecting our broader methodological approach to all forms of knowledge-making; Ellen Welch's chapter 4 of this volume explores how such emphasis on process can help us celebrate plurality in the subjects of academic study, working towards "different" rather than "better" choices and interpretations.[14] The trick, in Stratford, was finding ways to marry such an output-orientated framework with a process that was, well, just that: *process*. Perhaps we weren't asking about the "ends of PaR" but about its beginnings and middles: how do we record those without turning them into products? Keeping the re-iterative nature of the work in mind, we can push for new questions and recognition of what Welch sees as the "potential energy and the unrealized cultural and aesthetic directions" of the archive: "we can be unsettled by dwelling in that uncomfortable middle where nothing quite fits and yet many things could."[15]

Prior to participating in the Engendering the Stage workshop at Stratford, I was lucky enough to have had experience working with and documenting performance process as research thanks to Before Shakespeare's collaboration with Emma Frankland's (and collaborators) ongoing *Galatea* project.[16] Emma's work in progress workshops were characterized by regular group "check-ins" with all present in the room, alongside experimental and devised "play": costume catwalks and silent, unplanned collaborative creation (from any props, costumes, or random materials) of an effigy of the patriarchal deity, Neptune, who haunts much of John Lyly's play. These performance activities sat alongside read-throughs and stagings of the play-text itself. Over the course of the process, participants and theatre-makers generated a vision of *Galatea*'s world in dialogue and understanding with the individuals in the real-world room (or cliff or beach) itself. Emma was also integral to the experience in Stratford as one of the invited guest artists from outside of the Stratford Festival company who helped bring this sense of fluid, open-ended, and humane exploration to the week's PaR. My previous experience working with Emma was accordingly at the heart of finding ways to honour as much as possible sensitive personal investment in and response to ongoing processes of performance work.[17]

Indeed, in Stratford, process was emphasized repeatedly as a central tenet of the collaborative research work between performers and academics by then associate producer of Stratford Festival and our collaborator at the Festival Lab, Keira Loughran. It has also proved a key term for performance studies writers, who have long been concerned with the difficulties of documentation – practically and theoretically – for live art forms, from Phelan's observations on the inherent ephemerality of performance to Sven Spieker's exploration of the relationship between archive and art.[18] Barbara Hodgdon has explored how the "archive" that makes up performance – what Hodgdon calls "scraps, scribbles, drawings and fragments" – can reflect not only the "performance as product" but also "performance as process."[19] Rob Conkie, too, sets out new approaches to performance processes and also new modes of writing and publication for exploring "rehearsal materiality."[20] Both writers frame such documentation – what survives the rehearsal room, and what is created there and archived – as a "marginal zone" that is itself performative. Matthew Reason explicitly acknowledges that "the representation of performance forms a kind of audiencing of performance" – in other words, all kinds of *setting forth* create witnesses to past events and present documents.[21]

PaR (at least in our approach) presents a slightly different set of challenges to the recording of performance events, as it is constituted almost entirely by what Hodgdon helpfully calls "scraps": it dwells entirely in archival matter, playfully reiterated, and as such might be seen as pre-archived. In other words, there is no archive *of* PaR; PaR *is* archive: what I am conceiving of here both literally as the recorded or surviving "stuff" of the past (physically or digitally located records, words, things) but also, by extension, the processes associated with them – their modern and early modern narratives and performances (always in flux) and the meta-stories we have woven from them.[22] The liveness of PaR work, as with all liveness, is transient, but in a research process defined by the open-ended possibilities of bringing together fragments (historical, archival, performance, personal) resisting trajectory or final "output," there can be no separation of performance event and archival documentation (past or present).[23] Moving away from debates about the quiddity of PaR's "output," then, we were seeking to document its process, its reiterations, its "play."

Such processual work poses challenges to certain academic modes of enquiry. For instance, one fundamental tenet of the workshop at Stratford was to not let academic research lead or determine performer choices but to make it part of a spectrum of resources and expertise. Also on this spectrum, for instance, was stage manager Renate Hanson, without whom the "practice" would have been significantly less practical: another archivist, then. Moreover, unlike much traditional academic work, Engendering the Stage's recorded PaR resisted "conclusion" and encouraged open-ended "play" with both contemporary experiences of early modern texts and with historical evidence (broadly conceived). As a result, we were able to move between historical costume workshops and discussion of how to respect Two-Spirit beliefs, between staged sword fighting and both presentist and historical textual analysis. We could also explore what it was like to have a child actor play the spurned and suicidal Evadne before the adult king Amintor (as in early modern English troupes), while reflecting on company dynamics that meant the actors in question (Logan Brideau and Marcus Nance) worked together in very different professional roles elsewhere.[24]

Such open-endedness leaves room for the often underplayed research method of serendipity, but it can also put a vague pressure on practical participants to deliver something that has not been defined or explained: André Morin, reflecting on the workshop in a conversation with the volume's editors, asks, "Were we trying to create a piece and perform it? Or were we performing an experiment?" He also emphasizes, relatedly, the need for serious amounts of time properly to enable actors to explore texts in performance, giving those perhaps unfamiliar with the full texts requisite time to know and inhabit the plays, to develop their personal relationship with a character and situation. Marcus Nance similarly stresses the need for time as a key part of the process – both ahead of scholars coming in and during the first work with a text.[25] As Purcell observes of original practices work, "'research imperatives' often sit side-by-side, and not always comfortably, with 'creative or professional imperatives.'"[26] Engendering the Stage at the Stratford Lab was careful to make such imperatives the subject of ongoing conversation throughout the workshop (and beyond) – sometimes by design and sometimes by necessity – and to entertain the question, as Morin phrases it, *What are we doing here?* This is the same question that governs the documenting of performance as research: what is this archive for?

It is through such questions about recording that the Stratford workshop might help to articulate its "impacts": Engendering the Stage brought together UK and Canadian universities to work with leading theatre company Stratford Festival; it created a network of discovery and career opportunities among actors, theatre-makers, academics, artists, and people who fit none or every such description; it allowed exploration of early modern cruxes and questions and aligned them with modern theatre-making; it offered an institutional and international platform for previously marginalized performers to reimagine the canon; and it provided a space (sometimes private, sometimes shared) for personal engagement with what is at stake in classical performance: Who gets to be represented and how? What theatrical stories from the past are we not telling? Most importantly, it revealed the work yet to be done in all these areas. All these threads are drawn out across the different labours documented from the week at Stratford Lab, and out of these "paynes" comes reflection and action – at both individual and institutional levels.[27]

As Welch testifies, for instance, the week's working practices can prompt reappraisal of approaches to scholarly writing. These recognitions can be put into statistics and testimonials – and they were – but they inevitably mean more than fulfilling a research framework requirement: asking how we should document PaR begins to suggest why it might be a valuable methodology not only for contemporary theatre-making or performance studies but also for challenging traditional approaches to theatre history.

Sometimes private, sometimes shared. Because not everything in the PaRchive is visible. In order to allow for personal check-ins and the airing of thoughts uncommitted to video or audio memory, not all conversations were recorded. Moreover, PaR work is often personal, as our testimonials and video interviews on the Engendering the Stage website show, particularly when it is focused on trans and cis female roles in classical theatre. And so, while live recording, blog posts and tweets, and interviews seek to convey scraps as immediately as possible in the research moment, there are inevitable sensitivities in what can be written about – and how.

On top of ethical and personal questions, there are also institutional limits on documentation (beyond pressures exerted by academic and funding bodies). For instance, the collaborative week-long workshop was only possible thanks to the Stratford Festival, which committed a group of company actors who were, for this cycle, performing only one show (rather than the customary two) thereby freeing them to participate in the workshop with us. Their media and copyright policy meant they would support us in professionally videoing the workshop (except on occasions, as stated), but the arrangement with Equity was that, after the workshop, we would have to reduce the many hours of footage to only five minutes of publicly shareable film. The rest of the "archive" must, like live performance, be ephemeral and disappear from our hard drives and clouds. The PaRchive, then, unsurprisingly, begins to look a lot like any historical archive: shaped by institutional pressures and preferences, with an eye to either embracing or resisting dominant political and financial pressures, born from a complex group of people whose personal and professional lives are only glimpsed, and filled with a wealth of documentary and performance scraps cut down to … smaller scraps.

It is here where our PaRchive on the Engendering the Stage website advertises its affinity with historical archives, which, for Spieker, "do not record the experience so much as its absence."[28] The surrounding materials – lengthy blog posts written in real time the same day or the day after, testimonies, reflections, interviews that channel participants' conversations and the practice that arose from them – to some extent produce, to adapt Reason's phrase, "a representation of PaR": "the act of documentation makes disappearance visible."[29] But those "scraps" are also constitutive of the process, not a shadow or remnant of it; they are part of the iterative method, where reflection, digestion, and conversation takes place (in the room, on social media, on blogs) *at the same time as* performance practice unfolds. While this "live archiving" must therefore deal with inevitable absences and gaps, it is also more than a "representation" of practice.

Indeed, one key aim for the project's impact engagement was to amplify the work as much as possible while maintaining a safe space within the room for sharing and experimentation. When part of the impetus for a workshop is to increase awareness of diverse plays with major cis female, trans, and gender-nonconforming roles, it is important not only to reach those in the room who are exploring those roles but also to advertise to a wider industry and the public the complexity of historical gender identities, their fictional expressions, and their contemporary resonances. Indeed, events such as the Shakespeare Institute's annual play reading marathon (reading aloud through a particular canon of plays over two weeks) illustrate how place-specific PaR-adjacent work can extend beyond location into social media, through dialogue and performative exchanges. There are obvious limits on engagement by those outside the room, but we were aiming to create an open-ended repository of process, via social media and blog updates throughout the week, summarizing and showcasing different avenues (in as non-linear a way as possible). For Reason, representations of live performance create audiences afresh; for PaR, we hoped, they might create collaborators. The spike of engagement on Twitter (now X), with conversations between the project, workshop performers, and interested parties (academics and actors alike), and immediate and continued readership of the blog, indicated a breadth of interest and involvement with the available scraps of PaR activity.

What is our PaRchive, then? It is multivocal, multimedia, multitemporal, inconclusive, and scrappy. Like Hodgdon's "scraps," it is comprised of play-texts, performances, historical material, pictures, notes, videos, blogposts, tweets, interviews, emails, chapters, and the personal experiences and memories of those who "were in the room where it happened." Indeed, this latter sense of living repositories perhaps pushes beyond the philosophical scope of this chapter, but it nonetheless underpins the PaRchive described here as key to the different elements that compose archival performance work: not just documentary-led theatre history but individual recall, sentiment, lived and embodied experience – elements by their very nature in continual flux, in continual processes of revision. These scraps are part of the PaR event itself, which doesn't just leave behind "archival traces" but is constituted by them.

Processing Early Modern Scraps: *Scrap, 1588*

In 1588, three individuals, Fynchley, Pope, and Napton, were remiss in their duties of lopping the willow trees and cleansing and scowering the sewer on the "ground at ye new plaie house."[30] Fynchley is the alias of Philip Henslowe, builder of the Rose, and Pope and Napton owned connected ground and part of the adjacent Bear Garden grounds. Immediately beneath, in this Surrey and Kent Commission for Sewers (SKCS) record, is a request for John Rych and his tenant Thomas Parker to clean the sewer "lying behind the beare garden." We are now grateful for these residents' scrappy yard work, which helps to fill in our knowledge of south London and the responsibilities of the different individuals involved in the early modern entertainment scene. Not only does the SKCS concern scraps of land – sections of sewers divided up as they relate to land ownership or tenancy – but the documents themselves are arranged like scrapbooks: they offer various entries and records in loose geographical and chronological order. Many of the bureaucratic records surviving from Elizabethan England have a similar form, and memoranda-style record-keeping is inherently a matter of entering "scraps" of the larger business of a recorder or organization (and, too, of the ongoing matter at issue): the entry for Fynchley, Pope, and Napton in the SKCS in 1588 is, in the terms of the OED definition for "scrap," a "remnant; a small detached piece ... a fragmentary portion."[31]

If PaR provides challenges for both performance and scholarship, then theatre history, which can (sometimes uneasily) span these two fields, can learn from the construction of a PaR archive. Marvin Carlson laments the division (in the United States at least) between academic research and practice in universities; he identifies this separation as a historic bid to make "theatre history" more "*professional,* more specialized, more 'serious.'"[32] For Carlson, any such separation creates an unhelpful division between practice and so-called pure research.[33] PaR offers to bridge this gap, and in recent years, Rob Conkie's work, together with the Shakespeare and the Queen's Men, Before Shakespeare, Staging the Henrician Court, and Engendering the Stage projects (to name only a few), have sought to combine professional practice and creative theatre-making with theatre history. The documentation of PaR in a live archive, as described above, can also help reconceive our approach to the archives at the centre of "traditional" (documentary-focused) theatre history. Many of the surviving archival repositories that provide our narratives for the development of the early modern playing industry – for the purposes of this chapter, the SKCS and the City of London Corporation records – are "scraps" of process themselves. They warrant being approached in a similar way to Hodgdon's "scraps" of performance in two fundamental senses.

First, they represent a practice (Council management, sewer maintenance) continually in process. Items that deal explicitly with theatrical matters (such as those Henslowe records in the scrap above) are therefore part of a wider network of documentation that was frequently consulted and rewritten. These records were formed themselves from the live archiving of ongoing business in a period where bureaucratic and administrative culture burgeoned – part of what Peter Burke identifies as the rise of the "paper state."[34] Paul Griffiths observes, in turn, how such "books" were "very much working records."[35] Beyond their frequent consultation in courts, guildhalls, and houses, they were also revisited, reconstituted, revised: the administrative culture of early modern Bristol, for instance, is characterized by amendments to earlier decisions, with updates in the margins of different orders and precepts noting whether they continue "permitted" or are made "void"; the city also returns to much older documents, including the "Byffette" book and other materials, in order to consult on past precedents, and by 1614 they had resolved to collate and collect all such material into a revised "p{er}fecte booke of Ordynanc{es}."[36] In London, an Act of Common Council issued in 1579 was revised through an appendix to add a series of regulations that set a precedent for the London authorities' attempt to suppress playing entirely.[37] Like PaR and its archive, many of the early modern administrative books and records that survive in today's archives were (and are) themselves part of an iterative and open-ended process – one that is driven, here, by civic management but that nonetheless has attributes in common with the PaRchive: an emphasis on recognizing the flux and plurality of opinion and the multiplicity of approaches to a given issue (a textual crux or a governmental one); an impulse to speak squarely to contemporary concerns; and an albeit implicit resistance to a final and fixed record.

Theatre history, however, can sometimes seem to treat these documents not as an interrelated network of practice and process but as sources of separate, evidentially useful scraps (to be metaphorically torn out and reappropriated). The relational nature of these records has sometimes been obscured in both anthologized extracts (Malone Society, *Records of Early English Drama, English Professional Theatre 1530–1660*) and in theatre-historical narratives, where each record or sub-record can be read as a discrete entity – a scrap removed from its process – and treated as a "source" for theatre-historical research divorced from other city records. While this form of "excerptionalism" is essential, of course, for identifying and making available records of playing, it can also deify ostensible "theatre" records and consequently exclude a wealth of useful, sometimes essential, context that can inform readings of performance events and spaces – and their flux. To date, for instance, there has been no study of the relationship of theatre history to the totality of London City Corporation records, in their full breadth and scope. Yet conceiving of the totality of these records as scraps from a larger, related practice opens up valuable wider contexts: what we might call – modifying Ott, Tucker, and Buckler – "material manifestations of institutional *process*" for studies of performance in London (and the chance to rebut some persistent myths).[38] Such a conceptualization also helps to avoid anachronistically bracketing off theatrical performance as a uniquely distinct activity.

Second, these records do not offer historians closed outputs, events, or narratives, but remain open-ended. Thinking of them in relation to the similarly end-product-less PaRchive therefore heeds the call of William Ingram, Peter Holland, and other methodologically conscious theatre historians to think about the structure and theoretical bases of the discipline. Theatre history, like its sources, is a process – one (broadly speaking) invested in teasing, telling, and/or resisting narratives about and asking questions of the cultural past, in generating hi*stories*. While historians since the late 1970s have explored what it means to *do* or *write* history, Ingram observes that theatre history has been a little late to the party.[39] There is growing acknowledgment in the wider discipline that narrative and rhetoric are central to creating historical knowledge (beside mere "fact" or "evidence"). Nancy Partner notes that "historians characteristically interpret evidence (itself a metaphor of visual perception) into some special version of what Elizabeth Bowen meant by the 'realisations along that course,' which are never 'quite whole, quite final.'"[40] Partner's characterization of how historical evidence is used sounds a lot like the process of the PaRchive. This chapter champions Partner's sense that both evidence and narrative are scrappy – never quite whole or final – but it also suggests that those scraps are organic and original to early modern bureaucratic sources, which are a testament to institutional process. If historical sources are scraps from the very start, then how might they inform our interpretations and narrations? Rather than seeing scrappiness as a product of 400 odd years of distance, decay, dispersal, and disappearance, what if we restore the scrap-in-process as the central essence of many of our most important surviving Elizabethan sources?

The Scrap as Process in the Early Modern Archive: *Scrap, 1592*

A few years after Henslowe and fellow landowners were charged for their neglect surrounding the "new playhouse," the SKCS recorder notes that the Bear Garden had shifted hands and that there was some complication in levying accumulated fines:

> Whereas Morgan, Pope or [blank] Napton and Captaine Barnaby were amerced att xxxv[s] for default{es} done att the bearegarden wharfe, long before the tyme of Richard Reve now Tenaunte of the beare garden ... the sayd Richard pleseth he is not able to paye the fyne; by reason he was commaunded to dep*ar*te into the country w{i}th his game, to his great hinderaunce and almost vndoing and for that the fault{es} were don before he came to the garden remitted the fyne to —x[s].[41]

These wider records show a long-term (if unclear) relationship between the Rose and Bear Garden in the late 1580s and early 1590s (before Henslowe's own interest in the latter site) and mutual infrastructural obligations. This entry also reveals mutual influence between Bankside entertainment institutions; in line with much current work in theatre history, scraps offer ways to acknowledge the complexity of the past and the nuances and contexts of the nascent leisure industry. Indeed, Reve's comments suggest that the touring model we ascribe to playing companies had parallels with bearbaiting businesses.[42] In 1592, several playing companies were themselves on extended tours "into the country" – probably Sussex's, Pembroke's, and Admiral's Men. It is not clear why or by whom Reve was commanded to "depart into the country" – likely at the Master of the Game's command. Yet at the same time, as with playing companies, there may also be related commercial reasons coinciding with Reve taking his business out of town (albeit unsuccessfully) following a bad plague year. As Andreas Höfele notes, "stage, stake, and scaffold ... are in collusion."[43]

Seeing the SKCS as an archive generated by the administrative practices described above – a repository of process – indicates the business, geographical, and interpersonal relationships between those in and adjacent to early modern playing. The records' assortment of scrappy activity necessitates putting different entries into relation with one another, across space and across time, to reveal their status as fragments of administrative process that help us identify the "paynes" of early modern performance and its related industries.

The SKCS's "repository of process" also presents parallels with Henslowe's "Diary." Neil Carson observes that the term "diary" is a "misnomer": much of the volume "is given over to non-theatrical affairs" including "memoranda, receipts, recipes, and notations," and S.P. Cerasano sees it as a memorandum book rather than a strict accounting system.[44] In 1588, Hugh Oldcastle described memorandum books as documents "used and compiled of many things,"[45] a scrapbook quality noted above that works equally for Henslowe's "Diary" and the SKCS. The "Diary," like the multimedia PaRchive, is witness to a cumulative array of scraps, fragments, performances, and conversations.

Henslowe's "scraps of communication," in Joel Altman's words,[46] encourage scholars to situate plays within wider material exchanges, what William Ingram has called "the other community – the network of social, and hence economic, interdependencies that formed among the men who provided these early Elizabethan entertainments."[47] That is true, too, of the SKCS, which loosely records personal landownership, the running of entertainment businesses, and the daily responsibilities of individuals within parishes and suburban communities. We might see its scrappiness as an extension or parallel of the "Diary," which itself records scraps of Bankside activity and is marked and remarked endlessly, not always in linear or chronological order. This constant, in-the-moment updating of administrative information means that these records as they come down to us are not reflections or representations of "loss" or markers of absence – they are the scrappy, piecemeal, still-in-process archive they were from their very genesis.

The City of London's Corporation records present a parallel case study to the PaRchive and the SKCS records and Henslowe's "Diary," and they reveal how attitudes to the playing industry did not arc through the sixteenth-century in a chronological narrative but are textured at all stages by open-ended debates about playing, plague, and practicalities and show how the regulation of playing is inextricably related to a number of other wide-ranging concerns. Indeed, far from a theatrical exceptionalism in the City Corporation, restrictions on playing are in line with and informed by attitudes to all forms of perceived social deviance – records overlooked by cutting and repasting "playing" records. Chief concerns are "youth," "strangers," and provision for vagrants. There are various orders for a "pryvye searche [a night-time hunt for vagrants] to be made … in all Innes, Alehowses, Victuallinge howses, and all other suspect places" in language directly related to that used about playing.[48] The wider framework of playing entries in these records therefore adds overlooked contexts to our understanding of Elizabethan performance and its reception.

These records further demand reappraisal of the persistent notion that the City was an "enemy" to theatricality. Numerous scraps testify to a fear of plague, and so this concern underpins the City's attempts to limit public gatherings. It is tempting to see the rise of playing as a narrative of counterculture, transgression, and displays of anti-authority (a social reading to match many literary ones). Yet at the same time – aside from the pressure of numerous other forms of authority – the mayors and City Corporation were dealing with epidemic, disorder, and discontentment, alongside changes in the economic and social order (even as their politics can often seem objectionable). Seeing theatrical extracts as one scrap among many – and constantly revised – helps remind us that responses to playing were not always driven by "antitheatricalism" but borne from more practical considerations.

Viewing City Corporation records as a live repository of process – a parallel to the PaRchive – resists an overarching narrative predicated on the anachronistic centrality or uniqueness of "playing" and opens a wider contextual field for theatre and performance history – one that can link topics as diverse as breadmaking, victualling, begging, and the building trade (as, for instance, they are subject to questions about their commercial legitimacy, licensing, and regulation). An extended stand-off between Mayor Nicholas Woodrofe and Ambrose Warwick about Warwick's servant building a bowling alley points to wider London-specific issues with construction, building, and managing recreational activity.[49] Other entries show the City pushing back against such Privy Council pressure, including in the awarding of freedoms or reversions.[50] This tension is surely relevant to its attitude towards performance during a period when London was resisting the appointment of a non-City officer to approve plays and playing spaces in a pre-Tilney role.[51] This significant debate, leading to the expanded role occupied by Tilney, has scarcely been touched in histories of the Master of the Revels to date. Embracing the iterative quality of the administrative processes behind these records can serve as a prompt to embrace, resume, or adapt them through re-iterative approaches like PaR and so encourage theatre history to incorporate obscure or overlooked "scraps" into its many possible narratives.

Leftovers

The practices that characterize many early modern records make them an organically scrappy and fragmented archive. Nothing is "lost" if the scrap is a sign not of partially obscured product but a part of iterative administrative process. This is precisely the governing logic underlying the documentation of PaR at Stratford, where Hodgdon's "scraps, scribbles, drawings and fragments"[52] constitute the stuff of practice, not its detritus or remainder. "The leftovers that fascinate me," Hodgdon writes, "are not indexical signs of a theatrical past; rather, the work they do is neither strictly archival nor documentary but performative – sites of re-performance for which I together with other readers constitute a present audience."[53] Perhaps we might start to think of the historical records of sixteenth- and seventeenth-century England in a similar vein as they relate to the stories we tell about its playing industry – as organic scraps whose work is and always was iterative, open-ended, and performative. As with all narratives about the past, the urgent question remains: how are they made to perform and who gets to perform them?

NOTES

1 Suffolk Record Office C/4/3/1/2, fol. 15r, fol. 14v.
2 Loughran, "The Meeting of Art and Academia," chapter 1 of this volume, explores these tricky cross-communications, particularly with regard to bridging differences between artistic practice and academia.
3 Cockett, "Performing the Queen's Men," 241.
4 Purcell, "Practice-as-Research and Original Practices," 429.
5 This slogan's origins are not easy to pin down; see Charlton, *Nothing About Us Without Us*. Oucharek notes that she picked up the phrase through Carmen Aguirre (Denise Oucharek in conversation with Cockett and Gough, unpublished interview, 2019). See also Loughran, "The Meeting of Art and Academia," chapter 1 of this volume.
6 Some of them can be viewed on the Engendering the Stage in the Age of Shakespeare and Beyond website.
7 Steedman, *Dust*.
8 Nelson, *Practice as Research in the Arts*, 8–9.
9 Purcell, "Practice-as-Research and Original Practices," 425.
10 Purcell, 426–7.
11 Clarke, "The Impact Market."
12 Nelson, *Practice as Research in the Arts*, 69. See also Melissa Trimingham's emphasis on the need for methodology in her "Methodology."
13 Phelan and Lane, *Ends of Performance*.
14 Welch, "Potential Energies," chapter 4 of this volume.
15 Welch, "Potential Energies."
16 See Before Shakespeare, "Galatea." I was particularly involved during the period 2017–18.
17 Workshops for Emma Frankland's *Galatea* project had in its long-term view a full-scale professional production, which premiered at the Brighton Festival in May 2023. While the project's workshops were markedly not about determining immediate production choices, they nonetheless had "ends" – unlike the Stratford research.
18 Phelan, *Unmarked*; Spiecker, *Big Archive*.
19 Hodgdon, *Shakespeare, Performance, and the Archive*, 4–5.
20 Conkie, *Writing Performative Shakespeares*, 28–9.

21 Reason, *Documentation*, 27.

22 I lean here on Jacques Derrida by way of Steedman, *Dust*, in particular Steedman's engagement with *Archive Fever* at 6–10.

23 The very existence of this piece and this volume, however, paradoxically constitute a "product," even as they resist finality and embrace scrap.

24 For further discussion, see this volume's "Introduction" by Cockett and Gough, as well as chapter 13, "A Question to Be Asked," by Barker and Munro.

25 André Morin in conversation with Peter Cockett and Melinda Gough, unpublished interview, 2019; Marcus Nance in conversation with Peter Cockett and Melinda Gough, unpublished interview, 2019. See also Cockett and Gough, "Introduction," in this volume.

26 Purcell, "Practice-as-Research and Original Practices," 432.

27 Denise Oucharek tweeted, "One of the most thought-provoking weeks of my career and my life. Forever changed" (22 September 2018); and Keira Loughran (Stratford Festival's then associate producer) noted in an interview that the workshop would prompt the organization to look to diversify their "canon" further (Engendering the Stage, "In Conversation with Keira Loughran").

28 Spieker, *Big Archive*, 3.

29 Reason, *Documentation*, 27.

30 SKCS 18. 3 Jan. 1569–25 Apr. 1606. MS. London Metropolitan Archives, London, fol. 148v.

31 *OED*, "scrap," n1: 2. https://www.oed.com/dictionary/scrap_n1.

32 Carlson, "Inheriting the Wind," 119.

33 Carlson, 122.

34 Burke, *Social History of Knowledge*.

35 Griffiths, "Local Arithmetic," 125.

36 Bristol Archives M/BCC/CCP/1/2, fol. 48r.

37 See Archer, "City of London."

38 Ott, Tucker, and Buckler, "Introduction to the History of Scrapbooks," 3.

39 Ingram, "Introduction: Theatre History."

40 Partner, "Making Up Lost Time," 94.

41 SKCS 18. 3 Jan. 1569–25 Apr. 1606. MS. London Metropolitan Archives, London, fol. 184r; 1592.

42 The touring practices of baiting are explored in comparison to touring players in Davies et al., "Bear Journeys."

43 Höfele, *Stage, Stake, and Scaffold*, 62.

44 Carson, *Companion to Henslowe's "Diary,"* 5; Cerasano, "Henslowe's 'Curious' Diary," 72.

45 Oldcastle, *Briefe instruction*, B4v.

46 Altman, *Improbability of Othello*, 250.

47 Ingram, *Business of Playing*, 15.
48 COL/CC/01/01/020-21. MS. 07 Nov. 1572–01 Aug. 1579. London Metropolitan Archives, London, fols 377, 487v, 606r.
49 COL/RMD/PA/01/001. MS. 1579–1592. London Metropolitan Archives, London. 131–33 (Sep. 1580).
50 COL/RMD/PA/01/001. MS. 1579–1592. 85 (6 Feb. 1579).
51 COL/CA/01/01/020. MS. 16 Apr. 1573–28 Oct. 1575. London Metropolitan Archives, London, fol. 168v; Cotton CH 26. 2 Mar. 1573. MS. British Library, London (March 1573).
52 Hodgdon, *Shakespeare, Performance, and the Archive*, 4.
53 Hodgdon, 6.

6   A Note to Mary Frith

SL GRANGE

The archival video of the January 2020 performance of SL Grange's A Note to Mary Frith *is accessible at Shakespeare's Globe.[1] It is funny, moving, and totally on topic for this book, and we strongly recommend taking the time to view it should you be at or near the Globe. We are delighted to publish the script here for the first time and to share with readers Grange's insights on the context around the writing of the script, their larger project using emergent practice in research for and about the queer/unruly dead, and the performance at the Wanamaker Playhouse.*

A Note to Mary Frith was commissioned by Shakespeare's Globe as part of their winter 2020 *Notes to the Forgotten She-Wolves* series, curated by Athena Stevens.[2] The *She-Wolves* series consisted of 20 × 20 minute monologues, four per night, over five nights. Each piece by a different writer explored lost, misunderstood, or marginalized individuals whose identities fell within a broad definition of woman, assigned female at birth, or trans-femme. The performances all took place within the indoor, candlelit space of the Sam Wanamaker Playhouse. Some authors performed their own work, while others (including me) had professional actors bring their words to life. LJ Parkinson performed *A Note to Mary Frith*: a request I made since LJ – as well as being an actor – is also an established drag king (LoUis CYfer), and I knew the piece needed the kind of conversational relationship with the audience that drag and cabaret styles do so well.

 A Note to Mary Frith, performed on 29 January 2020, ended the first night of the series. That evening's preceding writers and subjects were Jenet Le Lacheur on Mary Anning; Sabrina Mahfouz on Griselda Blanco, Nesmut, Ching Shih, and Linda Calvey; and Catherine Mayer on Paula Yates. Having previously produced and performed in *Moll and the Future Kings* – a one-off hour of anarchic drag king and improvised performance – in the Wanamaker the previous year, I had some sense of what the space could do. I also knew Mary Frith loved it in there, and I wanted to create a framework that allowed Mary to step into the space and own it. I, in turn, am in love with Mary Frith and attempt to meet them via various emergent, magical, and improvisatory practices. This includes the performance work described here but can equally involve tarot, astrology, shamanism-inspired work, mudlarking, and hanging out in pubs and other locations connected with Mary.[3] The commission came at the end of about ten years of working at Shakespeare's Globe in the less visible roles of shop assistant, stage-door keeper, and education admin assistant, so I also had my own conversation and history with the building and the institution. *A Note to Mary Frith* was an amalgamation of all these layers of history, relationships, and archives.

I wrote the piece pretty quickly once I'd keyed into the atmosphere I wanted to create and brought in some improvisatory techniques gleaned from my work with Improbable, a theatre company specializing in emergent processes, with whom I have worked for well over a decade.[4] The most important aspect of my creative practice is conversation. I believe that performance work is at its best when it is a direct engagement with the audience, when there is room for communication to go both ways, and when we acknowledge what is really happening. For *A Note to Mary Frith*, I also needed to open up a channel to Mary and invite them back onto a stage that felt at least a little familiar, some 409 years after their performance at the Fortune.[5] This multilayered understanding of who is present on and off stage is really crucial to the monologue. As the (co) author, I talk directly to the performer in the stage directions, and I ask them to talk directly to Mary, and to the audience, and back to me.

The game of what is "real" and what isn't is also a key part of this piece: LJ brought on my own dog-eared copy of *Better a Shrew than a Sheep*,[6] had space to talk about the thing that was genuinely making them angry in the improvised section, but also tore up the script because the script instructed that it be destroyed. The doublet that hung over a chair throughout the monologue was one that I had already used in a short film to represent Mary's presence in spaces around Bankside and that I myself had worn when I stood in for Mary in *Moll and the Future Kings*. Theatre is always already haunted, after all. These objects, histories, and emergent moments were also about shifting into a queerer time, acknowledging the living archive of that particular location as well – for me personally and for Mary.

The original scripted ending for the piece involved LJ encouraging the audience (particularly those who experienced marginalization) to carry out a stage invasion, but sadly this action was not allowed for safety reasons (fair enough, but I live in hope!). In the end, it was LJ who replaced this ending with the rallying cry of "Better a shrew than a sheep!" and instead got everyone stamping, shouting, and roaring along. Whether you believe in ghosts or not, there was certainly a strong spirit present in the playhouse, and I like to think we managed to open up some kind of connection and to invite at least a few genderqueer ghosts into the space.

Mary Frith, aka Mal or Moll Cutpurse, Mary Markham, or Mary Thrift, was born around 1590 in London and gained notoriety/celebrity for dressing in "men's apparel" as well as behaving in a "disorderly and licentious" fashion.[7] Frith pursued something of a performance career in the early 1600s, including at least one gig at the Fortune Theatre in 1611 during a production of Thomas Middleton and Thomas Dekker's *The Roaring Girl*, a play in which Moll Cutpurse is a central character. *A Note to Mary Frith* includes one title page for this play, included in the script below as Figure 6.1, and references a second title page, included elsewhere in this volume as Figure 2.2. Frith faced discipline from the church courts, following which they seem to have moved into criminal-adjacent activity, operating a "lost property" office whereat stolen items were fenced or sold back to their owners. A publication claiming to be at least in part Mary Frith's "diary" was published three years after Mary Frith's death in 1659, and Frith's will is preserved at the National Archives.[8]

NOTES

1 Grange, "Note to Mary Frith."
2 Shakespeare's Globe, *Notes to the Forgotten She-Wolves*. See also Shakespeare's Globe, "Giving Voice to Forgotten Women in History."
3 For more on such research practices, see Grange and Kesson, "A Bit Lit 15."
4 See Improbable (website).
5 Mulholland, "Date of *The Roaring Girl.*"
6 Brown, *Better a Shrew than a Sheep.*
7 While published scholarship gives an earlier birth date, my doctoral research, forthcoming, suggests that Frith was likely born up to six years later than is typically supposed.
8 Todd and Spearing, *Counterfeit Ladies*. Frith's will is at the National Archives, ref PROB 10/926.

A Note to Mary Frith

The performer is an AFAB person. They might identify as non-binary, GNC, or transmasc, as lesbian, gay, bi, pan, or queer.

The performer enters from within the audience – probably from the side of the stage, clambering over the railing. You wear a full skirt with a belt. You carry the script tucked into your waistband or belt and a book called Better a Shrew Than a Sheep *by Pamela Allen-Brown.*

Performer: Hi, hello. Hang on. Here I come. Right.

Get an audience member to help you onto the stage. Keep up chat as you do this. An informal, scrappy-happy entrance. Once on the stage, plant yourself in the centre of it and give yourself a moment to absorb the audience, look them in the eye. Clear your throat. Look down. Perhaps the skirt has got in the way of the entrance? Swish it about a bit. Grin at the audience. Take the hem of the skirt and tuck it up into the waistband front and back – thus transforming the skirt into makeshift breeches. If you need a hand from an audience member to do this, that is absolutely fine, and you should take all the time you need to do it. You are absolutely not sorry for the time required to make this clothing adjustment.

That's better. Ok. Good. (*Pull the script out of your waistband and shake it out, smooth it out.*) A Note to Mary Frith, alias Mal Cutpurse. Oh, first, who wants to hear an authentic Tudorbethan joke? Alright then.

Put the script back into your waistband and pull out the book. Flick to the marked page.

"A citizen that was more tender of himself than his Wife, did use to make her first to bed in the winter time and lie in his place to warm it, and when he came, to remove to her own, and for this cause did always call her, His warming pan; which she not very well relishing, went one night (according to her custom) to warm his bed, and when he was ready to come, she (Sir reverence) shit in his place. He suddenly leaping into it, and finding himself in a stinking pickle, Wife, quoth he, I am beshit: No husband, says shee, it is but a Coal dropt out of your warming pan."

Good innit? Earthy. A joke for women to laugh at. Better a Shrew Than a Sheep. A popular proverb from the sixteenth century. Here, I want to show you something else.

Pull the picture page [Figure 6.1] *out of this script and hold it out to the audience. (It should be stapled in – genuinely rip it out. Maybe have a couple and send them out in different directions.)*

Mary Frith, alias Moll Frith – pass this round – Moll Cutpurse, Mary Markham, Maria Thrift, Margaret Markham, Frith, Thrift alias Margaret Malcutpurse. Some other names she's been called: notorious baggage, infamous virago, cutpurse drab, merry, honest … mad.

So many names, yet somehow, despite rampaging through seventeenth-century London for nearly eight decades, she left barely a trace of her real self behind her. A lot of opinions and stories – a whole play, and an alleged biography – but hardly any of her own words. A myth, a lie, or a fiction even in her own lifetime.

She didn't rule a nation or invent something wonderful, she didn't write poetry – as far as we know – or compose operas. She might have been a pickpocket, a conman, or a highwayman. She was definitely a lutenist, and a trader in stolen goods. A troublemaker, a brawler, and a survivor. She was also a cross-dresser … or a trans man …? or a butch dyke? A gap. An unanswerable question.

The Roaring Girl.

Beat

What made me first fall in love with her was that picture. But then someone said, (*pedant voice*) "This is most likely the boy actor who played her in *The Roaring Girl.* Because girls weren't allowed to act in them days." Because they weren't, were they? The All Male Stage! Plays written by men, for men, we're told. Women were subordinate to their husbands. Daughters married off against their will. Scold's bridles. Ducking stools.

It was against the law for women to act. I hear that everywhere. Guided tours. History books. All those movies and plays and tv shows. Gwyneth Paltrow cutting her hair off and getting into trouble.

Beat

You know, there is another picture of the Roaring Girl. More rakish, but sort of coy. And yeah, a bit mad looking. I didn't want that to be my Moll, then – sixteen years ago when we first met. I wanted her squared up to the world. Full frontal.

But I can see something else in that other picture, now. Something Puckish maybe. A trickster. She's got a wicked glint in her eye. And she

Figure 6.1. Title page, Thomas Dekker and Thomas Middleton, *The Roaring Girl* (London, 1611). Woodcut, Folger Shakespeare Library, STC 17908.

knows how to hold a sword properly. She's taken the scabbard off, for a start. She's more dangerous somehow when she's looking at you side-on.

This is an invitation to flirt with the audience.

The theory is, that other picture shows the real Moll, but the publishers had to replace it because it was too scandalous, an actual cross-dressing woman on stage.

> "The Roaring Girl herself some few days hence
> Shall on this stage give larger recompense,
> Which mirth that you may share in herself does woo you,
> And craves this sign: your hands to beckon her to you."

Beat

Love, I can't celebrate your birthday because I don't know the date. So you spring full-formed into the Bankside mud. Your cradle – the tavern counter. Your swaddling – the petticoats of whores. A hubbub baby, a market-call, a brawl, and knife-to-the-neck dark alley dream of torchlit, hard-bit ale-washed streets. Subtle-fingered, stealing time from the pocket of *history*, making it *hers*. Ours.

And, love, I can't lay a flower on your grave. St. Brides is burnt out and bomb shattered, bodies dug up and shoved aside. No rest in London's listless shift and heave. So instead, I stand where the-stage-of-the-Fortune-might-have-been. I walk the Bankside alleys, spill beer in the George. I fold the ground over like a playbook page, and shove my fingertips down deep in the foreshore muck, scrabble through pipe stems and potsherds to find perhaps, possibly, pieces of you.

Beat

I met her once, in a dream. She was maybe sixty or so, wearing a really good hat. She turned to me, gave me a slow smile and a nod.

Last June I found her will in the National Archives, exactly 360 years to the day that she'd signed it, sealed it in red wax with her signet ring. A tiny, jewel-bright eagle spread-winged on grubby paper in a dull cardboard box; the great filing cabinet of humanity.

I put my hand over the paper where she'd scrawled oak gall ink into a spidery monogram, six weeks away from death, and just for sharp second I fell through a hole in time and I felt her skin under my palm. Whoosh.

History is nothing. Time: nothing at all. Just the movement of air and the glitter of dust motes in slow suspension, waiting to be stirred up again into the light.

They're all right here, the she-wolves … or they-wolves. You're breathing them in right now. They're in your lungs and your hair, under your fingernails. They're whispering in your ears.

(*To some cis men, naughtily*) They're shitting in your beds.

Beat

In 1611 Mary Frith took to the stage of the Fortune Playhouse "in man's apparel and in her boots and with a sword by her side. Immodest and lascivious speeches she used at that time. And also sat there upon the stage in the public view of all the people there present in man's apparel and played upon her lute and sang a song."

The church authorities gave her six months beating hemp in Bridewell. It's a horrible job. The coarse fibres get in your eyes, makes the skin on your hands red raw … get in your lungs, your hair, under your fingernails. You'll cough it up the rest of your life. After that, she had to do public penance, sackcloth and ashes in the marketplace. She did it drunk.

All that for wearing "men's apparel," for telling men's jokes.

She walked out of Bridewell wearing her plain penitent's dress, out to St. Paul's. And she tucked her skirt up between her legs to make britches, put on a man's cloak, and gave not one fuck about it.

Beat

The fortune-teller and the ballad-seller both know the truth – stories are living things. To speak of you is a resurrection, an insurrection. Codpiece daughter, shameless sister. Burn the rules to a blister on your tobacco-hot tongue. Wear your britches out, dancing to the jig of the rebel shout. What echoes? What remains? A handful of words, a fistful of names.

When there's gaps, there's got to be a dialogue with the dead, not just epitaphs.

What would Moll say to us, now?

Time flows both ways. If you're witch enough, you can do it. You just need the right spell.

In the cracks between the boards, and in the wax that drips and scrawls. In the infinitesimal silence between the notes of the chords, in the dramatic pause as the tragic hero … falls. I call you back. I call you here.

Give me your hand, pipe-bowl warm, and step across the dark river. Re-member.

Beat

What would Moll say to us, now?

Beat

Let's ask her.

Listen; you're a medium. She's coming through …

She says, tell them to buy me a pint, I'm parched. Tell them to light up their pipes and tune the lutes and get their stomping clogs on. Tell them to make some noise and stop being so bloody polite.

   She says, tell them, this is really important, tell them it was never illegal for women to act. Never.

Be Moll, for a bit

Sure (*pedant voice*), the playhouses' companies were all "male," but that wasn't the law, and you can bet it wasn't the only story. We weren't sheep. We weren't all patient Griseldas waiting quietly in cold beds. No. We had voices, and filthy jokes, and some very dirty songs. We set up planks on barrels in the streets, we stood on chairs in taverns, we climbed on wagons and heckled from the galleries.

Can you get a little heckle out of the gallery now? A warm up?

We gave as good as we got. We always made ourselves heard. I remember Mother Bunch! The size of a cathedral and even more full of stories – as famous as Tarlton or Kemp. She brewed the ales and told the tales. There was Long Meg of Westminster! Beheader of Frenchmen – though I hear that's not the done thing now … And there was me. Moll Frith. A mad merry mess, a tomrig rumpscuttle. I made my way from the streets to the stage to the jestbook page. They named a bear after me. Bet none of you can say that.

   You know, when I performed at the Fortune, I was already an old hand. I'd been working the inns for years by then, challenging the gallants to drinking matches, and brawls. Singing their buttoned-and-braided-randy-dandy masculinity right back at them.

   Mal Cutpurse they called me. A very funny pun.

   They were scared of me.

Dressed in men's clothes, they said. But they weren't men's clothes, they were mine. My clothes. When they took them away, I changed my skirt into britches. When they made me do public penance, I thought, great, an audience! And I upstaged the priest – who by the way, was wearing a damn dress.

Men. They laugh at our anger, but you know what, they are *so* scared of our laughter.

Beat

That's what Moll says.

When I speak to her – them, him? – what I notice most is how powerful their anger is. The voice that comes through, across four centuries, is so defiant. Sometimes defensive, even. Being punished, villified, mocked every day for being themselves. Being erased then rewritten, constantly. So much to be angry about.

Beat

Have you noticed, whenever anyone mentions female anger, there's a kind of nervous laugh? Nervous.

You know what makes me angry?

Tell us what makes you angry, in your own words. Locate it in your body. Tell us the shape of it. Tell us what it does to you, how it feels. Find the energy of it, find out what quality it is giving you. It can be any kind of anger. Ice cold. Brittle. Burning hot. Angry laughing. Messy rage. Whatever is true at that moment. Tell us what it gives you – what's its message or power?

Give this moment some time.

I asked Mary, what did you do with your anger? What can I do with mine?

Use whatever quality/power your anger gave you to deliver this next bit – it will give you the quality of the sword you hold.

Learn how to hold a sword. Then even if you don't have one to hand, your body will always know. If you're made to wear the wrong clothes, change them to suit you. Wear them how the fuck you want. Get yourself a bloody big hat and wear it like a weapon; make yourself tall, one way or another – get up in their eyeline.

If everything else fails, shit in the bed. Be leaky. Be bloody. Be unruly. Be a mess. Be loud. Be brawling. Be wilful. Be froward. Be a notorious baggage. Be fat *and* happy. Be expansive. Take up more space. Be a state. Be big enough to declare yourself an independent fucking state. Roll yourself like a boulder through the crowds and up the streets. Don't move out of the way for anyone. If they tell you how to speak, what to say, tear up the script.

Tear up the script. Throw it to the ground.

If someone tells you, you're not allowed on here

Indicate the stage.

ignore them. Defy them. Come on. Up you come.

Get some AFAB audience on stage. Help them over the barrier. This next bit of speech you can ad lib and adjust in the moment. Make it your own, as long as you get people to make some noise and connect to their anger:

It's yours. It was always yours. You've got so many stories to tell. We've been waiting so long to hear them. Shout it out. Stand up. Shout it out. What is it you've never been allowed to say? Tell me. Tell Moll Frith. What is it you wish for? What is it that's getting in your way? What makes you angrrrrrrrrryyyyy???!!!!!

People start calling out. You might need to help them along, make invitations to specific audience members around you. Especially use your experience in the world to spot the folks who mostly likely don't get a look in and give them extra permission. Get some noise out of them.

Radiate. Take the space. Demand the space. Be a shrew, not a sheep! Be heard! Be seen!
Stop being so damn polite!

Get them to shout back at you "Better a Shrew than a Sheep!" or any other slogans you find that feel important in the moment. A call-and-response protest chant.
Soak up the noise.
Stamp stamp stamp.
Fuck yes!

PART FOUR

Skill, Power, and Swordplay

7 Drawing Your Weapon

PETER COCKETT AND MELINDA GOUGH, WITH CARMEN ALVIS,
EMMA FRANKLAND, LILY McEVENUE, AND DENISE OUCHAREK

The sword and its use was one means through which the middle and upper classes of early modern Europe defined masculinity at its intersection with social rank. As a prop in life and on the stage, the sword offered a key opportunity to embody gender.

Due to health and safety regulations, it was not possible to give the scholars in the room the opportunity to handle weapons, nor was there time to create stage combat for the scene work. Instead, Wayne Best, an actor and experienced fight captain at the Stratford Festival, ran a one-hour workshop for the actors, observed by the scholars, that focused on the basics of wearing and drawing a sword.

Best's workshop entwined teachings about the techniques of weapon management with information about the etiquette of sword carrying and the ways in which carrying a sword increased the stakes and consequences of actions in early modern Europe, both in life and on the stage. His work offered the actors a gestural language that could articulate non-verbal negotiations of power before any weapon was drawn. This language was gendered in that sword-wielding was conventionally associated with men, but in the workshop, actors of all genders worked with a sword and took that learning into their scenes featuring sword-wielding characters.

The swords used for the workshop were fencing rapiers. For anyone who has not worn a sword at their hip, the experience can be disorienting at first. The rapiers are relatively light and not hard to carry, but they extend behind the body and thus require a different bodily awareness, especially when moving in tight spaces. Best gave the actors time to acclimatize themselves to this extra appendage, encouraging them to move safely around the space and demonstrating how the left hand can be used to raise the hilt and bring the tip of the sword closer to the body to avoid contact with other people or furniture.

The workshop established the basic techniques of drawing a sword and returning it to the scabbard. As the actors became increasingly comfortable, Best taught them how to draw the sword quickly into an *en garde* position, ready to fight. It was an explosive movement through which the actors were suddenly taking up more space, and Best used it as a springboard to explore the storytelling possibilities of simply carrying and drawing a sword and the drama that can happen between sword-bearers, even when there is no fight. When walking towards each other armed, Best explained, the moment of contact occurs much earlier than expected since both parties require the length of a drawn sword between them and their potential opponent. In consequence, when armed, a person's spatial awareness is extended a good two metres in front of them. Armed people take up a lot more space, both physically and mentally.

If two people approaching each other sense the possibility of conflict before the moment of conflict, they will stop at that distance. Should one of the parties put their right hand to their sword, the conflict escalates. Half-pulling the sword out of the scabbard escalates the situation further without committing either party to a fight. Best taught all of this technique and gestural language to provide the actors with a vocabulary of action and gesture connected to their swords that could be drawn on in their later scene work.

Importantly, Best taught in a non-prescriptive way, clearly indicating the protocols and techniques that would best represent a character accustomed to sword-wearing and accomplished with their weapon but also allowing for the fact that not all people, actors, or characters would be equally adept with a sword. Their competency or lack of it could be a means to share aspects of their characters with the audience. In this way, Best encouraged the actors to develop a specific relationship with their sword, one they felt best aligned with their character in the scene.

This subtlety in Best's teaching gave space for the actors' embodied engagements with swords to become a sustaining element in their exploration of the embodiment of gender more broadly. Within the critical context established at the workshop, the actors connected their embodied responses to the weight of the sword to the cultural weight of this object, which carries the power, privileges, and oppressions inherent in Euro-patriarchal patterns of masculinity. This power was familiar to actors identifying as male who had handled swords previously in their work. Marcus Nance, for example, commented that "the sword gives you power because … it would be like … the right-wing Americans with the guns: you've got your weapon on you, you have the protection."[1]

In additional reflections below, other actors speak further about developing embodied relationships with their swords in which their lived positionalities became entangled with the gendered performance of their characters. Best's advice that sword "mastery" need not be the goal, depending on the character and on the actor's objectives in representing the character, opened additional creative space for the complexity of responses and relationships these actors developed with their stage weapons.

Artist Reflections

DENISE OUCHAREK (she/her, Canada)

Role: *Guzmán*
Play: *The Lieutenant Nun* (*La Monja alférez*, 1623)
Scene: *Act 3, lines 2420–2628*

In the scene we workshopped, Oucharek's character, who has lived as a man, is being asked to wear a dress in order to meet with the Visconde de Zolina. The scene ends with Guzmán responding to the sounds of fighting in the street by rushing out of the room, drawn sword in hand.

My swooooord! Oh, I loved my sword. Everyone knew how much I loved my sword. Up until that week, I had never ever had any opportunity to use any weaponry other than a handgun in a show. I had to shoot another actor every single night for months. And I never liked it. I always felt – because it was a comedy as well, it felt wimpy – there was no power in it. The power was in the gun; the power was not in me. Anyone could have done it. A child could have done it, an old woman could have done it, a big burly man could have done it. Anyone could have pulled that trigger with the same effect. So I actually didn't enjoy it at all. Not to mention the fact that you're firing blanks, and what if they're not – we've all heard those kinds of stories – and, you know, it didn't feel good, there was nothing proactive about

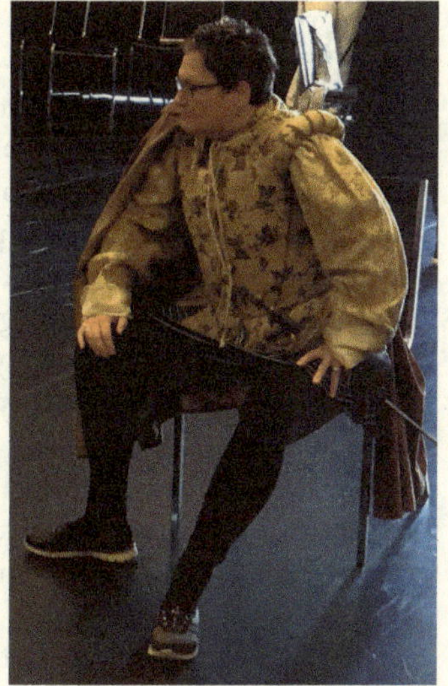

Figure 7.1. Denise Oucharek, 2018 Stratford Festival Laboratory participant, as Guzmán. Photograph by Callan Davies.

it for me, physically. But being a very physical actor, using a sword for the first time was, I think, one of the highlights of my entire career. It really was. And I didn't think it would be. I was like, "Okay, here we go – this is kind of – wow! – this takes a lot of energy." Realizing the kind of energy it required – even as an actor who is very physical. For example, I don't do a lot of TV and film because I'm usually too big. What I do is too big. It's too big for the camera, and I have to dial it back. So for TV and film I play a lot of outlandish characters, those really wacky zany people, because my work is big. My physical work is big, so they celebrate that and find that place to put me in – which I love, and it's great.

I categorize myself as a very physical actor, but – this felt like a great fit for me because the actual physical energy required to wield those weapons is immense. It's *immense*. And I felt it in my body after that first day. I felt it. I went home, and I was like, "Oh *wow*, that really, you know, stretched out my back." That really stays with you afterwards. The way you're walking, the way you have to shift your weight. All of that was fascinating to me. And I enjoy looking at swordplay on stage, but I never ever considered it. Ever. And so, to be a woman shouldering this same weight physically in weaponry typically wielded by men was incredible. It was really incredible. It was more work for the cis-women. It was more work for us to do that. But the sense of physical power you got from it, because the energy that was in your body had to be transferred to the sword in order for the move to work – and that's what I loved, that my energy had somewhere to go, right? Because I have that energy. If I wasn't given a sword, and I had to play Guzmán, there would have been places where I wouldn't know where to put my energy. It would have just been bubbling. But I had a place to put it. I had something to grab when I was getting angry, or frustrated, or feeling challenged. Even when I wasn't wielding it, I had something, I had a threat. I had a physical threat that I knew I could control at any time. And it gave me a sense of power that I hadn't experienced in any female characters I've played. And in any other largely physical roles I've played. And that was telling. And so – it was exciting, but then it made me sad as an actor, because I thought, "Damn it, I want that all the time." My only power should not be my brain or my emotions. I want that physical power. I'm a larger woman of stature, I should be able to have that power all the time if I want it and if the character suits it. But it's not something that's considered, usually. So even in a modern practical sense, that's not being employed and so – now I'm hungry for it. Now I want that all the time. But there are ways of finding it, there are ways of finding it. If I don't get to carry a sword in something, where can I find that physical power, and how can I translate it?

EMMA FRANKLAND (she/her, UK)

Role: *Moll Frith*
Play: *The Roaring Girl* (c. 1607–10)
Scene: *Act 3, scene 1*[2]

In this scene, Moll confronts Laxton, a lascivious gentleman who has come for what he thinks is a sexual liaison. Disguised as a man, Moll humiliates the would-be seducer, both outwitting and out-fighting him.

Figure 7.2. Emma Frankland, 2018 Stratford Festival Laboratory participant, as Moll Frith. Photograph by David Campbell.

I am an experienced sword fighter and have studied stage combat. In my earlier life I fenced, and as a young actor, I worked in historical costume at the Tower of London for seven years, often wearing and wielding swords and other weapons. On one occasion I played the role of Laertes and worked with a famous fight director who regaled us with hilarious tales of fighting Lawrence Olivier during the filming of Richard III … but I haven't picked up a sword in the ten years since I transitioned from male to female.

So when the entire Engendering the Stage company were invited to wear swords and engage with swordplay, it was an emotional experience. Firstly because, although holding a sword can be fun and feel cool, I was struck that the vast majority of the female-identified participants in the workshop were experiencing this sense of empowerment (the empowerment that comes from carrying a two-foot solid metal weapon) for the first time. Of course, there are many, many experienced female sword fighters and fight directors, but for most of the female-identified participants, the permission to pick up a sword and feel easy and relaxed was missing. For me, the emotion was coupled with a memory that what I had feared most about the prospect of gender transition was that it would mean an end to my acting and theatre career. So it was remarkable to be invited to explore a series of roles that utilized swordplay and to feel again the space and freedom to be playful that I always felt accorded as a young, white, non-disabled (perceived) male actor.

In the scene where I was playing Moll Cutpurse, I enjoyed subverting the expectations an audience would lay on that character – the assumptions of how a person assigned as female should behave. I suspect that an actor with less sword experience might have approached the scene differently, but my confidence with the sword allowed me a swagger and gave me power – it allowed me to be dangerous. I also combined this with notes from our fight director, Wayne Best, about how somebody experienced in the etiquette of dueling might behave (that is, drawing your sword is a final resort) versus how someone with skill but unrestrained by the rules of good sportsmanship might behave … This permitted me more of an unpredictable energy.

It was fun to play a character read as female but to explore stereotypically masculine traits – something I do often in my own performance practice, whether that be wielding knives (in "Hearty") or a circular saw (in "Don Quijote") or hurling heavy rocks and operating a jackhammer (in "We Dig"). These are not actions that are technically off-limits to women, but we are still not expected to embrace or delight in them, and particularly as trans women, the expectation is that we will distance ourselves from "masculine" behaviours in order to prove that our identity is valid. So it was tremendous to engage with early modern texts that have gender play and subversion at their core – and to be reminded that many of the gender constructs that we understand today are modern, colonial inventions – rather than innate truths.

LILY MCEVENUE (she/her, Canada)

Role: *Clara*
Play: *Love's Cure, or The Martial Maid*
Scene: *Act 2, scene 2*

In this scene, Clara, having grown up on the battlefield as a man, is forced to wear women's clothes – but refuses to relinquish her sword.

It was not Clara's choice to become a soldier or a war hero, yet she took great pride in it. Her duties were attributed with that of male identity, and therefore she started to identify as male. Clara was later forced into a reality completely different from the one that shaped her existence. It was a significant shift in her reality because now, as a female, she has lower status, no choice, and is obligated to fulfil the duties of what society deems appropriate for women. It was a challenge for me to tap into that reality. As a cisgendered, white, straight female, I do not hold the same risk if I were put in the same situation as Clara. The stakes were significant for Clara in transitioning from her role in public as male to her birth identity as female. I had to put myself in the emotional state of someone whose status was taken away and who was forced into becoming the image of what society expects.

Figure 7.3. Lily McEvenue, 2018 Stratford Festival Laboratory participant, as Clara. Photograph by David Campbell.

Holding the sword and gun immediately affected my posture. I quickly realized how much confidence and coordination is required to draw and sheath a sword. Your physicality has to be alert and strong. You need a sense of oppositional force between weight dropping into the floor and the upper body holding strong and lifting. If I stood with narrow footing, I would lose control of the weapons. Having a wide stance and feeling connected to the ground were important to establish if I wanted to embody feelings of confidence and authority. As a dancer, all story is expressed through movement. It is a natural process to explore character through physicality. This is why working on Clara was so satisfying for me.

CARMEN ALVIS (she/her, Two-Spirit, Michif)

Role: *Aspatia*
Play: *The Maid's Tragedy*
Scene: *Act 5, scene 3*

In this scene, Aspatia, dressed as a man, challenges the unfaithful Amintor to a duel.

Figure 7.4. Carmen Alvis, 2018 Stratford Festival Laboratory participant, as Aspatia. Photograph by David Campbell.

Aspects of myself I brought to Aspatia, particularly in the task of wielding the sword, include the burden of being required to perform as a man and enjoy typical male things. I have a female as well as male spirit, and at various points in my life I have been redirected by family, friends, and society to perform the role of a man to the exclusion of my femininity. For this scene, I brought my disdain for performative masculinity to the task of swordplay, given that Aspatia is convinced a sword fight is how she must die and is likely untrained in combat. It was refreshing when my forced and unnatural ability with overt masculinity became an asset to play the role.

Facilitator Reflections

Picking up a sword is an opportunity to express the complexity of a character's gender. Competency with the weapon reads as a complex cultural sign, and while the weapon has deep cultural associations with masculinity, the way the weapon is used can mean many things. Training in swordplay can thus be more than a technical exercise: it can be a means to expand understandings of the embodied performance of gender, then and now.

Sword training has traditionally been given to masculine-presenting actors. When expanding the possibilities for casting martial roles, any gaps in training should be addressed in the interest of equity. Managing a sword is complex: time to train, practice, and play are key to liberating the expressive possibilities of swordplay. Cisgender women and non-binary and trans people have generally not been granted the same opportunity to learn, and so theatre companies and theatre schools should consider committing resources to addressing that inequity.

For the actors quoted above, working with swords provoked affective responses tied closely to their gender identities. Cisgender female actors Denise Oucharek and Lily McEvenue speak to the liberating experience of carrying a sword and playing martial roles. Yet additional complexities arise when trans and Two-Spirit actors engage with activities like sword-play that are culturally coded as male, as becomes clear from Emma Frankland's and Carmen Alvis's reflections in this chapter.

From our PaR experimentation using early modern play-texts that feature sword-wielding characters, we learned first-hand that welcome additional performance complexities become available to directors and acting companies when cisgender female actors, as well as Two-Spirit and non-binary actors, are invited into the work as meaningful artistic col-laborators. At the same time, our experience in the workshop as a whole leads us to ask hard questions about the value of exercises like this on this land today. Does Turtle Island need more people of any gender demon-strating how the world can be ruled through force? Are we not imposing colonial narratives of violence, regardless of the gender of the actor? How might rehearsing gender in such scenes be subversive, and how might it be repeating dominant narratives through alternative means? How might it be both?

NOTES

1 Marcus Nance in conversation with Peter Cockett and Melinda Gough, unpublished interview, 2019.
2 Scene 5 in *The Roaring Girl*, ed. Kahn.

CLARE McMANUS

Late in the week of our Stratford Festival workshop, trans theatre-maker Emma Frankland as Moll and company actor Daren A. Herbert as Laxton faced each other, swords in hand, as they worked on scene 5 of *The Roaring Girl*.[1] In this scene, Moll, under the pretence of an assignation with the predatory Laxton, reveals her identity, lures him into a duel, and – to his surprise – is victorious. All three artists workshopping the scene drew from their professional experience to deploy skills of verbal and physical dexterity, gendered movement, and wit: both Herbert and Megan Caines, who played the braggart servant Trapdoor, are performers of musical theatre and were appearing in the festival's production of *The Music Man*; and Frankland could draw on her career "explor[ing] stereotypically masculine traits [in her devised shows] ... whether that be wielding knives (in "Hearty") or a circular saw (in "Don Quijote") or hurling heavy rocks and operating a jackhammer (in "We Dig")."[2] This combination of performers offered opportunities to explore the characters' spatial and verbal relationships to one another as they approached, assessed, circled, and withdrew from each other, their dynamic shaped by the two-foot prop of the swords they wore and by the etiquette dictating when it should and should not be drawn. Into this mix, Pamela Allen Brown introduced the idea of the verbal "zinger": short, sharp, witty one-liners that she has identified as a practice used by the *innamorata* in Italian commedia, which we found to be a very fitting practice for Frankland's Moll, who uses her wit and physical skill to survive in a dangerous world.[3]

As Frankland and Herbert focused on the sword fight itself (scene 5, lines 57–124), one particular moment offered an insight into the collision of early modern and modern codes of embodied femininity. As explored by these actors, Moll's challenge to Laxton unfolded over several phases. Frankland's Moll at first seemed uncertain of herself; she

Figure 8.1. Emma Frankland, 2018 Stratford Festival Laboratory participant, as Moll Frith. Photograph by David Campbell.

held her sword limply, standing with her feet close together and off balance, drawing her abuser closer to her through a performance of incompetence (lines 57–67). As soon as Herbert's Laxton was within range of her weapon, however, Frankland combined the shout "Win 'em and wear 'em!" (line 68) with an explosive, gleeful snap into a dynamic, athletic fencing pose, legs wide to balance her weight, sword firmly in her hand, ready to attack in a proud display of her training and skill (Figure 8.1).[4] The move was a joyous revelation of unexpected feminine skill, playing with assumptions about the capabilities of feminine bodies and the limitations placed on them. Above all, it abounded with what Frankland herself calls "swagger."[5]

The Roaring Girl is a stalwart of women's performance studies, and from the 1990s onwards, scholarship has offered important interpretations of the play as proto-feminist, exploring what it has usually defined as the cross-dressing of its cis female-identified protagonist and her manipulation of the gendering of clothing and costume to challenge the misogynist strictures of patriarchy.[6] Perhaps more written about than performed, the play has long been a touchstone for emerging iterations of gender studies, seemingly as compulsively attractive for scholars as its charismatic protagonist, based on the real life sword-wielding duellist Mary Frith, was for Middleton and Dekker. Extending these studies of gendered categories and epistemologies, emerging scholarship is beginning to unpack the play's trans valences: what Marjorie Rubright, deploying David Getsy's "keyword" for transgender studies, calls its "transgender capacity."[7] This chapter takes a cue from the Stratford Festival workshop to combine a triad of approaches – theatre history, feminist and trans studies scholarship, and practice as research – to explore the interactions of embodied actorly expertise, play-text, and inclusive casting in *The Roaring Girl*.[8] In bringing Rubright's textual "soma-semantics" into contact with the embodied somatics of performance, gender scholarship's challenges to the binary make themselves felt in the collision between the early modern archive and present-day performance. Key to this collision is the lived experience of actors and the risk that a trans performer in the central role of *The Roaring Girl* might experience both agency and violence.

The collaboration of practitioners and scholars has consequences for both groups' engagement with early modern drama. In what follows, I argue that we must broaden the early modern dramatic performance canon to include plays with more expansive possibilities for casting and gendered performance. Broadening means *Love's Cure* and *The Roaring Girl* rather than only *Twelfth Night* and *As You Like It*, and in an important corollary as yet unexplored in our Engendering the Stage workshops, it means drama authored by women.[9] Alongside this expansion of the repertory, critical editions of early modern plays must advocate for diverse, equitable casting by attending to possibilities in the play-texts, in the editing of the texts, and in commentary. In addition, we must also look again at familiar, canonical plays to expand the gendered performance codes of modern productions. What, for instance, might the duel scene in *Twelfth Night* (3.4) look like if Cesario were cast as a trans man, something which makes sense of his underexplained decision to wear masculine clothing in 1.2.52–8?[10] The misogyny of the duel scene when Cesario is cast as a cis female-identified character changes with this new casting to resemble the transphobic mockery of a trans man's inability to pass, radically shifting the stakes of this moment. And how might the final attempted imposition of a feminine identity on Cesario – to which, as Stephen Orgel pointed out long ago, the play never returns and which it hence never endorses – be played with a trans man in the role?[11]

An expanded theatre history that attends to diverse genders can offer precedents and necessary validation for diverse gender expressions now. For this chapter, expanding theatre history in this way entails seeking out performers who, in early modern binary terms, are identified as female by the historical record and whose performances of femininity as tumblers, rope-dancers, acrobats, and sword-dancers were as explosively energetic, muscular, and dynamic as Frankland's was when she snapped into the balanced, knowledgeable, dangerous, swaggering fighting pose that so unnerved Herbert's Laxton.[12] Frankland's physical exploration of skill, muscularity, sweat, and bodily labour has a historical parallel in the early modern period in the work of other performers of femininity who have been marginalized from theatre history. Acknowledging this parallel is part of the critical project of disassociating the category of femininity from intimations of weakness and passivity. Citing Julia Serano's *Whipping Girl*, Jack Halberstam writes: "Recognizing that femininity is co-constructed and coinhabited across bodies that are male and female, trans* and cis, Serano calls not just for an inclusive trans* feminism, but one that actively embraces femininity rather than leaving the concept stranded in lexicons for weakness, dependence, and fear."[13] This recognition, what Serano calls a prying away of femininity from "the insipid, inferior meanings that plague it," in turn can challenge binary depictions of femininity in modern productions of 400-year-old plays by energizing the transgender capacity that these texts possess. This chapter attempts such an approach by focusing on the circulation of performance skills between a remarkable triad of early modern and modern performers (Frankland, the boy actress, and tumblers and rope-dancers identified by the archive as women) to show the extent to which such skills did not pertain to one gender category or another but circulated in a queering commonality between distinct and diverse groups of performers.

In the introduction to this book, Peter Cockett and Melinda Gough discuss the difficulties of escaping terminology and the problematics of using the language of our time to think about past identities. For this chapter, terminology is the site where the dual pull of the archive is most felt. On the one hand, the evidence of early modern performance offers examples of performers behaving in ways that we have been taught to understand as unexpected; for example, performers whom the record identifies as women embody dynamic, muscular, agile femininities and offer a new, transformative narrative of early modern performance. On the other hand, the same evidence imposes constricting categories of identity on those performers, identifying them straightforwardly as women in ways that can push us to accept cis identities as normative and close down the possibilities of past trans identifications. Simone Chess has used the archive to open up such possibilities, identifying a "queer residue" around the careers of some celebrated seventeenth-century boy actors.[14] With Chess's argument in mind, I use the term "boy actress" to signal the potential that this professional category holds for multiple, potentially playful, gender expressions. Similarly, when in this chapter I write of performers whom the images, texts, and documents of performance figure seemingly straightforwardly as "women," I use foregrounding phrases such as "whom the archive has identified as women" to make visible the workings of that archive. This terminology does not mean that such performers might not have called themselves women, but it allows for the possibility that they may not have done and acknowledges the potential violence of the archive upon past identities.[15]

Hiring People to Be Themselves

Frankland's bravura "snap" into a trained fighting stance is, of course, less straightforwardly utopian than my description allows. Watching Emma as Moll from my own position as an attentive academic eager to learn from the verbal and embodied practice of the Stratford Lab practitioners, I saw a woman revelling in a skill that her aggressor could not conceive she would possess. As the rug was pulled from under Laxton's feet, I was reminded of the moment in *Raiders of the Lost Arc* when Indiana Jones brings a gun to a sword fight, blows the cobwebs off a dusty old film trope, and confounds expectations. Of course, the imperialism and orientalism of *Raiders'* depiction of Western technology overcoming Egyptian sword skill tipped me off to the complexities of this and similar moments, and when seen from Emma's lived and professional perspective, the complexities of her portrayal of Moll make themselves forcefully apparent. This section will consider the opportunities and risks of casting a trans woman in the title role of *The Roaring Girl*.

The play-text of *The Roaring Girl* has a remarkable inherent multiplicity and fluidity, and its charismatic central character can be played by a range of gendered performers: cis female-identified, male-identified assigned female at birth (AFAB), non-binary, genderqueer, or gender fluid, to name but a few. Hence, Frankland's fluid, ludic, and self-conscious manipulation of conventionally gendered positions reflects her character in *The Roaring Girl*. To quote from SL Grange speaking about *A Note to Mary Frith*, an important project on *The Roaring Girl* and Mary Frith (showcased by Shakespeare's Globe's "Notes to the Forgotten She-Wolves," the script of which appears in chapter 6 of this volume): "You can't fit Moll into any of the boxes we've constructed for gender or sexuality, and as a butch-bi/pan-feminist-genderqueer-drag-king myself, I love that."[16]

Casting a trans performer in this role, then, is *not* to read against the grain of the play-text. On the contrary, going *with* the grain – specifically, *with* the fluidity of the performer and the play-text – reveals much about a play that can be cast in diverse ways. In an allusive "wordscape," framed as a dictionary entry in homage to Dekker the playwright and lexicographer, Marjorie Rubright sketches the contours of the remarkable variety of names for the play's protagonist.[17] They range from the professional "Moll Cutpurse" (2.207) or "The Roaring Girl" (2.258); to the oppressive "a scurvy woman" (2.127), "a creature" (2.102), "a thing/ One knows not how to name" (2.130–1), "a strange idol" (2.120), a "bouncing Ramp" (7.7–8), or "whore" (7.222); the status-based "my Mistress" (5.183), "your Mistress" (5.174), "Mistress Mary" (3.230), "Mistress Moll" (3.376); the awestruck "the maddest fantastical'st girl" (3.211); and to terms of bodily fascination such as "Sweet plump Moll" (3.283) or "a stout girl" (8.24). As the list suggests, these swirling names centre for the play's first nine scenes on the name "Moll" and – except at moments of explicit disguise as a young lawyer (scene 5) or as a gallant rescuing Jack Dapper from the Counter (scene 7) – the vast majority of pronouns used by the protagonist and by other characters are feminine.[18] Importantly, there is a clear change in nomenclature in scene 10. Here, Jack Dapper suddenly begins to refer to his rescuer as "Master Captain Jack" (10.1). The consistently inconsistent Dapper, however, then swiftly names this captain "Captain mad Mary" (10.36) and even "Sirrah, Jack, Moll" (10.30). Such a blunt tool as counting cannot, of course, account for the play's constant efforts to reinscribe its protagonist in the discourses of conventional femininity, discussed below, but it gives a sense of the protagonist's potential fluidity with regard to gender categorizations, what Rubright identifies as the resistance to stable categories of gender evident in the discourse around its central character.

In line with her sense of the play's refusal to settle and its impetus to move through and "hover" over conventional gender categories, Rubright uses the philological detail of the discourses around the play's protagonist to take a distant reading of *The Roaring Girl*.[19] Stepping back from the detail of the play-text's structural to and fro, she names the protagonist "Moll | Jack." By avoiding the "either … or: formula of the forward slash (i.e., 'Moll / Jack')" in favour of a name that folds around the vertical slash, Rubright's formulation permits us to see how each name mirrors and coexists with the other, allowing "both … and" or "sometimes X … sometimes Y."[20] However, just as embodied theatrical practice brings the utopian abstract of gender fluidity into collision with the lived politics of transphobic violence, so the activated transgender capacity of *The Roaring Girl*'s discourse is opposed by its own structure as it tends inexorably towards its New Comedy conclusion in heterosexual, cisnormative marriage.[21] *The Roaring Girl* is a magnet for gender scholars perhaps precisely because of the poignant internal balance between a structure that closes down gender fluidity even while its own discourse resists any such closure.

The play's final scene contains a particularly significant crux. Moll | Jack enters, as Coppélia Kahn's editorial stage direction (SD) tells us, "[*dressed as a man*]" (11.96 SD) and offers to marry Sebastian. Goshawk and Greenwit greet their acquaintance:

> GOSHAWK: Life, here's Moll?
> GREENWIT: Jack!
> GOSHAWK: How dost thou, Jack?
> MOLL: How dost thou, gallant?   (11.96–8)

This small but snagging moment could easily be interpreted as Greenwit, somewhat more sensitive to the nuances of clothing than his companion, interjecting quickly to correct Goshawk as he publicly deadnames a trans man and subjects Moll | Jack to transphobic linguistic violence. Interpreted this way, these lines further italicize the significance of names in the play. The textual history of Q 1611, the sole textual witness for Middleton and Dekker's play, suggests that this crux is ascribable neither to textual error nor to the processes of collaborative authorship; yet neither it nor Jack's name have attracted much editorial attention.[22] Instead, the editorial history of a play that effectively calls its central character both "lower-class woman or whore" (Moll) and "lower-class man or rogue" (Jack) demonstrates equally binary responses that elide the subtleties of the play's nomenclature and gendering. In 1987, Paul Mulholland glossed Jack as follows: "A generic name for a man, *Jack* is apparently used as a familiar name for Moll when she wears male attire."[23] Coppélia Kahn in the Taylor and Lavagnino *Thomas Middleton: The Collected Works* (2007) glosses "Jack" as "Moll's name when she is dressed as a man" but repeats this gloss when Moll | Jack returns later in scene 11 dressed as a conventional bride, even though it is an editorial stage direction that has Moll | Jack "[*in female dress*]" (11.128 SD). The gloss recurs when Moll | Jack, unmasked, is again addressed by Noland as "Jack" (11.215). Hence, this gloss is used to explain the name "Jack" even when our central character is not in masculine dress. The ideological work of textual editing defines how early modern plays may be cast; critical editions must account for the sheer range of gendered possibilities depicted in this play-text and acknowledge the textual evidence for casting a trans man or – with particular care – a trans woman (see below), a boy actress, a genderqueer performer, a non-binary performer, a gender-nonconforming performer, or a cis female-identified actor in the central role.[24]

In a play full of references to soldiery and fencing, the emergence of Jack as a name for the central protagonist is clearly connected to the accruing of a soldierly identity, to prowess with the sword, fists, and feet. Productions could, indeed, pick up on what may seem like a consolidation of Moll | Jack's masculinity as the play progresses. The protagonist's first entrance in scene 3 is made in a mélange of masculine and feminine attire ("*Enter Moll in a frieze jerkin and a black safeguard*" [3.180 SD]), before shifting into masculine disguise, further consolidated by gallant acts of duelling ("*Enter Moll like a man*" [5.37 SD]) and the rescue of Dapper from the Counter (7.185–233).[25] This trajectory, however, is unstable; Moll | Jack ends the rescue of Dapper with the lines, "If any gentleman be in scrivener's bands, / Send but for Moll, she'll bail him by these hands!" (7.232–3). What's more, the trajectory is risky, curtailed as it is by generic convention and patriarchal hetero- and cisnormativity.

The play ends by forcefully returning Moll | Jack to an iteration of femininity that would be restrictive and marginalizing no matter the gender identity of character or performer, as Moll | Jack plays the role of unacceptable bride. Again, editorial practice plays a significant part, hardening this return to gendered convention in the wedding ceremony that concludes the New Comedy–influenced plot: "*Enter Moll [in female dress] masked, in Sebastian's hand*" (11.128 SD). This carnivalesque gender shaming is omni-offensive, marginalizing all non-normative performers and interpretations of the character. While a cis woman could perhaps deploy Moll | Jack's charismatic trickster status to satirize the construct of marriage itself, for a trans performer the mockery of a trans woman's ability to pass and the misgendering of a trans man is too violent a mirroring of our current transphobic climate to be acceptable, as the comic resolution marginalizes its charismatic go-between in a conventional comic celebration of hetero- and cisnormativity.

What, then, are the effects of casting Emma Frankland, a trans woman, in the title role and of the collision of the textual with embodied and lived experience? Moll | Jack's interaction with Goshawk and Greenwit exemplifies gender fluidity but also exemplifies the potential violence of the play-text when played by a trans performer working with moments of transphobia generated by an inconsistent, ultimately patriarchal text. To avoid replicating such violence in this chapter, I will use "Moll | Jack" for the character in the play-text – following Rubright in acknowledging the fluidity of the play-text to consciously open up the role for diverse casting imperatives, for cis female-identified, trans men, genderqueer, non-binary, and gender fluid performers – and I will use "Moll" for Emma Frankland's character as played in our workshopped duelling scene.

In the workshopped scenes, it soon became clear that access to a sword and the bodily decorums that such a prop required offered a measure of freedom for female-identified performers in the company who had not trained with the sword before. Company actor Lily McEvenue, who played the sword-wielding Clara of *Love's Cure* (a character AFAB, raised masculine, and vigorously resisting an enforced return to femininity), explained that, for her, it was "so empowering, as a woman, to adopt, for that time, what it meant to be a man."[26] The play-texts we worked with offered cis female-identified performers such as McEvenue a thrilling opening to explore physical strength and to play beyond the conventional markers of patriarchy – clothing, drinking, smoking, swearing, fighting, and an expansive and assertive physicality. Yet, while some female-identified performers experienced an emancipation into an expanded range of gender codes, for Emma Frankland, as she attests with great precision in this volume's chapter 7, "Drawing Your Weapon," taking up the sword was a return to her earlier professional experience as well as a pleasurable return to classical theatre, something she had feared would be lost with her transition.[27]

In our workshop, Frankland began working with the play-text from a position of positive fluidity, interpreting Moll as "someone unbothered by gender, despite the constraints and expectations that others place on Moll's body."[28] Coinciding neatly with Rubright's sense of the play's contingent epistemology of gender, Frankland at the workshop paraphrased Moll's declaration that

> Base is the mind that kneels unto her body
> As if a husband stood in awe on's wife;
> My spirit shall be mistress of this house
> As long as I have time in't (5.138–41)

to conclude at first that, for Moll, "My mind rules my body and I see through all of that stuff."[29] Later, however, Frankland articulates important reservations that show the complexity underlying her triumphant revelation of skill that layered her professional experience as a classically trained actor trained in stage combat with her lived experience as someone who describes herself as "a trans woman with inconsistent passing privilege (by which I refer to the way in which other people might read my gender)."[30] Here Frankland reflects on the riskiness of walking the line between bodily decorums that code as masculine and feminine, including sword fighting: for such a performer, forays into what might be thought of as conventionally masculine gestures are riskier than for many cis women.[31] Such skills are clearly differently freighted when they are an individual choice – as in Frankland's own devised shows – or when they are compelled by the collision of a play-text and institutional circumstance, such as a workshop at a national festival theatre strongly associated with a white male figurehead of colonial culture and watched by eager academics with their own expectations, agendas, and places within academic hierarchies.

The moment is made more loaded still by Frankland's ethical reservations about casting a trans woman as Moll, included in this volume's chapter 10, "Performing Gender 'From the Ground Up'": "there was something ethically uncomfortable for me about portraying a person who was assigned female at birth (AFAB) when I was not ... There was undoubtably space where mine and Moll's experiences might cross over. But there is a world of difference between the life of a twenty-first-century trans woman and a sixteenth-century gender-fucking butch."[32] This elision in our casting italicized the tension between perceived and lived allegiances and identifications colliding in an inconsistent and often hostile play-text. While I do not wish to limit the already small number of roles that the theatre industry currently deems a trans woman "should" play, with reflection it became clear that Frankland's vigorous, energetic, and charismatic Moll might not exist safely beyond scene 5, and perhaps not even within it. In his reflection on the Stratford Lab, company actor Marcus Nance, who played Amintor in *The Maid's Tragedy*, identified a similar violence in the racialized language of early modern plays that denigrated his Black identity.[33] In each case, the goal of expanding the early modern dramatic canon came into tension with the complexity of accounting for lived experience, as this experience interacts with, resists, and contradicts seventeenth-century play-texts.

The play-text of *The Roaring Girl* does not make its peace with its title character, whom it treats like a "blazing star" (2.136) or prodigy. Moll | Jack is surrounded by layer upon layer of containment strategies, perhaps most notably in the city comedy plot that divorces them from the sexual economy and renders them as what criticism has tended to see as a beneficent "monster" and useful plot device.[34] Though demonstrating no desire or sexual agency of their own, Moll | Jack is the subject of constant speculation, insistently gazed upon as an object of fascination for other characters. Both duellists are in fact subject to such scrutiny: Laxton, a character of perceived genital "lack" and bodily difference, is another target for the violence that the play-text aims at nonconforming bodies, while in our workshop, the nature of Laxton's fascination with Moll's body was especially problematic, as Frankland notes.[35] Indeed, a specular, eroticized fascination with Moll | Jack's body runs throughout the text, as Laxton imagines, "She slips from one company to another like a fat eel between a Dutchman's fingers" (3.213–14); or Sir Alexander declares, "The sun gives her two shadows to one shape" (2.134). Such eroticization has not escaped scholarly attention, but thinking of Moll | Jack as a "monster," even after the etymological and theatrical connections have been made to specularity and performance, still marginalizes both character and performer.[36] Emma Frankland's "Toward a Trans Canon," which reflects on her continuing work with the Stratford Festival in summer 2019, opens with a powerfully subversive reclamation of that fetishization performed in front of an audience made up of a Two-Spirit, trans, and cis company and is a necessary corrective to the play-text of *The Roaring Girl.*[37]

The keynote for the central character in that play-text may perhaps begin as fluidity, but any utopian category quickly finds its limits when it intersects with the lived experience of the actor. A central takeaway from our workshop is the importance of attending to the specific lived experience of actors and of consciously attending to the violence of canonical texts. To quote from the guidance document for working with trans artists at the Stratford Festival Lab in 2019: "When you hire people to be themselves, bring their own lived experiences, and represent their communities, additional care is required."[38] The violence that *The Roaring Girl* does to its protagonist highlights the crucial need to scrutinize and interrogate the imperatives of the play-text through the collaborative, embodied, vocal practices of workshopping and performance, giving it the time and attention that Frankland advises. As Frankland further outlines, when dealing with 400-year-old texts, we need to be free to edit, translate, co-opt, appropriate, rewrite and – when necessary to protect a performer – unwrite.[39] As my next section will discuss, one impetus for this creative interrogation is a revised, renewed theatre history.

Diverse Feminine Embodiments and a New Theatre History

The ground for the Stratford Lab's work on the duel between Laxton and Moll was laid in the early days of the workshop. On day one, company actors and guest artists had participated in a sword fighting class with the festival's fight captain, Wayne Best. "After all," as Callan Davies notes in his blog on the day's events, "all of the scenes being workshopped at the Lab involve elements of swordplay."[40] On day two, company actors, guest artists, and academics together were led by Peter Cockett in exercises on movement and footwork.[41] Focused primarily on exploring the gendered gaits of early modern aristocratic men and women, these exercises worked with the relationship between early modern costume and body. In this framework, femininity is perceived as constrained by gender and costume to short, small steps and careful movement, and masculinity uses longer, more energetic, and dynamic strides. The exercise explored possibilities for moving within and outside this binary division of feminine containment and masculine freedom, as did company actor André Morin in the role of Lucio for our scene work with *Love's Cure*. Lucio – a character assigned male at birth (AMAB), raised as feminine, and now strenuously resisting an enforced return to their assigned gender role – complains poignantly that

> This masculine attire, is most uneasie,
> I am bound up in it: I had rather walke
> In folio, againe, loose, like a woman.   (*Love's Cure*, 2.2.18–20)

With these lines, the text brings to the fore the physical constraints that seventeenth-century "masculine attire" placed on men.[42] Indeed, much is shared between what are perceived as conventionally binary early modern gender positions: corsetry and doublets kept both women and men upright, and ethical interpretations of the body valued this uprightness and the streamlined, straight lines created by corsetry. Further, Lucio's sense of being "bound up" in "masculine attire" and unable to walk "loose[ly]" like a woman is confirmed by the research of costume designer and clothing historian Jenny Tiramani. Reflecting on her designs for original practice productions at Shakespeare's Globe, Tiramani notes that actors who could not adapt their posture, gait, and movement to the strictures of their costume would often leave the stage with the back of their breeches ripped.[43]

The associations of constraint with femininity are, of course, well understood in theatre history. Farah Karim-Cooper identifies the "ideal posture of virtue" in which women would fold their hands "one across the other, demurely placed at the level of the waist"[44]:

> Actors playing noble women tend, for the most part, to fold their hands and rest them on their stomachs, or thereabouts, a gesture … meant to provide evidence of the sitter's modesty … [I]n the anonymous seventeenth-century cross-dressing pamphlet, *Haec Vir; or the Womanish Man*, the female speaker asks: "Because I stand not with my hands on my belly … am I therefore barbarous or shameless[?]"[45]

For the early modern boy actress wearing feminine clothing, this posture means that, when standing, their hands come to rest at the bottom of the corset and above whatever combination of farthingale, hoop, bum roll, and skirt was fashionable at the time.

If we are to seek out embodiments other than the modest ideal, one thing to observe is that the "hands on belly" posture does not appear in either the famous Peacham or de Witt sketches of early modern play-houses.[46] Furthermore, curves or twists of the body and loose folds of clothing on a boy actress were indeed staged, depicted as either tempt-ingly or grotesquely lacking in virtue – think of Desdemona unpinned in her smock, standing in place as Emilia labours around her to unpin her gown (*Othello*, 4.3), or of the witches in the antimasque of Jonson's 1609 *Masque of Queenes*, dancing "with strange gestures."[47] Reminiscent of the "looseness" longed for by Lucio in *Love's Cure*, such representations of femininity by the boy actress are inflected by a broader repertory of performances of femininity than has previously been recognized, in par-ticularly by the dynamic, flexible, and energetic production of femininity by rope-dancers, tumblers, sword-dancers, and acrobats in early modern England and Europe whom the documents of performance categorize as female.

Attending to the specificity of early modern performance culture, and acknowledging that it does not straightforwardly map onto a binary divide of "masculine" and "feminine" embodiment, allowed us to bring in an expanded theatre history when exploring our collaborative itera-tion of *The Roaring Girl*, scene 5. The archives of early modern English performance offer such a history for an extended range of feminine embodiment once we attend to records of "feats of activity" by perform-ers whom those archives identify as female, replete with evidence of mus-cular, agile, dexterous, explosively powerful physicality. "Feats of activity" is an umbrella term that includes tumbling, acrobatics, vaulting, leger-demaine or conjuring (also known as "juggling"), and rope-dancing.[48] Such practice was widespread across early modern England and Europe: the archives record female dancers and tumblers in Italian commedia dell'arte troupes; Spanish comedia actresses were known for their athleti-cism and agility; and in England, we have records of acrobats and rope-dancers identified as both male and female playing inside and outside the playhouses.[49] These are the activities that, as Frankland points out, nei-ther cis nor trans women are comfortably supposed to embrace; this is the physical activity that McEvenue found emancipating in her exploration of the character of Clara because of its close association with masculinity. Yet gendered embodiments such as these formed part of the repertory of performers whom the archive records as female across early modern Europe. Hence, when we expand what we think we know about how such early modern performers should or could move, stand, sit, leap, tumble, dance, hold a pose, use a sword, or climb a rope, we expand the options open to practitioners in productions now in ways that can support diverse and inclusive casting.

Early modern women's acrobatics stand in contrast to an idealized containment and verticality, suggesting instead a bodily decorum of forcefulness, agility, power, and energy. Female rope-dancers leapt, walked, and ran on the tight rope; they spun around the slack rope, hung from it by their legs or feet, or lounged on it in a performance of impossible leisure. As Edward Ward's description of a Black female rope-dancer in very early eighteenth-century London has it, this fair-booth performer played "at swing-swang with a rope ... hanging sometimes by a hand, sometimes by a leg, and sometimes by her toes."[50] On the ground, the movements of tumblers and acrobats are capaciously taxonomized in Robert Laneham's 1575 description of an Italian acrobat's display for Elizabeth I. Laneham mentions "turnings, tumblings, castings [a "throwing up" of the body], hops, iumps, leaps, skips, springs, gambauds [gambols; that is, leaps or capers], soomersauts [somersaults], caprettyez ["fantastic motion(s)"] & flyghts [movements through the air] ... with such wyndyngs ["undulating motions"], gyrings ["gyrations"] & circumflexions ["a bending round"].[51] Tumblers, then, leapt, turned, and twisted; they performed sword-dances and stood on their hands or their heads; they used their flexibility and core strength to hold inverted or curving positions. Period comparisons between fighting and dance are commonplace, and images of early modern female sword-dancers bring together the prosthetic and embodied decorum.[52] The long history of tumblers, acrobats, rope-dancers, and performers skilled in legerdemaine and magic evidences an early modern femininity that participates in the skills of the body and of props, in sword-dancing, fencing, acrobatics, and sword play.

Acknowledging the constraints of masculine costuming articulated in *Love's Cure* and the possibilities of dynamic, flexible feminine movement attested to in the history of rope-dancers, acrobats, and performers of "feats of activity" identified in the records as female added an important caveat to our day two movement exercise: the recognition that the discipline of theatre history has assigned overly rigid, binary gender positions to the skills of bodily movement on the early modern stage. The false binary of masculine energy and feminine stillness has found a place at the centre of the canon through the scholarly preoccupation with Shakespeare and the valorization of tragedy, particularly those tragedies staged by the King's Men c. 1600–13. From *Hamlet* to *The Duchess of Malfi*, such plays reify female-identified characters as corpses, statues, monuments, and skulls.[53] Once we set aside received theatre history notions of binary gender, however, alternative early modern repertories and potential bodily decorums are also revealed. We can see that, in fact, a range of early modern codes of femininity were available to be taken up by the early modern boy actress who played *The Roaring Girl*'s title role at the Fortune playhouse in late April or early May 1611 and that adopting a more vigorous somatic discipline might not have been straightforwardly gendered as transgressive but could speak instead of alternative performances of femininity. In England, this practice informed the depiction of femininity by the boy actresses of the commercial playing companies: either by contrast, as in the static, passive reified tragic femininity in the repertory of the early Jacobean King's Men; or by exploring shared skills, as did the boy actress playing Moll | Jack at the Fortune in 1611. Indeed, this performer's practice would have picked up both on the actorly skill of sword fighting and – crucially – on the muscular, explosively powerful and agile bodily somatics of paratheatrical performers of femininity, such as rope-dancers and tumblers.

I propose that the gender fluid duel of *The Roaring Girl* points to the potential for an altogether more dynamic, agile, flexible, occasionally explosive, and downright powerful feminine bodily stage decorum than the received image of the boy actress with hands crossed on the bottom of the stomacher might suggest. As the history of amazons and warrior women suggests, lack of training with the sword is not the only option for performances of duelling scenes involving female-identified or assigned-female characters. For a modern audience steeped in a Shakespeare cut loose from his contemporaries, the duel scene in *The Roaring Girl* undercuts what has come to look like the dominant trope, best exemplified in a conventionally cast *Twelfth Night* (3.4) of the cis woman in masculine clothing who is inept with the phallic, overdetermined sword. Yet an early modern audience would expect the boy actress to be trained in fencing, and the micro-skills needed for this activity are also those of rope- or earthbound acrobatics – muscularity, balance, strength, poise, agility, and dexterity. These various skills are brought together in what Evelyn Tribble calls the "kinesic intelligence" with which early modern actors underpinned "the seeming miscellany of mental and physical skills ascribed to them."[54] So, when the cross-dressed early modern boy actress performs a lack of ability, as in *Twelfth Night* (3.4), or reveals a sudden skilfulness, as *The Roaring Girl* prompted Frankland to assay in our scene work, audiences not only glimpse the self-referential performance of the boy actress performing inept or competent masculinity; they also receive an equally self-referential glimpse of the muscularly powerful, agile, dynamically flexible femininity performed by a diverse range of early modern performers whom the archive records as women.

Indeed, the play-text of *The Roaring Girl* gave Emma Frankland's Moll the cues to work with a dangerous, potentially violent, and powerfully agile and explosive physicality throughout.[55] For Frankland's Moll, the duel with Laxton is prefigured by her challenge to a gallant she claims insulted her in a tavern the previous night (3.225–37) and is immediately followed by her picking an altogether less formalized street fight with Trapdoor. Moll has mass, muscle, and weight, and she is never brought to heel or down to earth. When Goshawk calls her "the maddest fantastical'st girl," he finishes with the wondering compliment, "I never knew so much flesh and nimbleness put together" (3.185–6). Earlier, testing Trapdoor's potential as a servant, "*Moll trips up his [Trapdoor's] heels [and] he falls*" (3.334 SD). It is nimble, muscular, physically powerful Moll who inflicts a rupture of bodily decorum on Trapdoor rather than he upon her. Moll is physically competent and imposing, abundant in energy and skill.

Such performance and its effects on the representation of gender in *The Roaring Girl* are, though, not without risk. Early English images of tumblers and contortionists show women in slim-fitting but unrestrictive dresses (Figures 8.2 and 8.3). In all cases, there is a moral interpretation based on the visual accessibility, displayed or imagined, of the dancer's body that echoes the fetishizing specularity aimed at Moll | Jack's body in the play-text of *The Roaring Girl.* The visual record of female-identified acrobatics makes clear that these displays of skilled balance were erotic, voyeuristic experiences: both King Herod (Figure 8.3) and Marcellus Laroon's leering Jack Pudding (Figure 8.4) look or point to the women's genitals. The connection is made forcefully in scene 5 of *The Roaring Girl,* and before they demonstrate their physical agility and competence with the sword, Moll |Jack is given a speech that attempts to separate them from the play's specular fascination with their sexualized body – a forty-two line speech of challenge to Laxton in which they decry the sexual exploitation of impoverished women. Yet this speech, positioned as the lead-in to Moll | Jack's exhibition of virtuoso swordplay, is not divorced from the acts of physical skill that follow it; rather it is the trial of wit that precedes the trial of defence.[56] The player who takes up the performance skills required for virtuoso swordplay doubles down on the specular fetishization of the player in ways that, for a trans performer like Emma Frankland as Moll, radically raise the stakes.

Attending to early modern muscular femininities and their effect on canonical drama offers an expanded range of femininities for actors performing in early modern drama, pushing beyond gender binaries of bodily deportment. The accepted conventional range – reified in tragedy or played for humour in comedy – misrepresents the options available to early modern boy actresses. Early modern performers identified by the

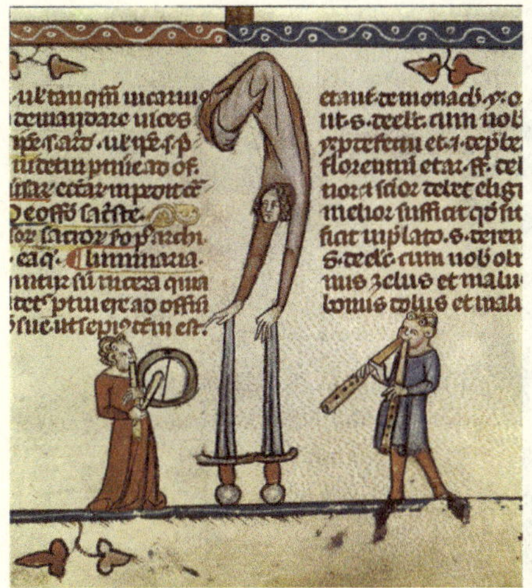

Figure 8.2. Medieval sword-dancer from the Smithfield Decretals [Decretals of Gregory IX], c. 1340. MS. Royal 10.E.IV, fol. 58, British Library, London UK. Bridgeman Images.

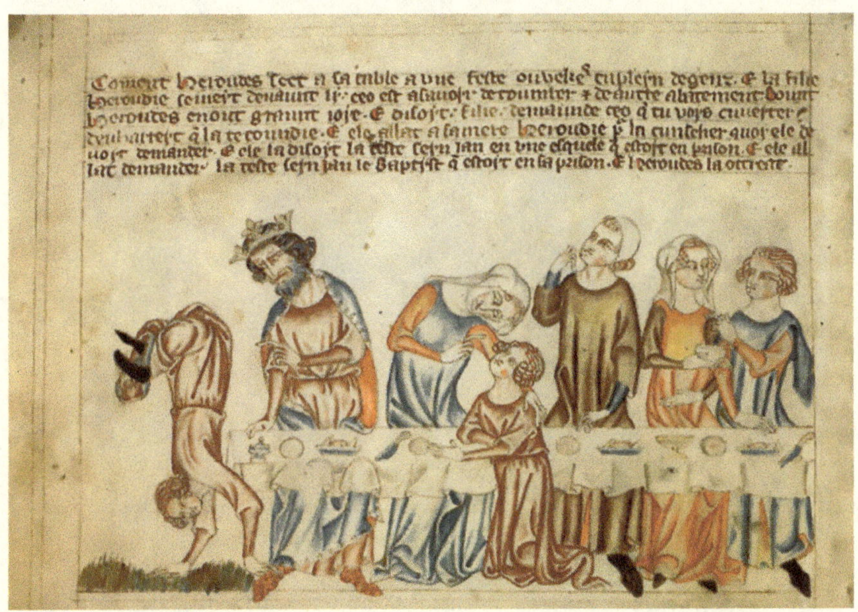

Figure 8.3. Salome dancing before Herod; cropped from fourteenth-century *Holkham Bible Picture Book*, fourteenth century. MS. Add. 47,682, fol. 21v. British Library, London UK. Bridgeman Images.

Figure 8.4. Rope-dancer and leering Jack Pudding: "The Famous Dutch Woman," Donna Thedesca, the trapeze artist, in Marcellus Laroon, *The Cryes of the Citie of London* (1711). British Library, London, UK. Bridgeman Images.

records as male and female both performed feats of activity: both could bend, be flexible, powerful, muscular, dynamic, energetic, agile, and dexterous. Though enacting these micro-skills as a performer whom the archive categorizes as female could certainly mean being bewhored, these embodied skills were part of the professional identities of performing women. Hence, challenges to the binary are variously found in the collision between the early modern archive and present-day performance, specifically, in the lived experiences of actors. The circulation of skills between these groups, who each take up balance, agility, flexibility, and explosive physical power and deploy them in their own circumstance – on the rope, in the Fortune playhouse, in the Stratford Festival Lab – is a cue to extend our framework of understanding of the range of gendered bodily decorums on both the early modern stage and in present-day productions of early modern drama.

Conclusion: Swaggering through History

The embodied performance practice of the unknown boy actress playing Moll | Jack in April 1611 brings together the fencing training of the early modern player with the dynamic, energetic swagger of the historical sword-wielding duellist Mary Frith, also a performer on the Fortune stage in April 1611, combining it in a performance practice that is itself inflected by the agile, skilful femininities performed by early modern performers of feats of activity. This history is behind Emma Frankland's swagger in September 2018, a swagger that can be read as part of the repertoire of feminine representation for the early modern period and, simultaneously, as risky for a trans woman performer in our current political reality. Bringing a trans performer into contact with this history in the present moment offers rewards but comes with risks that must be negotiated by an institutional embrace both of the utopian abstract – the text as it awaits activation in embodied performance – and of the personal. Hiring people to be themselves, as in the case of Emma Frankland at the Stratford Lab, means centring the trans performer to allow them to explore and to navigate their individual way through the risks posed in the meeting of the textual and the lived.

Rather than only uncovering a history of diverse performers, the circulation of the skills of performance between distinct performing groups – early modern performers of feats of activity whom the archive identifies as female, the early modern boy actress, and Emma Frankland – also challenges the binary assignment of gesture, posture, and deportment by revealing a shared stock of performance skills that are not in themselves rigidly gendered. The play-text of *The Roaring Girl* does not, then, offer a set of Linnean categorizations into which performers must fit. Rather, it is a witness to the protean production of early modern performative femininities to be taken up by diverse female-identified performers now.

NOTES

1 Middleton and Dekker, *The Roaring Girl, or Moll Cutpurse*, ed. Kahn. Throughout this chapter, I use Kahn's scene numbers. For the workshop at the Stratford Lab, we used Mulholland's edition, in which the equivalent scene is designated Act 3, scene 1.
2 Emma Frankland, in Cockett and Gough et al., "Drawing Your Weapon," chapter 7 of this volume. See also Frankland, *None of Us Is Yet a Robot*.
3 Brown, "Art of the Zinger," unpublished paper pre-circulated for our workshop. See also "Who's It? Acting the Actress in Shakespearean Comedy," in Brown, *The Diva's Gift*, 136–72.
4 One iteration is preserved in the *Engendering the Stage in the Age of Shakespeare and Beyond at the Stratford Festival Theatre Laboratory* video, timestamp 2.40–50.
5 Frankland, in Cockett and Gough et al., "Drawing Your Weapon."
6 For crucial interventions, see Korda, *Labors Lost*, and Korda, "Case of Moll Frith."
7 Rubright, "Transgender Capacity," 47–8.
8 I use the term "play-text" to refer to the textual witness as the composite product of collaborative authorship, compositors' labour in the printing house, and potentially, actors' labour in the playhouse.
9 Recent projects include Frankland and Kesson's production of John Lyly's *Galatea* performed at the Brighton Festival, 5–21 May 2023; see Brighton Festival with Emma Frankland, "Gather Round: Galatea." See also John Lyly, *Galatea*, ed. Kesson, adapted by Frankland and Joy. For this project in research and development, see Before Shakespeare, "Galatea."
10 Shakespeare, *Twelfth Night*, ed. Elam. Miranda Fay Thomas suggests that this moment "could be interpreted as a new lifestyle choice, reflecting a truer version of the person that Viola/Cesario is but has never before had the opportunity to present" (Thomas, "Queer Reading of *Twelfth Night*"). See also Shakespeare, *Twelfth Night*, ed. Korda (forthcoming).
11 Orgel, *Impersonations*, 50.
12 By "knowledgeable," I refer to Christian Billing's definition of the practitioner's "procedural" and "experiential" knowledge: "knowing *how* to do things and knowing *of* things which exist or have been done before" (Billing, "Rehearsing Shakespeare," 385).
13 Halberstam, *Trans**, 119; Serano, *Whipping Girl*.
14 Chess, "Queer Residue."

15 Kit Heyam's *Before We Were Trans* is alert to how alien the archive is to our present-day categories when we impose present-day terminology such as AFAB or "female-identified" onto the past. Heyam reminds us that no one in the early modern period was "strictly 'assigned' male [or female] in an institutional way, since the state kept no systematic record of individuals' gender in this period" (68). Offering the salient corrective that "'cis man' and 'cis woman' are modern categories as well" (20), Heyam pinpoints ways in which seeking for testimony can narrow trans history (21). I would like to thank E.M. Parry for productive comments on this chapter's terminology; any errors are my own.

16 Grange, quoted in Shakespeare's Globe, "Giving Voice to Forgotten Women in History." See also Grange, "A Note to Mary Frith," chapter 6 of this volume.

17 In its late stages, this essay has benefited greatly from considering Rubright's article alongside issues raised by embodied performance as research. For the "wordscape," see Rubright, "Transgender Capacity," 46, figure 1.

18 By my count, using Kahn's text in *Thomas Middleton: The Collected Works*, female pronouns (she or her) are used approximately 124 times; male pronouns (he) approximately 10 times; "we" once, by Moll | Jack when establishing a hierarchy with Trapdoor (3.370); and the dehumanizing article "it" and variants are used approximately 4 times.

19 Rubright, "Transgender Capacity," 47, invokes Jack Halberstam's use of "hover" to describe one effect of a "gender-variant language" system.

20 Rubright, "Transgender Capacity," 48–52.

21 David Getsy describes capacities as lying "in wait to be activated" (cited in Rubright, "Transgender Capacity," 47–8).

22 For the play's textual history and analysis of its collaborative authorship, see Taylor and Lavagnino, *Thomas Middleton*, 369–71, 610–11.

23 Middleton and Dekker, *The Roaring Girl*, ed. Mulholland, 5.1.1, n1.

24 See Rubright, "Transgender Capacity," 67, for a further important example of a silent editorial decision that closes down the play's transgender capacity.

25 Rubright interprets the safeguard as conveying "the virility of 'masculine womanhood'" (Rubright, "Transgender Capacity," 70n26).

26 *Engendering the Stage* video, timestamp 0.55–1.09.

27 Frankland in Cockett and Gough et al., "Drawing Your Weapon."

28 Frankland in Cockett and Gough et al., "Performing Gender 'From the Ground Up,'" chapter 10 of this volume.

29 *Engendering the Stage* video, timestamp 2.40–3.03.

30 Frankland in Cockett and Gough et al., "Performing Gender 'From the Ground Up.'"

31 Frankland in Cockett and Gough et al., "Performing Gender 'From the Ground Up.'"

32 Frankland in Cockett and Gough et al., "Performing Gender 'From the Ground Up.'"

33 Marcus Nance in conversation with Peter Cockett and Melinda Gough, unpublished interview, 2019.

34 This view is countered by SL Grange's important intervention; see Grange, "A Note to Mary Frith," chapter 6 of this volume.

35 Frankland in Cockett and Gough et al., "Performing Gender 'From the Ground Up.'"

36 See, in particular, Burnett's formulation of the terms in *Constructing "Monsters."*

37 Frankland, "Toward a Trans Canon."

38 This guidance document is published in Frankland, "Toward a Trans Canon."

39 Frankland, "Toward a Trans Canon."

40 Davies, "SF Day 1: Introductions, Swordplay, and Scenes." See also Cockett and Gough et al., "Drawing Your Weapon."

41 Cockett and Gough et al., "Performing Gender 'From the Ground Up.'"

42 Beaumont and Fletcher, *Love's Cure*, ed. Williams. See *Engendering the Stage* video, timestamp 1.32–45.

43 Tiramani, "Audio: Seventeenth-Century Costume," discussing doublet and satin breeches (England, 1630–49), museum no. 348–1905, https:// web.archive.org/web/20201028083755/http://www.vam.ac.uk/content /articles/a/audio-early-17th-century-costume/. See also Arnold, *Patterns of Fashion*, as well as Parry with Cockett and Gough, "Playing with Gender: Stance, Gesture, Embodiment, and Prosthetics," chapter 11 of this volume.

44 Karim-Cooper, *The Hand on the Shakespearean Stage*, 60.

45 Karim-Cooper, 93.

46 Aernout van Buchel's copy of de Witt's drawing is available from the British Library's *Discovering Literature* online collection: https://web.archive.org /web/20201111205709/https://www.bl.uk/collection-items/van-buchels -copy-of-de-witts-drawing-of-the-swan-playhouse. The Peacham image is reproduced in Levin, "The Longleat Manuscript."

47 Shakespeare, *Othello*, ed. McManus; see also McManus, "'Sing It Like Poor Barbary'"; Jonson, *Masque of Queenes*, A4v.

48 Butterworth, *Magic on the Early English Stage*, 26.

49 For a description of "La Vettoria the *cantimbanca*" in 1616, see Henke, "The Italian Mountebank," 27. For analysis of the athleticism of Spanish comedia actresses, see Mujica, "Actresses as Athletes and Acrobats."

50 Ward, *London Spy*, 185.

51 Laneham, *A letter*, 24; glosses are from the *OED Online*.

52 See, for example, the sword-dancer in Matthias Gerung's 1558 *Melancolia in the Garden of Life*.

53 For corpses, see Desdemona and Ophelia; for monuments, see Cleopatra and the Duchess of Malfi; for skulls, Gloriana in *The Revenger's Tragedy*; for statues, see Middleton's *The Lady's Tragedy* (1611) and the tragicomedy

The Winter's Tale. See also James Stokes's important argument on periodization, namely that the so-called high Renaissance was in fact a low point of women's theatrical exclusion and marginalization (Stokes, "Women and Performance").

54 Tribble, *Early Modern Actors*, 10–11.

55 Emma Frankland comments that her confidence with swordplay "allowed me a swagger and gave me power – it allowed me to be dangerous." Frankland in Cockett and Gough et al., "Drawing Your Weapon."

56 Tribble, *Early Modern Actors*, 13.

PART FIVE

Stepping Beyond Binaries

9 "Mincing Steps" and "Manly Strides": Practising Gendered Footwork on the Early Modern Stage

NATASHA KORDA

If standing and walking are fundamental features of the human animal and also those banal arts that might be failed, then the stakes of this artistry, and the consequences of its failure, could not be any higher.

– Gayle Salamon, "Passing Period: Gender, Aggression, and the Phenomenology of Walking" (2015)[1]

The epithet "treading the boards (or the stage)" has long been synonymous with actors' artistry, suggesting its reliance upon footwork and foot-skills.[2] For the majority of early modern playgoers, the vantage afforded by the elevated thrust stage of the public amphitheatres positioned bystanders at eye and ear level with actors' feet, bringing footwork to the fore and highlighting actors' practised skill at enacting both "banal" ways of walking and more specialized feats of footwork. Elsewhere, I have explored the design affordances of the Shakespearean stage as a "walkscape," arguing that the aesthetic practice of "treading the boards" had the potential to unsettle bystanders' understanding of the cultural and ideological work performed by everyday modalities of pedestrian movement in the world.[3] Here, I want to consider the potential of this practice for unsettling the performance of gender as what Gayle Salamon terms "a gestural phenomenon," focusing in particular on actors' footwork as "disclosive of gendered meaning."[4] After briefly surveying the role of footwork in gestural expression generally on the early modern stage, I analyse particular scenes that foreground the practice or rehearsal of gendered footwork and what they reveal about what Salamon terms "the stakes" of this practice and the "consequences of its failure." As Salamon's work demonstrates, these stakes "could not be any higher" for gender-nonconforming people in the past and present whose ways of walking are scrutinized and deemed to "fail," at times with lethal consequences.[5] I conclude by considering how the enactment of such scenes by cis, trans, and non-binary actors at the Stratford Festival's Engendering the Stage in the Age of Shakespeare and Beyond laboratory explored possibilities for disrupting such violence and, in so doing, illuminated the stakes of *practice* as a mode of embodied research into gender performance in the past and present.

Pedal Eloquence

> There's language in her eye, her cheek, her lip,
> Nay, her foot speaks.
> > – Shakespeare, *Troilus and Cressida* (4.5.55–6)[6]

Early modern descriptions of actors as "Stage-walkers" and "stalking-stamping Player[s]" remind us that performers did not merely stand and deliver orations onstage but conveyed meaning in motion from head to toe, or rather, from the ground up.[7] Effective delivery or *actio*, for the orator as for the actor, was a fully embodied activity. The term "gesture" encompassed everything from bodily posture, carriage, deportment, attitude, and countenance to the body's positioning and movement in and through space.[8] Contemporary usage reveals that orators and actors gestured "with their hands, with their eies, with their shoulders, and with their feet."[9] Any and every part of the body might become a vehicle of gesture, from the head ("The Shaking of the Head … is a Gesture of Slight Refusall")[10] and facial expressions ("Looke well what gesture I make with my mouth"),[11] down to the feet ("to gesture, to leap or skippe for joy").[12] Gesture rendered the entire body a vehicle of expression: "though they say nothing with their mouths, yet they speake in their gate, they speake with their eyes, they speake in their carriage of their bodies."[13]

In classical rhetorical theory, gestural expression, like verbal expression, was governed by the norms and dictates of social decorum. Quintilian insists on the importance of the entire body working together to produce "appropriate Delivery."[14] Regarding the feet, Quintilian observes that "both stance [*status*] and walk require attention" but cautions that the expressive repertoire of the orator is far more limited than that of the actor.[15] Oratorical decorum allows for only the most minimal and carefully controlled foot movements: "A step forward is quite in order, so long as it is opportune, short, and well controlled. So is a certain amount of walking up and down" but "only on rare occasions and not for long."[16] Excessive stomping or stamping of the feet, as well as "running up and down," jumping, hopping, standing "on tiptoe," "holding the feet too far apart," and so forth are proscribed as "gesture[s] of comedy rather than of oratory."[17] Expressive footwork of this kind is the purview of actors or pantomimes ("An orator has to be very different from a *saltatore* [pantomime performer]") and ought to be shunned not only by orators, Quintilian opines, but also by "more serious actors [*histrionibus … gravioribus*]."[18]

In developing a canon of gestural decorum for the stage, early modern players and playwrights sought to appropriate the prestige of classical rhetorical theory, while at the same time adapting it to suit the purposes of playing. The character of "An excellent Actor" (attributed to John Webster) thus maintains, "Whatsoever is commendable in the grave Orator, is most exquisitly perfect in him [the actor]; for by a full and significant action of body, he charmes our attention."[19] As in the rhetorical theory of *actio*, actors' "full and significant action of body" entailed expressive yet decorous movements, not only of the head and hands but also of the feet. In his advice to the players, Hamlet cautions that actors must be moderate, graceful, and seemly of foot as well as of hand and voice: in order to "o'erstep not the modesty of nature" (3.2.19), they must neither "strut," "saw the air," nor "bellow" onstage (ll. 32, 4, 33). Yet the bounds of decorum governing actors' expressive footwork were of necessity far more flexible than those of oratory and were not (*pace* Quintilian) confined to comedy, for tragedy too required "o'erstep[ping]," as Hamlet's leap into Ophelia's grave so memorably demonstrates.[20]

The activity of "treading the boards" thus continually tested the boundaries of pedal decorum, while at the same time elevating the feet above their typically lowly position in everyday life; in so doing, it reoriented theatregoers towards everyday pedestrianism in ways that had the capacity to unsettle what Salamon terms "the typicality of the world."[21] In foregrounding footwork as a *practice* – a set of skills that required practise to appear spontaneous and natural – and thereby heightening awareness of habitual modes of movement, the aesthetic "walkscape" of the early modern stage and the practice of "treading the boards" had the potential, as we shall see, to destabilize conventions of normative social decorum governing gendered footwork.

Practising Gendered Footwork

Practise footing.

– Richard Brome, *The Court Begger* (1632), SD[22]

Although stage directions (SD) in early modern play-texts are notoriously scarce, they nonetheless provide a surprisingly fertile source of information about the repertoire of theatrical footwork and foot-skills that comprised the practice of "treading the boards." A brief survey of Dessen and Thomson's *Dictionary of Stage Directions in English Drama, 1580–1642* reveals just how much attention was paid to actors' feet in play-texts of the period and confirms that in practice, as in theory, the actor's art required not only an ability to speak "trippingly on the tongue" (*Hamlet* 3.2.2) but to "*trip about the stage*" lithely while doing so.[23] There are, for example, almost 350 stage directions to "*dance*" (142) in early modern play-texts.

The specialized foot-skills deployed in dancing could be learned at the many dancing schools in early modern London, whose popularity created an audience deeply appreciative if not demanding of displays of expert footwork onstage. Indeed, playhouses and dancing schools are frequently described as catering to the same clientele,[24] a type giddily satirized in Barnabe Rich's *Faultes Faults, and Nothing Else but Faultes* (1606):

> But whom have we here, one, two, three, foure, five? One, two three, foure, five, and nothing else but, one, two, three, foure, five? O ho, I understand him now, this is one of the Skipping Arte, that is newly come from the Dauncing Schoole; this fellow had rather treade a tricke of one and twentie follies, than to performe one action that might increase wisedome: And yet to speake truly, there is no great harme in his witte, but it will serve him well enough to talke of the turne of the toe, of the caper above ground, of the lofty tricke, and he hath some smacke of judgement in vawting, tumbling, and in dauncing with the Iebie horse. And he will speake of Playes, Players, and who be the best Actors.[25]

The theatregoing gallant's study of the "Skipping Arte[s]" (for example, "Dauncing," "tread[ing] a tricke," "the turne of the toe," "the caper above ground," "the lofty tricke," "vawting," "tumbling," and so forth) renders him eager to see such skilful tricks displayed onstage, knowledgeable about "the best Actors" who perform them, and attuned to the rhythms of such performances ("one, two, three, four, five," and so on). In counting out his "newly" acquired steps, he draws attention to their status as a practised discipline; yet in doing so *aloud*, he betrays his lack of practised expertise. In associating him with a "Iebie horse" (a "jibby-horse" or show horse decorated with "parti-coloured trappings, plumes, streamers, &c.") and by extension with a "jibby" (a cant term for a "frisky, gadding, flaunting wench, full of fantastical and affected airs, and dressed in flashy finery"),[26] Rich links the gallant's fancy footwork to ostentatious effeminacy, while also suggesting the gendered stakes of perceived "failure" in its practice: to "fail" at gendered footwork by revealing its status as practised is to put one's gender at risk of being deemed inauthentic or affected.

Henry Fitzgeffrey's "Play-house Observation" of theatregoers at Blackfriars playhouse in his *Satyres* (1617) echoes Rich in satirizing a playgoing gallant who skips straight to the theatre "from the Dauncing-schoole."[27] So affected is his gait upon entrance that he steals attention away from the performers onstage: "Whereof, that all the world may notice take, / See! Every step an Honor hee doth make / That Ladyes, may denote him with their Fan, / As he goes by, with a Lo: Hee's the man."[28] Another dancing dandy "ushers in [to the playhouse], with a Coranto grace," and the female playgoers "solicite" him to demonstrate his newly acquired foot-skills: "Pray (Sir) a step or two. / A Galliard or a Jigg: Pox on't! cryes hee, / That ere I knew this Toylin[g]e faculty. / Yet marke! No sooner shall the Cornets blow, / But ye shall have him skipping too and fro."[29] Fitzgeffrey's satire places foot-skills at the centre of theatrical production and reception, while highlighting the practised "toil" involved in acquiring such skills and the *faux pas* (literally, the "false step") of affectation that potentially imperils the practitioner whose lack of expertise makes such toil overly apparent. The gallant's motion of "skipping too and fro" further suggests the superficiality of the "Skipping Arte[s]," while the spelling of "Toylin[g]e faculty" suggests that toil is being exerted over what amounts (in Fitzgeffrey's view) to mere frivolity or a "Toy," in the sense of "a playful or frisky movement … a capricious act or practice … A matter or thing of little or no value or importance, a trifle."[30] To "skip" is to "move lightly and rapidly" from one thing to another with "omission of what intervenes" and, in so doing, "to pass *over* with very slight or superficial treatment."[31] The gallant who skips to and fro in the audience is like the clown who in Hamlet's view causes playgoers to skip over "some necessary question of the play" (3.2.42). The "Ladyes" who praise the gallant as manly with the phrase "Lo: Hee's the man" and a flick of their fans are equally superficial in the view of Fitzgeffrey, who clearly does not share their assessment; in his eyes, the gallant's display of the "Skipping Arte[s]" is mere posturing – a shallow and frivolous affectation. Fitzgeffrey's satire nonetheless reveals the extent to which the norms of decorum governing gendered footwork were a site of continual contestation.

Several decades later, we find expertise in "vawting," decried as a "fault" of manhood by Barnabe Rich in 1606, extoled as its very epitome by Richard Godfrey in a dedicatory poem praising Will Stokes's manual on *The Art of Vaulting* (1641).[32] Godfrey contrasts the outdated "False capers" of the effeminate "French Courtier" with feats of footwork that will elevate English "Gallants" to new heights of masculinity when "th' have learn'd a sport" that will enable them to emulate the "Leap of *Hercules*." Of the vaulting Englishman, Godfrey extols, "He, he's the Man! He shall applauded be / 'Bove the gay sutes, and Tinsell-Poetrie [of the French]: / Mark how the Ladies drink to Him alone!" (B2v). Several other dedicatory poems in Stokes's manual likewise make the case that vaulting, properly executed, epitomizes elite masculinity: N.H. opines that it will "refine / Th'embased [debased] spirits to temper *Masculine*" (A2v), while Jo. Shearman maintains, "Thy Art I manhood stile" (B3r). Vaulting is here not merely a sign of elite manhood but a vehicle by means of which social aspirants may attain it: "let th'ambitious try / T'attaine this Art," Shearman counsels, "he'll quickly find, and say, / That Vaulting is the only Rising way" (B3r).

Gender (as inflected by national identity and racialized complexion) and social status (a term derived from the Latin *stare* meaning "to stand") were conveyed not only through specialized foot-skills such as vaulting, fencing, and dancing but also through stance, gait, and carriage (bodily "bearing or deportment")[33] as Autolycus facetiously acknowledges when he asks, "Hath not my gait in it the measure of the court?" and proclaims, "I am a courtier cap-a-pe" (*Winter's Tale*, 4.4.732, 736). Conduct manuals of the period stress the importance of a decorous gait and carriage as signifiers of "fair" (white) elite status: "There is no one thing that setteth a fairer stampe upon Nobilitie then evenesse of Carriage," advises Henry Peacham's *The Compleat Gentleman* (1622).[34] Richard Brathwaite's *The English Gentleman* (1630) similarly maintains: "The habit of the minde is to be discerned by the carriage: so as even in motion, gesture, and pace, is modestie to be observed."[35] Because the foot-skills that upheld elite status were learned and could therefore be acquired by social upstarts, however, the effort required to master them had to be dissimulated to make them appear natural, rather than affected or practised, through a kind of *sprezzatura* (or nonchalance) of the feet. Castiglione thus advises the courtier to avoid "over nimble footinges or to[o] busie trickes,"[36] which reveal the *work* of footwork. The "faire[] stampe" of (white) elite status must therefore eschew exaggerated "footinges" (such as actual stamping of the feet) so as to leave no trace behind.

In codifying the canonical norms of decorum governing footwork, conduct manuals made them accessible to social aspirants and actors who wished to "*practise [the] footing*" befitting a particular status or role. In the Induction to John Marston's burlesque comedy *Antonio and Mellida* (c. 1599), the boy actors of the Children of Paul's enter "*with parts in their hands*," but the boy playing Piero, Duke of Venice, complains: "Wee are ignorant in what mould we must cast our Actors." When instructed to "frame [his] exterior shape / To hautie forme of elate majestie," he replies, "If that be all, feare not, Ile sute it right. / Who can not be proud, stroak up the hair and strut!"[37] Key to the boy actor's enactment of the role of Duke is his haughty carriage and strutting gait.

Hamlet, as we have seen, cautions the "tragedians of the city" (2.2.328) against such strutting, which in his view "o'erstep[s] ... the modesty of nature" (3.2.19), yet himself "*leaps in [to Ophelia's grave] after Laertes*" (5.1.258 SD) because, he later explains, "the bravery of his [Laertes'] grief did put me / Into a tow'ring passion" (5.2.79–80). In its early modern meaning, the term "bravery" here conveys not simply courage but "swaggering; bravado ... in display of courage or daring, as a brag."[38] Echoing his earlier query, "What is he whose grief / Bears such an emphasis" (5.1.254), Hamlet undercuts Laertes's enactment of manly grief by intimating that it is overdone, ostentatious, or "showy"[39] in its display of "over nimble footinges." From the start, Hamlet expresses aversion to such affected "shows of grief" (F1, TLN 263) and is consequently castigated by Claudius for his inactive, "unmanly grief" (1.2.94) and "unprevailing [ineffective, impotent] woe" (1.2.107). The dilemma Hamlet faces as an actor "treading the boards," then, is how to enact a "tow'ring passion" in a "manly" manner without hamming it up with showy feats of footwork.

Hamlet casts Laertes's leap into Ophelia's grave as an attempt to "outface" (5.1.278) or one-up him – if not "Hercules himself" (l. 251) – with an exaggerated display of vaulting footwork, as noted above: "What is he whose grief / Bears such an *emphasis?*" (ll. 254–5; my emphasis), he demands, deflatingly. Far from simply renouncing such emphasis – from the Greek *emphainein*, "to exhibit, display"[40] – however, Hamlet audaciously vaults into Ophelia's now overcrowded grave himself and exponentially amplifies Laertes' rhetorical flourish with his own hyperbolic "rant" (l. 284):[41] "show me what thou't do" (l. 274), he dares, and boasts, "I'll do't" (l. 277). In this contest of "manly" footwork, Hamlet casts Laertes as one who can only *show* and himself as one who is now poised and ready to *do*.

The display of foot-skills in the final fencing match is cast and plotted by Claudius as a proof of manly grief that must be shown: "What would you undertake / To show yourself indeed your father's son / More than in words?" (4.7.124–6), he asks Laertes. Hamlet's encounter with the effete courtier Osric, whom he disparagingly calls a "water-fly" (5.2.83), just prior to his fencing match with Laertes helps to clarify the gendered stakes of this final display of footwork. The term "water-fly," although often glossed as a reference to Osric's silken, courtly attire (evocative of an insect's wings), may also refer to Osric's effeminate way of walking, as the insect was also known as the "Water Skipper,"[42] suggesting that Osric walks with a skipping or effeminate, "mincing" stride. At the end of the scene, Hamlet calls attention to his own gait ("Sir, I will walk here in the hall" [l. 172]), effectively contrasting it with that of Osric, setting up the play's final fencing match as a gendered contest over the foot-skills that define masculinity. What distinguishes Hamlet's footwork from that of Laertes is not that it is *unpractised* (he admits to having been "in continual practice" [ll. 210–11]) but its *readiness*: "If his fitness speaks, mine is ready," Hamlet nonchalantly responds to Osric, "now or whensoever … the readiness is all" (ll. 201–2, 222). Departing from the premeditative "gain-giving" such as "would perhaps trouble a woman" (ll. 215–16), which has troubled Hamlet throughout the play, he is now ready to perform a manliness defined by the "fitness" and "readiness" of his practised footwork.

Elsewhere on the early modern stage, the requisite "readiness" of gender performance is exposed as the product of practice in scenes that stage the rehearsal of *unready* footwork. Thus, for example, when the court-aspirants in Brome's *The Court Begger* (c. 1639–41) "*Practise footing*" onstage, they humorously highlight the arduous, yet ordinarily hidden, work of *readying* required to make gendered footwork appear ever-ready or nonchalant. That the "footing" in question in this scene is an impromptu dance lesson is indicated by Dainty, who says to Cit-wit and Swain-wit: "I'll make [devise] the dance and give you [instruct you in] all the footing."[43] The scene offers a glimpse into the sort of instruction that might have occurred in the dancing schools of early modern London, satirizing the disgraceful lack of finesse (or, to use Hamlet's term, "fitness") among Dainty's pupils as they "*practise about him*"[44] onstage. Cit-wit, in attempting to follow Dainty's choreography, thus "*dances, looking on his feet.*"[45] Whether Cit-wit is looking down at his own feet or is staring too fixedly at those of his instructor, his breach of decorum reveals by negative example the studied effort that apparently impromptu footwork elides. The scene concludes with Dainty ushering his pupils offstage, "*Footing*" as they go, to continue to "practise, and be ready" for the play's final masque.[46]

The unpractised foot-skills of Cit-wit and Swain-wit are contrasted with those displayed by Ferdinand in an elaborate dance routine in Act 4, scene 2; he "ris[es] from his chair and cavort[s] about" the stage boasting, "So now a Dance! I am all ayre – Ahaigh – Ahaigh / I thanke thee Mercury that hast lent thy wings / Unto my feete."[47] He proceeds to dance "*a conceited Countrey Dance, first doing his honours, then as leading forth his Lasse. He danceth both man and womans actions, as if the Dance consisted of two or three couples.*"[48] Although we can only imagine what this choreography might have looked like, the virtuosity of Ferdinand's feats of footwork clearly entails the performance of both male and female "*actions*." His readiness to perform such "over nimble footinges" counters the earlier scene of dance practice, as his multigendered footwork is expertly performed without "*looking on his feet*." Looking down at one's feet when putting gender into practice breaches decorum in revealing the gender performed to be not yet "ready" or "fit" (that is, to be in process). Scenes that expose this process by staging the ongoing practice of gendered footwork, as we shall see, have the potential to subvert the illusion of gender "readiness" and to expose the normative ideological work it performs by enacting genders that do not "fit" prescribed codes of conduct.

"Mincing Steps" and "Manly Strides"

> I know the boy will well usurp the grace,
> Voice, gait, and action of a gentlewoman.
> – Shakespeare, The Taming of the Shrew (Ind. 1.131–2)

Thus far, we have focused on the role of practised footwork in producing the illusion of gender as always already "ready" and able to perform the kinetic capacities required by socially prescribed parameters at any given moment. These capacities and parameters are not equitably allocated, however: certain types of gender expression are permitted to "o'erstep," while others are not. Polonius thus schools Ophelia in the perambulatory boundaries of elite masculinity versus femininity at the court of Elsinore when he instructs, "[Hamlet] with a larger teder may … walk / Than may be given you" (1.3.125–6). Not being a son, Ophelia cannot freely "walk i' th' sun" (2.2.184), much less "jig and amble" (3.1.144), without compromising her perceived chastity, Hamlet later concurs. Ophelia herself notes this double standard when she observes "the steep and thorny way to heaven" to which she is steered, while her "reckless" brother "the primrose path of dalliance treads" (1.3.49–50).

Hamlet's continual pacing of the stage, and running commentary on the faulty footwork of others with whom he shares it, takes on a quasi-metronomic, regulatory function, positioning him as an arbiter of pedal propriety who takes the measure of footwork that is "overdone, or come[s] tardy off" (3.2.24–5).[49] His enforcement of gestural decorum, and in particular his advice to the players, contains verbal echoes of George Pettie's popular 1581 translation of Stephano Guazzo's *The Civile Conversation*, which follows Quintilian in castigating excessive "libertie of … jestures" for "a playerlike kinde of lightnesse" (advising agreement "between the words and the countenance, and the countenance and the words").[50] Guazzo elaborates on the gendered stakes of such gestural "libertie" by recounting an anecdote in Macrobius about Cicero's derision of his daughter Tullia's and son-in-law Piso's wayward ways of walking:

> His sonne in law was so delicate of nature, that in his gate he used a slowe and mincing pace, like a woman: his Daughter on the other syde, stryd [strode] out lustilye like a man, which her Father seeing, sayde merrilye unto her, Daughter, goe [walk] as your Husbande doth: which is to be understood, not only of going, but of all other doings, wherein it is an unde-cent thing for a woman to resemble a man, or a man a woman … for it is a monstrous and naughtye thing, to see a young Gyrle use such libertye and boldnesse in her Gesture … as is proper to men … On the other side, it is the worst sighte that may bee, to see sonnes, who by their womanly gestures and countenaunce, make men doubt whether they are males or Females.[51]

Cicero's gender- and gesture-norming jest turns on Macrobius's ambiguous phrase *ambula tamquam vir*, which may mean "walk like a man" or "walk like your husband."[52] In Cicero's cisgendered view, his daughter walks "like a man" but should instead walk like her husband, who in turn walks "like a woman." In this roundabout way, Cicero snidely insinuates, Tullia would walk as she purportedly should "of nature," that is, with a "mincing pace." His quip seeks to cut Tullia's lusty stride down to size or, more precisely, to "mince" it, a term meaning to cut "into very small pieces" and, by extension, "to moderate or restrain … so as to keep within the bounds of … decorum" or decorous femininity.[53]

Because gender decorum dictated that the female gait should be modest in stride, a woman who "stryd out lustilye like a man" risked ridicule or worse. In Jonson's *Epicoene*, Truewit thus abhors women who "stalke i' their gait like an Estrich, and take huge strides," insisting, "I cannot endure such a sight. I love measure i' the feet" (4.1.45–7).[54] His comment underscores the extent to which the propriety of gender performance was literally *measured* through footwork: a "fit" gait had to be "of the right measure" and to "conform properly" to "particular dimensions" in order to re-produce the "standard or rule" of gender decorum.[55] What Truewit calls "measure i' the feet" was (and still is) a means of regulating how differently gendered bodies are variously allowed and required to move through and occupy social space. At stake in taking the "measure" of gendered ways of walking (or "going") is the regulation of gender performance more broadly in "all other doings."

Whereas in Macrobius, Cicero seems primarily concerned with correcting his daughter Tullia's masculine stride, in Guazzo's rendering the greater censure shifts to Piso's effeminate, "mincing pace": worse in his view than merely "monstrous and naughtye," it is deemed "the worst sighte that may bee." Although the *OED* maintains that "mincing" was not used as a pejorative descriptor "of a man" deemed to be "effeminate" until "later" (the examples it cites are from the twentieth century[56]), Pettie's use of the term to describe Piso's gait suggests otherwise, as he is clearly preoccupied with a perceived indeterminacy of gender expression (that is, a "doubt whether they are males or Females").[57]

When wayward ways of walking occasion transphobic "doubt" about gender-nonconformity, the stakes "could not be any higher" and, indeed, in the case of transgender people in the past and present are often lethal.[58] Because gendered ways of "going" are often read as signifiers of "all other doings," their "measure" is taken to be a means of assessing the "success" or "failure" of gender performance more broadly. By inviting heightened scrutiny of gender as a "gestural phenomenon" grounded in footwork, the elevated thrust stage of early modern amphitheatres encouraged playgoers to take the measure of players' gender-variant ways of "treading the boards," while also heightening awareness of the ongoing effort and practised skill that gendered footwork requires, particularly in scenes that foreground its rehearsal. Such scenes of rehearsal, I want to suggest, reveal the potential of *practice* as a form of embodied "research" (careful observation and knowledge production) or "*re*-search" (the iterative "action of searching again"[59]) by subverting the illusion of gender "readiness" in ways that invite actors and audiences to take pleasure in the transience or mutability of gender performance in general, and of gender fluidity in particular. Salamon's work underscores the importance of attending to such scenes when they occasion rhetorical derision or outright violence against trans and non-binary gender expressions in the past and present. Yet it is equally important to attend to scenes that depict the practice of gender-nonconformity as occasioning desire, rather than disgust. Certainly, the "womanly gestures" of boy actresses were excoriated by Puritan anti-theatrical writers like Stephen Gosson; yet even Gosson acknowledges the power of "effeminate gesture, to ravish the sence."[60]

Scenes in which characters first introduced as female (or, less frequently, as male) plot and later appear in "cross-dressed" disguise invited heightened audience attention to and heightened performance of gender as a "gestural phenomenon" precisely because they lay bare the labour of learning and inhabiting gender through practice – including habituation to a different stance, gait, and carriage as enabled or impeded by newly acquired masculine or feminine attire – and thereby reveal a gender in process. In *The Merchant of Venice*, Portia plots her transformation into Balthasar by noting that it will require her to "turn two mincing steps / Into a manly stride" (3.4.67–8). As Balthasar, she suggests, each of her strides will measure two of her "mincing steps" as Portia. Yet she also intimates that the gender to which she aspires is not an achieved masculinity defined by its "readiness" but rather the masculinity in formation of a "bragging youth" (l. 69), whose gender is "between the change of man and boy" (l. 66).[61] From beginning to end, the speech calls attention to the ongoing labour of gender transformation (for example, "I have work in hand" [l. 57]) and its status as a reiterative practice (for example, "I will practice" [l. 78]). And if masculinity must be proved through contest or competition (here, with Nerissa), her desired goal is to "prove the *prettier* fellow of the two" (l. 64; my emphasis), suggesting that her "delicate," "diminutive" appearance and mincing stride continue to shape her newly gendered persona.[62]

The potential for subversion in scenes that focus on the labour of learning gendered ways of walking occurs in Fletcher's *Love's Cure, or The Martial Maid* (probably written c. 1605 and revised by Massinger c. 1625), a play that unusually includes both male and female "cross-dressed" characters.[63] Even more unusually, siblings Lucio and Clara, who are separated by their parents and "cross-dressed" from childhood through puberty, have no interest in returning to their respective genders assigned at birth. Clara (in contrast to Portia, or Viola, or Rosalind) struggles to learn the habits of femininity, not masculinity, and Lucio vice versa. The scene in question (and the play more generally) is thus concerned with their reluctant and belaboured attempts to acquire gendered "habits," assumed to be natural but revealed to be performed and in need of continual practice.

Act 2, scene 2 – which was among the scenes workshopped at the Stratford Festival practice as research (PaR) laboratory on Engendering the Stage – stages the practice of gender in process. Lucio appears in male attire for the first time and has the following exchange with Bobadilla, a swaggering servant tasked with "mak[ing] a man" (l. 637) of "it" (Bobadilla's preferred gender-neutral pronoun for Lucio), a task that immediately centres on footwork:

LUCIO: What would you have me do? This scurvy sword
   So galls my thigh: I would 'twere burnt: pish, look,
   This cloak will ne'er keep on: these boots too hidebound
   Make me walk stiff, as if my legs were frozen,
   And my spurs jingle, like a morris-dancer:
   Lord, how my head aches, with this roguish hat;
   This masculine attire is most uneasy;
   I am bound up in it: I had rather walk
   In folio again, loose, like a woman.

BOBADILLA: In foolio, had you not?
   Thou mock to heaven, and nature, and thy parents;
   Thou tender leg of lamb: Oh, how he walks
   As if he had bepissed himself and fleares!
   Is this a gait for the young cavalier,
   Don Lucio, son and heir to Alvarez?
   Has it a corn? Or does it walk on conscience,
   It treads so gingerly?   (ll. 638–54)

The scene foregrounds the gendered "habits" of a masculine gait and of male attire as "uneasy" or " troublesome" in causing both "physical" and "mental discomfort," and in making the stage "difficult to traverse on account of ... obstacles."[64] The jingle-jangle of spurs produced by Lucio's mincing gait feminizes a sound ordinarily associated with a masculine stride. Lucio's stride is hobbled by masculine footwear he experiences as ill-fitting: his boots are "too hidebound" and produce a walk that is "stiff," rather than "loose, like a woman." In Bobadilla's view, however, Lucio's gait is not stiff enough; it remains "tender," which is to say "delicate," "frail," "immature," "sensitive," and "unmanly" or effeminate:[65] "Has it a corn?" Bobadilla asks, "Or does it walk on conscience, / It treads so gingerly?"[66] The dis-ease of Lucio's gait is read as symptomatic of a bodily infirmity rather than an external encumbrance, and the pronoun "it" is wielded not only to indicate that "sex is not particularized" but also to cast Lucio in a "*derogatory* or *humorous*" way as a young "child" that might "bepiss" itself, if not as a subhuman "thing."[67] The hostility of Bobadilla's derision is real and, like the mockery of Piso, helps to shed light on the prehistory of violence and demeaning rhetoric aimed at dehumanizing male effeminacy and trans femininity. Yet Bobadilla's association of Lucio's "tender" effeminacy with a reluctance to "walk on conscience" also aligns Lucio with moral rectitude and his own hyper-masculinity with callousness (an alignment that is maintained throughout the play). Seville, where the play is set, or "Civill" (as it is spelled in the 1647 Folio), has been riven by a blood feud between Lucio's father Alvarez and his rival Vitelli and is in dire need of civility to "preserve [the] commonwealth," and "not daring / Wherein men nowadays exceed even beasts," in order to bring an end to "the deadly and uncurable hatred ... and outrages daily arising" (5.3.2016–17, 2028, 2043–4). Bobadilla concludes the encounter above by posing as Vitelli in order to "accost" Lucio and train him to perpetuate the feud; Lucio refuses, suing for "love and peace" in the name of "Christianity" (ll. 676, 681).

Clara, who appears shortly thereafter for the first time in female attire, enters re-enacting a military march recollected from her "golden days" on the battlefield: "Ran tan tan ta ran tan ran tan tan, ta ran tan tan tan-tan. Oh, I shall no more see those golden days, these clothes will never fadge with me: a – o'this filthy farthingale, this hip hap: brother, why are these women's haunches only limited, confined, hooped in, as it were with these same scurvy farthingales?" (ll. 692–8). Clara strides out in ways deemed "too mannish" (l. 710), just as Lucio minces in ways deemed too womanish. Her cumbersome farthingale or hoop-skirt does not "fadge" or fit with wonted habits of masculine movement; indeed, her stride likely causes it to swing comically back and forth.[68] Bobadilla takes the measure of Clara's gait as he does of Lucio's, viewing it as un-"fit" and still in need of practice:

> Look you now, is this a fit trot for a gentlewoman? You shall see the court ladies move like goddesses, as if they trod air: they will swim you their measures, like whiting-mops [young fish] as if their feet were fins and the hinges of their knees oiled ... You cannot trot so fast, but he ambles as slowly. (ll. 716–20, 724)

Yet Bobadilla's detailed description of the mechanics of footwork (for example, well "oiled" knees) that produce "a fit trot for a gentlewoman" highlights the artifice of this display of femininity and, in so doing, seems to invite demonstration of its techniques and their effects onstage. Mark Harapiak, who played the role in the Stratford PaR lab, deftly demonstrated what it might look like to "swim" with ease as if treading air in slow motion with fins for feet.[69] The very deftness of the demonstration, however, revealed that Bobadilla's enactment of a gentlewoman's "fit trot" only serves to subvert the claim that the "fitness" of gendered footwork is a product of "nature" (ll. 648, 722).

Crucial to the significance of the scene is Bobadilla's status (or lack thereof) as a recently promoted servant whose authority as a "tutor" (l. 636) of gendered gaits is undercut by his confessed need to practise the stride appropriate to his new role as steward: "I am now to practise the steward's pace ... [E]very man must fashion his gait according to his calling" (1.2.231–3). The ongoing labour such fashioning requires is further exposed by the play's subplot in which Pachieco (a cobbler or shoe-patcher), Mendoza (a mender of stockings or "hose-heeler" [2.1.488]), and Metaldi (a metal smith or spur-forger) vaunt their intimate knowledge of "the length of every man's foot" (ll. 510–11) and "every man's step that walks" (l. 525). As "daily menders" (l. 512) who maintain the feet of the body politic, they lay claim to sustaining its foundation; yet in the process, they also lay bare its ailments ("scabs, chilblains, and kibed heels" [l. 505]), to which they contribute by leaving their honest (if lowly) trades and turning to thievery in the employ of the corrupt constable, Alguazier.

In the end, the governor of Seville/Civill restores civility to the vice-ridden state by disguising himself (like the Duke in *Measure for Measure*) to take the "measure" of its duplicitous deputies, exposing the ways in which they have "trod awry" (5.3.2244).[70] Bobadilla complains that his stewardship remains "not only not regarded, but also not rewarded" (5.2.2212). Notably, Clara's and Lucio's lovers desire them, not despite but because of their gender variance: when Vitelli kisses Clara, he admires her "soldier's arm" and "lips [that] appear *as if* / They were a lady's" (4.2.1602–3; my emphasis), a reference not only to Clara's masculinity but also to the boy actress playing the role. Genevora is ravished by Lucio's "sweet innocence" and tender delicacy, claiming "I ne'er saw / A lovely man, till now" (4.4.1755, 1760–1) when they kiss. In the end, it is Clara's masculinity and Lucio's effeminacy that effectively bring peace and civility to Civill by tempering the "inflamed blood" (4.2.1479) of its feuding factions.

Practised footwork plays a key role in this process, as both siblings demonstrate expert foot-skills in fencing to quell, rather than further to inflame, the blood feud that threatens the state. Clara uses her sword to subdue a scene of civil strife in which Vitelli and Piorato (a fencing-master) fight for the attentions of a sex-worker, Malroda. In Act 5, scene 1, "womanish Lucio" fights the "great duelist Lamorall" for Genevora and "*wins Lamorall's sword*" but refuses to take his life, renouncing the "bloody purpose" of the feud and leading Lamorall to say, "This courtesy / Wounds deeper than your sword can" and "I ne'er knew what true valour was till now" (ll. 1834–5, 1860 SD, 1876, 1880–1, 1901). Clara and Lucio are ultimately able to wield swords and display expert foot-skills in ways that re-envision gendered codes of decorum and are a source of admiration rather than mockery.

Engendering the Stage: Practising Footwork as Research

In this volume's chapter 7, "Drawing Your Weapon," Denise Oucharek, who was cast as Guzmán in the Engendering the Stage workshop's explorations of *The Lieutenant Nun*, exuberantly describes the elation – "one of the highlights of my entire career" – she experienced in the week's swordwork and footwork exercises, an elation she links to the licence to wield a sword and enact a different, more powerful way of walking. Although this way of walking is transient, re-searched and re-formed with each stride, it nonetheless "really stays with you" – it recreates a new gender, engendering it, step by step. In this same chapter, Lily McEvenue, who was cast as Clara in the workshop on Act 2, scene 2 of *Love's Cure*, similarly observes how widened footing and shifts in posture, rooted in "a sense of oppositional force between weight dropping into the floor and the upper body holding strong and lifting," helped her to "embody feelings of confidence and authority."

McEvenue's satisfaction of finding her footing and stride while wielding both a sword and a gun was nonetheless tempered by the corset and farthingale she had to wear in the scene. Asked (in an unpublished video recording of the workshop) by the costumer how the farthingale feels, McEvenue says, "It's awful! It's very restricting; how's someone supposed to mount a horse with this dress!" The protruding "hip hap," she realizes, not only restricts her movement but will also prevent Clara from wearing her prized sword at her hips. She mimics the awkward gesture of trying to draw a sword from a scabbard worn "very high up" and in the process rips the seam where the sleeve of her sword-bearing arm joins the bodice of the dress. "Oh no!" she says, and laughs with a mixture of embarrassment and mischievous excitement. Renate Hanson, the Stratford Lab's stage manager who is giving out the costumes, asks, "What happened? Did you rip it? Are you okay in there [that is, does it fit]?" to which McEvenue replies, "Yeah, I'm good," but then turns to the camera (and thus to the audience) and, grimacing, says under her breath, "but the costume's not good," and laughs again. In a subsequent interview, she elaborates: "I have never had to wear a dress as heavy and with so many layers before. I felt awkward and uncomfortable. It was especially challenging to avoid tripping or catching the sword on the many layers of fabric. Fortunately, this had a great effect on the character choices I made. The way I felt in the costume informed Clara's emotional state. She was also not familiar with being dressed in that fashion, and it significantly contributed to her identity crisis."[71] As McEvenue recognizes, it is the "sense of oppositional force" – this time between the (empowering) masculine weaponry and (inhibiting) feminine costume – that enables her to practise Clara's footwork in the scene as an ongoing process of discovery and engendering.

"Treading the boards" engendered the early modern stage by means of practised footwork: it extended the parameters of pedal decorum by staging gender-fluid ways of walking to "ravish" the senses of audiences and scenes of footwork-in-practice to foreground and elevate its techniques. In such scenes, the practice of footwork had the potential to become a means of re-searching gender roles and thereby of re-envisioning them. Such scenes provide an ideal template with which to conduct practice as research into gender performance on the early modern stage by foregrounding footwork as an ongoing practice of producing embodied knowledge about gender and by exposing the material constraints and affordances through which costume and staging shape the performance of gender from the ground up.

NOTES

1 Salamon, "Passing Period," 189; see also Salamon, *Life and Death of Latisha King*, 46.
2 The *Oxford English Dictionary* (OED) dates the earliest usage of "treads the Stage" to 1691. As Jonson's dedicatory poem in the First Folio attests, however, "to tread the stage" was in usage in Shakespeare's time. Michael Drayton uses the related phrase "strut the stage" in *Idea the Shepheards Garland*, H3v.
3 Korda, "Understanding Shakespeare's Shoes."
4 Salamon, *Life and Death of Latisha King*, 12, 14.
5 See Salamon, "Passing Period" and *Life and Death of Latisha King*.
6 All references to Shakespeare, unless otherwise indicated, are to *The Riverside Shakespeare*, 2nd ed.
7 Dekker, *Satiro-mastix*, I3v; W.S. [attrib.; Thomas Middleton?], *The Puritane*, F2r.
8 *OED*, "gesture, *n.*," 1.a., b., 2.a., 3.a.
9 From a description of the Roman actor Roscius (Lloyd, *Jubile of Britaine*, A2r).
10 Bacon, *Sylva Sylvarum*, 185–6.
11 Hollyband, *Campo di Fior*, 115.
12 Thomas, *Dictionarium*.
13 From a description of the role of gesture in inciting affect (Burton, *Anatomy of Melancholy*, 566).
14 Quintilian, *Orator's Education, Books 11–12*, 121 (11.11.69).
15 Quintilian, 149 (11.3.125).
16 Quintilian, 151 (11.3.126).
17 Quintilian, 149–52 (11.3.125–9).
18 Quintilian, 131 (11.3.88).
19 Overbury, *Sir Thomas Overburie*, M2r.
20 A funeral elegy for Richard Burbage published in 1619 finds this gesture particularly memorable, recalling "oft have I seene him, leap into the Grave" (cited in Nungezer, *A Dictionary of Actors*, 74).
21 Salamon, *Life and Death of Latisha King*, 66.
22 Brome, *Court Begger*, S3r.
23 Dessen and Thomson, *Dictionary of Stage Directions*, 237. All further references to stage directions, unless otherwise indicated, are to Dessen and

Thomson's *Dictionary*. Page numbers corresponding to the relevant entry will be cited parenthetically.

24 John Hall, for example, decries the "mis-education of our Gentry" in the "Playhouse, or Dauncing Schoole" in *Epistles*, 70. In Thomas Nabbes's *Totenham Court*, 27, James says, "Were it not for the dancing-schoole and Play-houses, I would not stay at the Innes of Court for the hopes of a chiefe Justice-ship."

25 Rich, *Faultes Faults*, C4v–D1r.

26 Rye, *Glossary*, 112.

27 Fitzgeffrey, *Satyres*, F7v, F5v.

28 Fitzgeffrey, F5v.

29 Fitzgeffrey, F2r–F2v.

30 *OED*, "toy, *n.*," 3., 4.a.

31 *OED*, "skip, $v.^1$," 2.b., 3.a., 3.b.

32 Stokes, *Vaulting-Master*.

33 *OED*, "carriage, *n.*," 23.b.

34 Peacham, *Compleat Gentleman*, 185.

35 Brathwaite, *English Gentleman*, 259.

36 Castiglione, *The Courtyer*, Zz1r.

37 M[arston], *History of Antonio and Mellida*, A3r.

38 *OED*, "bravery, *n.*," 1.

39 *OED*, "bravery, *n.*," 3.a.; "brave, *adj.*, *n.*, and *int.*," 2.

40 *OED*, "emphasis, *n.*"

41 Hamlet amplifies Laertes's "O, treble woe / Fall ten times [treble] on that [Hamlet's] cursed head" (5.1.246–7) to "Forty thousand brothers / Could not with all their quantity of love / Make up my sum" (269–71).

42 See, for example, "a Water Skipper, or Water Fly" in Holme, *Academy of Armory*, 358. Samuel Johnson glosses Hamlet's use of the moniker to describe Osric as follows: "A water-fly skips up and down upon the surface of the water, without any apparent purpose or reason, and is thence the proper emblem of a busy trifler" (Johnson, *Plays of William Shakespeare*, 295; also cited in Shakespeare, *Hamlet*, ed. Jenkins, 558 [at ll. 5.2.82–3]).

43 Brome, *Court Begger*, S3r.

44 Brome, S3v

45 Brome, S3r.

46 Brome, S4r.

47 Brome, R1r.

48 Brome, R1r.

49 *Hamlet* is often described as a play of inaction, but it might more accurately be called a play of pacing as it repeatedly calls attention to the simple act of walking "upon the platform" (1.2.251), from the "martial stalk" (1.1.66) of the Ghost to Hamlet's habit of walking "four hours together / … in the

lobby" (2.2.160–1). Modern editors often emend "four" to "for," but the original spelling in the quartos and folio underscores the sense that Hamlet paces throughout the entirety of the play.

50 Guazzo, *Civile Conversation*, vol. 2, 12–13. On the influence of Guazzo's treatise on Hamlet's advice to the players, see Korda, *Labors Lost*, 167–8, 263n77.

51 Guazzo, *Civile Conversation*, 3:40, citing Macrobius, *Saturnalia* (2.3.16).

52 Macrobius, *Saturnalia*, 344–5.

53 *OED*, "mince, *v.*," 1.a., 4.d., 6.a.

54 Jonson, *Epicoene*.

55 *OED*, "fit, $v.^1$," 5.a., 5.b.; "fit, *adj.*," 3; "measure, *v.*," 2.b., 13.a.

56 See *OED*, "mincing, *adj.*," 1.b.

57 See also J. Sylvester's roughly contemporaneous satire of effeminate gallants: "Who with a mayden voice, and mincing pace, / Quaint looks, curl'd locks, perfumes, and painted face, / Base coward hart, and wanton soft aray, / Their manhood onely by their beard bewray" (*Englands Parnassus*, 380).

58 Here I draw specifically on Gayle Salamon's analysis of the murder of Latisha King, a biracial, trans-feminine teenager, by a white, male, cisgendered high school classmate for the purported offense of dressing and "walking 'like a girl'" (Salamon, *Life and Death of Latisha King*, 12, 46). In light of the long history of violence targeting trans women of colour, violence that has reached record levels in recent years, it is incumbent upon early modern scholarship to attend to the *longue durée* of the complex entanglement of transphobia, transmisogyny, and anti-Black racism. For a groundbreaking example of such work, see the special issue of the *Journal for Early Modern Cultural Studies*, edited by Simone Chess, Colby Gordon, and Will Fisher, the introduction of which asks: "How do the forms of trans embodiment taking shape in early modernity illuminate genocidal histories of white supremacy, anti-blackness, Islamophobia and anti-Semitism, settler colonialism, and empire?" (Chess, Colby, and Fisher, "Introduction: Early Modern Trans Studies," 5).

59 *OED*, "re-search, $n.^2$"

60 Gosson, *School of Abuse*, B6v.

61 It should be added that her earlier gender is equally in process, for she describes herself as "an unlesson'd girl, unschool'd, unpractic'd" (3.2.159).

62 *OED*, "pretty, *adj.*, *n.*, and *int.*," 2.a.

63 All references are to Beaumont and Fletcher, *Love's Cure*, ed. Mitchell.

64 *OED*, "uneasy, *adj.*," 1.a., 1.b., 2.a., 3.c.

65 *OED*, "tender, *adj.*," 1.a., 2., 3.a., 3.c., 4, 10.b.

66 Philip Stubbes describes "dansing minions, that minse it ful gingerlie, God wot, tripping like gotes that an egge wold not brek under their feet" (Stubbes, *Anatomie of Abuses*, 1583, E8r).

67 *OED*, "it, *pron.*," I.1.a.i., I.1.a.iii.
68 In an interview for my *Norton Critical Edition* of *Twelfth Night*, actor Mark Rylance describes the fluid gait that characterized his Olivia as both inspired and constrained by costume: "it *was* the dress: when you have the hoops inside of a dress like that, if you don't keep yourself stable as you're moving, the dress rocks back and forth" (341).
69 Captured in the *Engendering the Stage in the Age of Shakespeare and Beyond at the Stratford Festival Theatre Laboratory* video, timestamp 2.22–8.
70 Pachieco and Mendoza are sentenced "To cobble and heel hose for the poor friars" (l. 2240) without pay and Metaldi to wear "shackles" and "lie by the heels a year" (ll. 2246–7) for their crimes.
71 Lily McEvenue in Cockett and Gough et al., "Performing Gender 'From the Ground Up,'" chapter 10 of this volume.

10 Performing Gender "From the Ground Up"

PETER COCKETT AND MELINDA GOUGH, WITH EMMA FRANKLAND,
LILY McEVENUE, ANDRÉ MORIN, MARCUS NANCE,
AND DENISE OUCHAREK

Lucio. What would you have me do? This scurvy sword
  So galls my thigh: I would 'twere burnt: pish, look,
  This cloak will ne'er keep on: these boots too hidebound
  Make me walk stiff, as if my legs were frozen,
  And my spurs jingle, like a morris-dancer:
  Lord, how my head aches, with this roguish hat;
  This masculine attire is most uneasy;
  I am bound up in it: I had rather walk
  In folio again, loose, like a woman.
Bobadilla. In "foolio," had you not? Thou mock to heav'n, and nature, and thy
  parents; thou tender leg of lamb. [Lucio walks.] O, how he walks as if he had
  bepissed himself, and fleers! Is this a gait for the young cavalier Don Lucio,
  son and heir to Alvarez? Has it a corn? Or does it walk on conscience, it treads
  so gingerly?

– Love's Cure, 2.2.9–21[1]

The very habit of the minde may bee best discerned and discovered by the state
and carriage of the body.

– Richard Brathwaite, The English Gentleman, 259[2]

Portia. I'll … turn two mincing steps / Into a manly stride.

– Merchant of Venice, 3.4.67–8[3]

Working on the performance of gender in a context that seeks to challenge the colonial gender binary demands language for the rehearsal room that avoids the description of movement as masculine or feminine. We therefore introduced workshop participants to the Laban system of movement analysis in an initial exercise on the first day.[4] Laban's system uses a combination of three ungendered binaries to create simple language to describe, direct, and generate physical action: heavy and light, sudden and sustained (sometimes teachers use fast and slow), direct and indirect. Combinations of the three produce common movement types that can be used in multiple ways within a performance process. A heavy, sudden, and direct movement, for example, is usually named a "punch," whereas a heavy, sustained, and direct movement is called a "press." The list of Laban "efforts" used for the workshop was as follows:

- **Press**: Heavy, Sustained, Direct
- **Punch**: Heavy, Sudden, Direct
- **Slash**: Heavy, Sudden, Indirect
- **Wring**: Heavy, Sustained, Indirect
- **Glide**: Light, Sustained, Direct
- **Poke or Dab**: Light, Sudden, Direct
- **Flick**: Light, Sudden, Indirect
- **Float**: Light, Sustained, Indirect

Having shared key concepts from Laban, we gave both the actors and the scholars time (admittedly very short) to familiarize themselves with the language system and the feeling that different combinations of energies had on and in their bodies. On day three, we applied Laban's principles in an embodied exploration of historical evidence for the gendering of footwork in the early modern period. This exercise drew on Natasha Korda's pre-circulated workshop paper "Gendered Footwork on the Early Modern Stage," a revised version of which appears in this volume.[5] Evidence from early modern etiquette manuals and play-texts constructs a style of movement for courtly elites and distinguishes between movements expected of men and of women. Simply put, the sources recommend lightness and grace as essential to courtly manners, irrespective of gender, and stipulate that men's and women's movements should be distinguished by their expansiveness: men stand with feet further apart and take longer strides.

Applying Laban's conceptual framework to this evidence, we explored light and sustained movements as a starting point for the idea of courtly grace, and heavy and sudden movements as constructing the movements of labourers as well as incompetent courtiers. There is no record of advice on posture or gait being given to those of the lowest ranks, and so we assumed a greater level of freedom in their movement and less commitment to balance, grace, and modest proportion. Numerous contemporary portraits provide ample evidence supporting such aspects of courtly posture, and we drew on these sources – and others – when teaching the group basics of noble gesture and embodied comportment as commonly accepted in classical movement training.[6] In these sources, such as the Arbeau image here (Figure 10.1), courtiers typically position their feet at right angles with the heel of the right foot pointing to the centre of the left foot. The women's feet, however, touch each other, while the men place their feet approximately six inches (15 centimetres) apart.

Figure 10.1. "Révérence," Thoinot Arbeau, *Orchésographie*, 1589. Wikimedia.

At the workshop, we worked from the premise that gentlemen placed their left hand on their sword and used their right to gesture, as in Figure 10.2, whereas gentlewomen often adopted a pose of hands folded right over left and resting just below the navel.[7] Such restraints on noblewomen's posture were likely not universal, however. In fact, this performance tradition is not supported by the evidence of contemporary portraiture, much of which features aristocratic women holding their arms in a variety of ways, including arrangements that mimic men's posture nearly exactly (see Figures 10.2 and 10.3). Furthermore, the famous pamphlets *Hic Mulier* and *Haec Vir* reveal that gender nonconformity was prevalent enough on the streets of London to attract the attention of conservative satirists. The title page for *Haec Vir* (Figure 10.4) depicts a "mannish" woman in an overcoat worn atop a shorter dress, revealing her long stride and the spurs on her heels. This image closely resembles Lily McEvenue's performance of the character of Clara at the workshop. The figure's long stride is used to denote masculinity, but the image also indicates the obvious fact that women could lengthen their stride at will.

Through this process, we developed a provisional movement language for exploring the performance of classed and gendered identities without resorting to the binary descriptors "masculine" or "feminine." Initially, Peter took the full group through the range of possible motions and encouraged them to explore multiple combinations, with particular attention to how the different ways of moving changed the way they felt about themselves and the way they were occupying physical as well as social space. Having opened up the possibilities of movement, we then asked the actors to use the dialectics of embodied movement that we had

Figure 10.2. Unknown artist [in the style of Marcus Gheeraerts (1561–1635)], Portrait of Henry Wriothesely, 1605. Oil on canvas. The Portland Collection, Harley Gallery, Welbeck Estate, Nottinghamshire. Bridgeman Images.

Figure 10.3. William Larkin, Portrait of Diana Cecil, later Countess of Oxford, c. 1614–18. Oil on canvas, 205.9 x 119.5 cm. English Heritage, Kenwood; Wikimedia.

established to develop a gendered presentation for their characters. Moving the full set of workshop participants into a circle, Peter invited pairs of actors into the centre space to conduct silent improvisations exploring their physicality and the power dynamics between them. Initially, the pairs were random, and characters from different scenes entered the space and playfully interacted. Next, the exercise progressed to improvised movements involving paired characters from specific scenes. Here, as earlier, the actors entered the space in character, bringing knowledge of their scenes together with physicalities developed through the movement exercises.

Adding costumes contributed further complexity to our explorations of movement within and outside of gendered binaries. Costumes were drawn from the Stratford Festival's stock of early modern pieces that demarcated gender and class following the sartorial codes of the period. The male-identifying and presenting characters were dressed in doublet and breeches, and the female-identifying and presenting characters in typical long dresses and stiff bodices. The costumes for higher status characters were more elaborate, weightier, and more substantially structured, while the costumes for lower ranking characters were made out of plainer, lighter, and softer materials. Provision of costumes for small group scene work and large group exercises introduced further creative opportunities for exploring embodied gender in performance. The actors were always moving within clothing that was designed to structure their relationship to social norms.

Figure 10.4. Title page image from *Haec Vir or the Womanish Man*, London, 1620. Wikimedia Commons.

As indicated by the commentaries and reflections gathered below, our gendered footwork exercises prompted new questions about the performance of gender both historically and today. These explorations resulted in feelings of empowerment for some actors and a renewed sense of risk and potential harm for others. Such commentary on the gendered movement workshop suggests that theatre practice creates expectations for gender conformity and limits gender expressions to a degree that, for many actors, may in fact be higher than that experienced in everyday life. Additionally, the commentary makes clear that the gender neutrality of Laban's language as a tool for the rehearsal room does not remove the concept of the gender binary from the heads of observers/audiences nor the normative assumptions that arise from it. Playing with the performance of gender, even in the performance as research (PaR) rehearsal room but especially in public performance, is not equally accessible for all. For people whose gender is challenged or questioned by society, such play carries a different level of risk. Below, the cisgender women actors Lily McEvenue and Denise Oucharek report feelings of weightiness but also liberation. The cisgender men actors André Morin and Marcus Nance express greater familiarity with the effects of the costuming and period movement but still question the limitations placed on their and their characters' genders, either by the play-texts or by the theatre profession. Similarly questioning these same limitations, trans artist Emma Frankland shares further complexities and challenges arising from our movement work.

Actor Commentary

LILY McEVENUE

It was not Clara's choice to become a soldier or a war hero, yet she took great pride in it. Her duties [on the battlefield] were those attributed to men, and therefore she started to identify as male. Clara was later forced into a reality completely different from the one that had shaped her early existence. This was a significant shift in her reality because now as a female, she has lower status, no choice, and is obligated to fulfil the duties of what society deems appropriate for women.

In *Love's Cure,* Clara is forced to wear a petticoat and farthingale. In my experience, I have never had to wear a dress as heavy and with so many layers before. I felt awkward and uncomfortable. It was especially challenging to avoid tripping or catching the sword on the many layers of fabric. Fortunately, this had a great effect on the character choices I made. The way I felt in the costume informed Clara's emotional state. She was also not familiar with being dressed in that fashion, and it significantly contributed to her identity crisis.

Figure 10.5. Lily McEvenue, 2018 Stratford Festival Laboratory participant, as Clara in *Love's Cure.* Photograph by David Campbell.

The gendered movement exercise also had a profound impact on my understanding of Clara and of womanhood in the early modern period. I had to walk with a narrow gait, make smaller footsteps, and hold my upper body very still. It felt restricting, unnatural, almost to the point of changing my use of breath. The experience informed an instinct towards a woman's emotional state if her duty was to present herself in that respect. It also gave me the perception that a woman's presence would have barely been noticed and that perhaps it was her duty to walk with the least amount of disturbance possible. This was an important exploration for peeling back some layers of Clara's character.

DENISE OUCHAREK in conversation with
PETER COCKETT and MELINDA GOUGH

DENISE: In the very beginning, we hadn't talked a lot about the material – "Let's just get up and do it. Let's be really physical." And that was great, but in our group, I would say we were closer to stereotypical movement. What we thought masculine, what we thought feminine was based on stereotypes. And then through all of the work during the entire session that changed, and I felt like stereotypes didn't apply anymore. Not only with that case [the particular *Lieutenant Nun* scene] but across the board, and the discovery was: Oh, yeah there are things that we call masculine and call feminine, for lack of exploring other terminology, that we've just allowed to exist that way, but I don't think they do. I think that that sliding scale is literally that. You know, I'm a very physical actor – and I always have been – but I felt like that was a moment where I will – I can't work any other way now, my brain can't be reversed after that discovery, after that sort of light bulb moment. I cannot approach anything any other way …

The costuming was fascinating to put on. It wasn't comfortable. [laughs] It wasn't comfortable, but I don't know that anyone's was. And I don't think this was a gender thing, I

Figure 10.6. Denise Oucharek, 2018 Stratford Festival Laboratory participant, as Guzmán in *The Lieutenant Nun*. Photograph by David Campbell.

think it was more a reflection of the time. Um, really restrictive. The female clothes in particular, but just in general the clothes were quite restrictive. And I thought, "How could" – for Guzmán, even in the masculine attire, I thought – "How could you have possibly fought in this?" I would have been whipping that off and just – there's no way. So it was not so much a gendered thing as it was a time period thing, which I found fascinating. The formality that existed in the apparel was really, really neat.

MELINDA: One of the reasons Guzmán has a sword is because he's *Don* Guzmán, right, so he's a noble.

DENISE: That's right.

MELINDA: So the formality of the weight of the sword and the constraint of the costume are these privileges and duties and honours. They are the things that give Guzmán freedom, and yet they're also the things that constrain him.

DENISE: Yeah, it's a freedom of appearance but … carrying a sword, it's a weight to carry – it's a weight to carry, so, you know, my character was in physical structure feminine, had less body bulk, so that would have been a difficult thing to do. The physical effort required to carry that around, to wear those garments, might have felt good and looked right, you know: when Guzmán looked in the mirror, looked right, that was correct. And yet, it was effort …

PETER: Did you ever actually put on the dress?

DENISE: *Never.* Not once. [PETER and MELINDA laugh] Not once … By choice, by choice. It was never suggested that I did – Danielle [Wade, who performed the part of Sebastian in the *Lieutenant Nun* scene work] tried to get me in it a couple of times – but there was no way, it was never going to happen. We threw it over the shoulder, we tied it around the body, I wore it as a scarf at once point, but never ever did I put it on. And luckily, again because we were going along with the text excerpt that we were given, because the process of getting into that dress is interrupted by the sword fight that I leave for, I would never have to. So I was protected by the excerpt. [Everyone laughs] So thanks for that too!

MELINDA: Well I don't think Guzmán ever appears in a dress.

PETER: I don't think he does.

DENISE: Yaaaaaaaaaaay! That's amazing. Well, he gets his dispensation from the Pope, so he doesn't have to.

PETER: That's right! Yeah …

The gendered footsteps exercise that I ran building on Natasha Korda's paper, where we explored the courtly way of walking, with the difference between men and women being in the length of the stride, basically: did that play into Guzmán?

DENISE: Yeah, I think it was really valuable. I think I naturally and instinctively was already taking larger strides, because on the polarized scale of binary gender that I was bringing to the scene work at the beginning of the week, that felt like the right thing to do because that was "masculine." Naturally, I would try to take up more space, is what I felt. And so just knowing through the exercise that movement and gender were connected historically – it's like having the tools: knowing this allowed me to feel comfortable in my instinct, which was really helpful. I felt like a lot of the information that came to us helped immensely because it solidified instinct. You can have an instinct about something, but if you don't have any facts or information to bear that out, it's just your gut. And that never feels good. Like, if you get all the way to a performance and you're going on gut, there's a problem. [laughs] You know, your confidence comes from the facts. Someone has to make the decisions, someone has to know the facts, and corral us all together. And having the scholars and the director helped that. We had someone who was allowing instincts to flow, and someone who was fielding information, and then someone who was corralling us all [laughs], you know, and letting us all be in the same place. So I think that exercise specifically was very helpful for me in terms of solidifying what felt like an instinct.

PETER: I was really struck by Danielle [Wade]'s performance of Sebastian: it was so elegant.

DENISE: Right.

PETER: And so light, but still within the realm of what might have been considered a courtly man of the day. So it encompassed what we've come to think of as traditionally feminine qualities, yet it worked really well in context –

DENISE: It was a great fit for Danielle, because she's a self-identifying tomboy. You know, she wears her overalls, her sweats, and puts her hair in a messy bun, and yet on stage plays all these feminine stereotypical roles. But she's a tomboy, she wants to get down and dirty in the mud, that's what she likes to do. So it felt like a great fit, because all her stage work as these hyper-feminine females gave her the deportment and the carriage.

PETER: Her courtliness. [Everyone laughs]

DENISE: And yet her natural instinct allowed her to have a little more weight to it than someone who wasn't a tomboy. It was a great fit for her. She loved it, too. She thought it was so much fun …

MELINDA: In our exercise at the end of the week led by Emma [Frankland],[8] you said something like, "I wonder how, how much

time I've spent like not acknowledging my masculinity," or something like that.

DENISE: For me, it was a big thing, that. I remember saying it, and
it was very specific, and it was something I wanted the group to
hear. It came from a place, throughout the week, of thinking about
my own position as an actor in the industry. I am a cisgendered
female who has rarely in her career fit into [laughs] the box of a
cisgendered female role that would be desirable by most actors.
Especially in classical theatre. I've never been the ingenue. I think
the last time I was an ingenue was when I was eighteen years old.
I was playing forty-year-olds when I was twenty; when I was forty, I
was already playing sixty-year-olds. It's always been the way. So, you
know, I'm really acting, because I'm never, never really close to
playing what I am.

And that being said, I've always fought the masculinity, the
strength that I have as a Ukrainian female, as a woman of a certain
stature – you know my dad always jokes, and he says things like [in
mock Ukrainian accent] "strong like bull, dumb like streetcar."
[PETER and MELINDA laugh] And I think that's hilarious because
it's *so* Ukrainian for me, but it's true! I can go in my backyard and
chop down a tree, I've done it. I can put floors down, I can drywall,
I've done it. The masculine arts, the strength arts, I have no problem
with them, and I've done them my whole life. I was raised to be a
very physically strong girl. And yet, from the time I was three, I was
a dancer, and I owned my own dance studio for five years, and I was
a choreographer and a teacher. And I'm a singer. And, you know,
all of these more "feminine" arts are a *massive* part of my existence.
They're my heart. That's where my vulnerability and my emotions all
lie because I'm a *massively* emotional creature. Very stereotypically
feminine in that way. So, what the week showed me was, with the
sword work and feeling that power: "See, this is what I'm missing!"
I'm missing the joy and the strength that someone like Guzmán was
able to live their life – I'm missing that, I've been apologizing for that
strength that I have for far too long. It's okay to be strong, it's okay
to have a big frame. It's okay. And maybe, had I chosen a different
career or if I had existed in another industry, I don't know if it would
affect me as much.

So at the end of the week, that's what I was thinking about. I was
thinking about where I am, where I'm at, the kind of work I get
offered, and that maybe I should enjoy that and embrace it instead

of resisting it and trying to prove otherwise all the time. That it's just a part of me, and it's an *awesome* part of me, you know, that I should hold up as a strength. It served me so well in the work on *Lieutenant Nun*. I had no problem jumping right in and doing that. Because I had permission, because it was the character's needs and not Denise's, right? So, embracing that, embracing the power, embracing what's stereotyped as masculine skills and masculine strengths – no, they're mine, and I'm fairly feminine – that this is me, this is who I am. And like it. I wanna like it. And I feel like I have, ever since, you know?

ANDRÉ MORIN in conversation with
PETER COCKETT and MELINDA GOUGH

ANDRÉ: I find that clothing from that time period [the age of Shakespeare] gives a lot of form to the human body, and I'm always liberated by it.

PETER: You get a kind of tight feeling – the form is a kind of "on your toes" kind of form?

ANDRÉ: Yeah! It's like "up, out, direct." These were direct people. They lived their lives directly. And they dressed … in a direct way.

MELINDA: In the video we made from our week, you as Lucio were like – "*how* do I wear this?"[9] You've got that gesture of being bound up. Like you're being *forced* to be direct.

ANDRÉ: Yeah, well Lucio wants to be a little more … curvy. He doesn't want these straight lines. Like, all that, sort of, all circles and curves, because I thought that's kind of where you might move if you were in a dress, in order to just mobilize.

PETER: That's kind of loose, like when they walk around "in folio."[10]

ANDRÉ: Yeah, yeah!

PETER: You have that kind of fluidity to it.

ANDRÉ: He wants to be able to curve! He wants the kind of freedom of motion, which is not necessarily what most dresses actually provide.

Figure 10.7. André Morin, 2018 Stratford Festival Laboratory participant, as Lucio in *Love's Cure*. Photograph by David Campbell.

MELINDA: Yeah, that's hilarious! [Everyone laughs]
ANDRÉ: But yeah, it was very informative. And it always takes you to the next level to have costumes on –
MELINDA: I wonder if you had had boots if that would have been even better?
ANDRÉ: Oh, it would have been more fun, with the "bepissed himself." We could have done a lot more with the boots to make "bepissed himself" work. [PETER laughs] That's such a good joke. God it's a good joke. [laughs] "O, he walks as if he had bepissed himself!" That's not a word! [PETER laughs] What an asshole [referring to the character Bobadilla]. It's kind of offensive, but it's funny though.

MARCUS NANCE in conversation with
PETER COCKETT and MELINDA GOUGH

MELINDA: Can you talk about how costume shaped your feelings of masculinity in the role of Amintor?
MARCUS: Even in modern times, if I put a suit on, I feel physically different. And move physically different. If I put swimming trunks on, I physically am moving in a different way. [As Amintor I was wearing] just this leather [doublet], and I think there was a bit of puffy sleeves, and it was weighty. It automatically gives you a sense of what that person probably felt. And for women, again, I think you were saying it's even more informed, you know, if they have a really tight corset, and for men I don't think it's as big a difference. I don't think I had boots, but there's something about boots that really makes you feel – like a *guy* [laughs] …

Nowadays, we have this idea of what a man is supposed to be, how a man is supposed to move, and it always bothers me because I see a lot of feminine men that are straight, you know? And I'm like, why … why on stage does it always have to be defined in a certain way?

Figure 10.8. Marcus Nance, 2018 Stratford Festival Laboratory participant, as Amintor in *The Maid's Tragedy*. Photograph by David Campbell.

EMMA FRANKLAND

To be honest, I wished that I had been cast as another character – there was something ethically uncomfortable for me about portraying a person who was assigned female at birth (AFAB) when I was not. Regardless of the fact that the character (and true historical figure) of Moll undoubtably subverted gender expectations and was gender-nonconforming, I would like to see a non-binary AFAB person exploring Moll and the potential in their story (something that SL Grange has brilliantly explored in the UK with their early modern drag king project "Moll and the Future Kings"!).[11] But: embracing the necessity of the casting choices within the workshop, I suppose I related to Moll as someone unfettered by gender. Or perhaps a better way to

Figure 10.9. Emma Frankland, 2018 Stratford Festival Laboratory participant, as Moll Frith in *The Roaring Girl*. Photograph by David Campbell.

say that is to say someone unbothered by gender, despite the constraints and expectations that others place on Moll's body.

In playing Moll, I engaged with more masculine traits than I choose to present in my day-to-day life, which for me, as a trans woman with inconsistent passing privilege (by which I refer to the way in which other people might read my gender – for more on this topic see S. Bear Bergman's brilliant book *The Nearest Exit May Be Behind You*) creates difficult territory.[12]

If an AFAB actor plays a cross-dressing character who is subverting gender expectations, then, in the case of Moll Cutpurse, any choices that actor might make are in line with those the character might choose. For an actor assigned male at birth (AMAB), if I choose to portray Moll in a masculine style – clothes, swagger, voice – then there is a danger that I may be perceived to be a cisgender man. This is a complexity of casting that there wasn't really sufficient space to cover and which proves a challenge to trans actors and productions working with them, as indeed it does for trans people in our real lives.

There was undoubtably space where my and Moll's experiences might cross over. But there is a world of difference between the life of a twenty-first-century trans woman and a sixteenth-century gender-fucking butch.

It was particularly challenging playing the scene with Laxton, where much of the humour comes from their mistaking of Moll's gender and their attraction to Moll, as well as their embarrassment at being caught out. More time allowed to explore the nature of cis attraction to trans bodies and the ways in which the latter are fetishized and have assumptions placed upon them would have been helpful.

Facilitator Reflections

PETER COCKETT

Reading Natasha Korda's draft paper, I was most struck by the fact that the foundational *decora* of lightness, grace, and modesty applied to both men and women of the upper classes. The only difference in the sources is in the simple length of a stride. Since lightness and grace are generally associated with women today, I wondered if all early modern courtiers, male and female, would appear "feminine" within contemporary stereotypical lenses. Would a male Elizabethan courtier walking through a shopping mall today appear masculine by our normative standards? I suspect not. What possibilities for the performance of masculinity on contemporary stages are opened through this PaR engagement with historical evidence? Given that the majority of roles in these plays are for male-identifying characters, can shifting our understanding of historical presentations of masculinity free actors and directors from the pressure to push performers to embody stereotypical modern ideas of masculinity? Our movement exercise and the scene work that built on it, establishing a sustained lightness as the courtly default for movement and defining gendered difference solely in terms of length of step and expansiveness, brought all the courtly characters further away from today's performances of a masculinity stereotypically associated with heavy movements: punch, press, slash/kick, and wring.

Conrad Alexandrowicz presents strong evidence for the ways that actor training needs to be more accessible for queer and gender-nonconforming students.[13] And so we wonder: Could insights gleaned by working through the movement implications of historical evidence, in workshops like the one we facilitated, be taken up in future rehearsal rooms and classical training contexts as a way of making casting and performance more inclusive and equitable? Can we imagine rehearsal processes that do not demand conformity to assumptions about gender presentation just out of habit? Marcus Nance's frustration that theatre enforces a clearer binary on the performance of straight men than he witnesses in everyday life is telling. How can our rehearsal rooms and stages resist normative pressures rather than enforcing more conservative articulations of gender? Questioning normative ideas of gender presentation can be exciting parts of a rehearsal process, liberating actors and directors to explore expressive possibilities not traditionally associated with these old plays yet amply supported by historical evidence on courtly movement.

MELINDA GOUGH

At one moment during our gendered footwork movement workshop, Emma Frankland's agile and explosive Moll Cutpurse, dressed as a man, was matched with Marcus Nance's contained, statuesque Amintor. Their silent improvisation contrasted in terms of energy, with Frankland's sudden, light, indirect movements set alongside Nance's more sustained, weighty, direct comportment. Despite Amintor's nobility obviously outranking Moll's status, it was not entirely clear which character was more powerful in this dynamic face-off of contrasting movement styles. In scene work prior to this movement exercise, I had witnessed Frankland's Moll shift from short to lengthy strides when, suddenly drawing and wielding her sword, she identified herself to her opponent Laxton.[14] Through this shift in gait, Frankland's Moll was claiming for herself a social space typically reserved for men. Our later movement exercise and its focus on intersections between gender and rank revealed how, via movement and physicality, Frankland's Moll transgressed received hierarchies of gender but also social rank or class. Seeing Moll best a young gallant like Laxton was deeply satisfying, but watching her steal observers' attention away from the much more admirable noble figure of Amintor, through movement alone, was simply stunning. It was thrilling to see a woman actor and her lower status character take up such space. And yet, Frankland's commentary above articulates some of the risks to trans performers whose characters' transgressive gender presentations might result in harmful audience misgendering of the actors themselves. How can future PaR explorations work to mitigate such potential harms?

Frankland suggests that dedicated discussion on the fetishization of trans bodies could be fruitful. Additionally, increased opportunities for scholars to participate in embodied PaR exercises might be beneficial. Getting up on my feet during our workshop's movement exercises certainly drove home to me the risks undertaken by all actors, and especially gender-nonconforming actors. Prior to our workshop, I had read about the period's gendered codes of comportment, movement, and gesture, but as an academic trained primarily in literary studies and early theatre history, I hadn't had much opportunity to bring embodied affect and physicality into my research in a professionally sanctioned way. Our gendered footsteps exercise was something I was really looking forward to, but I also experienced an uncomfortable self-consciousness. An actor's comfort level with being watched is likely greater than my own, but the vulnerability that comes with being observed by others must always still be there. As I watched Frankland, Nance, and the other artists working on their feet in character during the second part of the movement exercise, my affective experience of vulnerability moments earlier, as an embodied mover being observed by others in the first part of our exercise, brought home to me just how much actors risk merely by virtue of their craft and even more so when their identities, and/ or the characters they play, challenge received constructions of gender, class, race, or physical and attitudinal barriers. Above, Frankland explicitly names some of these risks, but awareness of such challenges also underlies Marcus Nance's questioning of the restrictive binaries that continue to shape stage masculinity more generally, as well as André Morin's, Lily McEvenue's, and Denise Oucharek's recollections of "being bound up" and "forced" into unnatural, restrictive, and heavy expectations about noble masculinity and femininity in their scene work as Clara and Lucio from *Love's Cure* and Guzmán from *The Lieutenant Nun*.

What other exercises could scholars and artists dream up together to help share both the discoveries and the risks of embodied experiments about gender on stage, past and present? We hope that planning for such exercises and workshops might find inspiration in Maddie Krusto and Kitoko Mai's chapter 16 of this volume, as well as the "Guidance Document for Creating Trans-Affirming Theatre Spaces," collaboratively authored by a group of artists that includes two of this volume's contributors: Carmen Alvis and Emma Frankland.[15]

NOTES

1 Fletcher and Massinger, *Love's Cure*, ed. Diez.

2 Brathwaite, *English Gentleman.*

3 Shakespeare, *Merchant of Venice*, in *The Norton Complete Shakespeare*, 3rd ed.

4 Laban's written publication of his system, originally dating to 1950, can be found in the unfortunately gendered book *The Mastery of Movement.* Ewan

and Sagovsky's *Laban's Efforts in Action* gives a more up-to-date analysis regarding applications of Laban's theories to the craft of acting specifically. Alexandrowicz, *Acting Queer*, also proposes the use of Laban's movement language in rehearsal to subvert normative assumptions about gender presentation.

5 A revised version of Korda's pre-circulated workshop essay that incorporates reflections on our PaR experiments appears in Korda, "'Mincing Steps' and 'Manly Strides,'" chapter 9 of this volume.

6 For this work, Peter drew on his experience with the Shakespeare and the Queen's Men project and training provided in that project by choreographer and dance historian Dr. Emily Winerock. Our explorations also drew on scholarship by Karim-Cooper, *The Hand on the Shakespearean Stage*, 60, 93. For further discussion, see McManus, "Casting *The Roaring Girl*," chapter 8 of this volume.

7 For a discussion of this conventional posture associated with courtly women and how it would have been taken up, or not, by early modern boy actors, see also McManus, "Casting *The Roaring Girl*," chapter 8 of this volume, which cites work by Karim-Cooper, among others.

8 For a description of this exercise, adapted by Frankland from Split Britches's "Porch Sitting" public address system, see this volume's Introduction.

9 *Engendering the Stage in the Age of Shakespeare and Beyond at the Stratford Festival Theatre Laboratory* video, timestamp 3.15–3.30.

10 "In folio" is a reference to Lucio's line quoted above (*Love's Cure*, 2.2.17). *OED* cites this line as an example for the meaning "in a full and loose dress" (II.5.b).

11 Grange, "Moll and Future Kings." See also Clerkinworks, "Moll and the Future Kings."

12 Bergman, *Nearest Exit*.

13 See Alexandrowicz, *Acting Queer*, for more evidence of this need and potential offers for making actor training more accessible for queer presenting and gender-nonconforming students.

14 For a more lengthy discussion of such moments, see McManus, "Casting *The Roaring Girl*," chapter 8 of this volume.

15 Alvis et al, "Guidance Document for Creating Trans-Affirming Theatre Spaces." This document is published as part of Frankland's essay "Toward a Trans Canon."

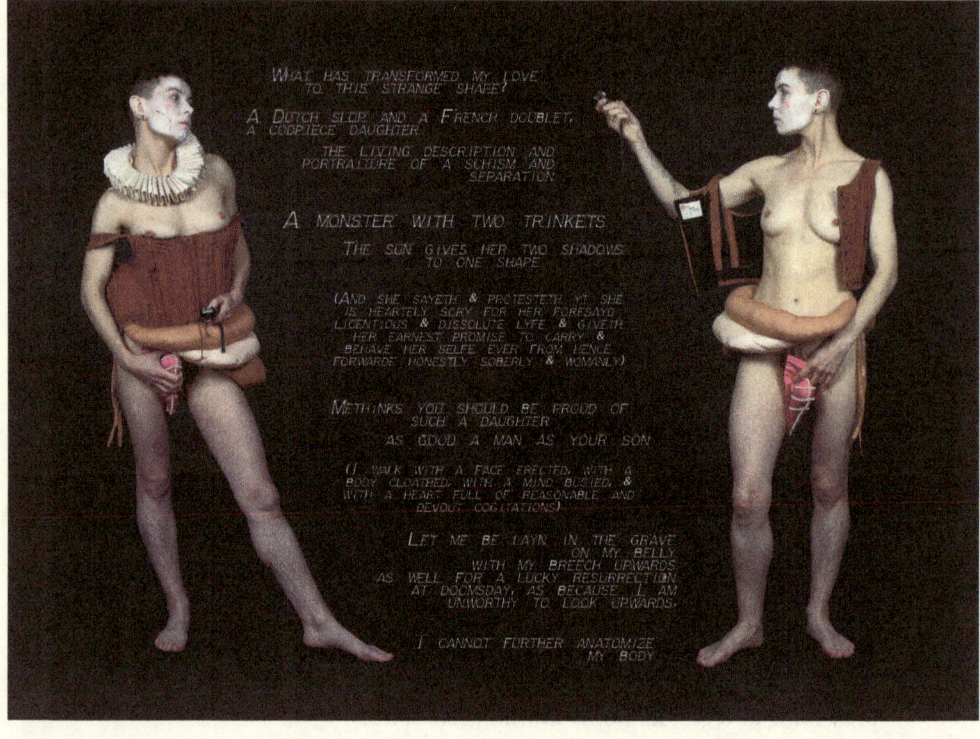

Two Shadows to One Shape, by E.M. Parry, 2022. Digital collage.

11 Playing with Gender: Stance, Gesture, Embodiment, and Prosthetics

E.M. PARRY WITH PETER COCKETT AND MELINDA GOUGH

MELINDA: Your piece "Two Shadows to One Shape" repurposes some photos from a series that you created several years ago, and in our conversations, you've mentioned that when you were first working on that series you were inspired by early modern portraits. Could you talk a bit about gender in portraiture and how that plays into your experiments here?

MAL: Most portraits that we encounter from that time are self-stagings of people. When I was working on these photos, I had been reading Anne Rosalind Jones and Peter Stallybrass on Renaissance materiality in connection with portraiture and self-fashioning, in particular the descriptions that they give of people sending their clothes to *sit for* them.[1] I had images in my mind of painting studios with lots of props and costumes, and I remembered my aunt, who's a drawing teacher, telling me about historical studios where they would have stock image books from which you could choose what kind of leaves or drapery, for example, you wanted in your painting. I was interested in the idea that this could also be the case for hands and bodies, and that clothes might be put onto a model or a dummy to be drawn separately from the sitter. So I was playing with ideas of a conglomeration of props and objects and bodies in a room, and how they might be put together in different ways. And then stance and gesture and posture become kind of additional props. There's also the overt gesture of actually taking the photograph, using the remote camera trigger as a prop in its own right – I'm clearly stating that I'm the one taking the photo and drawing attention to the skewed or layered temporality in the double image.

We're more used now, I think, to viewing portraits with the idea that they capture a moment in time or a moment of psychological insight. Deconstructing that idea by going back to how these images might actually originally have been created, you get something that's much more like an amalgamation of props and of objects and images, with a layering or blurring of different bodies and different temporalities as well. The portraits would be created over a long period of time in different stages. I felt there was something very queer and very trans about that: the intermingling of a conglomeration of temporalities, of props, prostheses, and bodies in order to construct an identity, to stage gender.

There's a connection, too, to my own body in flux. I was fairly early on in hormone transition at the point when I created the photos featured in the "Two Shadows" piece. By putting two images of my body opposite each other, as though they were sort of observing or encountering each other, I guess I was staging an entanglement of different objects, identities, events, and temporalities and drawing attention to their unfixity.

MELINDA: I'm intrigued by the way this piece speaks to questions of the materiality of gender, and of gender as not only performed but also prosthetic, both historically and today.

MAL: Yeah – I was also reading Will Fisher's book on *Materializing Gender in Early Modern English Literature and Culture* around the time that I was creating this image, I think. Fisher is looking at the material culture of gender in the period less as something that is performed than as something that's actually prosthetic or sort of external to the body, imposed or impressing on the body. Gender *exceeds* the body in some way.

My imagery here plays with active or performed stance, gesture, and physical embodiment, and I'm also playing with prosthetic gender signifiers that in some way impose on or exceed the body. That comes from thinking and research around early modern ideas of gender and the body framed by early modern medical understandings. When you look at clothing or costuming through the lens of humoral theory – which is very much about what you put into the body and what you take out of the body and an understanding of the body as this kind of porous, mutable situation – then clothing becomes very entangled with embodiment. It becomes entangled, literally, with the body. In the early modern period, they had this idea that what goes right next to the skin – the linen – absorbs some essences from the body, and I think you can flip that as well.

I take the concept of an interpenetrative relationship between body and clothes in this period as a key to understanding early modern anxieties around the gendered body and gendered cloth-ing. If you have this idea of the body as a porous situation, and that putting in and taking away from the body is literally influencing your essence, then adopting the clothing of the "opposite" gender is high risk. The stakes of putting on someone else's clothing and therefore potentially altering your identity – your gender, your rank, your status in society – are high. There's a material aspect to that, in the early modern period, that feels very different to how we think about gen-der now, when we're inclined to silo ideas of gender as behavioural and experiential, and sex as physical and biological – often for politi-cal reasons. But it also feels oddly adjacent to a contemporary under-standing of gender transition where there can be almost a fixation on bodily change. It speaks to my personal experience too, where I literally do absorb something into my skin that alters my sexed and gendered body. That was all swirling around in my thinking when I was creating these images.

They draw on my own experience, and my own embodied knowledge, as someone who works very intimately with cloth-ing, too, and with performing bodies, and with my own body as a performer. You quickly learn that bodies and clothing *are* co-pro-ducing and that, in the most basic way, wearing clothes affects the way you behave, how you hold yourself and take up space, the way you move and the way people move around you, the way you feel gravity act on you.

PETER: Can I ask a really specific question? The codpiece as a signifier is really clear, but I'm wondering about the doublet and bum rolls. I guess these are gendered things for you.

MAL: Definitely. The bum rolls! These weird sort of sausage things – they're worn under the skirts to pad out the hips, but I got really fascinated with them as objects by themselves – they almost look like organs have tumbled out of the body – they seem like a really weird, interesting, liminal object, I suppose. They're underwear in that they're not supposed to be seen, but they're also not exactly the kind of linen that is worn right next to the body and which soaks up fluids from the body and therefore almost becomes part of the body. So they take up some intermediary space, and I started using them in costumes, putting them outside rather than inside, which felt like a subversive thing to do, to put that kind of construc-tion on display.

The bodice is interesting too – it's actually called a "pair of bodies" in the early modern period, from which the word "bodice" derives, and the garment we'd probably think of as a corset would at this time have been called "stays" – so there's a sense of something multiple in the words themselves that reinforces an idea of clothing as very piecemeal, as assemblage. They're also interesting because they're very flattening to the bust, and wearing them feels a bit like wearing a binder. They actually compress and give a flattened and quite ambiguous silhouette that can feel quite masculine, although they're a female-signifying garment.

So many of the things that we would think of as very typically Elizabethan, I think, are very ambiguously gendered. The silhouette is quite similar: male and female chests are padded and squished; they flatten to become quite similar and then angle down to narrow waists and spreading hips. I get so fascinated by all of the compression and all of these distortions of the body and constructions and additions. As somebody who is interested in playing with gender in my work and my performance but also has lived experience of changing my body through both things I put on externally and things I absorb into it internally, this is all very sensitive, rich territory for me.

MELINDA: This makes me think about how, on the one hand, in our gendered movement exercise at the workshop, Peter was trying to draw attention to a kind of levelling out of gender difference through these coded class deportments: the idea that a need to level up in terms of class through movement – grace, stance, carriage – made for more similarities than differences along this continuum of gender. But at the same time, a lot of our scene work was wrestling with instances of rank being codified, and things like honour being upheld, through policing of a gender binary. I'm thinking of the *Love's Cure* scene, where family honour is upheld through teaching the children to embody rank in a very binary gendered way, like the honour won't be upheld if the gender binary isn't upheld. And the way that works itself out in the play is through prosthetic gender. Clara has to take off the sword and put on the farthingale, and Lucio has to take up the sword and put on boots that change his carriage. There was tension in our work between a more utopian and a not so utopian idea regarding the intersection of class with gender. Your image, Mal, makes me rethink what we were doing: because I think we initially wanted to talk with you about how, in your image, there is a binary, but actually it's more fluid. In this image but also in all of them.

PETER: I like what both of you are saying, this sense that the levelling up is about the higher classes, how they will be graceful, they'll be light on their feet. So they seem like they're closer to heaven, less attached to the dirtiness of the earth. They become these galactic beings who are operating on a different plane. But then, between those there's probably still a lot of space to say, "But men are going to be graceful in this way and women can be graceful in this way," where men wear these clothes and women wear these clothes, and there's a lot of language in the scenes that we did about the stiffness of the clothes that Lucio has to put on compared to the moving in folio in the women's dress and how much Clara hates the "scurvy farthingales."

MAL: This is interesting to me in that it tracks with what a lot of early modern conduct manuals suggest – that practice and habituation are essential to embodiment. There's an emphasis on gesture, posture, and gait *appearing* to be effortless, alongside an acknowledgment that it actually takes conscious effort and practice. The idea that Lucio and Clara both find the unfamiliar garments "stiff," constraining, or uncomfortable is quite equalizing – it's not the clothes or the bodies themselves that have an innate quality, or relationality, but their relative familiarity. It's a very Butlerian idea! Having experienced wearing those kind of clothes, they do have a stiffness, and a heaviness, but there's a sense in which that becomes less constricting as you learn to move *with* rather than *against* them. They have the potential to mould or impose behaviour. And the stiffness and heaviness definitely increases the further up the social scale you go. Working people of any gender would need more mobility – so we're probably encountering a manifestation of an idea here, too, that binary gender dimorphism is something aspirational and to do with culture and status. That tension between something inherent and something that has to be striven for and maintained. The conduct manuals seem to be acknowledging that moving gracefully and effortlessly in such clothing is a challenging feat.

Ruffs have become an important motif in my work too. Partly because they feel like such a classic signifier of Elizabethanness, and there's a campy, draggy aspect to the broad brush strokes of that which appeals to me – it's historical drag. But in their own era, they have a much more complicated iconography and politics to them, which is enmeshed with class and status – the higher up in the social hierarchy you are, the more likely you would be to have ruffs and the larger they would be. Making them was incredibly labour intensive, and ruffs led a slightly fluid life of their own because not only do they have to be sewn together, they also then have to be soaked in starch and set using ruff-setting tools (like long heated metal pokers) and then pinned together – or glued with blobs of wax. Their "unset" form is very different. Different hues could be temporarily added to them by colouring the starch. So they're quite unfixed, malleable objects. It's symbolic, perhaps, that they separate the head off from the body at a moment in history when Cartesian philosophy is emergent and when people are starting to think about the body in very different ways – ways that still inform how we think about gender, class, and race, and how we value different kinds of knowledge and intelligence. The body begins to be seen as something unruly, dirty, or animalistic that needs to be disciplined, controlled, even punished, by the mind. Which informs a kyriarchy of class, race, gender, etc., based on an aspirational idea of head/body dichotomy. And of course, ruffs are cutting heads off from bodies in metaphorical ways at a time when it would have been part of a lot of people's lived experience to literally see heads removed from bodies as a capital punishment.

PETER: Can you talk a little bit about costume fittings and how actors respond to wearing the clothes you design for them and what you see of this co-producing relationship?

MAL: It's something that I've always been so interested in, from when I first started out working in costuming. You know how much of a difference clothing makes to help people embody characters, and it's quite difficult often, within the way theatre is generally practised, to be able to rehearse with costumes as much as you'd like, so often actors meet their costumes quite late on in the process. But the more you're able to work with costumes, the more that informs the way people move, feel, behave, and, potentially, how they understand their characters. You move 100 per cent differently when you're breaking in stiff, heavy clothing than when it's worn in, and a lot of it is about what you're habituated to as well. If those clothes feel alien to you – which is quite interesting to think of in the context of *Love's Cure*, where each sibling is wearing clothing that feels alien, that isn't habituated …

Corsets in the early modern period are very structured, heavily boned things, and it's really important to get used to wearing that because initially it will likely feel stiff and restrictive. But the more people wear them, clothing of that kind actually moulds to the person's body and starts to feel like *part of* the body, and so it alters the way you move, but you also have an effect on it. People weren't buying clothes off the peg, so they had a much more personalized relationship to clothing, unlike anything we have now in a western clothing economy. Now we have clothing that's anonymized and worked out to standardized sizes. There's no idea of standard sizes in this era; everything would be either completely bespoke, or acquired second-hand, sometimes even inherited, and then adapted or altered to fit, and the more you wore those garments, the more they influenced your own behaviour and your own comportment, and the more your comportment seeped into them and influenced them too.

And I suppose that's actually quite an interesting parallel with the way theatre works, because if you're doing period shows, especially somewhere like Shakespeare's Globe, which has a lot of resources, either things will be specially made for an actor or they'll be second-hand, something that's been at some point specifically made for somebody else, which, in fact, has its own history: someone else's body has informed those clothes, at some point, and then either it'll fit perfectly or it'll have to be altered to fit your body – either way, you'll have a very embodied relationship with it. They have long runs at the Globe, so the actors get used to wearing those clothes for a season and really develop a relationship with them. They might feel quite alien the first time people are wearing them, but by the end of the season, you've worn it so many times, your sweat has soaked into it and there'll be some kind of actual literal physical exchange with that costume, and you'll both have informed and affected each other. And as with actual early modern clothing, a lot of it can't really be washed – so the clothes really are absorbing peoples' essence in a literal way. It's interesting seeing people get used to moving in these costumes. They have a real weight to them, they kind of drag through the air, so they can make people start to move almost in slow motion or in a dance-like sort of way – they give you a different relationship to gravity, to space, even to time.

I could go on for ages about how costumes and bodies affect each other … This has made me think of something that isn't related but I just would like to just drop in, which is how Natasha Korda's chapter on gendered footwork for this book made me think of my experience at the Globe. She talks about the feet being very important because they're on the eye-level of the groundlings, and that's absolutely true, I can attest as a designer. Footwear and shoes become very important on that stage, much more so than any other stage I've worked – it's generally very rare, in most contemporary theatre spaces, to put audience at shoe level – and so shoes as a kind of storytelling language started to become more important in the Globe shows I worked on. Especially in *Hamlet*, where we played some little games with who was wearing what shoes and how they linked certain characters to each other.[2] Shubham Saraf, who played Ophelia, is a cis male actor, and he was wearing an Elizabethan dress, but he wore little sneakers that were very similar to the ones Hamlet (who was in contemporary masculine clothing) was wearing.

On most stages, people wouldn't necessarily notice that beneath the long skirt, but on that stage, it definitely was something that people saw, and he would sometimes swing his skirt a little bit so you could get a little flash of sneaker. It was interesting collaborating with him on his relationship to gendered embodiment in that show through the costume choices we made – we talked in that rehearsal process about playing the character and the status of the character, and not necessarily "performing gender" but letting clothes do some of that work for the actor.

I've been in a lot of rehearsal rooms where people are talking about performing gender, and it becomes quite drag-like, almost, with the idea that men move in this way and women move in that way, and it can rely heavily on clichés. I remember Michelle Terry specifically pushing back on that idea, talking about past experiences where there's "cross-gender" casting and people are asked to "act like a man," and the cliché is "men take up more space, men sit with their legs apart, men make big gestures," and she's like, "well my husband is a man and he doesn't do any of that."

I talked about this with actors in their costume fittings, about allowing clothes to do that work, allowing them to guide the way you move, the way you take up space, letting the clothes take the lead, almost: rather than performing gender, allowing your garments to inform your embodiment and trusting that an idea of gender emerges. I think a lot about Shubham and how he played Ophelia. He wasn't particularly "performing gender"; rather, he was acting the part of someone who wears those clothes and moves in the way that you have to when you wear these clothes and have that particular role in the play and in the world, a place of gender imposed by other people mostly. By questioning what that means, and having that little touch of wearing contemporary footwear, that just gave it a little twist, which was interesting and began to subvert and deconstruct it. To question, I suppose, what agency Ophelia has in that world, how much her role – both within the imagined world of the play and within its dramaturgical structure – has been mapped out for her by other people and the moments when she might be trying to push back.

Once we've decided on the shoes in a fitting, I'm often asked by actors, "Can I have them for rehearsals?" A lot of actors seem to find shoes inform everything else, which makes a lot of sense. The way you tread and the way you move through space could be said to come from the ground – or the shoes – up.

Intriguing to think, then, that in this era there isn't necessarily a huge amount of differentiation between male and female footwear. The stylings are quite similar. Probably the most obvious kinds of differentiation aren't necessarily so much to do with gender as they are to do with social role and job, which then maps onto gender more secondarily. Another funny thing about shoes in the early modern period is that they're not left or right. I suppose over time, they would mould to someone's foot and *become* left and right through wear, so again there's the idea of bodies and clothes co-mingling, their boundaries blurring, clothes becoming an extension of the body.

MELINDA: Like corsets, as we discussed earlier!

I have a different question about your piece. I have been reading about actors and white make-up, and I'm wondering if that's a subtle marker of the boy actor, in your images here as well?

MAL: That's definitely in there – but on my face it becomes a more complicated layering of gender signifiers. Interestingly, when I was making them, I found that by painting my face, it brought out more gender ambiguity, and my face looked more androgynous, rather than more feminine, with that layer of paint on. Wearing make-up to look pale would have been associated with women, but it was also a class thing; elite men sometimes used cosmetics as well, and being paler was generally associated with being higher status and with an idea of purity – at a time when whiteness as a category and white supremacy as an ideology were beginning to be constructed (as I talk about in the conversation about "Boi-Actrx" in chapter 12 of this volume). We know that actors used cosmetics to alter their appearance in other ways than gender, and because cosmetics were understood more generally as feminized, then perhaps for actors – even actors portraying male characters – wearing them may have made them read, or feel, more gender-ambiguous. Cosmetics as a kind of drag, even if not intentionally deployed as such. I liked too the contrast between the made-up face and the naked body; to have my face "clothed" in a sense, and to put that alongside naked skin.

PETER: What about the dotted lines on the image on the left?

MAL: That's a reference to surgery, an idea of cosmetic surgery. I've had temporary fillers in my face since these pictures were taken, and in the consultations both me and the person doing them would draw on my face – another kind of collaborative gender-fashioning. They're like the dotted lines you cut along on clothing patterns too. I was thinking about other ways to manipulate appearance and refashion the body – alluding to that, alongside the paint and clothing and gesture and embodiment – presenting gender as a bricolage; showing the workings of gender construction.

It's interesting to talk about the images in this way and just sort of pull out things that were swirling around in my mind, stuff that I was reading and thinking about but not necessarily articulating in this way as I made them. They were made in a very instinctive, improvisational way. I mean that's the point, isn't it? They do something that an essay doesn't, and they speak in their own way, and I suppose, when I talk about them, it could sound as though very meticulous planning and staging went in. Which, in a sense, it did – there was a lot of gathering and a lot of thinking and researching and a lot of careful collating and curating, but then I didn't plan what the images were actually going to be. I had a collection of items, I had my body, and I had a space, and a certain, limited amount of time I was able to be in that space. So there was a sense of one-off performance to it on multiple levels, and the images came out of a playful, instinctive creative process, with very little time for reflection and editing as I was making them. And then I'm discovering what I made, afterwards – becoming an audience to my own work as well as coming to it with an artist's eye, and I'm reading and writing and speaking back into it.

PETER: I think that really speaks well to the way that performance as research works.

MAL: Yeah, you know, you put things in a room and you improvise, and accidents happen and ideas pop into your head and –

PETER: Because you've thought about it in advance and you've been thinking about these things for a long time, then that emerges in the work and that speaks back to a lot of thinking and reading that you've done.

MAL: Hopefully, the figures kind of speak for themselves, and they're an interesting image without needing to know or read about any of the stuff that we've spoken of, but I'd like to think these conversations can enrich the experience of looking at them.

MELINDA: I'll just ask one more question then. To what extent is *The Roaring Girl* and Moll Frith – or was it at the time – influencing how you play with stance and visual concepts?

MAL: What I find interesting is that I'm not sure their influence was on a conscious level when I was taking those particular photographs, but it was definitely present – Mary Frith's been part of my mental world for a long time. And around that time – possibly even the same day – I made some portraits of SL Grange actually posing as Moll.[3] But what was interesting to me about making this particular work for this volume was that I already had this image of the two figures facing each other. I'd been playing with stances and gestures from Renaissance portraiture imagery – so borrowing from and occupying the physical space of fairly elite and high-status men and women who had a lot of agency in their self-fashioning and presentation. And I'd chosen to place those two self-portraits face to face, but there was this space between them, and I knew that *something* needed to go in that space – it felt unfinished. I'd been playing around with different kinds of text, and nothing was quite landing.

Then when we started having conversations about Frith and *The Roaring Girl*, and I looked at some of those different texts, that's when it began to come into focus. I began chopping up the texts, putting them together in different ways, and placing them in the gap between the figures, and it felt like that drew the two images together and added additional layers that spoke to it, drew something out of it, that offered a reading of the image as a whole and made a new sense of it, somehow. I'm not sure that I see the figures as *versions of* Moll so much as adjacent. Like the text, they're commentary more than portraiture. It's not literal representation. It's more about occupying a space of Mollishness.

The text intersperses lines from *The Roaring Girl* with quotes from the consistory court records of Frith's trial for indecency and quotes from *The Life and Death of Mrs. Mary Frith.*[4] This purports to be an autobiography, although it was almost certainly ghost-written; how much direct involvement Frith actually had in it isn't known (it was published after her death – at least some of it may be recorded or remembered from actual conversations by someone who knew her, but we don't know). There are so many layers to Moll/Mall/Mary (SL Grange,[5] who's my go-to authority on M.F., has said they now prefer to use Mary rather than Moll, as that seems to have been Frith's own preference, and "Moll" might be considered a slur) – and to how they presented themself, how they were presented and staged and co-opted by others for their own purposes – sensationalism, celebration, moralizing … So the texts play with those different voices: words that report on Mary in what we might think of as the "official" archive – legal documents that (try to) fix her into a traceable, albeit troublesome subject – alongside descriptions of a fictionalized version of her – a fictionalized version that she may actually have shared a stage with when she performed at the Fortune Theatre – as well as text from *The Roaring Girl* that's spoken about, the *other* Mary in the play, so additional layers of slippage and confusion, alongside what may or may not be her own words.

The juxtaposition of the two images also references the two versions of the frontispiece to *The Roaring Girl* – which are theorized to depict the boy actress who played Moll (the more well-known image where she's very upright with a direct gaze) with the less well-known one depicting the real-life Mary (which has more litheness and movement to it, with the eyes kind of turned away); seemingly the depiction of M.F. herself onstage was considered too subversive for later editions.[6] When I think of M.F., I think of someone who seems determined to author themself in defiance of what anyone else might want them to be, in their own lifetime. But what we now have left of them are these projections by other people – like shells or skins they've outgrown and shucked off.

So with the two images, which play with layers and signifiers of gendered embodiment but don't fix them or present a clear binary, juxtaposed with the cut-up text, we get multiple layers and versions of Moll/Mal/Mary. A conglomerate – or gender assemblage, in the words of Rachel Hann[7] – which, I suppose, ultimately tells a story of identity, not as essence but as aggregate: multi-authored and multivalently material, precarious, performative, and malleable.

NOTES

1 Jones and Stallybrass, *Renaissance Clothing*.
2 Shakespeare, *Hamlet*, directed by Holmes and While, 2018.
3 For one such portrait, see Grange, "Moll Frith."
4 Middleton and Dekker, *The Roaring Girl*, ed. Mulholland. *Consistory of London Correction Book* for November 1611 to October 1613 (London Metropolitan Archives, DL/C/310, fols 19–20), transcribed and analysed in Mulholland, "The Date of *The Roaring Girl*," also reprinted in Mulholland's edition of the play. *The Life and Death of Mrs. Mary Frith* (London: 1662), reprinted in *The Life and Death of Mrs. Mary Frith*, ed. Nakayama.
5 I'm indebted to SL Grange, whose work on Mary Frith has and continues to inform and inspire me.
6 Ungerer, "Mary Frith, Alias Moll Cutpurse."

7 Parry explains further: "In a recent book chapter, Rachel Hann theorizes the work of artist and drag performer Sin Wai Kin as assemblage (after Jasbir Puar), arguing for scenographic practices as a lens and critical framework for revealing and deconstructing a phenomenology of gender. Hann's articulation speaks deeply to my own work exploring gendered embodiment and performance across drag, fine art, and scenography." See Hann, "Gender-Assemblages."

PART SIX

Disruptive Boys

Boi-Actrx #1: Self-portrait as Nathan Field, by E.M. Parry, 2022.
Performance-for-camera.

Boi-Actrx #2: Self-portrait as Nathan Field, by E.M. Parry, 2022.
Performance-for-camera.

12 Disruptive Affects: Portraiture, Staging, and Drag

E.M. PARRY WITH PETER COCKETT AND MELINDA GOUGH

Day two of the workshop began with a short video introducing the acting company and guest artists to the boy players of the professional London stages. These boys, especially the adolescents who acted the parts of girls and women in adult companies, were famous in their day. Stephen Hammerton, Richard (Dick) Robinson, and Nathan Field are just three examples. These were highly trained, virtuosic performers, and casting practices that featured such "boy actresses" made playful explorations of gender a particularly exciting feature of the London playhouses.[1]

Writers who opposed the theatre railed against such boy players, alleging their power to morally corrupt audiences through their erotic appeal and fearing the boys' capacity, when dressed in women's attire, to blur distinctions between male and female. Our video asked: what if Puritan assertions about the disruptive appeal of boy actors famous for feminine gender expression on stage, and sometimes off stage as well, were well-founded?

Our video invited workshop participants to take such hints of erotic and gendered complexity as an invitation to mine early modern plays, including those written originally for the "all-male" London commercial stage, for transformative affective potential. We laid down a provocation: if Shakespeare's theatre was an art form that centred queer, non-binary genders and provoked a complex range of desires from its heterogeneous audience, what might be possible if we embraced this subversive power and ran with it in our scene work and beyond?

The presentation of the video initially provoked a powerful – and to us unexpected – reaction among some participants. Questions arose about whether celebrating boy actors famous for playing women, and the potentially queer affects mobilized by their performances, risked whitewashing a historical period in which what we now call homosexuality was a capital crime. This discussion led to further questions about our workshop's goals as a whole: to what extent might a focus on women performers from the early modern period similarly risk glossing over an oppressive past?

We paused the day's activities to give time for extended discussion of these issues. Scholars and artists discussed how sodomy was defined and wielded in legal and political contexts from the period; noted the relative acceptance of homoerotic friendship and artistic collaboration between playwrights Francis Beaumont and John Fletcher, who "lived together on the Banke side, not far from the Play-house, both batchelors; [and] lay together"; and pointed to textual evidence of queer, trans, and gender-nonconforming plot lines and characters in Elizabethan plays such as John Lyly's *Galatea.*[2]

And yet questions remained. Reflecting on this thorniness, Stratford company actor André Morin, speaking with Peter and Melinda following the workshop, highlights some of the ongoing ethical questions at stake:

[Workshop participants were] pointing out successful moments in history where perhaps these two men [Beaumont and Fletcher] had a gay relationship living by the river together. Or perhaps this person [Antonio de Erauso] was given the freedom to express himself as a trans person in society or was allowed to be out in society in a dress [boy actresses]. And this person was given, or not given … "Given" is the wrong word for all three situations. These people *earned* their right to live as a gay couple along the Thames. This person *earned* their right to express themselves as a trans person in society. This person *earned* their right to run a theatre company and tour Europe. These people *earned* it. And they must have worked incredibly hard against unbelievable odds. And what I thought we were doing was saying, "Look at these examples; things weren't all that bad after all." It's a logical fallacy, like saying that because someone escapes poverty to live a successful life, that means that poverty isn't so bad after all because it produced a success story. But that does not express the reality of those people who are still trapped in that poverty system. So there are people who through their genius, their humanity, their familial identity are able to transcend the expectations of their worth and live as themselves, but those people are rare. They are few and far between. And what I experienced, what I thought, was that we were saying, "Look at these examples; life wasn't so bad."

And you don't really have to look much farther than Oscar Wilde to say, "Things could turn like that, and then it's all over." It's not very far off, and it happens like that [snaps fingers]. And then everything changes, and all those privileges disappear. And all you need is one person in power to make that choice, and then it's all over.

So those people, no matter how successful they were – and I don't know the history so I can't actually speak with any authority – in my imagination they were living on the razor's edge. And so that's why I reacted the way I reacted. Because I think in some ways it's a whitewash if you present it as "things weren't so bad." I think it does disservice to the people who really, really suffered because of who they were, who weren't brilliant geniuses and couldn't transcend the expectations of society. And had to live a life in constant fear or, you know, be burnt at the stake … The memory of those people, I think, deserves service.[3]

As Morin's comments indicate, our discussion at the workshop regarding these issues was expansive, emotional, and necessarily inconclusive. As facilitators, we were called upon to redefine our objectives and took the opportunity to affirm that our goals regarding scene work experimentation were not fixed, nor did we have a position to prove. We were left with the feeling that the company wanted more clarity of intention, more certainty of objective, than we were able to provide. Our hope was that, through commitment to the work, new understandings could begin to emerge.

As a way of inviting this volume's readers into such ongoing thinking about the messy ethical stakes of turning to the past in order to explore gender, sexuality, desire, and performance both in the early modern period and today, we shared our *Disruptive Boys* video with E.M. Parry. Prompted in part by the video's discussion of Nathan Field's portrait (Figure 12.1), Parry's "Boi-Actrx" artwork draws equally on their experience as a drag king, their knowledge of early modern art and theatre history, and their professional experience as a costume designer. Parry's "Boi-Actrx" diptych expands and extends questions raised at the workshop. Parry's pieces subtly frame, present, and deconstruct gender and complicate the relationship between artist/sitter and audience/viewer, and in these ways, challenge us to continue to think deeply about the affective complexities that gendered performances of these colonial texts have the potential to prompt today.

Parry's "Boi-Actrx" images stand alone as powerful examples of practice as research. In the spirit of this volume, however, we include the following conversation with Parry to give readers further insight into the collaborative inquiry and artistic techniques behind their creation.

PETER: How does your approach in this piece relate to your understanding of self-fashioning?

MAL: I've been interested in ideas of self-fashioning in early modern portraiture for a while. Anne Rosalind Jones and Peter Stallybrass talk about the amount of agency that sitters in portraits had over those portraits.[4] There was a collaboration between the person portrayed and the person portraying, and arguably, the person depicted in the portrait has more power and status and agency than the artist. A more modern idea is that the artist has the power and the agency, and the person in the image doesn't really have any agency and is potentially quite objectified. Artists – especially female, assigned female at birth (AFAB), queer, and other artists who have historically been marginalized, people who have historically been more likely to be historicized

Figure 12.1. British School, *Nathan Field*, c.1615, oil on panel, 56.5 × 42.2 cm, DPG385. Dulwich Picture Gallery, London.

or presented as subject than as agent – minoritized artists have often used self-portraiture as a way to repurpose that gaze.

And then today we have this situation where selfies are one of the most ubiquitous forms of imagery and self-fashioning that we have. The ability to take a good selfie is seen as a very important part of being a person in a lot of cultures and communities, and especially for performers. When you're a performer, you're presenting an image when you're actually onstage, but for a lot of drag performers, having a social media presence is also really important, and the ways in which people stage themselves on the little micro-theatres of social media become highly significant. A lot of that is about being able to take a good selfie.

So these images are me channelling Nathan Field into a contemporary drag king persona – using his portrait [Figure 12.1] as inspiration but then loosely messing with that. I really like what Natasha Korda says about that image of Field in her beautiful essay about Shakespeare's laundry list.[5] What feels striking about the Field portrait is this idea of empowerment. Field is staging himself as a gentleman, as someone of a certain social status, and Korda also argues that the white shirt is commenting on the sitter's moral and even spiritual status. This would have been quite an assertive statement for an actor, as someone who made their money doing this slightly disreputable or ungentlemanly thing. Especially for assigned male people who acted women's parts: we know there was social anxiety around that, as well as a lot of excitement and titillation. Field is known for this quite subversive, ambiguous career that people had very different opinions and emotions about. So this staging of himself as someone who possesses masculine, gentlemanly virtues and a particular socio-economic status makes this a thickly signifying image. I felt there was a lot to play with in restaging that, as somebody who was assigned female but who's transitioned to a more masculine and more ambiguous presentation and way of living in the world and as somebody who uses drag in their work and performs as a drag king – and my main drag king character is called Mal Content and he's an Elizabethan actor, so it nods to my existing practice. I suppose that's also true of Field's portrait – it portrays the actor, but people viewing it would have also had in mind characters that he'd played – it's multilayered. I invented a particular drag look specifically for these images. It draws on my regular drag character, but it's a lot more glamorized – a lot more glamorous, I would say. I'm leaning into more contemporary glamour in this piece, I suppose, and playing around with agency and self-fashioning and self-empowerment within portraiture.

The contouring: it's classic drag king contouring. Contouring has an interesting cultural history! Facial contouring has become a big thing in the last ten years or so – you can buy contouring kits from most high-street make-up outlets, and there are lots of make-up tutorials on how to do it. It's mainly used by women, but there are contouring kits marketed to men as well. It uses illusionistic painting techniques to alter the shape of facial features, using a palette of skin tones that range from light to dark. It's designed to be especially effective on camera, because it's to do with the play of light and shadow – so it can look quite exaggerated in the flesh, but that's now become a fashionable look in itself. It's become a very mainstream thing because being on camera has become such a big part of a lot of people's lives, but the techniques derive, originally, from theatrical make-up, and there's a significant influence from drag culture, especially, I think – drag queen make-up that's designed to reshape "masculine" features as more traditionally "feminine" – repackaged and sold back to cis women. (Often it's a version of "feminine" that's quite rooted in white, eurocentric, fat-phobic beauty ideals too.) It's a strange blurring of worlds and signifiers – what's basically theatre/drag make-up, repackaged and sold back to (mainly) cis women. It's a neat demonstration of the performativity, plasticity, and prosthetics of gender. But kind of a depressing example too of how one very narrow, homogenized version of drag – that exemplified by RuPaul's *Drag Race* (which notoriously excludes drag kings, AFAB performers, and, until very recently, trans women) – has been co-opted by capitalism, its subversive potential defanged and commodified. Drag kings have adapted these techniques to imitate or enhance traditionally "masculine" facial structure – so, emphasizing the jaw, painting the chin to look more square, emphasizing the bone structure of the nose, highlighting the brow bones. Broadly speaking, you're enlarging and squaring out facial features, whereas traditional drag queen contouring tends to be about softening and rounding the shape of the face and making certain features – nose, chin, brow – appear smaller. And everyone wants good cheekbones!

My usual drag make-up is more heavily theatrical and stylized, and quite painterly looking – you can see the brush strokes – and kind of comic-grotesque, a sort of Grand-Guignol clown vibe. I toned that down for these images, with subtler, more illusionistic/naturalistic levels of contouring – referencing what's become quite an iconic signifier of drag kings – but of course, it's in white-face, with a glitter beard and eyebrows, where drag make-up tends to be in more "natural"-looking skin tones. And it's still rough-looking, you can

see the sponge and brush marks – where contouring is traditionally
all about smooth blending. I said just now that contouring derives
from theatre make-up techniques, but theatre has borrowed these
techniques in turn from painting – the use of light and shade to
create the illusion of depth is what a painter would do in a portrait.
Introducing painting into a photographic portrait that I've lit and
staged to feel very painterly mixes the signifiers and confuses the eye.
It disrupts the viewer's sense of what is "real," draws attention to flesh
and paint and garments, and where they meet and blur.

In this piece, the contouring is signifying drag and also leaning
into a glamour more usually associated with drag queens – but showing its workings and artificiality. I'm broadly generalizing here –
there are so many different kinds of drag, and the drag king and
drag thing scenes are incredibly diverse in how they frame and
explore gender – but I'd suggest that drag kings are more often paro-
dying masculinity in a way that isn't especially glamorous or about
foregrounding beauty. So I was interested in doing something that
emphasized beauty and glamour, and mixed signifiers of gender, in
a way that demonstrated their plasticity and potential for movement
across genders.

Korda's essay also references the use of white in the original painting – the whiteness of Field's shirt setting off the exaggerated (and
potentially feminizing) whiteness of his skin as a signifier of moral
and spiritual purity at a time when ideas of racialized whiteness and
white supremacy were emergent in their construction. The use of
white face make-up, and the contrast with the rest of my unpainted
skin, alludes too to that history of race as sociopolitical construct,
co-terminous with gender, with the potential to be deconstructed as
drag.

There are other elements in both images that are important to
the deconstruction of drag – playing with masculine- and feminine-
coded signifiers and what's in the frame and what's outside of it. It's
clear that I'm the person taking the picture in each of these, staging myself with some agency – as Field is doing by commissioning
his own portrait. The first image is riffing on that, looking directly
into the camera, chin raised, and outside of the frame; the camera
remote control is standing in for a cock – or a codpiece. It's quite
a broad, draggy, performative masculinity, with a lot of swagger –
restaging Field as this rock-star celebrity persona. The other one,
where I'm turned to the side, channels and subverts Field's image
in other ways – the pose is closer, but exaggerated and camped
up, so it becomes more explicitly come-hither. And outside of the

frame, the shirt is pulled down to reveal taped-down breasts – again, it's a drag trope, revealing an absence or something that could be read as "false" or disguised.

In the original portrait, Field's eyes are looking at the viewer, but his head and body are three quarters on, so it's not a direct gaze, and there's something quite ambiguous about it. Korda reads it as modest; it could also read as coy, a little sultry or seductive, even. His chest and arms are visible through this slightly diaphanous shirt, and there's the pale skin (that would have had associations with femininity as well as with a more elite status). His hair is worn long and loose, but it's swept behind his back, so we can't see *how* long it is – it's another ambiguous feature and interesting to think about in the context of his playing female parts. There tends to be an assumption that male actors sort of "graduated" from playing female roles as they got older, but evidence suggests that some actors continued to play female roles into adulthood, possibly alternating them with male roles – as a designer and a performer it makes me wonder if that long hair was a feature of his female presentation and if this suggests that he was still playing female roles at this time. At the same time, the moustache and beard perhaps serve to reassert or remind us of his maleness. He's definitely staging himself as a gentleman, and as a masculine person, and simultaneously there's something sort of feminine about the way he's presenting as well – or, perhaps, being presented by the painter. It's not a straightforward image on any level. It's difficult to know how it would be read at the time, in the context of how masculinity was staged by different people, and ultimately there is no one way of staging masculinity, no matter how heavily policed gender is. I wanted to play around with that idea, riffing on the different ways in which Field's portrait stages his gender identity(s) and reimagining him through drag imagery.

PETER: I always think that Field's portrait has a lot of markers of what we might identify with femininity today, but hearing that the soft shirt also signified masculinity as well as class status tells us that, clearly, the markers of gender, and of rank as well, shift over time.

MAL: Yeah, and what is sexy really shifts culturally, doesn't it. There's potentially something quite subversive in Field wearing a shirt – essentially an undergarment – rather than a doublet (outer garment). Following Korda, who emphasizes the significance of garments worn next to the body within the context of humoral theory (in which the body is seen as a porous and fluctuating situation), we can read the shirt as a kind of liminal garment. Shirts or shifts were liminal too in that the design of them was less differentiated male to female than the outer garments, which again suggests the idea of gender and identity as perhaps working from the outside in rather than the inside out. Korda emphasizes the coding of the shirt in relation to spiritual purity, and racialized whiteness as well, but there's also something intimate, potentially titillating, in someone staging themself in what would be read as semi-dressed in a way that's less obvious to us now. It's a really ambiguous image.

PETER: I get a real sense from your pictures of the potential for the boys to be superstars, that they were a big part of the attraction for playgoers: not just the leading man, but the leading boy.

MAL: Yeah, it was really fun to embody that myself, to take on that glamour and specifically that cross-dressing glamour. The drag I usually do isn't particularly glamorous or celebrating beauty! And to get to play with ambiguous signifiers of glamour too – glitter, the pearl-drop earring … (my version is from Claire's Accessories and has a tiny unicorn suspended from a snow globe). And playing with being quite alluring, in the image with the exposed shoulder, in a way I associate more with performative femininity – repurposing that within a masculine presentation and where it's ambiguous who I'm trying to allure … Nice to take up that space as well because drag kings tend not to take up that much space, culturally. They're much more under the radar and kind of fringe performers, whereas drag queens, assigned male people crossdressing, are having a massive cultural moment, to the point where I would say drag has become kind of mainstream.

MELINDA: At the same time, we're in a terrible moment of intense, very real backlash against rights for queer and trans people, including far-right protests outside drag story hours at public libraries and even actual laws being passed at the state level in the United States prohibiting drag in public, prohibitions on children attending drag shows, and more.[6]

MAL: Yes. Things have really heated up here in the UK too since we first talked about these images – it feels important to acknowledge that, and the moment we're in right now. Power is always shifting, and things can change quickly and not for the better, just like that – as your workshop participant André Morin notes.[7] We can't take anything for granted. I have my own opinions and feelings about how much space, cultural capital, and money drag queens have managed to co-opt, from the perspective of a drag king and AFAB queer person making and watching queer performance within a more marginal drag community. But at the same time, we're seeing people's livelihoods, safety, and very existence being threatened. The increased visibility of drag and its commercialization within mainstream culture arguably makes it more threatening to some than the idea of it as an underground practice. And I need to complicate this binary of mainstream versus fringe, assimilation versus subversion: the backlash against, in particular, drag as family entertainment and accessible to children suggests that it's that slippage from something perceived as belonging to a deviant subculture into heteronormative family space that's seen as threatening. It's grimly funny that people talk about "indoctrination" of children, when binary gender and heteronormativity are the real indoctrination – in the case of children, that indoctrination is still in process and more easily disrupted … We're not trying to turn your children queer – we might be stopping you from turning them straight, though. Un-doctrination. And the hysteria – for want of a better word – that inspires … It shows the real power of drag as disruption: that it genuinely does have real-world, off-stage potential to undo and remake gender, that people literally want to legislate it! It's the same fears that the Puritans and anti-theatrical writers were expressing.

Drag culture isn't monolithic, and neither are the ways it's read or experienced. Ultimately, it's not about individual drag performers; it's about a system that privileges and profits off a narrow selection of AMAB artists, whilst marginalizing and erasing others and creating a scarcity situation that pitches queer artists in competition with each other for the tiny slice of capitalism-pie that we've been offered … because it's the same system, in the end, that's also creating and benefiting from the stigma and fear, and that wants to control us and shut us down when we start to spill out of the box that some of us have been permitted to occupy. We need to think and act intersectionally, I guess is what I'm saying, and support each other. I stand with all drag performers against fascists, and I support the right of drag queens to earn a living and tell stories to children – and I'd appreciate it if they supported kings by booking them and paying them equally. *Sound of the Underground* by Travis Alabanza and Debbie Hannan expressed a lot of this in a much more entertaining way than I'm managing to here![8] I saw it on the same weekend as counter-protesting a far-right demonstration against a drag story-time event at my local pub. Strange times.

NOTES

1 As Clare McManus notes, "Shakespeare's theatre layered gender roles to tantalise audiences, drawing on the virtuosic skill of the highly trained young

men (aged between 12 and 21 years old) who played these complex female characters" (McManus, "Shakespeare and Gender").

2 Historiography on sodomy and its representations in early modern Europe is extensive. An early influential monograph on this topic is Goldberg, *Sodometries*. The quote about Beaumont and Fletcher is from *Brief Lives, Chiefly of Contemporaries, Set Down by John Aubrey*, 1:95–6, as quoted in Masten, "My Two Dads," 303. On queer and trans potentialities in *Galatea*, see Frankland and Kesson, "Perhaps John Lyly Was a Trans Woman?"; Frankland, "Trans Women on Stage"; Lyly, *Galatea*, ed. Kesson.

3 André Morin in conversation with Peter Cockett and Melinda Gough, unpublished interview, 2019.

4 Jones and Stallybrass, *Renaissance Clothing*.

5 Korda, "Shakespeare's Laundry."

6 Gabriel, "After Roe." Since summer 2022, when this piece was published, such attacks have increased dramatically.

7 Morin in conversation with Cockett and Gough, in the passage quoted earlier in this chapter.

8 Alabanza and Hannan, *Sound of the Underground*.

13 A Question to Be Asked: Boy Actors, Performance as Research, and Theatre History

ROBERTA BARKER AND LUCY MUNRO

Introduction: "Aspects of Myself I Brought to Aspatia"

Like all the scenes explored at the Engendering the Stage workshop in Stratford in September 2018, the climactic scene of Francis Beaumont and John Fletcher's *The Maid's Tragedy* (c. 1610–11) features swordplay.[1] In this case, Aspatia, disguised as a young man, provokes her unfaithful beloved Amintor to a duel. Amintor is a seasoned swordsperson; Aspatia is so much the opposite that Amintor asks, "What does thou mean?" exclaiming, "Thou canst not fight: the blows thou mak'st at me / Are quite besides."[2] At first sight, the binaries of this scene seem obvious; the male-identified character is skilled with the sword, while the female-identified character is coded as incompetent with it. At Stratford, however, Marcus Nance as Amintor and Carmen Alvis as Aspatia brought insights to these characters' relationships with the sword that complicated such conclusions. In an interview with Peter Cockett and Melinda Gough, later revised and expanded on in chapter 3 of this volume, Alvis explains:

> Aspects of myself I brought to Aspatia, particularly in the task of wielding the sword, include the burden of being required to perform as a man and enjoy typical male things. I have a female as well as a male spirit, and at various points in my life I have been redirected by family, friends, and society to perform the role of a man to the exclusion of my femininity. For this scene, I brought my disdain for performative masculinity to the task of swordplay, given that Aspatia is convinced a sword fight is how she must die and is likely untrained in combat.[3]

Nance, in turn, remarked that, in his experience, "the sword gives you power," comparing the experience of wielding it with that of "the right-wing Americans with the guns: you've got your weapon on you, you have the protection."[4] However, Alvis's choices transformed the usual dynamic. Because of Nance's uncertainty about his adversary's gender and the instinctive "sympathy" between them, his Amintor responded with confusion rather than aggression to Aspatia's challenge. He reflected on "being a man, reacting as a man would react, but then there was that confusion," concluding, "I really was thrilled to have that scene because of that."[5] Thanks to the lived experiences of both Alvis and Nance, their personal histories and the ways in which those histories meshed in their working relationship, new possibilities emerged from *The Maid's Tragedy*'s final duel.

What of the earliest actors to play Amintor and Aspatia? Did their lived experiences of gender, sexuality, and violence affect their understanding of the roles, as did those of Nance and Alvis in 2018? How might the identities and relationships of these early modern actors have shaped the meanings of plays like *The Maid's Tragedy* when they were new, as the identities and relationships of Alvis and Nance did more than four centuries later? Because we generally cannot answer such questions as these with any certainty, scholars have often treated them as unaskable. William Ingram notes the "general avoidance of biographical study as a component of Elizabethan [and, by extension, Jacobean] theater history," observing that "conjectural reconstructions of playhouses abound today, much as they did a hundred years ago; yet equivalent conjectures about the users of those playhouses – another popular Victorian pastime – are today regarded as unscholarly or romantic."[6] As Alvis's and Nance's comments on their swordplay in *The Maid's Tragedy* emphasize, however, one of the key effects of performance as research (PaR) is to underline the problems inherent in this reluctance to grapple with the biographies – and bodies – of early modern performers.

To speak of the "meanings" of *The Maid's Tragedy* as they unfolded at the Engendering the Stage workshop without speaking of the perceptions that Alvis, Nance, and Logan Brideau (who played Evadne) contributed to it would be unthinkable, so directly did their insights and personae as actors affect the scene as it was rehearsed and played. This essay strives to show how their work might encourage us to ask deeper questions about the individual actors who generated theatrical meanings on the early modern English stage. With Anne Lancashire, we argue that "theater history more importantly concerns people and processes than wooden frames and plaster."[7] By using PaR as a lens through which to read (and re-read) early modern textual and archival sources, we argue, scholars and artists can learn to ask (or re-ask) long-neglected questions about the bodies and identities – including the gendered and sexual identities – of early modern performers. Focusing especially on the elusive, fascinating boy actors who created female-coded roles on the early modern English stage, we consider what working with contemporary actors might teach us about who these boys were, how they related to other performers, and how their labour helped to engender the early modern theatrical canon.

Individualizing the Actor

One of the first things that any experience of PaR – and, indeed, of any form of theatrical practice – tends to expose is the vital role that the specific people in a company play in shaping the meanings of the performance text. In our scene work on Beaumont and Fletcher's *The Maid's Tragedy* at Stratford, this role was particularly powerful. The professional backgrounds and lived experiences of the contemporary artists who took on the play's leading roles profoundly affected the group's explorations of this early modern text.

Marcus Nance, who played Beaumont and Fletcher's beleaguered young hero, Amintor, is an accomplished singing actor who was performing Olin Britt in *The Music Man* at Stratford's Avon Theatre during the season in which he contributed so much to Engendering the Stage. Logan Brideau, the fourteen-year-old actor who embodied the murderous and embattled anti-heroine Evadne, was playing Nance's son in *The Music Man* during that Stratford season. Carmen Alvis, meanwhile, brought her rich background as an experimental theatre creator and artistic leader of multiple companies to her performance as Aspatia, the spurned lover who triggers one of the scene's principal actions by challenging the faithless Amintor to a duel.[8]

In each of these cases, the actor's presence profoundly shaped the possibilities that arose as the group worked through the bloody denouement of *The Maid's Tragedy*. Each performer raised questions about the text and its characters that might not have arisen in another company. As Nance remarked in an interview with Peter Cockett and Melinda Gough, his experiences as an African American Canadian performer affected his responses to the pervasive binaries of "black" and "white" in Beaumont and Fletcher's tragedy; of Amintor's line to Evadne, "Black is thy colour now, disease thy nature" (5.3.135), he commented poignantly, "I still have a hard time with that." At the same time, his identity as a gay man helped him to find the complex layers of attraction between Amintor and Aspatia dressed as a man in this scene "very interesting and very natural."[9] The difference in height between Nance's Amintor and Brideau's Evadne was also relevant to his approach to playing his character as a betrayed husband. As Nance notes, "from a physical standpoint it was a little awkward."[10] No one who was in the room for the workshop will forget the sight of Brideau's slight, childlike, and vulnerable-looking Evadne, bloody dagger in hand, throwing herself at Nance's tall, dignified, and troubled Amintor, and Amintor's surprised, active resistance to that attempted embrace.[11]

Nor are they likely to forget the disgust and mockery with which Alvis's Aspatia handled the sword, that symbol of masculine prowess. As a "Two-Spirit artist with Métis-Chippewa, Irish-English heritage from Turtle Mountain who also identifies as transfeminine,"[12] Alvis explains how Marcus Nance convincingly playing Amintor falling in love with Alvis's Aspatia "as a *him*" helped "affirm the spectrum of my gender experience": "To collaborate with scene partner Marcus Nance as Amintor was excellent; he made me believe that when Aspatia presented herself to him as a man she remained deserving of love."[13]

Such exchanges between actors' and characters' identities are sometimes occluded in forms of PaR that encourage performers to forget their contemporary experiences in the name of original practices. By contrast, such synergies exemplified the work that took place over those few days in Stratford. By generously offering her lived insights to the room, Alvis invited a collective reconsideration of *The Maid's Tragedy*'s possible meanings:

> As part of the scene study, we used they/them pronouns to describe Aspatia, even though the colonial world view of the play asserts a fixed binary. While both the character Aspatia and I as an actor were given permission to be our whole selves through the use of inclusive pronouns, the play-text as written requires Amintor not to recognize Aspatia in man's apparel. One take of our scene study had Amintor being in knowledge of Aspatia's gender spectrum. This turn became an affirmation for Aspatia's male presentation, complete with a feminine spirit. Performing the scene as characters aware of the gender spectrum highlighted for me the folly evoked by gender as a binary within Aspatia and Amintor's jilted marriage and society at large.[14]

The tragedies of the "maid," Aspatia, and of her/their beloved, Amintor, were thus brought into new focus through the questions and possibilities raised by Alvis's – and her fellow actors' – perspectives.

This sense of the ways in which theatrical meaning is shaped by the specificity of individual performers often seems to be one of the key elements missing from our understanding of early modern theatrical performance, especially when it comes to discussions of the so-called boy actors who played female-assigned roles on the early modern English stage. Take, for example, the famous letter in which Henry Jackson praised the actor he saw playing Desdemona in Shakespeare's *Othello* in Oxford in 1610. "But that Desdemona," Jackson wrote, "murdered by her husband in our presence, although she always pled her case excellently, yet when killed moved us more, while stretched out on the bed she begged the spectators' pity with her very facial expression."[15] Writing in Latin, Jackson refers only to the character and to her socially assigned feminine gender. Although he is clearly praising the performer's art, he writes as if the performer had disappeared into the role altogether. To this day, Scott McMillin writes, we "do not know who the boy was, what roles he had played, how long he had been with the company."[16]

McMillin is clearly right that we are unlikely ever to know with certainty the name, background, or lived experience of Jackson's Desdemona. Thanks to surviving cast lists and to the groundbreaking archival work of scholars such as David Kathman, however, we *can* list the names of many boy actors of the King's Men, the company that created *The Maid's Tragedy* within a year of the performance of *Othello* witnessed by Jackson and continued to perform it for several decades. For example, Richard Robinson had joined the company as an apprentice by the time the play was first performed in 1610–11 and was playing leading tragic female roles by 1611; Richard Sharpe was the charismatic leading actress of many Fletcher plays in the late 1610s and early 1620s; and Stephen Hammerton was the star boy actress of the early 1630s.

Early modern sources offer us multiple glimpses of each of these actors. In Ben Jonson's *The Devil Is an Ass*, several characters praise the wit and style of the real-life Robinson, an "ingenious youth" who hobnobs with gentlemen and landladies of the city in the dress of a lawyer's wife. Declaring that Robinson wears women's clothes with an elegance "beyond / Forty o' your very ladies,"[17] Jonson underlines the performer's fluid gender presentation on and off stage. In the process, as Simone Chess argues, the playwright hints at a gender identity beyond the male/female binary, suggesting that "Robinson's out-in-the-world, better-than-the-cis-ladies gender is of his own ingenious invention and self-styling."[18] A surviving record from the London parish of St. Giles Cripplegate evokes another boy actor's sexuality, telling us that "Richard Sharpe Player," after he graduated from female to male roles, was the "reputed ffather" of an illegitimate son, "base borne of the Body of Margaret Smith singlewoman."[19] Right at the start of his career, Hammerton was the subject of a dispute between William Blagrave, deputy Master of the Revels and an investor in the Salisbury Court playhouse, and another investor, Christopher Babham, who was said to have "inveigled" Hammerton from Salisbury Court so that he might be "imployed at the Blackfryars playhouse."[20] James Wright's Restoration-era reminiscence of the English stage, *Historia Histrionica*, invokes the histrionic talent and physical attributes that apparently made Hammerton a valuable commodity, saying that he "was at first a most noted and beautiful Woman Actor, but afterwards he acted with equal Grace and Applause, a Young Lover's Part."[21] The epilogue of Sir John Suckling's comedy *The Goblins* (c. 1638–41), written after this transition had taken place, imagines the women in the audience crying, "*Oh if* Stephen *should be kil'd, / Or misse the Lady, how the plot is spil'd?*"[22] These are not the traces of faceless actors, forgotten and forgettable, but of performers with unique physical characteristics, histrionic gifts, and personae.

Given the popularity of *The Maid's Tragedy*, which appears to have remained in the repertory of the King's Men quite consistently from the 1610s through to the 1630s,[23] each of these actors probably appeared in the play in multiple roles over the course of their career. Robinson is one of the most likely candidates to have created a female role in the first cast of *The Maid's Tragedy*. Given that he remained a sharer in the company until the closure of the public theatres in 1642, played numerous documented male roles during his later career, and was one of the signatories of the Beaumont and Fletcher first folio in 1647, he seems likely also to have assumed an adult male role in one or more later revivals of the play. Wright tells us that Hammerton played Amintor as an adult actor,[24] but he may well also have taken on Aspatia or Evadne when the play was revived at court on 29 November 1636 during the period of his apprenticeship with the King's Men. Can we imagine the ingenuity and chic for which Jonson praised Robinson, or the beauty and glamour that rendered Hammerton so beloved, shaping and reshaping audiences' perceptions of roles like Aspatia, Evadne, and Amintor over the years? What of the offstage lived experiences of these actors: experiences like Hammerton's early situation of being bartered between playing companies, Sharpe's fathering of an illegitimate child, or Robinson's marriage in 1622 to Winifred Burbage, the widow of the titanic leader of the King's Men, Richard Burbage? Could these circumstances have affected these actors' understandings of dramas of power, sex, and marriage like *The Maid's Tragedy*? And might the fluidity with which they passed from female to male roles over the course of their careers have reflected a parallel fluidity in their own lived gender identities?

Simone Chess has argued that Robinson and Sharpe may indeed have had a "nonbinary affect" in life as well as on stage.[25] Shaped by the "queer residue of their extreme success as … wom[e]n," this non-binary affect could well have influenced not only their work as boy actors but also their careers as adult players after they moved from female to male roles.[26] If so, the queer perspectives these performers brought to their performances in plays like *The Maid's Tragedy* – or that spectators brought to their reception of these performances – could have had the potential to disrupt patriarchal ideologies of gender and sexuality. The critiques of early modern anti-theatrical writers like Philip Stubbes, who objected to the practice of casting boys as women on the grounds that for "one to weare the apparel of another sex, is to participate with the same, and to adulterate the veritie of his owne kinde,"[27] can be read as supporting such readings.

On the other hand, boy actors and their performances may also sometimes have reinforced normative gender roles. In some early modern plays – including *The Devil Is an Ass* – male-identified characters are shown donning female clothing in order to interact with women and engage in heterosexual seduction, with and without their consent. An anecdote about similar behaviour off stage, sent to the Earl of Rutland in 1611, around the time of *The Maid's Tragedy*'s premiere, is even more complex than the stage representations. The Earl's informant writes:

> Heare was latlye one of the players boyes found in a marchantes howse in wemens apparrelle, who offering his service was received into the howse uppone trialle, and so laye with all the wemen in the howse, and played to his one profit and pleasuer tell he was discovered, taken, and sent to Bridwell.[28]

This tale of cross-dressed transgression could reflect anything from consensual erotic play, to sexual assault on the part of boy players, to early modern prejudices against these same boy players along the pernicious lines that shape the transphobic "bathroom debate" in contemporary society.[29] More evidence might have been supplied by the records of Bridewell prison's Court of Governors, but they are lost for the period between July 1610 and July 1617. With fragmentary evidence, it is similarly impossible to be certain whether the gender and sexual identities of players like Sharpe, Robinson, and Hammerton challenged or confirmed patriarchal norms of gender and sexuality in the early modern period. PaR reminds us, nevertheless, that questions about these identities and their impacts are worth asking – and that they matter profoundly to the unfolding of theatre history.

Boy Actors in Company

Another key point that emerged from the Stratford workshop was the power, complexity, and importance of relationships between actors. Such relationships include professional interactions (such as the shared history of Marcus Nance and Logan Brideau or the interactions between boy actors of the early modern stage and the masters to whom they were apprenticed); personal bonds, correlations, and disparities of age; and the kinetic onstage dynamics of actors of varying shapes, sizes, and physiques. All of these factors played into our work at Engendering the Stage, not least in the sequence in which Evadne enters to meet Amintor, "*her hands bloody, with a knife.*" The dialogue here is replete with possibilities:

> EVADNE: Amintor, I am loaden with events
> That fly to make thee happy; I have joys
> That in a moment can call back thy wrongs
> And settle thee in thy free state again.
> It is Evadne still that follows thee,
> But not her mischiefs.
>
> AMINTOR: Thou canst not fool me to believe again,
> But thou hast looks and things so full of news
> That I am stayed.
>
> EVADNE: Noble Amintor, put off thy amaze;
> Let thine eyes loose, and speak. Am I not fair?
> Looks not Evadne beauteous with these rites now?
> Were these hairs half so lovely in thine eyes
> When our hands met before the holy man?
> I was too foul within to look fair then;
> Since I knew ill I was not free till now.
>
> AMINTOR: There is presage of some important thing
> About thee which it seems thy tongue hath lost:
> Thy hands are bloody, and thou hast a knife.
>
> EVADNE: In this consists thy happiness and mine.
> Joy to Amintor, for the King is dead!

(5.3.106–26)

As written, the sequence teeters on the boundary between tragic grandeur and grotesque butchery. This moment is the first time that spectators have seen Evadne since she murdered the King, tying him to an adulterous bed, stabbing him repeatedly, and abruptly departing. Her lover dead, she attempts to reconstruct her relationship with her husband on the back of this murder.

In our scene work, the lines were mediated through the visual spectacle of the interaction between the tall, imposing Nance and the slight Brideau. Productions of the play have often presented Evadne as a sexily lethal vamp, as the comments of reviewers across three decades suggest. In 1980, Sinead Cusack was described as "a predatory woman"; in 1997, Lyn Gardner dubbed Evadne "one of the great Jacobean she-devils"; and in 2005, Zoe Simon was labelled a "fire-and-ice maiden" by a reviewer who also drew attention to her "poise and sexual authority."[30] By contrast, Brideau offered an unsettling combination of ecstasy and unease, an effect that was heightened by the chaste decorum of his long white robe and close-fitting bonnet. When he spoke the lines, "Am I not fair? / Looks not Evadne beauteous with these rites now?" he called passionately for a spiritual recuperation that was ultimately out of reach because it was founded in the act of murderous regicide. The disjunction between his appearance and the actions of which he boasted was heightened by the onstage presence of the knife. Movement added to this effect. On the line "Joy to Amintor, for the King is dead!" Brideau flung himself into Nance's arms. Nance met this confident physical gesture with marked unease, his Amintor seemingly unable to decide what the appropriate physical or emotional response might be. Across the various renditions of the sequence within the workshop, the sense increasingly emerged that Brideau and Nance were so well able to exploit the incongruous aspects of their performance because their established professional and personal relationship allowed them space for joint creative discovery despite their differences in age, size, and affect.

We do not know precisely who played which roles when this sequence was presented by the King's Men around 1610–11, but the leading candidates to have played Amintor are Richard Burbage, the company's long-established leading actor, and William Ostler, a younger man who had recently joined the King's Men and was playing some important roles in their plays. We know, for example, that he played Antonio in Webster's *The Duchess of Malfi* around 1613, and his name appears second, after that of Burbage, in three actor-lists for plays of the Fletcher canon (Beaumont and Fletcher's *The Captain* and Fletcher's *Bonduca* and *Valentinian*), suggesting that the authors of *The Maid's Tragedy* appreciated his talents.[31] Further support for the casting of Ostler as Amintor can be seen in the use of another young actor, Stephen Hammerton, in the role in the late 1630s or early 1640s. Moreover, the King's Men appear in some cases to have believed that particular roles were better suited to a younger actor. For example, a prologue to Chapman's *Bussy D'Ambois* that was probably written for a late 1630s revival declares that the second actor to have played the fiery title role "is denied / By his grey beard to show the height and pride / Of D'Ambois youth and bravery."[32] However, early modern playing companies in general seem to have cared little for age-realistic casting: there is no evidence that Burbage gave up playing roles such as Hamlet as he aged, and he may well have played Amintor.

Both Burbage and Ostler probably mentored younger actors. Burbage seems to have acted as master to some of the boy actors within the company – Richard Robinson among them – while there is evidence that Ostler was training younger performers as early as 1609, just before he joined the King's Men. A set of records of payments to actors in Jonson's entertainment *The Key Keeper*, staged in April 1609, refer to "Ostler the player" and "his boye."[33] Ostler received £5, while the other leading player, Nathan Field, received £4, suggesting that Ostler's fee was increased because he had worked to prepare the boy Giles Gary – who received £2 – for his performance. Logan Brideau was not, of course, Marcus Nance's apprentice, but the close working relationship between these two performers, and the qualities that it brought to our scene work, invited us to think about the kinds of bonds that might exist between younger and older players, and the dynamic impact that they might have in performance.

Such dynamics almost certainly affected early performances of *The Maid's Tragedy* and were likely inflected by the presence of the specific actor playing Amintor. Burbage, born in 1568, was in his early 40s at the time when *The Maid's Tragedy* was first performed; Ostler was around twenty years younger. The two actors are likely to have had very different physiques, and they may have had different styles of performance: Ostler had begun his career with an all-boy troupe linked with a choir school, the Children of the Chapel, while Burbage probably served an apprenticeship in a company similar to the King's Men. As a result, these two evidently charismatic and successful performers would have inhabited the role of Amintor differently, and their relationships with the actor playing Evadne would have differed, shaped by factors such as personality, gender, sexuality, class, professional hierarchies, and roles within the company. It is tempting, perhaps, to imagine Amintor being played by Burbage and Evadne by his apprentice, but there are other possibilities. If the Evadne actor was apprenticed to Ostler, he must have been a recent addition to the company. On the other hand, Ostler may have played Amintor opposite an Evadne trained by Burbage, and Burbage's methods may not have been his own. He may, for instance, have been irritated by the Burbagian way – perhaps, to his taste, overly old-fashioned and mannered – in which the Evadne actor cried "Joy to Amintor, for the King is dead!" Though such interactions may now seem unrecoverable, PaR's underlining of the ways in which relationships between contemporary actors engender readings, gestures, and ideas in rehearsal can encourage us to consider how they might also have done so on the early modern stage.

Boys and Their Roles

Even as Nance and Brideau's scene work encouraged us to raise new questions about the relationships that existed between masters and apprentices, we were also fascinated by the differences between Brideau and Alvis, the actors who took on roles gendered female in the text of *The Maid's Tragedy.* Such roles are often referred to in general terms as "women's parts," and the actors who created them in the early modern period as "boy actors." But these terms may be inadequate. Through their widely varying ages, affects, and personae, Brideau and Alvis suggested that such totalizing descriptions fall short of the complexity both of the theatrical event and of the actor's role in it. Wry, melancholy, and restrained, Alvis's Aspatia seemed to carry within them a well of painful experience that was especially marked when they spoke of their "sister," both distancing themself from Aspatia's female persona and bringing it forcefully to mind. They declared, sorrowfully,

> till the chance of war marked this smooth face
> With these few blemishes, people would call me
> My sister's picture, and her mine: in short,
> I am the brother to the wronged Aspatia.   (5.3.37–40)

Nance's Amintor then responded by accepting the ability of the "brother" to substitute for Aspatia through both word and gesture:

> The wronged Aspatia! Would thou wert so too
> Unto the wronged Amintor! Let me kiss
> That hand of thine in honour that I bear
> Unto the wronged Aspatia.   (41–4)

The scene draws attention to Aspatia's physical appearance, teasing character and spectator alike with the resemblance between the staged "brother" and the remembered "sister"; these elements were brought to the fore in the sensitive interplay between Alvis and Nance. Later in the scene, Aspatia attacks Amintor when he declares that "death is not so terrible as thou: / Thine eyes shoot guilt into me," retorting,

> Thus she swore
> Thou wouldst behave thyself, and give me words
> That would fetch tears into my eyes, and so
> Thou dost indeed[.]
>
> (74–9)

Although Aspatia is dressed as a man, the character's female persona is also vividly present. In a personal interview, Alvis describes her spirit as "female, male, and free of gender," and in performance her Aspatia presented not a collision of binary genders but a gender spectrum.

If using the pronouns "they" and "them" for Aspatia opened up the text and our workshop to non-binary understandings of gender, the conventions of early modern English, in which the informal "thou" pronoun can signal shifting power dynamics, intimacy, and anger, became a channel through which Amintor's enduring love for Aspatia could be expressed. At the start of the scene, Amintor and Aspatia both address each other with the respectful "you," but – as the lines quoted above indicate – Amintor quickly moves into "thou" pronouns. Aspatia initially resists this development, maintaining the chilly formality of "you" throughout a nineteen-line speech (ll. 51–69), but in returning to the topic of the absent "sister" also shifts to "thou." These shifts reflect ambiguities and uncertainties in the relationship between the two characters that were heightened in the Stratford workshop by the gender fluidity of Alvis's Aspatia. In his interview with Gough and Cockett, Nance described his Amintor as "completely confused" by, but also deeply attracted to, the Aspatia he encountered in their scene together, adding, "I think I found that stimulating. And it brought another level to how I was responding to them [Aspatia / Alvis] in terms of my attraction for them." At such moments, Nance's Amintor powerfully conveyed Alvis's point that "when Aspatia presented herself to him as a man, she remained deserving of love."[34]

Alvis's delicate, gender-fluid performance contrasted powerfully with the youthful eagerness and energy of Brideau's Evadne; the two actors created not only different emotional worlds but also different versions of gender identity. Is it possible that the "female characters" of *The Maid's Tragedy* – and the "boy actors" who portrayed them – could have varied just as widely on the early modern stage? A close look at the leading women's roles in *The Maid's Tragedy* suggests that the play may have been written with two very different boy actors in mind. Evadne, the tragedy's largest female part, is a spectacular showpiece that seems designed for a mature and versatile player. She is initially presented as a courtly bride, her wedding to a young lord welcomed by the King and her kinsmen and celebrated with a spectacular masque at the end of the first act. Yet the second act reveals her instead to be the King's mistress, married for convenience to Amintor, whom she mocks on their wedding night, flaunting her sexual experience and laughing, "A maidenhead, Amintor, / At my years?" (2.1.194–5). Two acts later, rebuked by her brother Melantius, she repents her sin and abases herself before her husband. In the fifth act, at Melantius's urging, she decides to kill her seducer, stabbing him in bed, and at her last appearance, she enters half-crazed, "*her hands bloody with a knife*" (5.3.108 SD). Demure charm, brazen sexuality, love, grief, penitence, and frenzied violence: Evadne's role offers them all.

Aspatia's role is quite another matter. Considerably smaller than Evadne's, it plays for much of *The Maid's Tragedy* on a plangent note of lovelorn despair epitomized by the celebrated song that the character sings in Act 2, scene 1, as Aspatia helps to prepare Evadne for her wedding night:

> *Lay a garland on my hearse*
> > *Of the dismal yew;*
> *Maidens, willow branches bear;*
> > *Say I dièd true.*   (2.1.72–5)

Unlike that of Evadne, much of Aspatia's role fits neatly into Carol Rutter's vision of the training of early modern boy actors as dependent in large part upon their mastery of the highly gendered, conventionalized rhetorical tropes taught in grammar schools.[35] Many of her words, tones, and gestures mimic those of the forsaken-yet-constant classical heroines whose Ovidian speeches such boys might have memorized, a point Aspatia herself underlines when she reels off a list of these heroines (Oenone, Dido, Ariadne) in Act 2, scene 2. Compared to the flamboyant array of passions and attitudes required by Evadne's role, for much of the play Aspatia's voice is powerful but her range is circumscribed. It is only when Aspatia impersonates her own brother in Act 5, scene 3 that she is allowed to occupy another dramaturgical space and to move – albeit fleetingly – beyond the circumscribed role of the classical heroine.

The sharp differences between Evadne's and Aspatia's roles may help us to catch a glimpse of the contrasting ages, experiences, and personae of the boy actors apprenticed to the King's Men when Beaumont and Fletcher wrote *The Maid's Tragedy* around 1610–11. As Kathman's painstaking archival research has recently underlined, this time was a moment of transition for the King's Men. The company's leading boy players of the peak Shakespearean years, 1603–10 – John Rice, William Ecclestone, and possibly John Underwood – were "nearing the ends of their apprenticeship terms."[36] Rice in particular had clearly had an illustrious career as a boy actor with the King's Men; the company had chosen to feature him in at least two well-documented, high-prestige performances for royal spectators.[37] This prominence makes him a likely candidate for the creator of many great female roles of the 1603–10 period.[38] It is tempting to imagine Beaumont and Fletcher designing Evadne's wide-ranging role as a kind of "greatest hits" for the celebrated boy player who might well already have played such roles as the chaste Desdemona, the bewitching Cleopatra, and the murderous Lady Macbeth. Since Evadne's part features major scenes with Amintor, Melantius, the King, the ladies of the court, and numerous other minor characters, it could also have offered an experienced actor like Rice a chance to showcase his well-evolved relationships with his fellow company members.

The year 1611 saw Rice's departure from the King's Men, along with that of his contemporary Ecclestone; on 29 August of that year, both men signed a bond with Philip Henslowe as sharers in a new company, the Lady Elizabeth's Men.[39] As this generation grew up and departed, the company took on a new cohort. Walter Haynes and George Birche were both apprenticed to members of the King's Men in 1610, and Kathman suggests that Richard Robinson was likely apprenticed in the company at around the same time.[40] We know little about Haynes's repertoire, while Birche's recorded female roles include the comic parts of Doll Common in *The Alchemist* and Lady Politic Would-Be in *Volpone*.[41] Robinson, on the other hand, is noted as playing leading tragic roles as early as 1611, when he appeared as the Lady in Middleton's *Second Maiden's Tragedy* (seemingly so dubbed by Sir George Buc, Master of the Revels, because of its resemblance to the earlier *Maid's Tragedy*). In the same year, Robinson is listed as one of the "principal Tragoedians" in Ben Jonson's *Catiline*.[42] The archival record probably simplifies the careers of both Birche and Robinson, each of whom is likely to have been required to take roles in comedies and tragedies, but the picture of the exuberant Birche and heart-rending Robinson that it presents may nonetheless preserve something of each actor's strengths as a performer.

Might Robinson have been a tragedienne in training in the previous year, when *The Maid's Tragedy* likely premiered? If so, then perhaps the plangent simplicity of Aspatia's role speaks to this point in his development. Almost all of Aspatia's lines are delivered either to other female characters, including Evadne and other court ladies, or to Amintor. For a young actor of thirteen – a typical age for "play-boys" to be apprenticed[43] and about Richard Robinson's age in 1610–11 – this limited circle of scene partners might have created a strong environment for training and relationship building. Aspatia's part reflects some of the training structures identified in the "restricted" roles designed for boy actors that Scott McMillin identifies, which are "largely rehearsable with one or two master actors, perhaps with a second boy," and the "scaffolded" roles – of which "restricted" roles may be a subset – that Evelyn Tribble analyses in the plays of Christopher Marlowe.[44] Her pathos, meanwhile, would surely have been an accessible mode to master, especially when it was offset in performance by the emotional variety required of the actor playing Evadne.

If Evadne was created by an older actor and Aspatia by a younger one in 1610–11, this dynamic was reversed at the Stratford workshop. There, Alvis's experience brought an edge of bleak humour to Aspatia's melancholy, while Brideau's youth gave the blood-stained Evadne an aura of wide-eyed vulnerability. Though this reversal of easy expectations might be read as an example of so-called miscasting, it also encourages us to ask new questions about the company that played *The Maid's Tragedy* in the early decades of the seventeenth century. When the play was first published in 1619, its title page stressed that it had already been "diuers times Acted at the *Black-Friers* by the KINGS Maiesties Seruants."[45] Over subsequent decades, it seems likely that many "diverse" versions of Aspatia and Evadne appeared on the Blackfriars stage, at court, and on tour. For example, if Richard Robinson played Aspatia as a young tragedienne in 1610, did he retain the role when *The Maid's Tragedy* played at court as part of the festivities for the marriage of Princess Elizabeth and the Elector Palatine in the winter of 1612–13, or had he by then graduated to the larger part of Evadne, his predecessors Rice and Ecclestone having left the field? In the latter case, might his Evadne have carried with it some of Aspatia's pathos – perhaps in contrast to the more savage or seductive Evadne of the older actor who had taken the role before him? Alternatively, did Robinson's contemporary, George Birche, who appeared memorably as Lady Politic Would-Be and Doll Common, and probably had a very different energy in performance from that of Rice or Robinson, move into the role of Evadne? If so, he may have presented an Amazonian or a playfully seductive figure, offering yet another version of theatrical femininity and contrasting yet more strongly with Robinson's Aspatia. In how many different ways might a privileged London theatregoer of the 1610s, 20s, and 30s have seen such contrasts play out as a sequence of apprentice actors took up and discarded these roles, and how disruptive, pleasurable, or productive were these varied performances of femininity for diverse early modern audience members? It is impossible to answer these questions with certainty, but the interpretative possibilities underlined at Stratford by the casting of Alvis and Brideau remind us that they can and should be asked.

Conclusion: Engendering Questions

Like all theatrical cultures, the culture of the early modern English stage was profoundly affected by the bodies, personalities, experiences, and relationships of its actors. These actors' lives, identifications, perceptions, and assumptions were so different from those of contemporary performers like Carmen Alvis, Marcus Nance, and Logan Brideau that we cannot confidently expect the discoveries of such performers to correlate directly with, or to offer unassailable evidence for, the discoveries of their early modern forbears. Nevertheless, by reminding us of possibilities that lie latent in the early modern theatrical archive – in its play-texts, cast lists, playhouse accounts, legal documents, and much more – these contemporary discoveries can have a transformative effect on our thinking, not only about what early modern drama can mean in our historical moment but also what it might have meant in its own. As Carmen Alvis eloquently commented of her decision to participate in Engendering the Stage, PaR experiments such as this one invite artists to "shine a light into … deliberately unlit areas." By bringing "the voices of the formerly marginalized (a term coined by Donna-Michelle St. Bernard of Ad Hoc Assembly)" to bear upon the early modern canon, these artists show us what that canon has engendered, for good and for ill, in the present.[46] At the same time, they also help us to think afresh about the ways in which the early modern stage and its dramas were themselves engendered.

NOTES

1 On the play's date, see Turner, Jr., "Textual Introduction," 3; Craik, "Introduction," 2; and Wiggins with Richardson, *British Drama, 1533–1642,* vol. 6, 180.
2 Beaumont and Fletcher, *The Maid's Tragedy,* ed. Craik, 5.3.99–101. All quotations are from this edition.
3 Carmen Alvis in conversation with Peter Cockett and Melinda Gough, unpublished interview, 2019. The interview is revised and expanded in Alvis, "We Tell Our Stories. We Continue to Exist," chapter 3 of this volume.
4 Marcus Nance in conversation with Peter Cockett and Melinda Gough, unpublished interview, 2019.
5 Nance in conversation with Cockett and Gough.
6 Ingram, *Business of Playing,* 24.

7 Lancashire, review of Gurr, *Shakespearian Playing Companies*, 435.

8 Among the companies Alvis has led are lemonTree creations, manidoons collective, and Ad Hoc Assembly.

9 Nance adds, "I don't know what it would be like if I had been straight – I would have [hoped] that it would be the same" (Nance in conversation with Cockett and Gough).

10 Nance in conversation with Cockett and Gough.

11 As Cockett and Gough note in their Introduction to this volume, provision of a paid childminder was important for mitigating the risks of casting a fourteen-year-old actor in the role of a sexual(ized) adult woman in this scene – risks for Brideau but also for Nance, given homophobic conflations of queerness with pedophilia. For further discussion of these and related questions, please also see Parry with Cockett and Gough, "Disruptive Affects: Portraiture, Staging, and Drag," chapter 12 of this volume. The moment we describe, where Amintor raises his arms and steps back, leaving Brideau's Evadne clinging to empty space, is captured in the *Engendering the Stage in the Age of Shakespeare and Beyond at the Festival Theatre Laboratory* video, timestamp 0.21–0:27. The complex nature of this moment in performance recalls the complex sexuality – and the disquieting sexualization – that scholars have often seen at work in the careers of early modern boy actors. For pioneering treatments of the sexualization and gender ambiguity of the boys, see, for example, DiGangi, *Homoerotics*; Orgel, *Impersonations*; and Zimmerman, *Erotic Politics*. For more recent treatments of the vulnerability of early modern boy actors to exploitation and objectification, see Mamujee, "'To Serve Us in That Behalf'" and van Es, "Captive Children." McCarthy offers an important corrective to these arguments, emphasizing the skill and virtuosity of boy actors (McCarthy, *Boy Actors in Early Modern England*).

12 Alvis in conversation with Cockett and Gough.

13 Alvis, in conversation with Cockett and Gough.

14 Alvis, "We Tell Our Stories. We Continue to Exist," chapter 3 of this volume.

15 Jackson, "Letter of 1610."

16 McMillin, "Sharer and His Boy," 234.

17 Jonson, *The Devil Is an Ass*, 2.8.64–77.

18 Chess, "Queer Residue," 251.

19 Baptism of Richard Sharpe, 6 September 1631, Parish Register, St Giles Cripplegate, London Metropolitan Archives, P69/GIS/A/002/MS06419/002; Bentley, *Jacobean and Caroline Stage*, 1:571.

20 Records of the Lord Chamberlain ... Petitions, TNA, LC 5/183, fol. 128v; see Nicoll and Boswell, "Dramatic Records: The Lord Chamberlain's Office," 408.

21 Wright, *Historia Histrionica*, 4.

22 Suckling, *The Goblins*, D8v.

23 For an account of these revivals, see Bentley, *Jacobean and Caroline Stage*, 1:113.

24 Wright, *Historia Histrionica*, 4.

25 Chess, "Queer Residue," 249.

26 Chess, 251.

27 Stubbes, *Anatomie of Abuses*, ed. Kidnie, 118.

28 *Manuscripts of His Grace the Duke of Rutland*, 1:429.

29 At least one erstwhile boy actor, Christopher Beeston, was publicly accused of rape soon after the end of his apprenticeship. In 1602, Margaret White, a widow accused of "getting a childe in whoredom," told the court of Bridewell that "one xpofer Beeston a plaier at one winters house in Star alley without Bishoppesgate had the use of her bodie but as she saithe hee did it forciblie for said hee I have lyen wth a hundred wenches in my tyme" (quoted in Salkeld, "Literary Traces," 381). For White's allegations and Beeston's response, see Griffith, "Christopher Beeston," 610–11.

30 Gussow, Review of *The Maid's Tragedy*, Section 2, 5; Gardner, Review of *The Maid's Tragedy*, 2; Jones, Review of *The Maid's Tragedy*, 77.

31 Webster, *Tragedy of the Dutchesse of Malfy*, A2v; *Fifty Comedies and Tragedies*, 3A1r, 3Y4v, 5C4r.

32 Chapman, *Bussy D'Ambois*, ed. Evans, Prologue, ll. 17–19.

33 Hatfield House Archives, Family & Estate Papers, Bills, 35/7, cited from *The Cecil Papers* (ProQuest).

34 Nance in conversation with Cockett and Gough; Alvis in conversation with Cockett and Gough.

35 See Rutter, "Learning Thisby's Part."

36 Kathman, "John Rice," 259.

37 In 1607, Rice appeared in a show offered by the Merchant Taylors' Company to King James and Prince Henry. Described as "a very proper child well spoken being clothed like an Angell of gladness," he was paid five shillings for his efforts, while his master, John Heminges, was paid forty shillings "for his direccion of his boy." Three years later, in 1610, Rice appeared as Corinea, "a very fayre and beautifull Nimphe," in a water pageant offered by the City of London to Prince Henry. For both of these appearances, see Kathman, "John Rice," 248–9.

38 Kathman, 258.

39 Greg, *Henslowe Papers*, 18–19.

40 Kathman, "John Rice," 259.

41 See Gurr, *The Shakespeare Company*, 220; Kathman, "John Rice," 259.

42 Jonson, *Catiline His Conspiracy*, 238.

43 Kathman, "How Old Were Shakespeare's Boy Actors?" 244–5.

44 McMillin, "Sharer and His Boy," 236–7; Tribble, "Marlowe's Boy Actors."

45 Beaumont and Fletcher, *The Maides Tragedy* (1619), title page.

46 Alvis in conversation with Cockett and Gough.

PART SEVEN

Rehearsing, Teaching, Translating

14 Calling Across from Our Difference: Teaching (Gender)-Nonconforming Characters in Early Modern English Drama

JESSICA SWAIN

After participating in the Engendering the Stage Lab in September 2018, I was inspired to put into practice the teachings of guest artist Emma Frankland, a trans actor/director who took an important leadership role during our time at the Stratford Festival and generously shared her own theatrical practice as an artist and actor. For the fourth-year seminar on non-Shakespearean Renaissance drama that I taught in Winter 2019 at McMaster University, my syllabus design took as a primary impetus Frankland's active reclaiming of space for trans and non-binary bodies through work on John Lyly's *Galatea* (1588).[1] In this course, students studied a range of genres in early modern English plays from the 1580s to the 1660s, paying particular consideration to transgressive or gender-nonconforming characters. Questions that framed our class included the following: How are these characters represented on the stage and to what ends? How might our examination of what makes these characters transgressive connect with pressing issues of our own contemporary moment (that is, consent, violence, "unruly" behaviour, strategies of resistance, self-surveillance)? In this chapter, I share my experience developing and teaching this class with the focus on these unorthodox characters and my students' intellectual discoveries while reading these plays. In particular, I explore how, by translating the Stratford Lab's intellectually playful performance as research (PaR) method of thinking through performance possibilities into a method for teaching in a literature classroom, we can call attention to textual potentialities that allow for greater inclusion around gender nonconformity.

Representation(al) Matters

Participating in the Engendering the Stage workshop, with its attention to challenges queer and gender-nonconforming actors face when performing early modern plays today, raised questions for me about the material conditions that are brought to bear on productions of classical plays: the kind of bodies we, as theatregoing audiences at venues similar to the Stratford Festival, usually see cast in early modern English plays; how audience expectations can perpetuate such limited casting practices for the works of Shakespeare and his contemporaries; and, as conveyed by guest artist Carmen Alvis, an Indigenous actor and theatre-maker, how we need to be aware of the colonial implications of performing these early modern English plays on Canadian ground. In this collection, Alvis notes that historically "the Stratford Festival of Canada has been telling itself stories that assert settler-colonial legacies responsible for the ongoing displacement and subjugation of the Indigenous peoples of Turtle Island."[2] Reflecting on the workshop, Frankland also observes that "the experience further highlighted for me how violent it is that the European early modern canon is widely considered to represent a universal human experience when these plays were written at a time when the West was enacting genocide and atrocities on Indigenous people on Turtle Island and around the world. So the action of visiting these plays on land that was colonised by Europeans and then expecting the plays to carry some sort of meaningful resonance with the Indigenous artists seemed fraught with the potential for further violence." Frankland concludes that, at the workshop, "this was something that I felt we navigated together as a group,"[3] but the question remains: why are we looking at these plays, indeed?

In a seminar on early modern English drama taught at a Canadian university, these conditions press in. Why are these texts important to teach, and in what ways should we go about teaching them? In other words, how do we, as teachers, make these texts matter? At the Stratford Lab, Frankland asked the actors, *What is your duty of care as an artist?* In her view, that duty of care was to *speak honestly of your experience to the world, as you see it.* Her words resonated with me, and I found myself asking myself a corresponding question, "What is your duty of care as a teacher?" As a teacher, I do my best to be attentive to the ways in which my students may not see themselves in these plays, as texts or performances. I am not saying that identification is necessary for the study and/or enjoyment of these works. That being said, not seeing *any* representation of one's self in a literature course can lead to, at a minimum, a feeling of disengagement.

In an attempt to counteract this potential estrangement, the starting point for my seminar design was *Galatea*, and more specifically, Frankland's new approach to the play. As embodied by the two leads, Galatea and Phillida, this pastoral comedy has been held up as a celebration of female-to-female same-sex love.[4] Michael Pincombe has gone as far to say that "*Galatea* [is] a clear candidate for the first 'lesbian' play on the English stage."[5] Although disguised as male shepherds in a wood setting, Galatea and Phillida are attracted to each other, according to Denise A. Walen, because of feminine traits:

> They are not drawn to stereotypically masculine attributes but to each other's feminine qualities ... Scripting the women's mutual appeal toward feminine qualities in each other firmly establishes the homoerotic nature of their desire. Each woman is attracted to female attributes, to the woman beneath the disguise, rather than to male characteristics the disguise might represent.[6]

Even when each begins to suspect the other is a woman, even when both are revealed to be women, Galatea and Phillida remain in love and wanting to be together.[7] Since this play is an early modern English comedy, however, genre conventions demand a heterosexual marriage at the ending. Venus, the goddess of love, steps in with a solution by offering to "turn one of them to be a man" (5.3.151–2) offstage,[8] and the audience is left not knowing which character undergoes this transformation. Scholars are divided on how to interpret the play's ending, wondering if this offstage biological metamorphosis undoes the positive portrayal of sexual desire and love between two women.[9]

At the Stratford Lab, Frankland outlined how her performance explorations of *Galatea* aimed to *keep the ending productive* by opening up space to imagine characters in ways they have not classically been portrayed. What happens, Frankland asked, if one or more of these characters is played by a trans or non-binary actor, and then at the end of the play, he/she/they *get to remain that way*? In other words, what if Venus does not actually transform Galatea or Phillida, but the woman "turned" man is really an expression of gender fluidity that is ambiguous enough to allow the community within the play's fiction to view the couple as heterosexual? In the play-text, when asked what she thinks about the love between the two women, Venus says, "I like [it] well, and allow it" (5.3.143). Why change what she receives favourably? This "transformation," in Frankland's interpretation, could be a strategy put in place to mitigate possible social objections to the relationship. Embracing Lyly's fluid depiction of gender in the play in a similar manner to Frankland, Simone Chess argues that "though the text is deliberately evasive as to whether or not either lover knows the truth of the other's sex, it nevertheless shows them playing together with the queerness of their genders and their relationship," meaning that "the play is less about any one fixed sexual identity or attraction, and more about the partnered project of creating and maintaining gender."[10] In Frankland's interpretation, this "partnered project of creating and maintaining gender" continues with Galatea and Phillida getting to remain in whatever gender they identify with, while also garnering heteronormative social approval to feel sexual desire for each other. Frankland's effort to recover trans and non-binary possibilities in Lyly's work makes plays like *Galatea* feel more reflective of and relevant to a modern audience.

By adapting Frankland's approach as an artist to my own approach as an instructor for an English literature seminar, I too wish to push towards finding evidence in these texts that is more inclusive than has previously been imagined. My own research involves female performance, boy actresses, and gender performativity on the early modern stage, and these interests impacted the plays I selected for the seminar. In each of these plays, I focused on reading one or two "subversive" characters gendered female (at least at one point) by the text: Queen Isabella in Christopher Marlowe's *Edward II* (1594); the previously discussed lovers in Lyly's *Galatea*; Bel-imperia in Thomas Kyd's *The Spanish Tragedy* (c. 1582–92); Alice Arden in *Arden of Faversham* (1592); Epicene in Ben Jonson's *Epicene* (1609); Moll in Thomas Middleton and Thomas Dekker's *The Roaring Girl* (1611); Mariam and Salome in Elizabeth Cary's *The Tragedy of Mariam* (1613); the Duchess in John Webster's *Duchess of Malfi* (1614); and Lady Happy and the Princess in Margaret Cavendish's *The Convent of Pleasure* (1668).[11] We investigated how these characters' gender behaviour was portrayed in the genres they existed within. When covering Cary and Cavendish, for example, we discussed such questions as why these two women playwrights wrote closet dramas; what being a closet drama meant for the performance of these texts; how a playwright's gender identification might affect character representation; what rhetorical space female characters could take up in such a genre; and what these characters talked about in relation to their gender performativity. *Mariam*, for example, is particularly unusual for a tragedy in the way that female characters have a lot of speaking time – which is more characteristic of early modern comedy. The first four scenes in *Mariam* have only women onstage, talking in long passages of verse either by themselves or to one another. Although Herod, Mariam's supposedly dead husband, takes up much space in these women's words, the play's opening hinges on the complexities of female experience. Having female speech spearhead this play arguably had the potential to nudge an early modern understanding of normative female gender behaviour in drama.

This course was designed to promote students' understanding of how the texts did and could operate, to foster students' engagement with the act of investigation, and in the vein of Frankland's work on *Galatea*, to address how the class might read these texts in a more inclusive manner. Expanding on our knowledge of the text and its historical context, we discussed potentialities in the play by thinking through the "what if's": "what if a character was like this," "what if a character was played by this person," or "what if this happened that way"? Then we discussed what we gained with certain choices, as well as what we lost. This dialogical teaching approach worked well in our small seminar. Engaging with the playfulness of PaR in a literature classroom engendered, I believe, a teaching methodology in the spirit of what Ellen Welch in this volume calls "a less goal-oriented way to frame the significance of academic research."[12] Performance is not as formalized as the written text would have you believe. When teaching drama as literature, we can sometimes lose sight of the variation within a play. The spontaneity and intuitiveness of PaR, where practice is the method of inquiry, allowed the class to mobilize the texts by trying out various approaches to these plays and talking through the aftermath of these choices. Centring my seminars on gender-nonconforming characters gave my students a model to delve more deeply into these characters, into who these characters could be, what the casting of actors to play them could look like, and how these changes in representation could shape the text as a whole. This structure gave the students the outline to then branch out and rethink the roles of other characters in the texts.

Learning Continues

In practice, the class posited how and why these characters' transgressiveness might stem from their gender ambiguity, and in what manner genre might impact their nonconforming existence in the plays. In each of the texts we covered, these nonconforming characters take on masculine and feminine gender traits in order to function outside strict individual, social, and at times, political expectations. This uncertainty or playfulness with regard to the characters' gender lasted, for the most part, until the last act of their respective plays. At this point, there was a strong push to make their gender ambiguity largely unambiguous and/or non-threatening. In comedy, it was usually done through a heteronormative marriage, and in tragedy,[13] usually through the death of the character. There were exceptions to this generalization: Isabella in Marlowe's *Edward II* is locked away in a tower; Epicene in Jonson's play of that title remains unattached, as does Moll in Middleton and Dekker's *The Roaring Girl*; and Salome in Cary's *The Tragedy of Mariam* lives. Yet key questions kept resurfacing throughout the semester: What conditions are required for such characters to exist? And what lessons are we to draw from the fact that, for the most part, at each play's ending characters such as these either conform or die?

In line with Frankland's interpretation of *Galatea* and her attempt at *keeping the ending productive*, I endeavoured to present each play as more open-ended. This task proved easier with the comedies since, on a basic level, the nonconforming characters still *existed* in some manner at the end of these plays. In other words, they were not dead. For the tragedies, I stressed this open-endedness by drawing attention to the impact of the characters' nonconformity on their communities, an impact that lingered in the text even after the characters' deaths.[14] For example, an early modern audience would not necessarily see Alice Arden's death as tragic but rather as the reinforcement of patriarchal ideology, of putting an end to a "disloyall and wanton wyfe."[15] A modern audience, however, might find her sympathetic since so much of her transgressive behaviour stems from her oppressive patriarchal society. Moreover, the fact that the non-complicit, gender-complying Susan Mosby also receives a death sentence at the end of the play demonstrates the lack of space in this community for either gender-conforming or nonconforming women to exist. With regards to viewing Frankland and Denise Oucharek's various approaches to one scene of *Galatea* in the Stratford Lab, Welch notes that "more compelling than any one version of the scene was the juxtaposition and accumulation of diverse possibilities generated through the process of experimentation."[16] Portraying Alice Arden's death as a tragedy is not a "better choice, only a different choice," and our understanding of the play-text can grow with these different choices.

Act 5, scene 3 of *The Maid's Tragedy* (1619) was the only tragic scene we focused on at the workshop, and the actors working on it noted how isolated they felt from the other groups looking at comedies. Structurally speaking, our workshop had separate groups made up of both actors and academics, with each of these groups tackling a play. While the academics could move from group to group if they wished, the majority chose to remain with one group. I personally decided to continue with the group exploring *The Roaring Girl*; staying with one group, I found, allowed for a greater appreciation and nuanced understanding of how the actors' character choices developed. Then, we would come together as a whole and share what we had been working on in our smaller groups. In these moments of sharing, a few of the actors performing *The Maid's Tragedy* expressed discontentment with having such humourless audience reactions, compared to the reactions the comedies received. The seriousness of the material, especially in the death scenes, made their performance powerful and engaging but also upsetting. There is a hopefulness in comedy that lends itself to Frankland's kind of intervention. Genre is a contextual factor in the reception of nonconformity. In tragedy, non-conforming characters are made to play the part of the villain, the scape-goat, the outcast, the mad, the murdered. At the end of the tragedy, there is usually some understanding that the removal of these characters is a critique on the rigidness of their communities, an appeal to make alterations. But the fact that such characters no longer are around to put this new-found knowledge into practice can make this realization seem hollow. Although transgressive characters in comedy are disruptive, this disruption generates the possibility of finding love. The formation of this bond leads to the subsequent integration of that deep affection back into what had been, effectively, a stagnate or reactionary community. The love of gender-nonconforming characters ends up restarting and resituating their societies, prodding them – even if only slightly – to be more adapt-able. Before teaching comedy and tragedy through this lens, I was not aware of how much labour genre was doing.

This playfulness in comedy engendered insightful and *productive* readings by my students. One striking example was an exchange of analyses during our study of Cavendish's *The Convent of Pleasure*. Reading the Princess as gender fluid, Madeleine Krusto asserted that the pastoral space of the convent acted as a place for "queer bodies to exist with the relationship between the Prince/Princess and Lady Happy as two women in love, and for the Prince/Princess to live as a gender-fluid individual." Rather than viewing the marriage between the two characters as the play's world enforcing heteronormativity, Krusto posited that this marriage is "a way to allow Lady Happy and the Prince/Princess's relationship [to continue] and their queer bodies to exist in this world." Building on Krusto's reading in class, Emily Meilleur-Rivers brought up the possibility of the Princess being a trans woman. Meilleur-Rivers further postulated that this interpretation greatly changes the revelation of the Princess being the Prince. Instead of 5.1 revealing the Princess as a "him," this moment is actually an outing of the Princess. That is to say, rather than exposing the Princess's true self as the Prince, this scene could be read as a moment of misgendering.

As a class, we close read this scene as outing the Princess, and this reading proved to be quite generative. When Madam Mediator comes racing in to tell the ladies that "there is a man disguised in the con-vent" (5.1.2), the stage directions read, "*They all skip from each other, as [if] afraid of each other. Only the Princess and the Lady Happy stand still together*" (5.1.3.1–2). In this play, the Princess gives no asides telling us she is really the Prince; the Princess's gender does not textually shift until many lines after this "reveal" when the Princess is identified as the "*Prince*" (5.1.11.1 SD), nor, as Sara Gorman notes, do we receive any "'preparation' scene" common in cross-dressing plots where "the audience is privy to the description of the particular act of donning and doffing disguise."[17] While there are hints that the Princess may not be who she claims to be, the characters' shock when the Princess is revealed to be the Prince should be contemporaneous with the audience's shock. Yet Lady Happy is not shocked. As a class, we noted how the Princess and Lady Happy are the only two people who do not jump away from each other's presence, perhaps because Lady Happy is already aware that the Princess is a trans woman. Their familiarity with and acceptance of each other registers physically.

Such cumulative readings not only made this closet drama seem very performable but also seemed in keeping with the joyous spirit of Frankland's work. By focusing on the transgressive characters in these plays, the students and I were able to find moments like the one above where this slight shift in perspective opened up new and exciting approaches. Incorporating the playfulness of PaR in the literature classroom resulted in the reading of speculative possibilities in the texts, discussing the revelations from such interpretative possibilities, and broadening our understanding of what these texts could mean. Our present concerns about equitability in professional theatre also have resonance for the literature classroom in terms what we read and how we read it. Rather than being overly concerned about being "faithful" to standard interpretations of these texts, this class celebrated readings that were actively trying to create more inclusive spaces in the plays and, in doing so, developed interpretations of these plays that better reflect the people who read and study them.

Acknowledgments

I would like to thank the organizers and participants of the Engendering the Stage conference. The conference was a singular experience, and it left me full of the intention to do better. I would also like to acknowledge that this conference held at McMaster University (Hamilton, ON) and the Stratford Festival (Stratford, ON) was conducted on the traditional lands of the Huron-Wendat, the Haudenosaunee, and the Anishinaabe nations and the Mississauga and Haudenosaunee nations, territories that are within the lands protected by the "Dish with One Spoon" wampum agreement. That a "spoon is not a knife" has been pointed out to me on several occasions. The "Dish with One Spoon" is not about carving up and dividing but about mindfully caring for and sharing resources – and the conference was in that spirit of exchanging and developing knowledges and experiences.

To the students in our seminar, English 4RD3: Renaissance Drama, Excluding Shakespeare, I give my gratitude for their engagement with the texts we studied. In particular, a big thanks to Madeleine Krusto and Emily Meilleur-Rivers who agreed to have their wonderful ideas cited.

NOTES

1 As early as 2009, the professional troupe Release the Hounds centred questions of gender nonconformity and queerness in a production of *Galatea* with accompanying workshops focused on sexuality, sex, and gender. For more on this aspect of the play's stage history, see Lyly, *Galatea*, ed. Scragg, 26n43. Research in print that discusses and disseminates subsequent work on the play by Emma Frankland with Andy Kesson and others includes Frankland and Kesson, "'Perhaps John Lyly Was a Trans Woman?'"; Lyly, *Galatea*, ed. Kesson. See also Lyly, *Galatea*, edited by Kesson, adapted by Frankland and Joy. This edition is based on a collaborative production at the 2023 Brighton Festival.

2 Alvis, "We Tell Our Stories. We Continue to Exist," chapter 3 of this volume.

3 Emma Frankland in conversation with Peter Cockett and Melinda Gough, unpublished interview, 2020.

4 See Scragg, *Metamorphosis of "Gallathea,"* 23; Rackin, "Androgyny," 31; Shapiro, *Gender in Play*, 94–7; Jankowski, "'Where There Can Be No Cause of Affection,'" 260–7; Jankowski, "'Virgins' and 'Not-Women,'" 82–4; Jankowski, *Pure Resistance*; Pincombe, "*Galatea*: We May All Love," 130, 139–43; Pincombe, "Lyly and Lesbianism"; Cartwright, "Confusions of *Gallathea*," 217–19; Dooley, "Inversion"; Wixson, "Cross-Dressing"; Chess, "'Or Whatever You Be.'"

5 Pincombe, "Lyly and Lesbianism," 90.

6 Walen, "Constructions of Female Homoerotics," 424. A revised and reprinted version of Walen's article is available in Walen, *Constructions of Female Homoeroticism in Early Modern Drama*; pages of particular note are 5–7, 287–8, 327–30.

7 Some scholars have also read this relationship as an example of male-to-male same-sex love. See Billing, *Masculinity*, 60–2.

8 The class used Scragg's edition of John Lyly's *Galatea*. All following in-text citations of the play are from this edition.

9 Traub, in "Renaissance of Lesbianism in Early Modern England," remarks, "Although the play leaves unspoken which girl will be transformed into a boy, it makes clear that such a transformation is the only means for a happy conclusion" (251); while the play "gestures towards the enactment of erotic passion for one's own sex," in the end it "reproduces social orthodoxy"

(252). Other scholars view the ending as observing the same ambiguous portrayals of gender and sex held throughout the text. Jankowski, for example, notes how "the arbitrary nature of the change – no one knows who will become the 'real boy' and the women do not seem to care – serves to call attention to the nature of the marriage being made here ... Venus' cavalier attitude toward gender ... trivializes the whole notion of the traditional patriarchal marriage" (Jankowski, "'Where There Can Be No Cause of Affection,'" 267). In a similar vein, Dooley discusses how "no such sex-change takes place [on stage] and Lyly goes out of his way to call into question whether the promised metamorphosis will ever occur ... [This] raises serious questions about the validity of Venus's offer [to transform either Galatea or Phillida into a man]" (Dooley, "Inversion," 63). Dooley postulates that "Venus will not metamorphose *either* of the girls; she is merely pulling the wool over Neptune's eyes" (70).

10 Chess, "'Or Whatever You Be,'" 158, 146.

11 The three texts required for the seminar were as follows: *English Renaissance Drama: A Norton Anthology*, ed. Bevington et al.; Cavendish, *The Convent of Pleasure*, ed. Jansen; and Scragg's edition of *Galatea*.

12 Welch, "Potential Energies in the Early Modern French Repertoire," chapter 4 of this volume.

13 Although a history play, I am including *Edward II* in this category.

14 That being said, I am still grappling with how best to approach teaching tragedies when trying to reclaim space for characters representing minorities.

15 From the title page of the 1592 quarto, as found in *Arden of Faversham*, ed. White, 1.

16 Welch, "Potential Energies," chapter 4 of this volume.

17 See Gorman, "Theatricality of Transformation," 12. Tomlinson, "'My Brain the Stage,'" asserts that the male gaze associated with such cross-dressing conventions is pushed aside by the genre of the closet drama; the distance created by Lady Happy and the Princess acting in a play within a play never meant for the stage makes space for "a fleeting fantasy of what we would call lesbian love" (151, 154). Tomlinson also observes how Cavendish closes with a reference to the Princess as female in the *dramatis personae*, uniquely appended at the end of the play (155). Perhaps in not needing actors to perform, the closet drama is able to maintain a fictive space for gender nonconformity and queer desire. My thanks to E.M. Parry for recommending this chapter.

15 Rehearsing *The Lieutenant Nun*: Translation in Action

EDWARD McLEAN (MAC) TEST

The question of Guzmán's gender identity in *The Famous Play of the Lieutenant Nun* (originally published in 1626 as the *Comedia famosa de la monja alférez*) arose every day we rehearsed a scene at the 2018 Stratford Festival Laboratory workshop, Engendering the Stage.[1] There are many possibilities for identifying Guzmán's gender as the protagonist of the play and for identifying the gender of the historical figure Antonio/Catalina de Erauso, on whose life the character and play is based (Figure 15.1).[2]

This Spanish Golden Age play was first attributed to the Spanish playwright Juan Pérez de Montalbán. More recently, scholars attribute the play to the Mexican-born playwright Juan Ruiz de Alarcón. Erauso was born female in 1592 and died as a male in México in 1650 under the name Lieutenant Antonio de Erauso. Circa 1600, around the age of fifteen, Erauso escaped a Dominican convent in San Sebastian, Spain, dressed in the clothes of a boy with shortened hair, and jumped aboard a ship bound for the Americas. Fighting in the wars against the Mapuche in Chile at a time of intense colonial violence, Erauso rose to the rank of *alférez* (lieutenant), living the life of a soldier, gambler, and swashbuckler. In 1617, after having committed a crime, Erauso was obliged by the bishop of Huamanga (now Ayacucho, Peru) to enter a convent. Shortly after, Erauso asked the authorities in San Sebastian to send evidence that they had never taken vows as a nun. Around 1624, Erauso returned to Spain. They travelled to the court of Madrid to petition the Council of the Indies for a military pension and to continue living as man. Around 1626, Erauso visited Pope Urban VIII and asked to receive an indulgence to live and dress as a man. Reportedly, the impressed pope stated, "If you bring me another Lieutenant Nun, I'll grant the same." In 1630, Erauso was in Seville, Spain, ready to embark again to the Americas. A recently discovered document from 1639 reveals that Erauso asked to receive the

Figure 15.1. Juan van der Hamen, Portrait of Antonio/Catalina de Erauso, c. 1626. Fundación Kutxa/WikiArt.

complete amount of their royal pension while in México, consisting in part of taxes collected from several *encomiendas* of Indigenous people of Oaxaca, Puebla, and Hidalgo. In México, Erauso also worked as a mule driver between the seaport of Veracruz and the City of México until 1649 (a date preserved in the records of a lawsuit for the inheritance of Antonio de Erauso) and had enslaved individuals working for them. Erauso became an instant celebrity at the Spanish court in Madrid, as well as in important enclaves within the viceroyalties of Peru and México.

Together, the historical figure of Erauso and the fictional character of Guzmán (representing Erauso) provide a view of the depictions of gender in the early modern world. In this essay, I have chosen to refer to the historical person with "they/them" pronouns, which reflects the alternating gender markers present in the original seventeenth-century archival documents about Erauso. I have chosen to use the pronouns "he/him" when referring to the dramatic figure, Guzmán, since that is how the character speaks of himself and is referred to by others within the play.[3]

Through the character of Guzmán, *The Famous Play of the Lieutenant Nun* features one of the first dramatic roles of a transgender character. It is also one of the first plays to feature the daily life and business of Spanish colonial soldiers and conquistadors in the Americas, revealing a complex and intriguing urban world. Furthermore, it features a Basque protagonist whose identity within the Spanish colonial world is negotiated as a strong minority figure. The play delves into the complex identity of Erauso, an individual assigned female at birth (AFAB) who left behind high social status of noble stock, choosing instead to live as a layman and a soldier in order to gain freedom.

Miguel Martínez, in his critical edition of the autobiography of Catalina de Erauso (*Vida y sucesos de la monja alférez*, 2021), brings to life new documentation yet also highlights that there are still unknown details about Erauso's life today. Eyewitness accounts, the autobiography, and the play all offer different takes, fictionalized and conditioned by the literary genres in which they were inscribed. Martínez has also argued very convincingly about the problems of situating the autobiography as a point of comparison with the play. The autobiography was highly modified when it was printed. Editors and readers added names, dates, and details that they found in the documentation about Erauso held at the General Archive of the Indies (Archivo General de las Indias) in Seville, Spain, and in eyewitness accounts of Erauso's life published during the early seventeenth century (most of them when Erauso was still alive). Luzmila Camacho Platero's recent edition of the play (2006) establishes a comparison between the autobiography and the play, and notes the places in which they differ. We need to bear in mind, however, that the play chronologically precedes the extant manuscripts of the autobiography, as Martínez emphasizes.

Before the Engendering the Stage workshop, I saw the character Guzmán as a cross-dressed woman, but through working with trans and non-binary advisors, I came to see Guzmán as a trans man. It is important to recognize that the character of Guzmán is not the same as the real person and to acknowledge that I am not trying to determine the gender of the historical figure; rather, I am focusing on the possible gender identification of the character within the play. The experience of the workshop in Stratford helped inform the decision by my co-translator, Marta Albalá Pelegrín, and I to identify Guzmán as a trans character for our edition of the play.[4] It is important to note, however, that during the Stratford workshop the role was performed by Denise Oucharek, a cisgender woman. She approached the role with an open and exploratory attitude, fascinated by the gender possibilities of the character, but quite rightly situated her process in the perspective of her own gender identity:

> Is this a woman who's gay, who wants to be more masculine? Is this a woman who's cisgendered but wants to appear masculine? Is this a transgendered individual? What is Guzmán? In order to play the role, you have to make decisions for Guzmán. What does Guzmán think inside? When Guzmán was younger and presenting as female in society, there were behaviours and responses that were learned that don't change. So, I layered onto Guzmán the question: when does the female Catalina surface?[5]

For Denise, playing the role of Guzmán involved self-reflection about her own gendered upbringing and the complexities associated with an identity switch. Denise had to get to know Guzmán and translate the character into performance. As Nerea Aresti points out, "the changes in Catalina's nature were less striking [to contemporaries] than the changes in society over the centuries that separate us from her."[6] Remarkably, in 1622 Erauso's mother refers to her child as a "son" in her will, and when returning to San Sebastián briefly in 1629, Erauso signed a notarized document with the name Antonio de Erauso.[7] In this particular instance, the historical records suggest that Erauso considered themself a man, and apparently even his mother viewed them as male.[8]

Traditionally, in Spanish drama of the seventeenth century and across the stages of Europe, Guzmán would be labeled a *mujer varonil* (manly woman). The *Lieutenant Nun*'s portrayal of non-normative gender, however, is unique in that Guzmán only appears as a male on stage. His identity is not a disguise. In seventeenth-century Spain, cross-dressed women were popular in theatre. Spanish comedias were performed in open courtyard spaces known as *corrales*; nobles and aristocrats sat in house balconies; women peopled the first floors of the surrounding *cazuelas*, or stewpots; and *mosqueteros* (akin to English groundlings at the London theatres) sat on benches just in front of the stage. A striking difference from English theatre is that women were allowed to perform on the Spanish stage (indeed, women were sometimes stakeholders in the theatres). On the title page of one extant version of *The Famous Play of the Lieutenant Nun* (attributed to Montalbán; see Figure 15.2), for example, the part of Guzmán is immediately advertised as being performed by Luisa Robles, a beautiful and renowned actress of the time period.

The most famous playwright of Spanish Golden Age drama, Lope de Vega, wrote more than 100 plays with this type of character and promoted the *mujer varonil* in his *Arte nuevo de hacer comedias en este reino* (*The New Art of Writing Plays*), where he affirms that cross-dressing women are a crowd-pleaser.[9] No other character from the Spanish comedia, however, so steadily exhibits a gender not assigned at birth. Lines are written for Guzmán (not Catalina), and he appears on stage only in male attire. Throughout the play, he refuses to be misrecognized as a woman, making statements such as "I'll die before making public that I am a woman" and "I am not a woman."[10] The only staged moment of cross-dressing in *The Lieutenant Nun* is not Catalina donning male attire; rather, it is the reverse: Guzmán is asked to wear female clothes. But notably, he refuses. As M.G. Allan asserts, "Guzman is neither a woman nor, as some readings intimate, simply a man; he is a transman who struggles for recognition."[11] Typically, in Golden Age plays, female characters cross-dress as male to achieve a goal within the context of their play (a lover, revenge, temporary power, and so on), but almost always, even the toughest *mujer varonil* conforms to her gender role within society by the end of Act 3.[12] Seventeenth-century Spanish audiences were also aware of the everyday realities blurring gender identities and sexual desire. Emilie L. Bergmann notes, "The historical documentation of the cases of Catalina de Erauso, known as the '*Monja Alférez*' (Lieutenant Nun) and Elena/Eleno de Céspedes reveal more than rebellion by women against the roles imposed on them; they also reveal an instability of gender roles that literary critics have traditionally dismissed as inconceivable."[13] Unstable gender roles and the representation of non-normative gender identity were a familiar aspect of life on and off stage in Renaissance Spain. In the comedias, the *mujer varonil* commonly gives up violence and cross-dressing to be reintegrated back into the community, but not so with Guzmán, who presents contemporary audiences and readers with a familiar yet different spectacle.

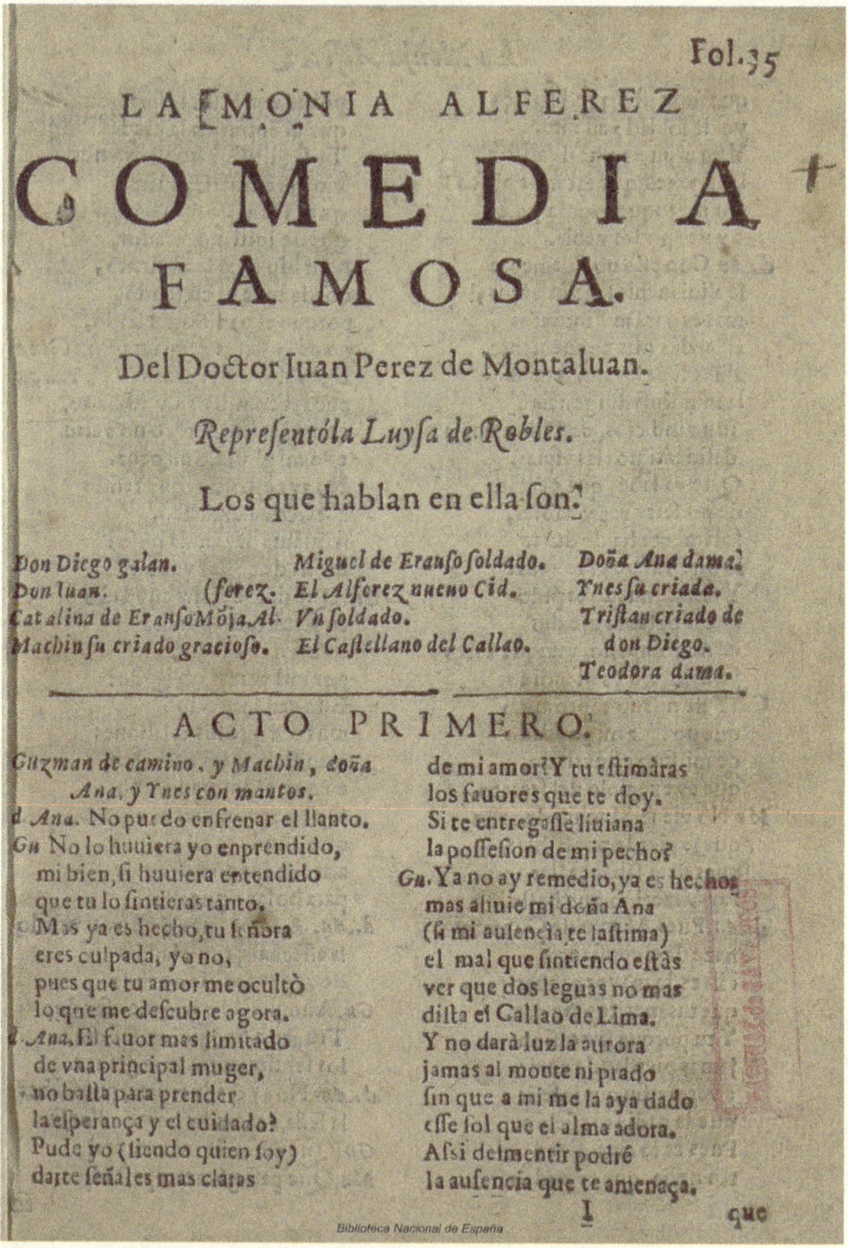

Fol.35

LA MONIA ALFEREZ

COMEDIA

FAMOSA.

Del Doctor Iuan Perez de Montaluan.

Representóla Luysa de Robles.

Los que hablan en ella son.

Don Diego galan.	*Miguel de Erauso soldado.*	*Doña Ana dama.*
Don Iuan. (*ferez.*	*El Alferez nueuo Cid.*	*Ynes su criada.*
Catalina de Erauso Mōja Al-	*Vn soldado.*	*Triftan criado de*
Machin su criado graciofo.	*El Caftellano del Callao.*	*don Diego.*
		Teodora dama.

ACTO PRIMERO.

Guzman de camino, y Machin, doña
Ana, y Ynes con mantos.

d *Ana.* No puedo enfrenar el llanto.
Gu No lo huuiera yo enprendido,
  mi bien, fi huuiera entendido
  que tu lo fintieras tanto.
  Mas ya es hecho, tu feñora
  eres culpada, yo no,
  pues que tu amor me ocultò
  lo que me defcubre agora.
d *Ana.* El fauor mas limitàdo
  de vna principal muger,
  no bafta para prender
  la efperança y el cuidado?
  Pude yo (fiendo quien foy)
  dajte feñales mas claras

de mi amor? Y tu eftimàras
los fauores que te doy.
Si te entregaffe liuiana
la poffefion de mi pecho?
Gu. Ya no ay remedio, ya es hecho,
  mas aliuie mi doña Ana
  (fi mi aufencia te laftima)
  el mal que fintiendo eftàs
  ver que dos leguas no mas
  difta el Callao de Lima.
  Y no darà luz la aurora
  jamas al monte ni prado
  fin que a mi me la aya dado
  effe fol que el alma adora.
  Afsi delmentir podré
  la aufencia que te amenaça.

A

que

Figure 15.2. Title page for *La Comedia famosa de la monja alférez*, c. 1626. Attributed to Juan Pérez de Montalbán. Madrid. Biblioteca Nacional de España.

The cross-cultural process of translating and staging *The Lieutenant Nun* today in English reveals a myriad of possibilities and contextual difficulties, arising especially from the importance of gender to the play combined with the grammatically gendered Spanish language. The most frequent struggle we encountered as translators centred on the fact that English frequently requires a gendered and marked pronoun before a verb (he or she), while Spanish does not. We encountered challenging phrases with no pronoun or impersonal and passive reflexive constructions that English language demands we attribute a gender. As the translator of Catalina de Erauso's memoir, Michele Stepto readily admits: "There is no English equivalent for the gender inflections of the Spanish adjective, which make a primary, grammatical notation of gender with practically every sentence, thus setting up a drumbeat of sexual self-identification that reverberates from one end of the text to the other."[14] The same can be said of translating the play.

Translating historically distant drama presents difficulties because the author is not around to clarify intention; the stage is no longer there; many of the sayings are no longer current; and even the simplest cultural markers may no longer apply. At Stratford, we workshopped a painful scene where a nobleman, Sebastián de Illumbe (played by Danielle Wade), forces Guzmán (Denise Oucharek) to dress in female clothing, while Guzmán's *gracioso* sidekick, Machín (played by Mariah Campos), looks on and provides pointed commentary. By this point in the play, all three characters are aware that Guzmán was assigned female at birth. In the following exchange, Guzmán expresses anger at having to dress in women's clothing, while Machín reminds him of his former position as a novice in the convent. The opening lines below point to Guzmán's frustration at becoming a "monstrous" object of the public gaze. Here is our initial translation:

GUZMÁN: What does he want from me?
  Am I some monster never seen before,
  or the beast they claim was spotted
  in the Polish Kingdom with pen and sword?
  Haven't you seen a man without a beard?
MACHÍN: A man? Could it be that you have
  plainly forgotten the *memento Mulier,*
  the Trinitarian's habit, that they dressed
  you with in Lima?[15]

When Mariah read these lines, she stumbled over "memento Mulier" and "Trinitarian." Moreover, Mariah asked why Machín, a lesser educated sidekick, would speak Latin (Spanish servants were often more like stewards and could be well educated). As frequently happens with translation, we were presented with the issue of fidelity to the original text versus the liberty of eliminating words, while maintaining the general intention of the playwright. The scholar in me explained to Mariah the probable joke between the common Latinate phrases of the Renaissance, "memento mori" and "memento mulier." We opted for a better phrased line that both communicated the meaning and propelled the action forward by communicating Machin's challenge to Guzmán's assessment of his own gender more clearly for a modern audience (while explaining what was lost in a scholarly footnote). We decided to simplify the speech as follows:

> MACHÍN: A "man"? Have you forgotten
>   the Nun's dress you wore in Lima?

This choice in translation is easy to comprehend and was further emphasized by the comical way Denise opted to play Guzmán's dilemma of how to put on the dress, something he was completely unaccustomed to wearing. Of this moment, Denise remarks:

> Guzmán felt threatened by having to change clothing … vulnerability came up. Playing Guzmán, I thought, "If I'm not allowed to exist and look and present the way that I want to, I suddenly feel powerless, like a little girl." Guzmán felt the younger Catalina again … [and] could be more petulant, which is more fun than just being angry. That's the childishness, right? You want me to wear the dress? Fine! Look, I'll tie it around my boobs. If I were directing this piece, I would encourage people to go for humour because the audience would see it and laugh. But it is also dark. In this scene, Guzmán deals with the exasperation of all the people just going, "Can't you just do this?" and me realizing as Guzmán, "No, I can't. It's not quite as cut and dry as you think it is, you know, it's actually painful for me to do this." That was fascinating.[16]

Exploring the interplay of actors, speech, and a multiplicity of emotions in the workshop helped us edit the play-text through collaboration. It was a quite explicit form of "communal translation through rehearsal," as Christian Billing writes of the theatrical methodology of practice as research (PaR). It is more about process than product. While the final published translation will follow the original text closely and contain singular choices, some annotations will provide alternative translations. As Billing notes, PaR creates "an embodied, spatial, and temporal refuge in which both the communities of the past (those who first wrote and acted the play, as well as those who have subsequently interpreted it) and those of the present (those who now interpret, as both scholars and actors) seek collaboratively to reconstruct a semantic assemblage of its elements for those communities who will see and feel it live in the future."[17] The Engendering the Stage workshop at the Stratford Lab provided us with an important opportunity to work with trans and non-binary artists, including the director for our *Lieutenant Nun* scene work who encouraged Denise to pursue all the uncertainty of Guzmán's gender. These artists made it abundantly clear to me that trans and queer elements are already present in early modern culture. "In contemporary translation studies," Emily Rose writes, "the translator is expected to reconcile constant and ongoing renegotiations between texts and cultures, instead of simply reproducing a text in a different language."[18] A translator of historical drama should work to make trans lives visible if the text doesn't already do that work, especially when the trans histories have been forgotten or overlooked.

Although Billing speaks of translation as a metaphor, his description of PaR as it relates to older texts is most apt: "In attempting to create a modern performance from a historically distant play-text, to make a translation of that text that renders its dialects intelligible to modern ears and its spectacle interesting to modern eyes, one must always attend to form – both in terms of what is possible in a modern theatre and to how those forms relate to the originals."[19] Billing seems to channel Walter Benjamin, who writes, "Translation ultimately serves the purpose of expressing the central reciprocal relationship between languages."[20] This reciprocal relationship between languages is exactly what Billing suggests by making an older play intelligible to modern ears. Finding this "central reciprocal relationship" is fraught with complexities between old and new language, written and performed language, and none are free from influences of power and constantly coloured by personal and cultural assumptions. The now famous Italian phrase "*Il traduttore è un traditore*" (The translator is a betrayer) speaks to the dark cloud that hangs above each translator's head: a translation will never be the same as the original. In this case, the real betrayer might be seen as a language that embeds a gender binary and misrepresents the complexity of gender identity.

The issue of gender identity is further complicated by the almost 400 years that separates our translation from the historical moment of 1626 when the play was composed. Today, scholars question whether we can use modern concepts of "transgender" or "trans man" before these terms even existed because "to do so would risk divesting past gender practice of what made it meaningful in its own time and place."[21] Indeed, by imposing modern understandings of gender on the past, we in effect erase language of the past; however, as the "trans" in "translation" indicates, it is a process of "carrying over" concepts and meaning from one language to another, which includes carrying over historical terms from the past in one culture to the present in another culture. "The translator," Emily Rose writes, "has the power to shape transgender identity in their translations."[22] As translators, we considered the "different methods for excavating pasts that certainly contained gender-variant cultural practices, without necessarily imposing the name 'transgender' on those historical moments."[23] The historical documentation mentioned above (that Erauso's mother referred to her child as a "son" in her will, that the pope and king likely provided papers for Erauso to dress as a man, and that Erauso signed their own name as "Antonio") clearly implies that viewing the dramatic character Guzmán as a "man" is in accordance with the historical Erauso's perceived legal status, even if the term "trans man" did not exist at the time.[24] In this manner, we are not introducing modern terms to the text but aligning with Guzmán's historical nature and with the gender of his character within the play-text by referring to him as a male in our translation. While Guzmán is a character who is trans before the modern trans concept existed, Joseph Gamble's brilliant research reveals the seventeenth-century use of the word "trans." Gamble notes: "Thomas Blount recorded both 'tran- sexion' and 'transfeminate' in his *Glossographia or a Dictionary* (1656). The entry for 'transfeminate' reads: 'Transfeminate (from trans and fœmina): to turn from woman to man, or from one sex to another. Dr. Br.' (sig. Rr4v)."[25] Further, there were seventeenth-century French and Spanish medical theorists who believed that men could become women.[26] The early modern scholar Kathleen Long puts it so elegantly: "Gender is one of our oldest systems of classification of embodied experience, yet this experience itself always escapes such classification and lives beyond the realm of regulation and containment. Our more generous and generative selves confound the systems that purport to define us, creating ever more possibilities for life, adapting to new circumstances and environments; this is how we survive."[27] Admittedly, even today we are still learning about gender variability, so any application of present knowledge to the past runs the risk of imposing a concept rather than listening to what history tells us.

Dealing with the gendered grammar of Spanish presented yet another difficulty and led to many discussions with trans guest artists at the workshop. We decided that Guzmán wants to be seen as and referred to as a man, so we opted to use a masculine-gendered translation, except in moments when the play-text purposefully changes the feminine ending of a particular word. In the original Spanish, the playwright notably switches Guzmán's masculine-gendered words to feminine-gendered words at certain points in the play. The change occurs for comedic effect, when characters discuss Guzmán as being female and when Catalina's brother, Miguel, refers to Catalina as female. In English, we did not translate the feminine and masculine endings, except for one moment where the gendered words were elemental to the text. This switch was most evident during the following exchange, which I will first illustrate in Spanish so that the gendered ending is clear:

MACHÍN: ¿Quieres acaso vestirte sobre la espada?
GUZMÁN: Estoy tan acostumbrad**o** …
Quítase la espada y pónese el manteo al revés.
MACHÍN: Acostumbrad**a**.
GUZMÁN: También
    lo estoy de tratarme hablando
    como varón.

Note the humour surrounding the word "acostumbrad**a/o**": Guzmán uses the masculine ending "o" and Machín immediately corrects him by using the feminine ending "a." We originally resolved this issue by inserting script directions for modulating the voice:

SEBASTIAN: Would you like to dress atop the sword?
GUZMÁN: [*Speaking in a man's voice.*] I'm used to it.
He takes off his sword and puts on the dress backwards.
MACHÍN: [*Imitating a woman trying to speak like a man.*]
    Used to it?
GUZMÁN: Also, I am learning to speak like a man.

When the actors attempted to intonate stereotypical "male" and "female" voices for this passage, laughter ensued. The comedic effect, however, was generated by the ridiculousness of modulating the voice, not because of the gendered word play. We discussed how we might rephrase the lines so that the gendered and comedic aspect of the exchange is maintained but not in such a gratuitous manner. Working together, we came up with the following:

SEBASTIAN: Are you putting the dress over the sword?
GUZMÁN: As a man, I am accustomed to dressing with my sword.
Guzmán takes off the sword and puts on the dress backwards.
MACHÍN: Accustomed as a man? Do you mean as a woman?
GUZMÁN: No. I always carry myself as a man.

The choice of "carry myself as a man" is in keeping with our strong sense of Guzmán's preferred identity as a male throughout the text. He has always spoken with male endings up to this point in the play. It also stays true to the gendered language of the original Spanish text. Given that Guzmán is based upon the real-life person, Antonio/Catalina de Erauso, one wonders if Spanish speakers of the seventeenth century made similar plays with language and gender.

The violent wars against the Indigenous people of South America provided an arena where Spanish women could take on traditionally male roles. As remarkable as Erauso's story may seem, other persons assigned female at birth also fought with the conquistadors in the Americas, a point that serves as evidence for the complexity of gendered identities in early modern Spain. Inés Suárez, the famous lover of Pedro de Valdivia, fought in the conquest of Chile; María de Estrada fought alongside Cortés during the "Sorrowful Night" massacre; and many other women fought with Cortes, some openly presenting as female and others concealing their sex: Beatriz Ordaz, Juana Martín, María de Vera, Elvira Hernández, Isabel Rodríguez, Beatriz Hernández, Catalina Márquez, Beatriz Palacios Parda, Juana López, Violante Rodríguez, Catalina González, and Antonia Hernández.[28] Isabel Barreto was the first known woman in European history to hold the position of admiral.[29] The history of the conquest of the Americas is replete with warriors who were assigned female at birth.

The first two acts of *The Lieutenant Nun* occur in Lima, Peru (the third and final act is set in Madrid, Spain). When Erauso arrived in 1604, Lima was a bustling metropole of 25,000 inhabitants. Lima's port of Callao (where Guzmán is stationed in the play) was the centre of a vast trade network that integrated Peru with the rest of the Americas, Europe, and the Far East. The silver mining around the city of Potosí (at the time, the largest city in the Americas with a population over 150,000) brought extraordinary wealth to the Spanish empire. Lima had a theatre, a printing press, a hospital, a cathedral, and even a university. It was a cultural hub of the Spanish colonial empire. Life was much less organized outside of the major settlements. The Araucanian wars against the Mapuche went on for most of the sixteenth and seventeenth centuries, with a final insurrection against the colonial oppressors occurring in 1655. According to Erauso's memoir (which adopts feminine pronouns), when Erauso was stationed at Fort Paincaví in Chile's frigid south, Erauso's bravery on the battlefield helped Erauso gain the rank of lieutenant. Within the context of the play, the Indigenous people known as the Araucanians are mentioned only in passing, but the wars are ever present for soldiers like Guzmán. While these women and trans men enjoyed relative freedom in the Americas, this liberty was obtained at the expense of massive cultural devastation: slavery, genocide, as well as societal and environmental destruction. "Native populations suffered an important decline during the first century of the Spanish rule, mostly as a result of epidemics, but also through violence and wars."[30] Guzmán, while exhibiting masculine violence in the killing of his brother and a soldier, is not as violent as the historical counterpart, Antonio/Catalina de Erauso, who kills and maims numerous Spanish and Indigenous people. As the editors of *Trans Historical: Gender Plurality before the Modern* note, the archival absences of trans histories are "compounded in the medieval and early modern periods in particular by the realities of slavery and colonialism, which actively sought to erase the voices of African and Native peoples who found themselves the target of European and broader settler colonial violence and expropriation."[31] As translators of the play, we had to constantly recognize that the trans history of Erauso is layered in colonial violence. Indeed, Erauso is not a likeable character but a product of the Spanish colonial project that aimed to subject non-Christian peoples in the Americas. The play papers over this violence, focusing instead on Guzmán's chivalry and his desire to protect Ana. Acknowledging these complexities, the dramaturgical material included in the forthcoming edition of our translation will provide directors with specific Indigenous and colonial cultural markers that can be explored in a stage production.

Translating *The Lieutenant Nun* has been a long process, and the journey will not end with submitting the text for publication. Adaptions of the translation for theatrical productions will follow, as will class discussions. I taught one draft in a theatre class, pairing up *The Lieutenant Nun* with play-texts such as Thomas Middleton and Thomas Dekker's *The Roaring Girl* and the Spanish play written by Ana Caro, *The Courage to Right a Woman's Wrongs*.[32] The students were unfamiliar with Spanish drama and were particularly struck by how contemporary *The Lieutenant Nun* was to our society's discussions about gender fluidity. We discussed how Guzmán likely felt like an oddity at home but felt most free in the Americas. As mentioned above, this freedom came at a great cost for the Indigenous peoples, including Two-Spirit individuals with whom Guzmán (and Erauso) may have found a certain kinship. In real life, Catalina returned to Mexico in 1630 as Antonio de Erauso and died there in 1650. According to the Mexican Friar Nicolás de la Rentería, in 1645 he met "the Lieutenant Nun Catarina de Araujo (who at that time went by the name Don Antonio de Araujo) working as a muleteer with black people ... dressed in male clothing, carrying a sword and dagger ornamented in silver, and looking about 50 years old, with a strong body ... and a mustache with a few hairs."[33] Whether on stage, in Spain or in the

Americas, whether a fictional character or a real person, Guzmán and Erauso stretched and blurred literary, historical, and societal categorizations. To borrow from Gamble's work on trans histories, "there is not one sex/gender system, but a multiplicity; not a stable multiplicity but only a perpetual multiplication of sexes and genders. Trans is the perpetual extension of the elements of gendered existence. Perpetual extension: that is, a process without a set product."[34] Translating *The Lieutenant Nun* is likewise a process, one that is still ongoing today.

NOTES

1 The original title in Spanish is *La famosa comedia de la monja alférez*. At the workshop, we used a working draft of the English translation of this play, now published as Ruiz de Alarcón, attrib. *The Lieutenant Nun*, in *The Lieutenant Nun, Annotated Translation of the Play, Historical Accounts and Documents about Antonio/Catalina de Erauso*, ed. and trans. Albalá Pelegrín and Test. In addition to being used for scene work in 2018 at the Engendering the Stage Stratford Festival Laboratory, this translation was workshopped at UCLA in 2017 (Cella, "Translation Workshop [October 17]"), and staged readings took place at Boise Contemporary Theater in 2019 and at Cal-Poly Pomona in 2022. The play's author has traditionally been considered to be Juan Pérez de Montalbán, and the two extant printed copies of the play have his name on the title page. However, *The Lieutenant Nun* is not included in either of the two collections of Montalbán's works that appeared in 1635 and posthumously in 1638. Recently, some scholars consider Luis Belmonte Bermúdez in contention as a possible author; Gabriel Andrés and Miguel Martínez, among other scholars, consider the possibility of a second play about Erauso that could have been authored by Luis Belmonte Bermúdez (Andrés, "Estudio introductorio," 8; Martínez, "Introducción," 20–1). Germán Vega García-Luengos affirms that the author is Juan Ruiz de Alarcón (Vega García-Luengos, "Juan Ruiz de Alarcón recupera 'La monja alférez,'" 101–3).

2 Velasco identifies Erauso as a masculine woman in *The Lieutenant Nun: Transgenderism*. Aresti, "Gendered Identities," argues that the play is ambiguous about Erauso's gender and sexuality. Allan, "Un Hombre Sin Barbas," and Rose, "Keeping the Trans in Translation," contend that Erauso is a trans man. Rose also notes that Rutter-Jensen in "La transformación transatlántica de la Monja Alférez" argues for Erauso as transsexual. Rose further notes that Leslie Feinberg considers Erauso to be an early "transgender warrior" in *Transgender Warriors*. See also Rose, *Translating Trans Identity*.

3 For more information about these pronoun decisions, see Albalá Pelegrín and Test, "Introduction."

4 I want to acknowledge that the historical person is not present to give us consent for the chosen gender reference. Although the concept of trans as we understand it today didn't exist 400 years ago, historical documents make clear that Erauso (on whom the character of Guzmán is based) lived their adult life as a man. For more in-depth discussion, see Albalá Pelegrín and Test, "Introduction."

5 Denise Oucharek in conversation with Peter Cockett and Melinda Gough, unpublished interview, 2019.

6 Aresti, "Gendered Identities," 404.

7 Aresti.

8 While Erauso signed this document using their male name, Antonio, there are other historical documents where Erauso signs with Catalina. It is important to note that historical documents configure the male and female subject according to bureaucratic requirements of the seventeenth-century Spanish empire and do not necessarily reflect personal preferences. For more information on this topic, see Goldmark, "Reading Habits."

9 See Lope de Vega, *New Art of Writing Plays*, 142. *Arte nuevo de hacer comedias en este tiempo* was written by Lope de Vega in 1609. He writes, "Las damas no desdigan de su nombre, / y, si mudaren traje, sea de modo / que pueda perdonarse, porque suele / el disfraz varonil agradar mucho." It roughly translates as "Ladies don't step out of character, and if they change to male clothing, it is in a manner that allows them to forgive themselves because a woman dressed as a man is a crowd-pleaser."

10 These quotes are from lines 2011 and 3210, respectively, in Ruiz de Alarcón, attrib., *The Lieutenant Nun*, and correspond roughly to Act 2, line 1724 and Act 3, line 2730.

11 Allan, "Un Hombre Sin Barbas," 122. I follow the GLAAD Media Reference Guide, 11th ed., "Glossary of Terms: Transgender," in using "trans man" and "trans woman" (not "transman" or "transwoman").

12 A few other plays from the time period push the limits of the *mujer varonil*. These include Lope de Vega, *La varona castellana*; José de Cañizares, *La señora Mari Pérez*; and Luis Vélez de Guevara, *La serrana de la Vera*.

13 Bergmann, "Folklore as Queer," 72.

14 Erauso, *Lieutenant Nun*, trans. and ed. Stepto and Stepto, xlvi.

15 Ruiz de Alarcón, attrib. *The Lieutenant Nun*. The Spanish text used for this translation is *La Monja alférez*, ed. Andrés. The lines read as follows:

> GUZMÁN: ¡Qué ha de verme!, ¿soy acaso
> algún monstruo nunca visto
> o la fiera que inventaron,

> que con letras y con armas
> se vio en el reino polaco?
> ¿No ha visto un hombre sin barbas?
> MACHÍN: ¡«Hombre», oh qué! Tú has olvidado
> sin duda el memento mulier
> de aquel monjil trinitario
> que te pusieron en Lima.

16 Oucharek in conversation with Cockett and Gough.

17 Billing, "Historiography," 23.

18 Rose, "Keeping the Trans," 495.

19 Billing, "Historiography," 12.

20 Benjamin, "Task of the Translator," 174.

21 DeVun and Tortorici, "Trans, Time, and History," 520.

22 Rose, "Keeping the Trans," 496.

23 Stryker and Aizura, "Introduction: Transgender Studies 2.0," 11.

24 The story of this permission in the form of a bull or indulgence by the Pope to Erauso has been repeated by scholars over the years, although no official documentation about this matter has surfaced.

25 Gamble, "Toward a Trans Philology," 29.

26 Kathleen P. Long notes that "certain forms of what we might call transgender were accepted in French [seventeenth-century] culture; a number of medical theorists believed that women could become men." Long also writes, "In medical and philosophical discourse of sixteenth- and seventeenth-century Europe, particularly France, there were intense debates over the nature of gender, and whether it was a simple binary of male and female, or whether it was more capacious and more mobile" (Long, in Bychowski et al., "'Trans*historicities': A Roundtable Discussion," 663, 678). The Spanish physician Juan Huarte attests to this belief, writing in 1578: "El hombre ... no difiere de la mujer ... mas que en tener los miembros genitales fuera del cuerpo" [The man isn't different from the woman except that his genitals are outside of the body; translation my own] (Huarte, *Examen de ingenios para las ciencias*, 315). And the physician Ambrose Paré "dedicated an entire section of one of his works to the subject of 'women who have degenerated into men'" (Soyer, *Ambiguous Gender*, 24). For early modern examples of historical and literary transitions of male to female, see Long, "Case of Marin le Marcis"; Chess, *Male-to-Female Crossdressing*; Cressey, "Gender Trouble"; Levine, *Men in Women's Clothing*; Garber, *Vested Interests*; Smith, *Homosexual Desire*; Dekker and van de Pol, *Tradition of Female Transvestism*; Schleiner, "Male Cross-Dressing"; Bray, *Homosexuality*.

27 Long, in Bychowski et al., "'Trans*historicities': A Roundtable Discussion," 672.

28 This list of women warriors in the Americas derives from Barjau's "El Papel
de las Mujeres en la Conquista." Barjau bases his work largely upon the
contemporary chronicle of the Spanish conquest by Francisco Cervantes de
Salazar. A book that mentions many more women who fought during the
conquest is Maura's *Españolas de ultramar.*

29 This citation is from Constenla Fontenla, "Ellas también hicieron las
Américas."

30 Ortiz-Sotelo, "Peruvian Viceroyalty," 879.

31 LaFleur et al., *Trans Historical.*

32 The original Spanish title is *Valor, agravio y mujer.* The translation referenced
here is from Caro, *Courage to Right a Woman's Wrongs.*

33 The English translation is mine. The full quote in Spanish is as follows:
"Que en el año 1645, siendo seglar, fue en los galeones del Genera D. Pedro
de Ursa: i que en la Vera-Cruz vido i habló diferentes vezes a la Monja
Alférez Da Catarina de Araujo (que entonces allí se llamava D. Antonio de
Araujo) I que tenía una requa de mulas en que conducía con unos Negros
ropa a diferentes partes: i que en ella, i con ellos le trasportó a México
la ropa que llevaba: i que era sujeto allí tenido por de mucho corazón y
destreza: i que andava en hábito de hombre, i que traía espada i daga con
guarniciones de plata: i le parece que sería entonces como de cinquenta
años, i que era de buen cuerpo, no pocas carnes, color trigueño, con
algunos pocos pelillos por bigote" (Erauso, *Vida I Sucesos de la Monja Alférez,*
ed. de Vallbona, 126).

34 Gamble, "Toward a Trans Philology," 36.

Dreaming PaR Futures

16 To Degender Is to Decolonize

MADELEINE KRUSTO AND KITOKO MAI

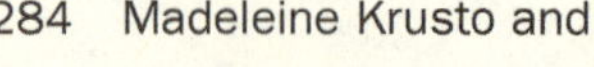

Who
are
We
?

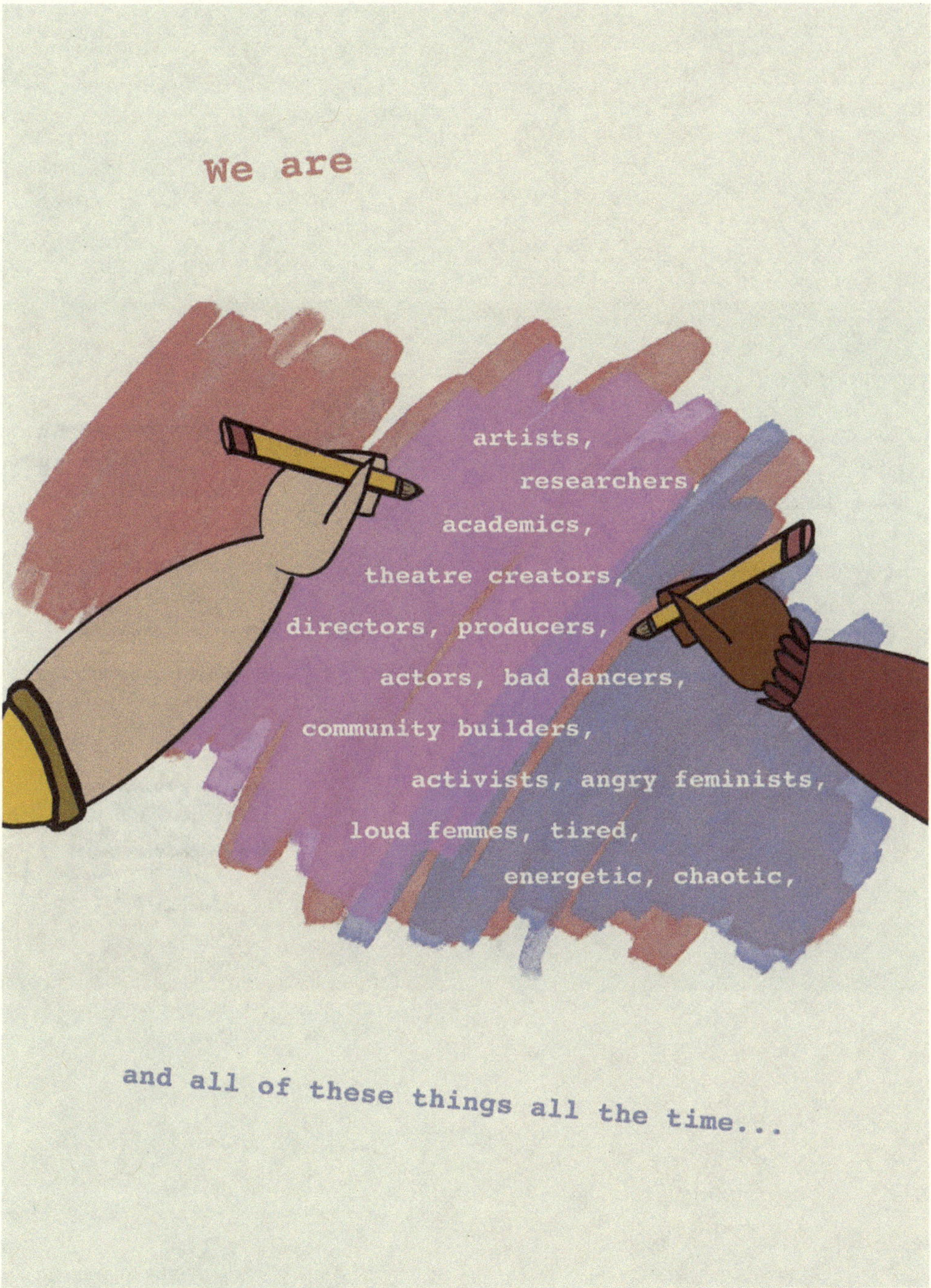

We are

artists,
researchers,
academics,
theatre creators,
directors, producers,
actors, bad dancers,
community builders,
activists, angry feminists,
loud femmes, tired,
energetic, chaotic,

and all of these things all the time...

MADDIE
She/her
Age: 23
Mood: Tired
Kitoko
They/Them
Age: 25
Mood: Black in the Year 2020
AKA: livid

We are young
emerging artists
based in
Hamilton and
Toronto.

We also were participants
at the Engender Stage Stratford Lab
in September 2018.

The lab was our first
formal research experience.

We were genuinely
excited to be there.
Not because we love
Shakespeare.
But because...

Gender
is
fake

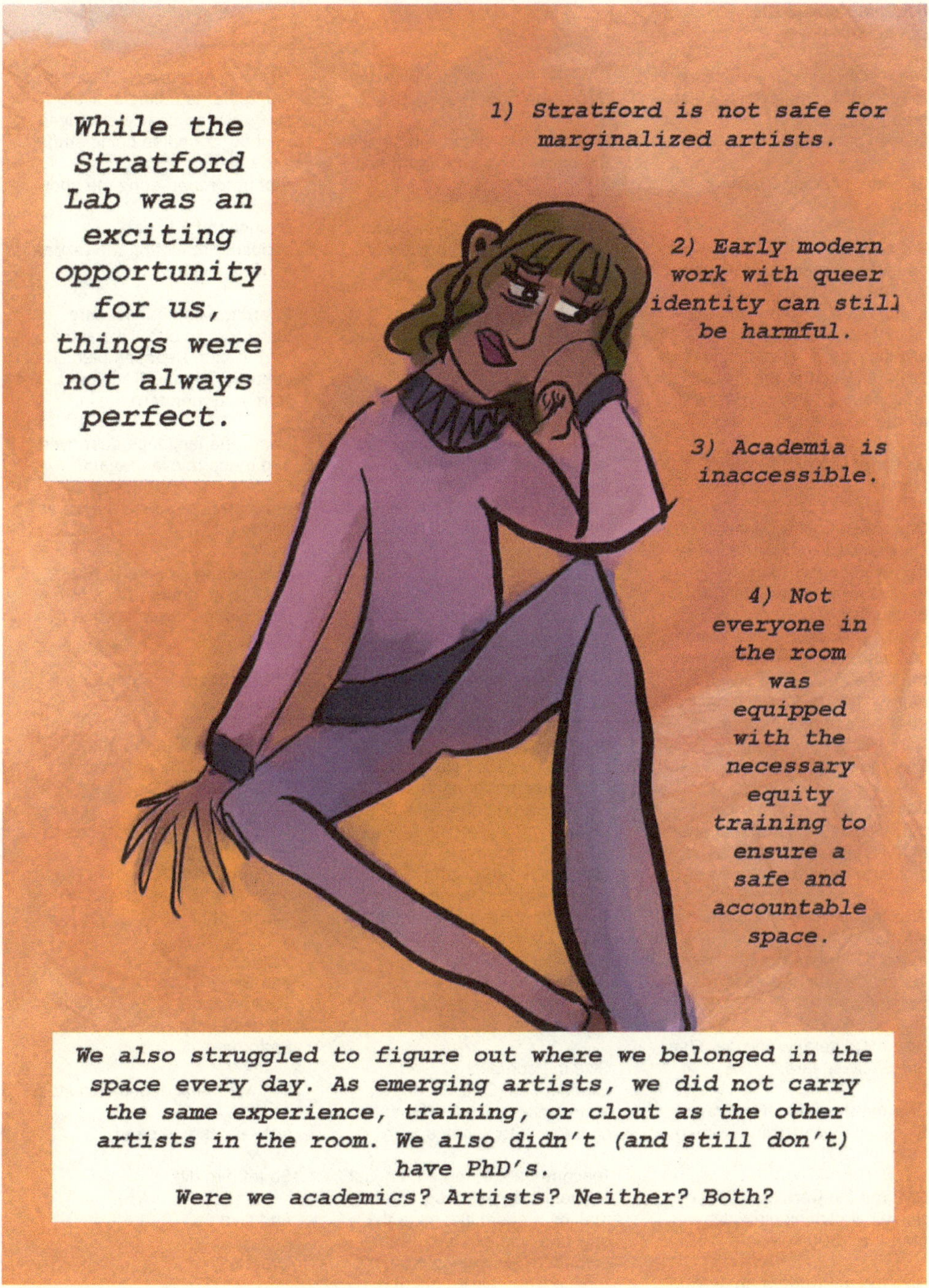

While the Stratford Lab was an exciting opportunity for us, things were not always perfect.

1) Stratford is not safe for marginalized artists.

2) Early modern work with queer identity can still be harmful.

3) Academia is inaccessible.

4) Not everyone in the room was equipped with the necessary equity training to ensure a safe and accountable space.

We also struggled to figure out where we belonged in the space every day. As emerging artists, we did not carry the same experience, training, or clout as the other artists in the room. We also didn't (and still don't) have PhD's.
Were we academics? Artists? Neither? Both?

Let Shakespeare Die
by Kitoko Mai

When will we lay Shakespeare to rest. When he gives his last breath, maybe then there will be space For me to offer my own.

Give me. Literally. Anything. Else.

But another director putting me on stage to recite text written for a white male body. Having those words bounce off my queer black feminine body. No significance or alteration just lazily leaving it to the imagination. "The words will do all the work."

Give me. Literally. Anything. Else.

Other than another adaptation of shakespearean text that believes it's revolutionary because they've reversed the genders. Because there are only two genders. Or an all female cast because having women perform the roles of classical kings is more inspiring than writing strong contemporary Queens.

Give me literally anything else.

But another strong female role that includes a handful of scenes and a tragic death after being driven to romantic insanity.

Give me anything but queering up that story and giving me a tragic queer death and romantic insanity. Visual representation is not enough.

Give me. Literally. Anyone. Else. But Shakespeare.

Give me the work of a Straight Black Quebecois trans woman from the 2010's.

Give me the work of a Queer Non-binary Latinx playwright from the 1800's

Give me the work of an Asexual Genderqueer Egyptian performer from the 60's.

Give me the work of a Bisexual trans man from the 1500's.

Give me the work of a Disabled Chinese-Cuban poet from the 70's.

Give me the work of a Filipina playwright before her country was colonized.

Give me the work of a Blackfoot Woman before her country was colonized.

Give me the work of Indigenous people around the globe before their countries were colonized. Before their art forms were deemed lesser. Before performance and community and ritual had to be defined as theatre....

Give me a Queer Nonbinary Congolese performer playing a role for a Queer Nonbinary Congolose performer. Give them a thousand more roles written for a Queer Nonbinary Congolese performer. Give them a thousand more roles that don't depend on Queer Nonbinary Congolese suffering or archaic, outsider representations of their identity.

Give them a thousand more roles that don't ignore their Queer Nonbinary Congolese existence in favour of "keeping it relatable."

And then pay them ... With money.

Give me complex experiences. Give me an abundance of narratives and characters to become.

Teach me about more than just shakespeare in school. Stop making it seem like he is the only one who existed. I want somebody else's name on my tongue when asked about classical theatre. Anyone else's work on my mind when someone says the word theatre.

I want to see diverse faces on a stage that is telling a diverse story. Not an unacknowledged rainbow of bodies being stuffed into binaries except for marketing the show.

Casting them is not enough. Presenting the text as is, is not enough.

I want to see shakespeare being torn to bits. Like actually torn to bits. Reassembled. Then destroyed again. Translated. Torn. And then torn again.

I want the language destroyed and made relevant again. Because no one fucking understands unless they're an academic.

I want shakespeare to return back to its orgins. Back to the dirty places where anyone can access him.

Shakespeare was not for the elite

Yet here we are, the elite, discussing. The privilege of discussing.

I am ready for other voices to be incorporated into the conversation. Of what is Classic and what is Theatre and who is Worthy of being

Included.
and Seen.
Spoken about.
Remembered.
Performed.

Or I want shakespeare to stop.

shakespeare is dead.

So let him die.

And give us.

Literally.

Anyone.

Else.

Engendering the Stage @Enge… · 6m
This was amazing from @JamieMilay. A spoken word piece that urges: give us anyone else but Shakespeare. A clarion call for diverse voices from across the world, across genders and sexualities, across eras. 🔥

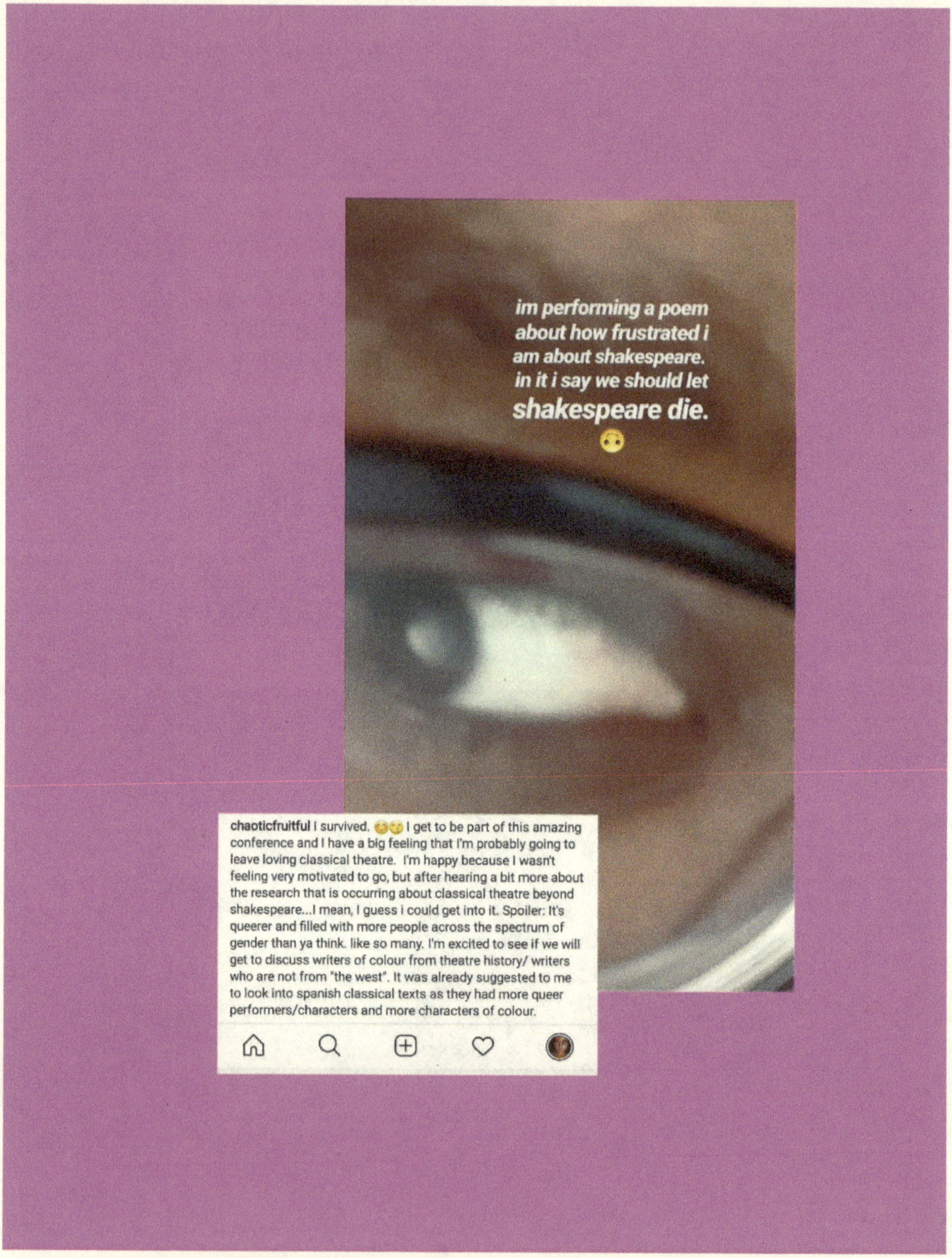

im performing a poem
about how frustrated i
am about shakespeare.
in it i say we should let
shakespeare die.

chaoticfruitful I survived. 😭😭 I get to be part of this amazing conference and I have a big feeling that I'm probably going to leave loving classical theatre. I'm happy because I wasn't feeling very motivated to go, but after hearing a bit more about the research that is occurring about classical theatre beyond shakespeare…I mean, I guess i could get into it. Spoiler: It's queerer and filled with more people across the spectrum of gender than ya think. like so many. I'm excited to see if we will get to discuss writers of colour from theatre history/ writers who are not from "the west". It was already suggested to me to look into spanish classical texts as they had more queer performers/characters and more characters of colour.

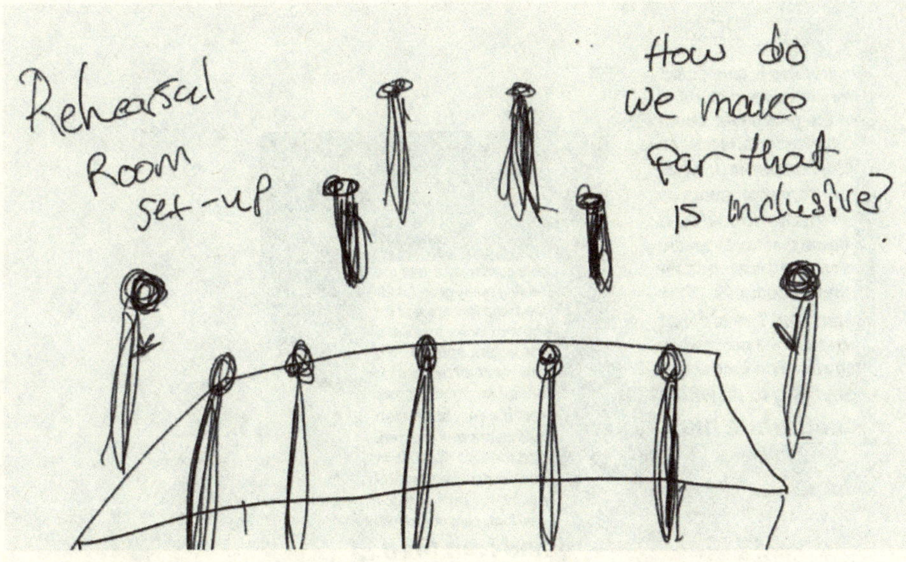

We didn't know where to stand in the room when actors performed and the scholars workshopped.

The Performance as Research (PaR) method that we witnessed did not feel inclusive or accessible.

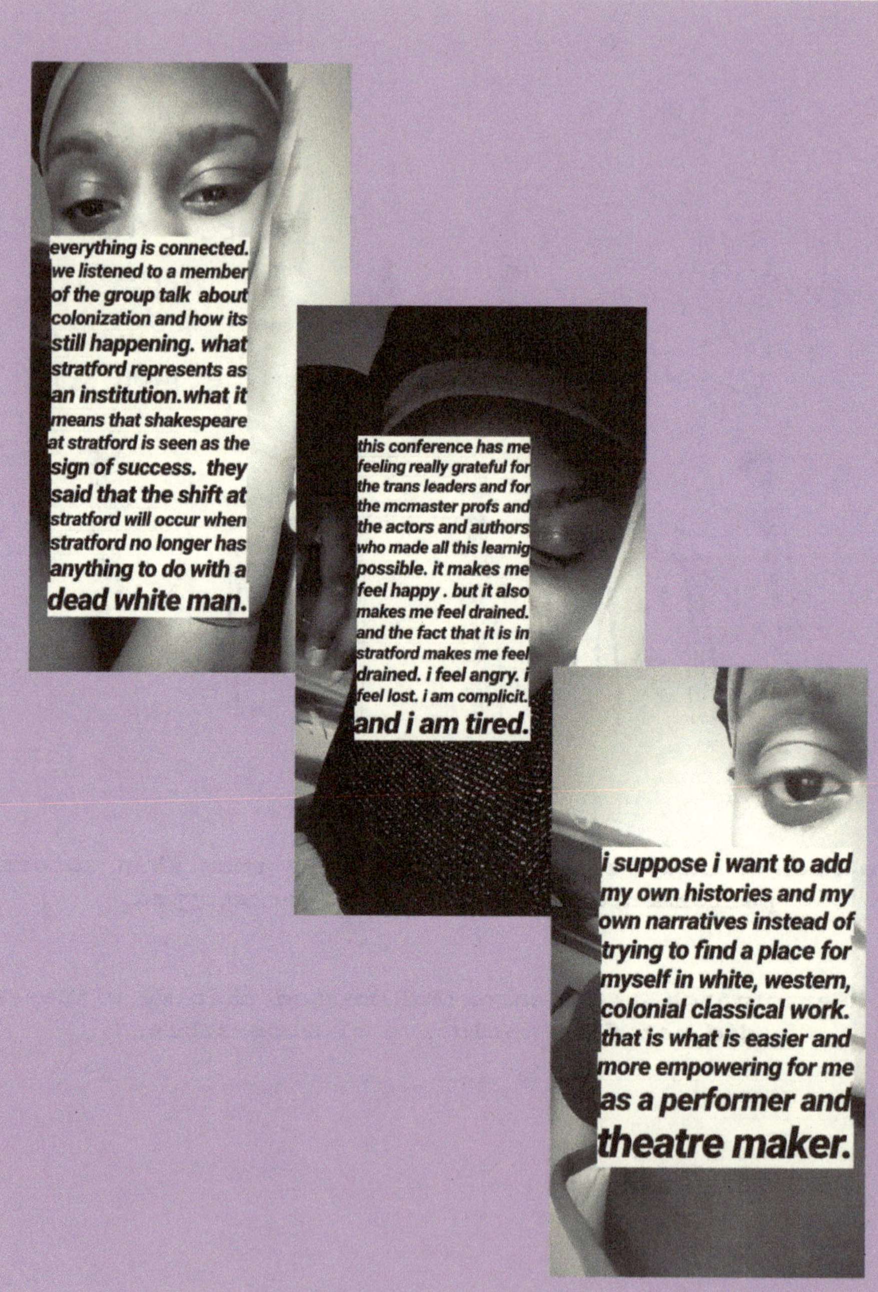
everything is connected. we listened to a member of the group talk about colonization and how its still happening. what stratford represents as an institution. what it means that shakespeare at stratford is seen as the sign of success. they said that the shift at stratford will occur when stratford no longer has anything to do with a dead white man.

this conference has me feeling really grateful for the trans leaders and for the mcmaster profs and the actors and authors who made all this learnig possible. it makes me feel happy . but it also makes me feel drained. and the fact that it is in stratford makes me feel drained. i feel angry. i feel lost. i am complicit. and i am tired.

i suppose i want to add my own histories and my own narratives instead of trying to find a place for myself in white, western, colonial classical work. that is what is easier and more empowering for me as a performer and theatre maker.

We are the future of PaR. We are the future of art-making. We are the future of academia.

Does inclusive, decolonial, PaR theory mean we rid ourselves of the power dynamics of the spectating (white) academic?

Who gets to document discovery?
Is it to preserve?
Is it to exploit intellectually or economically?

Who is doing the research and what gives you the right to do the research?

How do we decolonize PaR?

What is the future of PaR that is inclusive?

We do not have the answers, but we invite you to engage in this process and questioning with us.

Okay so... we said we don't have the answers... but just hear us out...
PaR should be grounded in the present as we look to the past.
What are the needs of the community? Is this research meaningful?
We look to Shakespeare productions featuring queer femme, BIPOC (Black, Indigenous, People of Colour) as lead roles. These productions feature work from the past that is grounded in the present. Give us a Black, queer, trans, femme Hamlet (i.e. someone please cast Kit as Hamlet)
We should be working towards a future that we all want.

Just as PaR should be grounded in the present, we should also be preparing for the future…

We want to see a PaR that is decolonial, degendered, collaborative, anti-capitalist, community-based, an ongoing process with no end

How do you create a shared language amongst everyone in the room?

Build a container in your workshop room that is built around community care and community needs before you go into the space. Not every room will be the same because we all enter the room with different trauma, identity, experience and needs. We have to collectively do the work to support each other and keep each other safe.

What is a researcher? What is an artist? Are people being labelled in specific roles (or subconsciously being labelled)

Who is responsible for care? Who is being held accountable? Who is doing the equity labour?

What do you want?.

girl / not a girl /
/ not a girl / n
not a girl / n
not a girl /not a
girl / not a girl /
/not a girl / n
not a girl / not a

WE LOVE IT WHEN WE
GET PAID TO BE
ARTISTS

Acknowledgment

We wish to thank Claud Spadafora for her help with final edits and formatting.

(Non)Conclusions

PETER COCKETT AND MELINDA GOUGH

On our final day at the Stratford Festival Laboratory, Clare McManus stated: "One of the really clear results of this [collaboration] is that this work pushes us to articulate our methodologies and to do that responsibly."[1] McManus has previously called on scholars to not simply change the focus of our theatre historical research but to "change the terms on which that history is written."[2] Taking up this challenge in creating this book and reflecting on interactions with the many brilliant artists and academics with whom we have collaborated both at the workshop and subsequently, we have begun to articulate for ourselves some guiding thoughts for future performance as research (PaR) collaborations and some related questions regarding repertoire and training. Many of these future orientations are represented throughout the volume, but a few such issues call for additional exploration. As our title "(Non) Conclusions" suggests, these thoughts are in no way exhaustive and will undoubtedly morph and change as we try new things together.

PaR in Early Theatre Studies: Scholars, Actors, Public Performance

PaR work is an integration of artistic and academic practice and inquiry, and the theories and practices governing these integrations are varied and emergent. The respective functions of scholars and performers, and the role of public performance, remain for us complex issues worthy of further discussion. Bruce Barton's assertion that PaR work should have equal investment from all participants, an idea articulated in Keira Loughran's chapter 1 of this volume,[3] has value, but it is also potentially restrictive. We accept that roles and expectations for all participants should be more clearly laid out than was the case for our Engendering the Stage workshop in Stratford, but we also want to hold space for future projects that imagine a multiplicity of relationships between partners who bring distinct skill sets and need a variety of ways to engage with the research. Barton's work also does not involve theatre historians or theatre histories, and these added elements in our research invite additional complexities into PaR work.

Scholars remain important to PaR work in early theatre studies because making early modern drama a space in which all can play depends on ongoing research dedicated to shattering the "all-male" stage myth. This myth is persistent, and breaking it down will require continued advocacy and innovative scholarship. Positivist theatre history mythologizes the all-male stage by insisting on the weight of surviving evidence. But since the patriarchal bias of European culture defines what evidence is made available, this methodology perpetuates imbalanced views of the past, including a distorting emphasis on the plays of William Shakespeare. The plays of other writers, especially those deriving from other cultures, offer more richly representative pictures of human diversity, and including them in our syllabi and theatre programming opens exciting possibilities for exploration. Equally, embracing liberatory historiographic work within early modern feminist and trans studies, built on previously ignored works and traces of lives lived within familiar texts, creates space for previously marginalized students and performers to find themselves and their ancestors in the works of this period. Such understandings open up (theatre) history as a process of imagining and revisioning in which all can participate, and participate in different ways.

Our workshop aimed to break down barriers between scholars and performers but also prompted a desire in some for a more radical approach, for an elimination of any division between observer (scholar) and active participant (performer). When Emma Frankland ran a subsequent workshop at the Stratford Festival, all participants engaged as performers, regardless of their level of expertise. Writing about that experience, Madeleine Krusto, who attended both workshops, observed the complexities of moving between the roles of performer and observer through the workshop process:

> As a cisgender woman invited into this space, a workshop series on the trans canon, it felt important to take up as little space as possible while also not sitting on the sidelines and simply watching the PaR work as if I was situating myself as an expert on transgender lives. When I was a performing participant, such as performing a nymph and ripping the pages from that RSC collection, I was still taking up space in some ways but also sharing the space with the artists in the room. Together we were unified and working toward something.[4]

Krusto goes on to argue that to "sit on the sidelines and watch PaR in action is to take more than you are giving to the work." On one level, we agree with this statement. Actors give something intimate of themselves in performance – their own bodies and emotions become the object of the research – and we feel it is important for every participant in a PaR experiment to share in the risk of this giving in some way. But can the ability to observe, and connect feelings generated by watching performance to other histories, contexts, and knowledges, also have a role to play?

Embodied engagement has immense value in PaR, but is the role of the audience not another important modality in this research? In fact, Frankland's Toward a Trans Canon workshop concluded with a performance that included the artistic director and other members of the Stratford artistic management in its audience. Invited guests and Stratford actors, playing nymphs digesting pages of Shakespeare's First Folio, were asked to enact, in front of the most powerful person in the institution, a radical performative statement about the (literal) deconstruction of the classical canon. That workshop thereby reintroduced the separation of audience and actor, and the related power dynamics, as a way of amplifying research impact.

Systemic biases and expectations that can cause distrust and misunderstanding between scholars and performers certainly need to be addressed within any PaR project, but we maintain there is value in participants coming to the problem from different angles. It is easy to fall into stereotyping when considering both groups. Not all actors are the same. The training necessary and the expectations placed on actors in musicals, for example, are immensely different from those of actors working in devised theatre and the collective creation of new works. Traditional rehearsal practice for musicals demands performers learn previously designed choreography: choreographers determine the steps and teach them to actors, who learn the steps and practise until they perform them with conviction and in time with each other and the music. Devised theatre processes usually have no determined scheme of choreography and begin with improvisational movement games. This description is both a generalization and a simplification but hopefully indicates that PaR practitioners should consider what kind of actors are being invited into the space and why. What training do they have already? What expectations will they have of the rehearsal room? For our workshop, several festival company actors arrived with the expectation that they would use their skills to make a complex text work for the stage. Finding themselves in an experimental workshop presented unexpected challenges, given the differences between preparing a role for public performance and the orientations required of actor-researchers. This dilemma sets up another false dichotomy but one worthy of further consideration.

For workshop scholar Pamela Allen Brown, this kind of confusion tangled up with unsustainable definitions of actors and scholars was potentially the "most impactful" aspect of the experience: "It's been useful as a scholar to hear the actors speak from their point of view; it's very different to how we speak as scholars. With PaR you have the actors and the scholars together in that same place, speaking about the same issues, but from different perspectives." Brown felt that the "division between scholars or academics or whatever we're called and the players or actors is not really bridged," but for her this division was a potential advantage for the research:

> I take the point that what they [actors] think they're here for is different from what we think we're here for ... but that can be a creative friction, and I think it has been. I just think we're here for a very different reason than they are here ... Frankly, I'd love to call myself an artist too! The PaR model itself makes me envy actors who can justify doing that and forces us as scholars to be modest and take a back seat. Not sure that's entirely good in an increasingly anti-intellectual world, however. And while I learned and felt a ton more than at other conferences, I did get the message that working scholars should learn from actors working, but vice versa, not so much ... How might the group improve actor/scholar interplay in the future?[5]

Brown asks a key question for imagining more reciprocal ways of harnessing not only commonalities but also differences in subsequent cross-sectoral PaR work. The dynamic of embodied engagement in performance and embodied observation of performance is a core element of theatre, perhaps *the* core element. Institutionalized power structures and unexamined habits of thought can make this exchange imbalanced and inequitable, but by acknowledging these aspects of the work, and using techniques to build trust such as those shared by Frankland and other guest artists and described in our volume's Introduction, we believe PaR can facilitate opportunities for performers and observers to engage in mutual exchange. The errors we made in the planning of this workshop, related in part to the conventions and regulations of the institutions of the academy and the theatre profession, created inequities in our PaR practice, but we hope questions arising through this process and shared via this book can lay the ground for future PaR work that embraces, more equitably, the opportunities latent in collaboration between experts drawing on a diversity of knowledges, lived experiences, and professional training.

"Why Be Chained to the Play?": Liquid Dramaturgies

Carmen Alvis's interjection early in our workshop, and described in the book's Introduction, articulated her caution while working at an institution expressly created to impose English culture on her people. This intervention has had a long-lasting impact on us as settler scholars working on the lands now known as Canada. Is it possible to engage with these colonial texts and their histories without continuing harm? Kitoko Mai's poem, included in chapter 16 of this volume, presents a stark choice: find more inclusive ways to work with these texts or stop producing them and make space for others. The latter provocation is an entirely valid option.

(Re)Setting the Stage: The Past, Present, and Future of Casting Practices in Canada delves into this dilemma in depth, engaging diverse artists working on these lands at their 2023 symposium "Recasting Shakespeare in Canada."[6] The project's podcast, *Shaking Up Shakespeare*, brilliantly highlights the conflicting and conflicted attitudes for IBPOC artists working with the plays of Shakespeare alongside the voices of others who call for resources to be diverted away from productions of Shakespeare in favour of producing new works. Episodes 5 and 6 specifically challenge listeners to consider both the value and the potential harm of engaging with colonial texts today.[7] Discussions in the podcast are wide ranging, and the diverse arguments and practices of the artists featured offer a deep and critical reflection on Canada's continuing attachment to the work of William Shakespeare. The colonial legacy of Shakespeare lives on within Canada today. Although we can imagine a time when that will not be the case, for the foreseeable future theatre companies on these lands will continue to produce early modern plays, and schools and universities will continue to study them. Providing a critical framework to do so without exacerbating potential harms is therefore a matter of urgency.[8]

At its best, our workshop's movement towards such a framework in relation to the performance of gender contributed to an ongoing "conversation," as imagined by Mai's spoken word poem, in which participants from historically marginalized communities could be "Included/Seen/Spoken About/Remembered."[9] And yet, there was much additional labour within our process for Two-Spirit and trans guest artist participants, in part because these plays remain full of colonial and patriarchal attitudes, alongside gender binary–enforcing plots and characters, and so their potential for repeating harmful oppressions is strong, even when artists and scholars approach the work with the intention to "dull the sharp edges of the problematic stories and humour," as Alvis suggests in *Shaking up Shakespeare*.[10]

In a post-workshop interview, Natasha Korda pointed out that the gendered violence in texts from the period is

> a real challenge in our present moment, both in performance and in teaching ... There's a lot of violence in these texts, violence that we often want to avoid in order to focus on the more hopeful aspects of the text. But it's equally important – and powerful in performance – to connect the violence of the past to the present, to make its ongoing presence felt. I think it's better to think carefully about how to do that than simply to say that we shouldn't perform these texts because they're violent and they're misogynist.[11]

At the workshop, André Morin, who played Lucio, a victim of mockery and abuse from his family's steward in *Love's Cure*, struggled to align the action of the play with the positive perspective on gender fluidity and empowerment in the historical period that he felt was presented in our short videos. "There's something really exciting about trying to make it about the ideas we were exploring," he said, "but I don't know if the play itself contains that." Morin embraces the possibilities for modern interpretations of classical texts but argues that "when we try to take a really modern idea and put it on a play, and not change anything about the play, then that's an entire production in bad faith." He goes on to clarify:

> That's an entire cast that's being forced to cram words into their mouths and say it as if that's not the words that they're saying, or to cram actions that take place in the play into their bodies and into their relationships ... I think that when we want to learn something about the world through classical texts that's one thing, but if we're dishonest about what they are, then I think the art suffers. So why ... why not – well, not why do it, necessarily, but why be chained to the play? Why be chained to the play?[12]

Morin's discomfort with modern interpretations of classical plays that sit uncomfortably with the actual words and actions in those play-texts is mirrored in Denise Oucharek's response to the same line of questioning. She speaks passionately as actor and playwright about the industry's tendency to change the setting of a production without fully engaging with the consequences:

> "Now we're doing this in the 1950s." Okay, there are certain conventions that come with that, but if you don't change the text to reflect that, who cares? It's meaningless. It's just costumes and scenery, and nobody's going

to be affected in a different way. Yes, change the context, that's wonderful. But change everything else about it as well. We're so precious about our texts, we don't like to alter and cut. But – I'm a playwright and my work is always malleable. I'm not precious with it. Please take it, please chop it up, please do something with it. That's going to keep it alive. When we preserve things and we don't allow them to evolve, I think they die.[13]

Morin's and Oucharek's perspectives lend weight to Nora Williams's call for "liquid dramaturgy": an approach to producing Shakespeare that enacts the kind of structural changes that are necessary to ensure that casting and other production choices do not end up inadvertently "propping up the same oppressive structures" they seek to dismantle.[14]

Williams calls out approaches to casting Shakespeare's plays that place female-identifying actors in male-identified roles but then leave the action of the play unchanged, thereby repeating patterns of oppression. Such casting might help facilitate critical perspectives on gender oppression, but the oppression itself remains. Williams asserts that, to change such patterns, Shakespeare's play-texts should be treated as freely as Oucharek suggests, and producers should be encouraged to edit them. This orientation aligns strongly with the tenor of the *Shaking Up Shakespeare* podcast and many of the artists' commitments to adapting Shakespeare rather than just staging it.[15]

Moreover, if the study and production of early modern drama is to live up to its transformative potential, we need to embrace what Sawyer Kemp terms "holistic dramaturgy," dramaturgy that pays attention not only to texts but also to the built environments in which they are performed and the regulations that accrue to those environments. Processes designed to meaningfully include previously marginalized artists, audiences, and communities require such a holistic approach to ensure auditions, rehearsals, and performances occur in contexts and spaces that are welcoming and accessible to all.[16]

Diversity, Representation, and Exploration

Imagining a room constructed equitably and accessibly, in keeping with Kemp's principles, there remain pressing questions about roles and representation within that room. The value that lived experience brings to the process of performance was powerfully manifested at our workshop, but so was the depth of learning to be derived from exploration into territory beyond our lived experience. Is there a way to hold both of these affordances within the complex politics of theatre practice in the profession and the academy?

In our interview with Oucharek, we asked whether she felt she would take the role of Guzmán in a professional production of *The Lieutenant Nun*. Her honest answer is deeply informative:

My 2019 artist existing in this industry says no. I couldn't … We're living in a time where people who are under-represented across the board in the theatrical world are fighting for their time. And rightfully so. I worked with Carmen Aguirre this year: brilliant, wonderful, powerful.[17] And she made a statement that I'm going to attribute to her because she's the one I heard it from, but I don't know who said it originally. And the statement was, the rule in theatre should be "nothing about us without us."[18] [I]t doesn't always mean literally "I have to always play this, you have to always play that." But because there's so much under-representation, until everyone gets a chance to do everything, the pendulum's not coming back to the middle. And I think we're a long way away from that. That being said, as an actor, what makes me really sad about living in this time where that pendulum's in motion is that what drew me to acting in the first place – which is why I enjoyed the work of Guzmán – is this idea about the power of transformation. And if we're all playing roles that are more literally us, where's the transformative power? That doesn't mean we can't learn something from a character, but if everything becomes more literal, we lose that part of the art form. So, I don't know what the answer is, but our work this season has continued that in our brain. And again, I think it's just that pendulum swing, and until everyone has representation, and until everyone has their stories told and their voices heard, we're going to have more literal … casting. And then it will right itself, and the transformative power will come back.[19]

In institutional settings where directors or researchers can hold open auditions through which they can find actors whose identities align with their roles and can pay them appropriately, this need for equitable representation and opportunity should take precedence.

In some settings, however, committing to a strict alignment between gender of actor and gender of role might paradoxically result in inequities and exclusions. For our McMaster University Fall 2022 adaptation of *The Force of Habit*, we were able to recruit a wonderful cast of genderqueer performers by engaging in significant outreach that attracted trans and queer students who may not otherwise have auditioned. But we were working in a context where we could draw actors from the campus community at large. McMaster's Theatre and Film Studies program is a BA program that does not have a fixed cohort of BFA actors needing roles in each year's productions. When programmers must find roles for a cohort of actors with a fixed demographic at a given moment in time, an unbending adherence to alignment of the identity of the actor with the character's identity, whether that be along the axes of race, gender, sexuality, and/or ability, could result in more conservative selections of plays.[20] Selecting plays for a season in a BFA program that provides every student with an appropriate learning opportunity is notoriously difficult. Insisting on strict alignment of role and character makes this challenge that much harder. Theatre educators in Canada are grappling with these issues and exploring a multiplicity of ways to make season selection more equitable and accessible, but this remains a pressing challenge.[21] The issue requires bravery and sensitivity from all parties, but from our present vantage point, we wonder whether the principle of identity-aligned casting within training contexts may place oppressive restrictions on the learning experience for queer and IBPOC actors, and others, who may want to explore roles beyond their own socially constructed identities. Is it possible to hold space for the importance of lived experience in the representation of character *and* create opportunities for actors to develop their craft, including by working on characters who do not align with their own identities? Are there ways to move beyond a binary approach to this dilemma?

Canadian playwright, actor, and advocate Donna-Michelle St. Bernard offers a way to think complexly about such issues in relation to race. She has committed to writing fifty-four plays, each inspired by research on specific African nations. One key element of this ambitious 54ology, for our musings here, is the fact that St. Bernard's plays, inspired by African stories, are set in fictional locations and imagined worlds, and actors of any ethnicity can play their characters. St. Bernard started the project in 2006 in part as a resistance to the argument that plays about Africa could not be performed because there were not enough Black actors. As she acknowledges, times have changed, and companies are now producing plays by "diasporic Africans" like "Tawiah M'Carthy and Mumbi Tindyebwa Out [Obsidian Theatre artistic director], who are manifesting culturally specific stagings."[22] St. Bernard acknowledges the deep value of this work, but her plays, by not insisting on the same cultural specificity, open a productive cultural space for creators and performers of all ethnicities to engage with her stories and the important issues she researches in African politics, past and present.

While historical distance and freedom from the imperative to respect the playwrights' words make early modern drama an exciting potential playground for training and for research, St. Bernard's decision to create new worlds that are distinct and different from our own while maintaining connection to real-life situations and stories shows that classical plays are not the only option.[23] Within a rehearsal room holistically constructed to allow each participant to bring their own knowledges and experience, we can see immense value in having actors play characters sometimes inside and sometimes outside of their lived experience, learning from and with each other while working across differences. We remain excited by Kemp's argument that old plays in such a context can offer a "holistic opportunity to see an ecosystem in which gendered meaning is being actively constructed in the moment of live performance."[24] Choosing to engage with colonial texts provides an opportunity to grapple with oppressive structures of meaning that continue to influence us today, to unpack those structures, to discover queer and trans ancestors marginalized by patriarchal histories, and to imagine futures in which such structures are subverted, reimagined, rebuilt as something new. At the same time, we acknowledge there are multiple ways that insights such as these may be achieved without restricting ourselves to classical texts. Mai's demand that we "let Shakespeare die," with its implicit call to move on to the work of new playwrights, remains compelling.

NOTES

1 McManus, quoted in Engendering the Stage, "Futures for Practice, Performance, and Research."

2 McManus, "Early Modern Women's Performance," 167.

3 Loughran, "The Meeting of Art and Academia," chapter 1 of this volume.

4 Krusto, "Towards a Trans Canon."

5 Brown, quoted in Engendering the Stage, "Future for Practice, Performance, and Research."

6 The project as a whole "seeks to situate debates about theatrical representation and the politics of casting in Canada within a broader historical context, advancing dialogue with directors, playwrights, actors, educators, students, and other creators who are actively transforming professional Canadian theatre and university-level theatre training." See the website (Re)Setting the Stage: The Past, Present, and Future of Casting Practices in Canada, https://castingcanadiantheatre.ca/.

7 Ziyana Kotadia argues that "as much as the master's tools will never dismantle the master's house, people have to live in that house. People are actively moving through the systems that we've designed, systems that are designed to exclude them and to marginalize them and to orient power towards the people who've built the systems. But they are the systems we move through. And so I do think that it's important to do work on the master's house at the same time that we're coming up with alternatives to living in that house. And I think a way that we can do work on the master's house is by taking up those colonial tools. And if we think about Shakespeare's work as a colonial tool, and we reorient it to give voice to communities and experiences that have historically been relegated to the margins." At the same time, Carmen

Alvis reflects on conversations with Yvette Nolan at Native Earth Performing Arts who raised questions about the "labour that's involved in making these problematic narratives less harmful versus commissioning new work." See (Re)Setting the Stage, *Shaking Up Shakespeare*, episode 5, "Something Rotten: Shakespeare and Colonialism," transcript, 9, 11.

8 Kim Solga's *Women Making Shakespeare in the Twenty-First Century* takes up this urgency by profiling and analysing work by women theatre-makers from historically marginalized communities whose engagements with plays by Shakespeare and his early modern contemporaries meaningfully address such challenges.

9 Kitoko Mai, "Let Shakespeare Die," reproduced in textual form in chapter 16 of this volume.

10 (Re)Setting the Stage, "Something Rotten: Shakespeare and Colonialism," *Shaking Up Shakespeare*, episode 5, transcript, 11.

11 Korda, quoted in Engendering the Stage, "Futures for Practice, Performance, and Research: A Conversation."

12 André Morin in conversation with Peter Cockett and Melinda Gough, unpublished interview, 2019.

13 Denise Oucharek in conversation with Peter Cockett and Melinda Gough, unpublished interview, 2019.

14 Williams, "Incomplete Dramaturgies," 5.

15 In (Re)Setting the Stage, *Shaking up Shakespeare*, episode 6, "Adaptations and the Politics of Language," artists articulate a multiplicity of ways that adapting Shakespeare's plays has proven to be a liberating approach: from Why Not? Theatre's *Prince Hamlet*, which incorporated Deaf actors and ASL in its bilingual staging; to Reneltta Arluk's *Pawâkan Macbeth*, developed with the Frog Lake First Nation in Treaty 6 territory; to Joseph Jomo Pierre's engagement with his relationship to Shakespeare as a Black man through the characters of Aaron and Othello in his play *Shakespeare's N###a*; to Jeff Ho's play *Cockroach*, which examines the restrictive influence Shakespeare has had on his development as an English-speaking queer Chinese person from Hong Kong.

16 Kemp, "Transgender Shakespeare Performance." See also Solga, *Women Making Shakespeare in the Twenty-First Century*.

17 See Aguirre's website: https://www.carmenaguirre.ca/.

18 For additional discussion of this saying in the context of our PaR work at the Stratford Lab, see Carmen Alvis, "We Tell Our Stories. We Continue to Exist" (chapter 3), Callan Davies, "The PaRchive and Scraps: Archiving Process in Practice as Research and the Work of Theatre History" (chapter 5), and Keira Loughran, "The Meeting of Art and Academia" (chapter 1) of this volume.

19 Oucharek in conversation with Cockett and Gough.

20 Recently, Drew Hayden Taylor (Ojibwe) published a playful and thoughtful article in *The Globe and Mail* suggesting that he might have to "stop writing plays with Native characters" (Hayden Taylor, "I May Have to Stop").

Hayden Taylor claims schools and universities often are unwilling to stage the work of Indigenous playwrights because they do not have a cohort of Indigenous students. Hayden Taylor reports he was consulted by the UBC MFA program because settler students were refusing to perform Thomson Highway's *The Rez Sisters*, demanding instead that they be allowed to stage Michel Tremblay's *Les Belle Soeurs*. "The professor asked them why they were apparently more comfortable with pretending to be working-class French Canadian women than they were with playing Indigenous women." The answer is obvious but also complex. Hayden Taylor acknowledges the dangers of settler teachers and students producing his plays, yet chooses to encourage teachers to "run with it" in the hope they may "learn about a people, or a culture." Not all playwrights would agree.

21 See Dobbie et al., "'Transformation Is Imperative.'" Contributors describe practices ranging from season committees with student members paid to contribute, to decisions at York University, to commissioning of new works devised specifically for the student cohort at Dalhousie, to the creating of a new play database at Studio 58, Langara College. The teachers at the National Theatre School are the only ones to challenge the orthodoxy of identity-aligned casting, arguing: "First and foremost, it is important that students have the opportunity to experience playing characters of their expressed identities. But if we carry forth the logic that only actors of specific ethnicities can play roles written for those ethnicities, then we would only be able to produce *Hamlet* if we had several Danish actors in our cohort, or Angelina Weld Grimké's play *Rachel* if we had several actors of mixed race" (53). In this same special volume of *Canadian Theatre Review*, Sadie Berlin presents a powerful counter argument: "As forms of dramaturgy that lean into cultural specificity are all the rage, the casting process in such a context can lead to what some will call extremes, like the old chestnut, the time-honoured mockery, that one must find a Danish prince to cast the character of Hamlet. As theatre moves toward greater specificity in performance, the endeavour is not based only on concerns of intersectionality and social justice; precision in cultural considerations adds to the quality of the work" (Berlin, "Outcast," 41).

22 Quoted from Nestruck, "54ology playwright."

23 St. Bernard's finished plays in the 54ology series are accessible from Canadian Playwrights Press, and works in development can be accessed on her 54ology website: https://54ology.wordpress.com/. St. Bernard is open to developing works in progress with collaborators. Other options that could be powerful alternatives to classical plays can be found at The Pledge Project, https://www.pledgeproject.ca, which features large cast plays by Canadian women, Two-Spirit, trans, and non-binary creators; and at Abundance of Works, https://abundanceofworks.ca/, a database of plays by equity-seeking performing arts creators. Many thanks to Donna-Michelle St. Bernard for sharing these resources.

24 Kemp, "Transgender Shakespeare Performance," 281.

Bibliography

Manuscript Sources

Baptism of Richard Sharpe. 6 September 1631. Parish Register, St Giles Cripplegate. London Metropolitan Archives, P69/GIS/A/002 /MS06419/002.

Bristol Archives, M/BCC/CCP/1/2, fol. 48r.

COL/CA/01/01/020. MS. 16 Apr. 1573–28 Oct. 1575. London Metropolitan Archives, London, fol. 168v; Cotton CH 26. 2 Mar. 1573. MS. British Library, London (March 1573).

COL/CC/01/01/020-21. MS. 07 Nov. 1572–01 Aug. 1579. London Metropolitan Archives, London, fols 377, 487v, 606r.

COL/RMD/PA/01/001. MS. 1579–1592. 85 (6 Feb. 1579).

COL/RMD/PA/01/001. MS. 1579–1592. London Metropolitan Archives, London. 131–3 (Sep. 1580).

Consistory of London Correction Book for November 1611 to October 1613. London Metropolitan Archives, DL/C/310, fols 19–20.

Frith, Mary. Will. National Archives, ref PROB 10/926.

Hatfield House Archives, Family & Estate Papers, Bills, 35/7. In *The Cecil Papers* (ProQuest). https://about.proquest.com/en/products-services /cecil_papers/

Records of the Lord Chamberlain … Petitions, The National Archives, LC 5/183, fol. 128v.

SKCS 18. 3 Jan. 1569–25 Apr. 1606. MS. London Metropolitan Archives, London, fol. 148v.

SKCS 18. 3 Jan. 1569–25 Apr. 1606. MS. London Metropolitan Archives, London, fol. 184r; 1592.

Suffolk Record Office C/4/3/1/2, fols 14v, 15r.

Other Sources

A Bit Lit. "Engendering the Stage: Making Space for an Inclusive Performance History." A Bit Lit, 24 November 2021. https://abitlit.co/history /engendering-the-stage-making-space-for-an-inclusive-performance-history/.

Abundance of Works (website). https://abundanceofworks.ca/.

Adams, Annalisa. "'His Play Shan't Ask Your Leave to Live': Following the Ghosts of Trans Embodiment in Restoration Drama." MA Thesis, Georgetown University, 2013.

Alabanza, Travis, and Debbie Hannan. *Sound of the Underground.* Bloomsbury Publishing, 2023.

Albalá Pelegrín, Marta, and Edward McLean Test. "Introduction: Translating a Trans Ancestor: Antonio/Catalina de Erauso." In *The Lieutenant Nun: Annotated Translation of the Play, Historical Accounts and Documents about Antonio/Catalina de Erauso,* translated and edited by Marta Albalá Pelegrín and Edward McLean Test, 1–58. Routledge, 2025.

Alexandrowicz, Conrad. *Acting Queer: Gender Dissonance and the Subversion of Realism.* Palgrave MacMillan, 2019.

Allan, Gabriela Madera. "Un Hombre Sin Barbas: The Transgender Protagonist of *La Monja Alférez* (1626)." *Journal of Spanish Cultural Studies* 17, no. 2 (2016): 119–31. https://doi.org/10.1080/14636204.2016.1165850.

Altman, Joel. *The Improbability of Othello: Rhetorical Anthropology and Shakespearean Selfhood.* University of Chicago Press, 2010.

Alvis, Carmen (Cole), Samson Bonkeabantu Brown, Rhiannon Collett, Emma Frankland, Cassandra James, Beric Manywounds, and Subira Wahogo. "Guidance Document for Creating Trans Affirming Theatre Spaces." In "Toward a Trans Canon," by Emma Frankland, *HowlRound Theatre Commons,* 26 May 2020. https://howlround.com/sites/default/files/2020-05 /Guidance%20Document%20for%20Creating%20Trans-Affirming%20 Theatre%20Spaces%20%20.pdf.

Andrés, Gabriel, ed. "Estudio introductorio." In *La monja alférez. Famosa comedia atribuida a J. Pérez de Montalbán,* 7–27. Metauro Edizioni, 2020.

Archer, Ian. "The City of London and the Theatre." In *The Oxford Handbook of Early Modern Theatre,* edited by Richard Dutton, 407–8. Oxford University Press, 2010.

Arden of Faversham. Edited by Martin White. W.W. Norton, 1990.

Aresti, Nerea. "The Gendered Identities of the 'Lieutenant Nun': Rethinking the Story of a Female Warrior in Early Modern Spain." Translated by Rosemary Williams. *Gender & History* 19, no. 3 (November 2007): 401–18. https://doi.org/10.1111/j.1468-0424.2007.00491.x.

Arnold, Janet. *Patterns of Fashion: The Cut and Construction of Clothes for Men and Women, c. 1560–1620.* Macmillan, 1985.

Bacon, Francis. *Sylva Sylvarum, or, A Naturall Historie in Ten Centuries.* London, 1627.

Barjau, Luis. "El Papel de las Mujeres en la Conquista." *Relatos e Historias en México,* no. 110 (October 2017): 24–9. Editorial Raíces, S.A. de C.V.

Barton, Bruce. "Introduction I: Wherefore PAR? Discussions on a 'Line of Flight.'" In *Performance as Research: Knowledge, Methods, Impact,* edited by Annette Arlander, Bruce Barton, Melanie Dreyer-Lude, and Ben Spatz, 1–19. Routledge, 2018.

Bay-Cheung, Sarah. *Shared Narrative Report in Theatre.* 1 April 2021. https://ampd.yorku.ca/shared-narrative-report-in-theatre/.

Beaumont, Francis, and John Fletcher. *Love's Cure.* Edited by Marea Mitchell. Nottingham Drama Texts, 1992.

– *Love's Cure, or the Martial Maid.* Edited by George Walton Williams. Vol. 3 of *The Dramatic Works in the Beaumont and Fletcher Canon,* edited by Fredson Bowers. Cambridge University Press, 1976.

– *The Maides Tragedy.* London, 1619.

– *The Maid's Tragedy.* Edited by T.W. Craik. Manchester University Press, 1988.

Before Shakespeare: The Beginnings of London Commercial Theatre, 1565–1595 (website). https://beforeshakespeare.com/.

– "Galatea." https://beforeshakespeare.com/category/galatea/.

– "John Lyly's *Galatea.*" https://beforeshakespeare.com/tag/emma-frankland/.

Benjamin, Walter. "The Task of the Translator." In *Illuminations,* translated by Harry Zohn. Pimlico, 1968. Republished in *Transatlantic Literary Studies,* edited by Susan Manning and Andrew Taylor, 172–81. Edinburgh University Press, 2007.

Benserade, Isaac de. *Iphis et Iante.* Edition of the play with commentary. *L'avant scène théâtre,* no. 1341 (April 2013).

– *Iphis et Iante, comédie.* Edited by Anne Verdier with the collaboration of Christian Biet and Lise Leibacher-Ouvrard. Editions Lampsaque, 2004.

Bentley, Gerald Eades. *The Jacobean and Caroline Stage.* 7 vols. Clarendon Press, 1941–68.

Bergman, S. Bear. *The Nearest Exit May Be Behind You.* Arsenal Pulp Press, 2009.

Bergmann, Emilie L. "Folklore as Queer, Vélez de Guevara's *La serrano de la Vera.*" In *Women Warriors in Early Modern Spain,* edited by Susan L. Fischer and Frederick A. de Armas, 66–88. University of Delaware Press, 2019.

Berlanstein, Lenard R. *Daughters of Eve: A Cultural History of French Theater Women from the Old Regime to the Fin de Siècle.* Harvard University Press, 2001.

Berlin, Sadie. "Outcast: Limits and Possibilities in Casting Black Performers in the Age of Granular Dramaturgy." *Canadian Theatre Review* 193 (February 2023): 41–4. https://doi.org/10.3138/ctr.193.009.

Bevington, David, Lars Engle, Katherine Eisaman Maus, and Eric Rasmussen, eds. *English Renaissance Drama: A Norton Anthology.* W.W. Norton, 2002.

Bicks, Caroline. "Repeat Performances: Mary Ward's Girls on the International Stage." *Renaissance Drama* 44, no. 2 (Fall 2016): 201–15. https://doi .org/10.1086/688688.

Billing, Christian M. "Historiography, Rehearsal Processes, and Performance as Translation; or, How to Stage Early Modern English Drama Today?" Paper presented at Performance as Research in Early English Theatre Studies: *The Three Ladies of London* in Context. John Douglas Taylor Conference, McMaster University, Hamilton, ON, Canada, 23–25 June 2015. http:// threeladiesoflondon.mcmaster.ca/par/ChristianMBilling.htm.

– *Masculinity, Corporality and the English Stage, 1580–1635*. Ashgate, 2008.

– ed. *Rehearsing Shakespeare: Alternative Strategies in Process and Performance.* Special Issue of *Shakespeare Bulletin*, 30. no. 4 (Winter 2012).

– "Rehearsing Shakespeare: Embodiment, Collaboration, Risk and Play ..." *Shakespeare Bulletin* 30, no. 4 (Winter 2012): 383–410. http://www.jstor.org /stable/26354890.

Brathwaite, Richard. *The English Gentleman, Containing Sundry Excellent Rules or Exquisite Observations, Tending to Direction of Every Gentleman, of Selecter Ranke and Qualitie; How to Demeane or Accommodate Himselfe in the Manage of Publike or Private Affaires.* London, 1630.

Bray, Alan. *Homosexuality in Renaissance England.* Columbia University Press, 1982.

Brief Lives, Chiefly of Contemporaries, Set Down by John Aubrey, Between the Years 1669 and 1696. Edited by Andrew Clark. 2 vols. Clarendon Press, 1898.

Brighton Festival with Emma Frankland. "Gather Round: Galatea." 21 April 2023. https://brightonfestival.org/news/gather-round-galatea/.

Britland, Karen. *Drama at the Courts of Queen Henrietta Maria.* Cambridge University Press, 2006.

Brome, Richard. *The Court Begger. A Comedie Acted at the Cock-Pit by His Majesties Servants, Anno 1632.* London, 1653.

Brown, Pamela Allen. "Art of the Zinger: Female *Sdegno* and Cut-and-Thrust *all'italiana*." Unpublished paper. Abstract at https://engenderingthestage .humanities.mcmaster.ca/conference/participant-bios/pamela-allen-brown -art-of-the-zinger-female-sdegno-and-cut-and-thrust-allitaliana/.

– *Better a Shrew than a Sheep: Women, Drama, and the Culture of Jest in Early Modern England.* Cornell University Press, 2003.

– *The Diva's Gift to the Shakespearean Stage: Agency, Theatricality, and the* Innamorata. Oxford University Press, 2022.

– "The Travelling Diva and Generic Innovation." *Renaissance Drama* 44, no. 2 (Fall 2016): 249–67. https://www.jstor.org/stable/26562704.

Brown, Pamela Allen, and Peter Parolin, eds. *Women Players in England, 1500–1660: Beyond the All-Male Stage.* Ashgate, 2005.

Bruce, Awanigiizhik. "Anishinaabe Gender Terms." Instagram, 13 December 2021. https://www.instagram.com/p/CXbxiN2vkR1/.

Burke, Peter. *A Social History of Knowledge from Gutenberg to Diderot*. Oxford University Press, 2000.

Burnett, Mark Thornton. *Constructing "Monsters" in Shakespearean Drama and Early Modern Culture*. Palgrave Macmillan, 2002.

Burton, Robert. *The Anatomy of Melancholy*. London, 1621.

Butler, Judith. *Who's Afraid of Gender?* Knopf Canada, 2024.

Butterworth, Philip. *Magic on the Early English Stage*. Cambridge University Press, 2010.

Bychowski, M.W., Howard Chiang, Jack Halberstam, Jacob Lau, Kathleen P. Long, Maria Ochoa, C. Riley Snorton, Leah DeVun, and Zeb Tortorici. "'Trans*historicities': A Roundtable Discussion." *TSQ: Transgender Studies Quarterly* 5, no. 4 (2018): 658–85. https://doi.org/10.1215/23289252-7090129.

Campbell, Julie D. "'Merry, Nimble, Stirring Spirit[s]': Academic, Salon and Commedia dell'arte Influence on the *Innamorate* in *Love's Labour's Lost*." In *Women Players in England: 1500–1660: Beyond the All-Male Stage*, edited by Pamela Allen Brown and Peter Parolin, 145–70. Ashgate, 2005.

Candy, Linda. "Practice-Based Research: A Guide." Creativity and Cognitions Studio Report. V1.0, November 2006. https://www.creativityandcognition.com/wp-content/uploads/2011/04/PBR-Guide-1.1-2006.pdf.

Carlson, Marvin. "Inheriting the Wind: A Personal View of the Current Crisis in Theatre Higher Education in New York." *Theatre Survey* 52, no. 1 (2011): 117–23. https://doi.org/10.1017/S0040557411000093.

Caro, Ana. *The Courage to Right a Woman's Wrongs* (*Valor, agravio y mujer*). Translated by the UCLA Working Group on the *Comedia* in Translation and Performance. Juan de la Cuesta, 2020.

Carrión, María M. "Legally Bound: Women and Performance in Early Modern Spain." *Renaissance Drama* 44, no. 2 (Fall 2016): 233–48. https://doi.org/10.1086/688690.

Carson, Neil. *A Companion to Henslowe's "Diary."* Cambridge University Press, 1988.

Cartwright, Kent. "The Confusions of *Gallathea*: John Lyly as Popular Dramatist." *Comparative Drama* 32 (1998): 207–39. https://www.jstor.org/stable/41153910.

Castiglione, Baldassarre. *The Courtyer of Count Baldessar Castlio Divided into Foure Bookes. Very Necessary and Profitable for Yonge Gentilmen and Gentilwomen Abiding in Court, Palaice or Place, Done into English by Thomas Hoby*. London, 1561.

Cavendish, Margaret. *The Convent of Pleasure*. Edited by Sharon L. Jansen. Saltar's Point Press, 2016.

Celik, Olivier. "A contre-courant: Entretien avec Jean-Pierre Vincent." *L'avant scène théâtre*, no. 1341 (April 2013): 75–6.

Cella, Paul. "Translation Workshop (October 17): Professor Edward 'Mac' Test (Boise State University) Visits UCLA." Diversifying the Classics, 18 October 2017. https://diversifyingtheclassics.humanities.ucla.edu/translation

-workshop-october-17-professor-edward-mac-test-boise-state-university-visits
-ucla/.

Cerasano, S.P. "Henslowe's 'Curious' Diary." *Medieval & Renaissance Drama in England* 17 (2005): 72–85. https://www.jstor.org/stable/24322721.

Chapman, George. *Bussy D'Ambois.* Edited by Maurice Evans. Ernest Benn, 1965.

Charlton, James. *Nothing About Us Without Us: Disability, Oppression, and Empowerment.* University of California Press, 1998.

Cherbuliez, Juliette. "Waking Early: Toward an Untimely Study of Character in Performance." Unpublished talk. University of Carolina, Chapel Hill. 9 April 2015.

Chess, Simone. *Male-to-Female Crossdressing in Early Modern English Literature: Gender, Performance, and Queer Relations.* Routledge, 2016.

– "'Or Whatever You Be': Crossdressing, Sex, and Gender Labour in John Lyly's *Gallathea.*" *Renaissance and Reformation* 38, no. 4 (2015): 145–66. https://doi.org/10.33137/rr.v38i4.26377.

– "Queer Residue: Boy Actors' Adult Careers in Early Modern England." *Journal of Early Modern Cultural Studies* 19, no. 4 (Fall 2019): 242–64. https://doi.org/10.1353/jem.2019.0046.

– "Teaching Transfeminisms: Avoiding Trans Exclusion in the Teaching of Women Writers." *Studies in Medieval and Renaissance Teaching* 28, no. 2 (2021): 41–52.

Chess, Simone, Colby Gordon, and Will Fisher. "Introduction: Early Modern Trans Studies." *Journal of Early Modern Cultural Studies* 19, no. 4 (2019): 1–25. https://doi.org/10.1353/jem.2019.0035.

Clarke, Paul. "The Impact Market: The Complicity of Practitioner-Researchers in 'the Spread of the University Beyond the University.'" *Performance Research* 20, no. 4 (2015): 112–21. https://doi.org/10.1080/13528165.2015.1071048.

Clerkinworks [Angela Clerkin]. "Moll and the Future Kings." https://clerkinworks.com/theatre-making/moll-and-the-future-kings/.

Cockett, Peter. "Performing the Queen's Men: A Project in Theatre Historiography." In *Performing the Queen's Men: Material Practices and the Conditions of Playing,* edited by Helen Ostovich, Holger Syme, and Andrew Griffin, 229–42. Ashgate, 2009.

Conkie, Rob. "Rehearsal: The Pleasures of the Flesh." *Shakespeare Bulletin* 30, no. 4 (Winter 2012): 411–29. https://www.jstor.org/stable/26354891.

– *Writing Performative Shakespeares: New Forms for Performance Criticism.* Cambridge University Press, 2016.

Conroy, Derval. "The Cultural Politics of Disguise: Female Cross-Dressing in Tragicomedy (1630–1642)." *Seventeenth-Century French Studies* 24, no. 1 (2002): 135–49. https://doi.org/10.1179/c17.2002.24.1.135.

Constenla Fontenla, Tereixa. "Ellas también hicieron las Américas." *El Pais,* 19 May 2012.

Craik, T.W. Introduction to *The Maid's Tragedy*, by Francis Beaumont and John Fletcher, 1–46. Edited by T.W. Craik. Manchester University Press, 1988.

Cressey, David. "Gender Trouble and Cross-Dressing in Early Modern England." *Journal of British Studies* 35, no. 4 (1996): 438–65. https://doi.org/10.1086/386118.

Darge, Fabienne. "Mariage pour tous, à la mode d'antan." *Le Monde*, 15 April 2013.

Davies, Callan. "SF Day 1: Introductions, Swordplay, and Scenes." Engendering the Stage in the Age of Shakespeare and Beyond, 21 September 2018. https://engenderingthestage.humanities.mcmaster.ca/2018/09/19/sf-day-1-introductions-swordplay-and-scenes/.

– "SF Day 3: Scenework, Walking, and Sharing." Engendering the Stage in the Age of Shakespeare and Beyond, 21 September 2018. https://engenderingthestage.humanities.mcmaster.ca/2018/09/21/sf-day-3-scenework-walking-and-sharing/

Davies, Callan, Anna Bloxam, Hannah O'Regan, Sophy Charlton, Liam Lewis, and Elizabeth Wright. "Bear Journeys in Early Modern England." *The Seventeenth Century* (March 2025): 1–20. https://doi.org/10.1080/0268117X.2025.2461368.

DeGrazia, Margreta. "Hamlet Before Its Time." *Modern Language Quarterly* 62, no. 4 (2001): 355–75. https://doi.org/10.1215/00267929-62-4-355.

Dekker, Rudolf M., and Lotte C. van de Pol. *The Tradition of Female Transvestism in Early Modern Europe.* Palgrave Macmillan, 1989.

Dekker, Thomas. *Satiro-mastix. Or the Untrussing of the Humorous Poet. As It Hath Bin Presented Publikely, by the Right Honorable, the Lord Chamberlaine his Servants; and Privately, by the Children of Paules.* London, 1602.

Della Valle, Pietro. *Viaggi di Pietro della Valle il Pellegrino. Descritti da lui medesimo in Lettere familiari. All' erudito suo amico Mario Schipano. Parte Terza.* Gioseffo Longhi, 1672.

Dessen, Alan C., and Leslie Thomson. *A Dictionary of Stage Directions in English Drama, 1580–1642.* Cambridge University Press, 1999.

DeVun, Leah, and Zeb Tortorici. "Trans, Time, and History." *TSQ: Transgender Studies Quarterly* 5, no. 4 (November 2018): 518–39. https://doi.org/10.1215/23289252-7090003.

DiGangi, Mario. *The Homoerotics of Early Modern Drama.* Cambridge University Press, 1997.

"Dish with One Spoon." Best Endeavours, n.d. https://nandogikendan.com/dish-with-one-spoon/.

Dobbie, Courtenay, David Hudgins, Shannon Blanchet, Quincy Armorer, Jani Lauzon, Alisa Palmer, Sue Miner, Jamie Robinson, and Roberta Barker. "'Transformation Is Imperative': Play Selection and Casting at Theatre

Training Institutions." *Canadian Theatre Review* 193 (2023): 49–54. https://doi.org/10.3138/ctr.193.011.

Dooley, Mark. "Inversion, Metamorphosis, and Sexual Difference: Female Same-Sex Desire in Ovid and Lyly." In *Ovid and the Renaissance Body*, edited by Goran V. Stanivukovic, 59–76. University of Toronto Press, 200.

Drayton, Michael. *Idea the Shepheards Garland Fashioned in Nine Eglogs*. London, 1593.

Dupas, Mathieu. "Lesbianism in Benserade's *Iphis et Ianthe* (1643): Gallantry and the Making of Heterosexuality in Seventeenth-Century France." In *Ovidian Transversions: Iphis et Ianthe, 1300–1650*, edited by Valerie Traub, Patricia Badir, and Peggy McCracken, 241–60. Edinburgh University Press, 2019.

Egginton, William. *The Theater of Truth: The Ideology of (Neo)Baroque Aesthetics*. Stanford University Press, 2010.

Engendering the Stage in the Age of Shakespeare and Beyond (website). 2018–present. https://engenderingthestage.humanities.mcmaster.ca/.

– "Futures for Practice, Performance, and Research: A Conversation." 5 March 2019. https://engenderingthestage.humanities.mcmaster.ca/2019/03/05/futures-for-practice-performance-and-research-a-conversation/.

– "In Conversation with Keira Loughran." 11 October 2018. https://engenderingthestage.humanities.mcmaster.ca/2018/10/11/in-conversation-with-keira-loughran/.

– "Reflections on Practice, Performance, and Research: A Conversation." 18 February 2019. https://engenderingthestage.humanities.mcmaster.ca/2019/02/18/reflections-on-practice-performance-and-research-a-conversation/.

Engendering the Stage in the Age of Shakespeare and Beyond at the Stratford Festival Theatre Laboratory (video). Edited by Peter Cockett, Callan Davies, and Melinda Gough. 2019. https://engenderingthestage.humanities.mcmaster.ca/.

Englands Parnassus: or the Choysest Flowers of Our Moderne Poets. Edited by Robert Allot. London, 1600.

Erauso, Catalina de. *Lieutenant Nun: Memoir of a Basque Transvestite in the New World*. Translated and edited by Michele De Stepto and Gabri Stepto. Beacon Press, 1997.

– *The Life of Catalina de Erauso, the Lieutenant Nun: An Early Modern Autobiography*. Translated by Sonia Pérez-Villanueva. Fairleigh Dickinson University Press, 2014.

– *Vida i sucesos de la Monja Alférez*. Edición, introducción y notas de Miguel Martínez. Castalia Ediciones, 2021.

– *Vida i sucesos de la Monja Alférez: Autobiografía atribuida a doña Catalina de Erauso*. Edited by Rima de Vallbona. Ediciones Perro Azul, 1999.

Erdman, Harley. Introduction to *The Mountain Girl from La Vera/La Serrana de la Vera* by Luis Vélez de Guevara, translated by Harley Erdman, 1–34. Liverpool University Press, 2019.

Evain, Aurore. *L'Apparition des actrices professionnelles en Europe.* L'Harmattan, 2001.

Evans, G. Blakemore, ed. *The Riverside Shakespeare.* 2nd ed. Houghton Mifflin. 1997.

Ewan, Vanessa, and Kate Sagovsky. *Laban's Efforts in Action: A Movement Handbook for Actors with Online Video Resources.* Bloomsbury, 2018.

Fayard, Nicole. "Shakespeare with a *Différance:* Daniel Mesguich and the Revisiting of the Canon in Late 20th-Century Theater." *Contemporary French and Francophone Studies* 10, no. 3 (2006): 321–30. https://doi.org/10.1080 /17409290600889685.

Feinberg, Leslie. *Transgender Warriors: Making History from Joan of Arc to RuPaul.* Beacon, 1996.

Festival Designs by Inigo Jones. An Exhibition of Drawings for Scenery and Costumes for the Court Masques of James I and Charles I. Introduction and catalogue by Roy Strong, forward by Thomas S. Wragg. International Exhibitions Foundation, 1967–68.

Fifty Comedies and Tragedies Written by Francis Beaumont and John Fletcher, Gentlemen. London, 1679.

Fisher, Will. *Materializing Gender in Early Modern English Literature and Culture.* Cambridge University Press, 2006.

Fitzgeffrey, Henry. *Satyres: and Satyricall Epigrams with Certaine Observations at Black-Fryers.* London, 1617.

Fleishman, Mark. "The Difference of Performance as Research." *Theatre Research International* 37, no. 1 (2012): 28–37. https://doi.org/10.1017 /S0307883311000745.

Fletcher, John, and Philip Massinger. *Love's Cure, or The Martial Maid.* Edited by José A. Pérez Díez. Manchester University Press, 2022.

Forestier, Georges. *L'Esthétique de l'identité dans le théâtre français (1550–1680): Le déguisement et ses avatars.* Droz, 1988.

Frankland, Emma. *None of Us Is Yet a Robot.* https://www.emmafrankland.co.uk /work/noneofusisyetarobot.

– "Toward a Trans Canon." *HowlRound Theatre Commons,* 26 May 2020. https:// howlround.com/toward-trans-canon.

– "Trans Women on Stage: Erasure, Resurgence and #notadebate." In *The Palgrave Handbook of the History of Women on Stage,* edited by Jan Sewell and Clare Smout, 775–805. Palgrave Macmillan, 2019. https://doi.org /10.1007/978-3-030-23828-5_34.

Frankland, Emma, and Andy Kesson. "'Perhaps John Lyly Was a Trans Woman?': An Interview about Performing *Galatea*'s Queer, Transgender Stories." *Journal for Early Modern Cultural Studies* 19, no. 4 (2019): 284–98. https://doi.org/10.1353/jem.2019.0048.

Fuchs, Barbara. "The *Courage* to Transform: Diversifying the Classics Translates *Valor, agravio y mujer.*" *Renaissance Drama* 50, no. 2 (Fall 2022): 233–44. https://doi.org/10.1086/723005.

Gabriel, Trip. "After Roe, Republicans Sharpen Attacks on Gay and
    Transgender Rights." *New York Times*, 22 July 2022. https://www.nytimes
    .com/2022/07/22/us/politics/after-roe-republicans-sharpen-attacks-on
    -gay-and-transgender-rights.html.
Gamble, Joseph. "Toward a Trans Philology." *Journal for Early Modern Cultural
    Studies*, 19, no. 4 (Fall 2019): 26–44. https://doi.org/10.1353/jem.2019.0036.
Garber, Marjorie. *Vested Interests: Cross-Dressing and Cultural Anxiety*. Routledge, 1992.
Gardner, Lyn. Review of *The Maid's Tragedy*, directed by Lucy Bailey,
    Shakespeare's Globe, London. *Guardian*, 27 August 1997, 2.
Gethner, Perry, and Melinda Gough. "The Advent of Women Players and
    Playwrights in Early Modern France." *Renaissance Drama* 44, no. 2 (Fall 2016):
    217–32. https://doi.org/10.1086/688689.
GLAAD. "Glossary of Terms: Transgender." In *GLADD Media Reference Guide*.
    11th ed. https://www.glaad.org/reference/trans-terms/.
Glinski, Marie Louis von. *Simile and Identity in Ovid's* Metamorphoses.
    Cambridge University Press, 2012.
Goldberg, Jonathan. *Sodometries: Renaissance Texts, Modern Sexualities*. Fordham
    University Press, 2010.
Goldmark, Matthew. "Reading Habits: Catalina de Erauso and the Subjects of
    Early Modern Spanish Gender and Sexuality." *Colonial Latin American Review*
    24, no. 2 (2015): 215–35. https://doi.org/10.1080/10609164.2015.1040278.
Gorman, Sara E. "The Theatricality of Transformation: Cross-Dressing
    and Gender/Sexuality Spectra on the Elizabethan Stage." *CUREJ: College
    Undergraduate Research Electronic Journal* (21 May 2006): 1–39. https://
    repository.upenn.edu/curej/11.
Gosson, Stephen. *The School of Abuse*. London, 1579.
Gough, Melinda J. "Courtly *Comédiantes*: Henrietta Maria and Amateur
    Women's Stage Plays in France and England." In *Women Players in England,
    1500–1660: Beyond the All-Male Stage*, edited by Pamela Allen Brown and Peter
    Parolin, 193–218. Ashgate, 2005.
Gough, Melinda J., and Clare McManus. "Introduction: Gender, Cultural
    Mobility, and Theater History Inquiry." *Renaissance Drama* 44, no. 2 (2016):
    187–200. https://doi.org/10.1086/688687.
– eds. *Transnational Mobility and Female Performance in Early Modern Europe*.
    Special section, *Renaissance Drama* 44, no. 2 (Fall 2016): 187–276.
Graham, Katherine M. "'[N]or Bear I in This Breast / So Much Cold Spirit
    to Be Called a Woman': The Queerness of Female Revenge in *The Maid's
    Tragedy*." *Early Theatre* 21, no. 1 (2018): 107–26. https://doi.org/10.12745
    /et.21.1.3257.
Grange, SL. "Moll and Future Kings." SL Grange, 10 August 2019. https://
    slgrange.com/portfolio/moll-and-the-future-kings/.

– "Moll Frith: In Search of Renaissance Drag Kings." Society for Theatre Research, 17 November 2021. Online poster: https://www.str.org.uk /product/online-moll-frith-in-search-of-renaissance-drag-kings/. Recording available via the Society for Theatre Research's YouTube channel: https:// www.youtube.com/watch?v=olA7bGgc7WY.

– "A Note to Mary Frith." Voices in the Dark: Notes to the Forgotten She-Wolves, 29 January 2020. Shakespeare's Globe Archives. Ref no GB 3316 SGT/ED/LIB/REC/2019-20/8/1.

Grange, SL, and Andy Kesson. "A Bit Lit 15: SL Grange on History, Queer Lives and Performance." A Bit Lit, 14 April 2020. https://abitlit.co/conversations /sarah-grange-on-history-queer-lives-and-performance/.

Green, Eugène. *La Parole baroque.* Brouwer, 2006.

Greg, Walter W. *Henslowe Papers: Being Documents Supplementary to Henslowe's Diary.* A.H. Bullen, 1907.

Griffith, Eva. "Christopher Beeston: His Property and Properties." In *The Oxford Handbook of Early Modern Theatre,* edited by Richard Dutton, 607–22. Oxford University Press, 2009.

Griffiths, Paul. "Local Arithmetic: Information Cultures in Early Modern England." In *Remaking English Society: Social Relations and Social Change in Early Modern England,* edited by Steve Hindle, Alexandra Shepard, and John Walter, 113–34. Boydell and Brewer, 2013.

Guazzo, Stephano. *The Civile Conversation.* Translated by George Pettie. London, 1581.

Guevera, Luis Vélez de. *The Mountain Girl from La Vera/La Serrana de la Vera.* Translated by Harley Erdman. Liverpool University Press, 2019.

Gurr, Andrew. *The Shakespeare Company, 1594–1642.* Cambridge University Press, 2004.

Gussow, Mel. Review of *The Maid's Tragedy,* directed by Barry Kyle, at The Other Place, Stratford-Upon-Avon. In "An Innovative Season at Stratford-Upon-Avon," *New York Times,* 27 July 1980, Section 2, 5.

Halberstam, Jack. *Trans*: A Quick and Quirky Account of Gender Variability.* University of California Press, 2008.

Hall, John. *Epistles. The Third and Last Volume Containing Two Decades.* London, 1611.

Hann, Rachel. "Gender-Assemblages: The Scenographics of Sin Wai Kin." In *Analysing Gender in Performance,* edited by J. Paul Halferty and Cathy Leeney, 293–310. Palgrave Macmillan, 2022. https://link.springer.com/chapter/10.1007 /978-3-030-85574-1_19#citeas.

Harding, Sandra. "Rethinking Standpoint Epistemology: What Is 'Strong Objectivity'?" In *Feminist Epistemologies,* edited by Linda Alcoff and Elizabeth Potter, 49–82. Routledge, 1993.

Harris, Joseph. "Disruptive Desires: Lesbian Sexuality in Isaac de Benserade's *Iphis et Iante* (1634)." *Seventeenth-Century French Studies* 24, no. 1 (2002): 151–63. https://doi.org/10.1179/c17.2002.24.1.151.

– *Hidden Agendas: Cross-Dressing in Seventeenth-Century France.* Gunter Narr Verlag Tübingen, 2005.

Hayden Taylor, Drew. "I May Have to Stop Writing Plays with Native Characters." *The Globe and Mail,* 21 April 2024. https://theglobeandmail.com/arts /theatre-and-performance/article-i-may-have-to-stop-writing-plays-with-native -characters/.

Henke, Robert. "The Italian Mountebank and the Commedia dell'Arte." *Theatre Survey* 38, no. 2 (1997): 1–29. https://doi.org/10.1017/S0040557400002052.

Heyam, Kit. *Before We Were Trans: A New History of Gender.* Seal Press, 2022.

Historia de la Monja Alferez, doña Catalina de Erauso, escrita por ella misma, e ilustrada con notas y documentos por D. Joaquin Maria de Ferrer. Julio Didot, 1829.

Hodgdon, Barbara. *Shakespeare, Performance, and the Archive.* Routledge, 2016.

Höfele, Andreas. *Stage, Stake, and Scaffold: Humans and Animals in Shakespeare's Theatre.* Oxford University Press, 2011.

Hollyband, Claudius. *Campo di Fior or Else the Flourie Field of Foure Languages.* London, 1583.

Holme, Randall. *The Academy of Armory, or, A Storehouse of Armory and Blazon.* Chester, 1688.

Huarte, Juan de San Juan. *Examen de ingenios para las ciencias.* Madrid, 1578.

Improbable (website). https://www.improbable.co.uk/.

Ingram, William. *The Business of Playing: The Beginnings of the Adult Professional Theater in Elizabethan London.* Cornell University Press, 1992.

– "Introduction: Theatre History: Where Are We Now, How We Got Here, Where We Go Next." In *Oxford Handbook of Early Modern Theatre,* edited by Richard Dutton, 1–15. Oxford University Press, 2009.

Jackson, Henry. "Letter of 1610." Edited and translated by D.F. Sutton. The Philological Museum, 31 July 2002. http://www.philological.bham.ac.uk /jackson/.

Jankowski, Theodora A. *Pure Resistance: Queer Virginity in Early Modern English Drama.* University of Pennsylvania Press, 2000.

– "'Virgins' and 'Not-Women': Dissident Gender Positions." In *The Lesbian Premodern,* edited by Noreen Giffney, Michelle M. Sauer, and Diane Watt, 75–89. Palgrave Macmillan, 2011.

– "'Where There Can Be No Cause Of Affection': Redefining Virgins, Their Desires, and Their Pleasures in John Lyly's *Gallathea.*" In *Feminist Readings of Early Modern Culture: Emerging Subjects,* edited by Valerie Traub, M. Lindsay Kaplan, and Dympna Callaghan, 253–74. Cambridge University Press, 1996.

Johnson, Samuel. *The Plays of William Shakespeare.* Vol. 8. London, 1765.

Jones, Ann Rosalind, and Peter Stallybrass. *Renaissance Clothing and the Materiality of Memory*. Cambridge University Press, 2000.

Jones, Emma. Review of *The Maid's Tragedy*, directed by Claire Lovett at the White Bear, Kennington, London. *Time Out*, 29 June 2005, 77.

Jonson, Ben. *Catiline His Conspiracy*. In *The Workes of Beniamin Ionson*. London, 1616.

– *The Devil Is an Ass*. Edited by Peter Happé. Manchester University Press, 1994.

– *Epicoene, or The Silent Woman*. Edited by R.V. Holdsworth/ New Mermaids. A & C Black, 1990.

– *The Masque of Queenes*. London, 1609.

Joubin, Alexa Alice, ed. *Contemporary Transgender Performances of Shakespeare*. Special Issue, *Borrowers and Lenders* 14, no. 2 (2023). https://borrowers -ojs-azsu.tdl.org/borrowers/issue/view/31.

– "Shakespearean Performance Through a Trans Lens." *Borrowers and Lenders* 14, no. 2 (2023): 65–89. https://borrowers-ojs-azsu.tdl.org/borrowers /article/view/350.

– "Trans as Method: The Sociality of Gender and Shakespeare." *Borrowers and Lenders* 14, no. 2 (2023): 3–21. https://doi.org/10.18274/bl.v14i2.314.

Karim-Cooper, Farah. *The Hand on the Shakespearean Stage: Gesture, Touch and the Spectacle of Dismemberment*. Arden Shakespeare, 2016.

Kathman, David. "How Old Were Shakespeare's Boy Actors?" *Shakespeare Survey* 58 (2005): 220–46. https://doi.org/10.1017/CCOL0521850746.021.

– "John Rice and the Boys of the Jacobean King's Men." *Shakespeare Survey* 68 (2015): 247–66. https://doi.org/10.1017/CBO9781316258736.020.

Kemp, Sawyer. "Transgender Shakespeare Performance: A Holistic Dramaturgy." *Journal of Early Modern Cultural Studies* 19, no. 4 (Fall 2019): 265–83. https://doi.org/10.1353/jem.2019.0047.

Kontatewenní:yos ne Tyonathonwí:sen (*The Women Are Free*). McMaster University, Hamilton, ON, Fall 2021. Digital production at https://www.youtube.com /watch?v=TejUDd1vRKc.

Korda, Natasha. "The Case of Moll Frith: Women's Work and the 'All-Male Stage.'" In *Women Players in England, 1500–1660: Beyond the All-Male Stage*, edited by Pamela Allen Brown and Peter Parolin, 71–88. Ashgate, 2005.

– *Labors Lost: Women's Work and the Early Modern English Stage*. University Pennsylvania Press, 2011.

– "Shakespeare's Laundry: Feminist Futures in the Archives." In *Rethinking Feminism in Early Modern Studies*, edited by Ania Loomba and Melissa E. Sanchez, 93–112. Routledge, 2016.

– "Understanding Shakespeare's Shoes." In *Shakespeare's Things: Shakespearean Theatre and the Non-Human World in History, Theory, and Performance*, edited by Brett Gamboa and Lawrence Switzky, 36–53. Routledge, 2020.

– "Women's Involvement in Theatrical Production." In *A New Companion to Renaissance Drama*, edited by Arthur F. Kinney and Thomas Warren, 282–94. Wiley-Blackwell, 2017.

Krusto, Madeleine. "Towards a Trans Canon: Reflections on Emma Frankland's Workshop at the Stratford Festival, 2019." Engendering the Stage in the Age of Shakespeare and Beyond, 15 November 2019. https://engenderingthestage .humanities.mcmaster.ca/2019/11/15/towards-a-trans-canon-reflections-on -emma-franklands-workshop-at-the-stratford-festival-2019/.

Laban, Rudolf. *The Mastery of Movement*. Edited by Lisa Ullman. MacMillan, 1971.

Lacour, Léopold. *Les premières actrices françaises*. Librairie française, 1921.

LaFleur, Greta, Masha Raskolnikov, and Anna Klosowska, eds. *Trans Historical: Gender Plurality Before the Modern*. Cornell University Press, 2021.

Lancashire, Anne. Review of *The Shakespearian Playing Companies*, by Andrew Gurr. *Shakespeare Quarterly* 49, no. 4 (1998): 434–5. https://doi.org/10.2307/2902240.

Laneham, Robert. *A letter. Whearin, part of the entertainment unto the Queenz Maiesty, at Killingwoorth Castl, in Warwik Sheer, in this soomers Progress 1575 is signified* [...]. London, 1575.

Leibacher-Ouvrard, Lise, and Anne Verdier. "Pièce d'hier, question d'aujourd'hui." *L'avant scène théâtre*, no. 1341 (April 2013): 81–5.

Lemkin Institute. "Statement on the Genocidal Nature of the Gender Critical Movement's Ideology and Practice." 29 November 2022. https://www .lemkininstitute.com/statements-new-page/statement-on-the-genocidal -nature-of-the-gender-critical-movement%E2%80%99s-ideology-and-practice.

Leverhulme Trust. "Engendering the Stage: The Records of Early Modern Performance." Research Project Grant, 2019. https://www.leverhulme .ac.uk/research-project-grants/engendering-stage-records-early-modern -performance.

Levin, Richard. "The Longleat Manuscript and *Titus Andronicus*." *Shakespeare Quarterly* 53, no. 3 (2002): 323–40. https://doi.org/10.1353/shq.2003.0011.

Levine, Laura. *Men in Women's Clothing: Anti-Theatricality and Effeminization, 1579–1642*. Cambridge University Press, 1994.

The Lieutenant Nun: Annotated Translation of the Play, Historical Accounts and Documents about Antonio/Catalina de Erauso. Translated and edited by Marta Albalá Pelegrín and Edward McLean Test. Routledge, 2025.

The Life and Death of Mrs. Mary Frith. Edited by Randall S. Nakayama. Garland, 1993.

Lloyd, Lodowick. *The Jubile of Britaine*. London, 1607.

Long, Kathleen P. "The Case of Marin le Marcis." In *Trans Historical: Gender Plurality Before the Modern*, edited by Greta LaFleur, Masha Raskolnikov, and Anna Kłosowska, 68–94. Cornell University Press, 2021.

– "Illegible Bodies; Reading Intersex and Transgender in Early Modern France (the Case of Benserade's *Iphis et Iante*)." In *Ovidian Transversions:*

Iphis et Ianthe, 1300–1650, edited by Valerie Traub, Patricia Badir, and Peggy McCracken, 213–40. Edinburgh University Press, 2019.

Lope de Vega y Carpio, Félix. *The New Art of Writing Plays.* Translated by Marvin Carlson. In *Theatre, Theory, Theatre: The Major Critical Texts from Aristotle to Zemi and Soyinka and Havel,* edited by Daniel C. Gerould, 135–45. Globe Pequot /Applause, 2003.

Lyly, John. *Galatea.* Edited by Andy Kesson, adapted by Emma Frankland and Subira Joy. Bloomsbury, 2023.

– *Galatea.* Edited by Leah Scragg. Manchester University Press, 2012.

Lyons, John D. *A Theater of Disguise: Studies in French Baroque Drama, 1630–1660.* French Literature Publications, 1978.

Macrobius, *Saturnalia.* Vol. 1, Books 1–2. Edited and translated by Robert A. Kaster. Loeb Classical Library. Harvard University Press, 2011.

Mai, Kitoko. "Let Shakespeare Die." Engendering the Stage in the Age of Shakespeare and Beyond, 2018. https://engenderingthestage.humanities .mcmaster.ca/2018/10/09/let-shakespeare-die/.

Making Treaty 7 Cultural Society (website). 2022. https://makingtreaty7.com/.

Mamujee, Shehzana. "'To Serve Us in That Behalf When Our Pleasure Is to Call for Them': Performing Boys in Renaissance England." *Renaissance Studies* 28, no. 5 (2015): 714–30. https://doi.org/10.1111/rest.12046.

The Manuscripts of His Grace the Duke of Rutland, G.C.B., Preserved at Belvoir Castle. Vol. 1. Eyre and Spottiswoode, 1888.

M[arston], J[ohn]. *The History of Antonio and Mellida. The First Part. As It Hath Beene Sundry Times Acted, By the Children of Paules.* London, 1602.

Martínez, Miguel. "Introducción." In *Vida y sucesos de la monja alférez,* 9–122. Castalia, 2021.

Masten, Jeffrey. "My Two Dads: Collaboration and the Reproduction of Beaumont and Fletcher." In *Queering the Renaissance,* edited by Jonathan Goldberg, 280–309. Duke University Press, 1994. https://doi.org/10.1215 /9780822382607-014.

– "'Reading 'Boys': Performance and Print." In *Queer Philologies: Sex, Language, and Affect in Shakespeare's Time,* 109–49. University of Pennsylvania Press, 2016.

Maura, Juan de. *Españolas de ultramar en la historia y en la literatura.* Universitat de València, 2005.

McCarthy, Harry. *Boy Actors in Early Modern England: Skill and Stagecraft in the Theatre.* Cambridge University Press, 2022.

McKellips, Jenna. "'Immodestly in Mans Apparrell': Queer Possibility and Tagging Gender in the Cambridgeshire Records." REED This!, 6 October 2022. https://reedproject.blog/category/gender-study/.

McKendrick, Melveena. "Representing Their Sex: Actresses in Seventeenth-Century Spain." In *Rhetoric and Reality in Early Modern Spain,* edited by Richard Pym, 72–91. Tamesis Books [Boydell & Brewer], 2006.

– *Woman and Society in the Spanish Drama of the Golden Age: A Study of the Mujer Varonil.* Cambridge University Press, 1974.

McManus, Clare. "Early Modern Women's Performance: Towards a New History of Early Modern Theater?" *Shakespeare Studies* 37 (2009): 161–77. https://pure.roehampton.ac.uk/portal/en/publications/early-modern-womens-performance-towards-a-new-history-of-early-mo.

– "Shakespeare and Gender: The Woman's Part." British Library. 15 March 2016. https://web.archive.org/web/20160320064253/https://www.bl.uk/shakespeare/articles/shakespeare-and-gender-the-womans-part.

– "'Sing It Like Poor Barbary': *Othello* and Early Modern Women's Performance." *Shakespeare Bulletin* 33, no. 1 (2015): 99–120. https://doi.org/10.1353/shb.2015.0013.

McMillin, Scott. "The Sharer and His Boy." In *From Script to Stage in Early Modern England,* edited by Peter Holland and Stephen Orgel, 231–45. Palgrave Macmillan, 2004.

Middleton, Thomas, and Thomas Dekker. *The Roaring Girl.* Edited by Jennifer Panek. W.W. Norton, 2011.

– *The Roaring Girl.* Edited by Paul A. Mulholland. Manchester University Press, 1987.

– *The Roaring Girl, or Moll Cutpurse.* Edited by Coppélia Kahn. In *Thomas Middleton: The Collected Works,* edited by Gary Taylor, John Lavagnino, et al., 712–78. Clarendon Press, 2007.

La Monja alférez: Famosa comedia atribuida a J. Pérez de Montalbán. Edited by Gabriel Andrés. Metauro Edizioni S.r.l., 2020.

Mujica, Barbara. "Actresses as Athletes and Acrobats." In *Prismatic Reflections on Spanish Golden Age Theater: Essays in Honor of Matthew D. Stroud,* edited by Gwyn Elizabeth Campbell and Amy R. Williamsen, 229–41. Peter Lang, 2016.

Mulholland, Paul A. "The Date of *The Roaring Girl.*" *Review of English Studies* 28, no. 109 (1977): 18–31. https://doi.org/10.1093/res/XXVIII.109.18.

Munro, Lucy. "Women's Investment and Performance at the Fortune Playhouse." Engendering the Stage in the Age of Shakespeare and Beyond, 11 December 2022. https://engenderingthestage.humanities.mcmaster.ca/2022/12/11/womens-investment-and-performance-at-the-fortune-playhouse/.

Nabbes, Thomas. *Totenham Court. A Pleasant Comedie.* London, 1638.

Ndo-Mshkawgaabwimi – We All are Standing Strong: Stories of Endurance, Resilience and Resistance from Members of the Indigenous Circle at Stratford. Video. Stratford Festival, 20 June 2020. https://www.youtube.com/watch?v=jHzm7sbJ6Ck.

Nelson, Robin. *Practice as Research in the Arts: Principles, Protocols, Pedagogies, Resistances.* Palgrave Macmillan, 2013.

Nestruck, J. Kelly. "54ology Playwright Donna-Michelle St. Bernard's Lifelong Theatrical Project Is Hitting Its Stride." *The Globe and Mail,* 1 March 2024.

Updated 3 March 2024. https://www.theglobeandmail.com/arts/theatre
-and-performance/article-54ology-playwright-donna-michelle-st-bernards
-lifelong-theatrical/.

Nicoll, Allardyce, and Eleanore Boswell, eds. "Dramatic Records: The Lord
Chamberlain's Office." *Malone Society Collections* 2, no. 3 (1931): 321–416.
https://ia600900.us.archive.org/10/items/p3collections02malouoft
/p3collections02malouoft.pdf.

Nungezer, Edwin. *A Dictionary of Actors and Other Persons Associated with the Public
Representation of Plays in England Before 1642.* Yale University Press, 1929.

OED (Oxford English Dictionary). Online ed. Oxford University Press, 2025.
https://www.oed.com/.

Oldcastle, Hugh. *A Briefe Instruction and Maner How to Keepe Bookes of Accompts
After the Order of Debitor and Creditor* [...].. London, 1588.

Onondaga Nation. "Two Row Wampum – Gaswéñdah." Accessed 29 May 2023.
https://www.onondaganation.org/culture/wampum/two-row-wampum-belt
-guswenta/.

Orgel, Stephen. *Impersonations: The Performance of Gender in Shakespeare's England.*
Cambridge University Press, 1996.

Ortiz-Sotelo, Jorge. "The Peruvian Viceroyalty and the Pacific." In *The Sea in
History: The Early Modern World,* edited by Christian Buchet and Gérard Le
Bouëdec, 879–90. Boydell & Brewer, 2017.

Ott, Katherine, Susan Tucker, and Patricia P. Buckler. "An Introduction to the
History of Scrapbooks." In *The Scrapbook in American Life,* edited by Susan Tucker,
Katherine Ott, and Patricia P. Buckler, 1–20. Temple University Press, 2006.

Overbury, Sir Thomas. *Sir Thomas Overburie his Wife with New Elegies upon His
(Now Knowne) Untimely Death: Whereto Are Annexed, New Newes and Characters.
Written by Himselfe and Other Learned Gentlemen.* London, 1616.

Palfrey, Simon, and Tiffany Stern. *Shakespeare in Parts.* Oxford University Press,
2007.

Partner, Nancy. "Making Up Lost Time: Writing on the Writing of History."
Speculum 61, no. 1 (1986): 90–117. https://doi.org/10.2307/2854538.

Peacham, Henry. *The Compleat Gentleman.* London, 1622.

Performance as Research in Early English Theatre Studies: *The Three Ladies of
London* in Context. John Douglas Taylor Conference, McMaster University,
Hamilton, ON, Canada, 23–25 June 2015. http://threeladiesoflondon
.mcmaster.ca/home/index.htm.

Petersen, Elizabeth Cruz. "Swordplay Uncloaked: Women as Active Agents in
Ana Caro's *Valor, agravio, y mujer* and Lope de Vega's *La pobreza estimada.*"
Comedia Performance 16, no. 1 (2019): 86–102. https://doi.org/10.5325
/comeperf.16.1.0086.

– *Women's Somatic Training in Early Modern Spanish Theater.* Routledge, 2017.

Phelan, Peggy. *Unmarked: The Politics of Performance.* Routledge, 1993.

Phelan, Peggy, and Jill Lane, eds. *The Ends of Performance.* New York University Press, 1998.

Pincombe, Michael. "*Galatea*: We May All Love." In *The Plays of John Lyly: Eros and Eliza,* edited by Michael Pincombe, 129–45. Manchester University Press, 1996.

– "Lyly and Lesbianism: Mysteries of the Closet in *Sappho and Phao.*" In *Renaissance Configurations: Voices/Bodies/Spaces, 1580–1690,* edited by Gordon McMullan, 89–107. Macmillan, 1998.

Platero, Luzmila Camacho. *La Monja Alférez de Juan Pérez de Montalbán.* Juan de la Cuesta, 2006.

Pledge – A *P*roduction *L*isting to *E*nhance *D*iversity and *G*ender *E*quity (website). https://www.pledgeproject.ca.

Poulsen, Rachel. "Women Performing Homoerotic Desire in English and Italian Comedy: *La Calandria, Gl'Ingannati* and *Twelfth Night.*" In *Women Players in England, 1500–1660: Beyond the All-Male Stage,* edited by Pamela Allen Brown and Peter Parolin, 171–92. Ashgate, 2005.

Pruden, Harlan. "August 4, 2020 'TWO-SPIRIT' Turns 30!!" *Two Spirit Journal,* 3 August 2020. https://twospiritjournal.com/?p=973.

– "Explanation of Two-Spirit Terminology." Best Endeavours. https://bestendeavours.ca/two-spirit/.

Purcell, Stephen. "Practice-as-Research and Original Practices." *Shakespeare Bulletin* 35, no. 3 (2017): 425–43. https://doi.org/10.1353/shb.2017.0033.

– "Whose Experiment Is It, Anyway? Some Models for Practice-as-Research in Shakespeare Studies." In *Stage Matters: Props, Bodies and Space in Shakespearean Performance,* edited by Annalisa Castaldo and Rhonda Knight, 15–33. Fairleigh Dickinson University Press, 2018.

Pyle, Kai. "Naming and Claiming: Recovering Ojibwe and Plains Cree Two-Spirit Language." *TSQ: Transgender Studies Quarterly* 5, no. 4 (2018): 574–88. https://doi.org/10.1215/23289252-7090045.

Quintilian. *The Orator's Education, Books 11–12.* Edited and translated by Donald A. Russell. Loeb Classical Library. Harvard University Press, 2001.

Quirot, Odile. "Un mariage homo ... en 1634." *Le Nouvel Observateur,* 16 April 2013.

Racial Equity Tools. "Racial Equity Tools Glossary: Caucusing (Affinity Groups)." https://www.racialequitytools.org/glossary.

Rackin, Phyllis. "Androgyny, Mimesis, and the Marriage of the Boy Heroine on the English Renaissance Stage." *PMLA* 102, no. 1 (1987): 29–41. https://doi.org/10.2307/462490.

Reason, Matthew. *Documentation, Disappearance, and the Representation of Live Performance.* Palgrave Macmillan, 2008.

Reeser, Todd W. "TransFrance." *L'Esprit Créateur* 55, no. 1 (2013): 4–14. https://doi.org/10.1353/esp.2013.0007.

(Re)Setting the Stage: The Past, Present, and Future of Casting Practices in Canada (website), https://castingcanadiantheatre.ca/

– *Shaking Up Shakespeare*, podcast co-created by Marlis Schweitzer, Liam Lockhart-Rush, and Hope Van Der Merwe, episode 5, "Something Rotten: Shakespeare and Colonialism." https://castingcanadiantheatre.ca/shaking-up-shakespeare#Episode_5.

– *Shaking Up Shakespeare*, podcast co-created by Marlis Schweitzer, Liam Lockhart-Rush, and Hope Van Der Merwe, episode 6, "Adaptations and the Politics of Language." https://castingcanadiantheatre.ca/shaking-up-shakespeare#Episode_6.

– *Shaking up Shakespeare*, podcast co-created by Marlis Schweitzer, Liam Lockhart-Rush, and Hope Van Der Merwe, episode 10, "Shakespeare and Beyond." https://castingcanadiantheatre.ca/shaking-up-shakespeare#Episode_10.

Rich, Barnabe. *Faultes Faults, and Nothing Else but Faultes*. London, 1606.

Román, David. "Archival Drag, or the Afterlife of Performance." In *Performance in America: Contemporary U.S. Culture and the Performing Arts*, edited by David Román, 137–78. Duke University Press, 2005.

Rose, Emily. "Keeping the Trans in Translation: Queering Early Modern Transgender Memoirs." *TSQ: Transgender Studies Quarterly* 3, no. 3–4 (2016): 485–505. https://doi.org/10.1215/23289252-3545179.

– *Translating Trans Identity: (Re)Writing Undecidable Texts and Bodies*. Routledge, 2021.

Row, Jennifer E. "Queer Time on the Early Modern Stage: France and the Drama of Biopower." *Exemplaria: Medieval, Early Modern, Theory* 29, no. 1 (2017): 58–81. https://doi.org/10.1080/10412573.2017.1284366.

Rubright, Marjorie. "Transgender Capacity in Thomas Dekker and Thomas Middleton's *The Roaring Girl* (1611)." *Journal for Early Modern Cultural Studies* 19, no. 4 (2019): 45–74. https://doi.org/10.1353/jem.2019.0037.

Ruiz de Alarcón, Juan, attrib. *The Lieutenant Nun*. In *The Lieutenant Nun, Annotated Translation of the Play, Historical Accounts and Documents about Antonio/Catalina de Erauso*, translated and edited by Marta Albalá Pelegrín and Edward McLean Test. Routledge, 2025.

Rutter, Carol Chillington. "Learning Thisby's Part – or – What's Hecuba to Him?" *Shakespeare Bulletin* 22, no. 2 (Fall 2004): 5–30. https://www.jstor.org/stable/26349129.

Rutter-Jensen, Chloe. "La transformación transatlántica de la Monja Alférez. *Revista de estudios sociales* 28 (2007): 86–95.

Rycroft, Eleanor. *Facial Hair and the Performance of Early Modern Masculinity*. Routledge, 2020.

Rye, Walter. *A Glossary of Words Used in East Anglia*. Oxford University Press, 1895.

Salamon, Gayle. *The Life and Death of Latisha King: A Critical Phenomenology of Transphobia*. New York University Press, 2018.

– "Passing Period: Gender, Aggression, and the Phenomenology of Walking." In *Performance and Phenomenology: Traditions and Transformations*, edited by

Maaike Bleeker, Jon Foley Sherman, and Eirini Nedelkopoulou, 186–203. Routledge, 2015.

Salkeld, Duncan. "Literary Traces in Bridewell and Bethlem, 1602–1624." *The Review of English Studies* 56, no. 225 (June 2005): 379–85. https://doi .org/10.1093/res/hgi056.

Schleiner, Winifred. "Male Cross-Dressing and Transvestism in Renaissance Romances." *Sixteenth Century Journal* 19, no. 4 (1988): 605–19. https://doi .org/10.2307/2540989.

Schneider, Rebecca. *Performing Remains: Art and War in Times of Theatrical Reenactment.* Routledge, 2011.

Scott, Virginia. *Women and the Stage in Early Modern France, 1540–1750.* Cambridge University Press, 2010.

Scragg, Leah. *The Metamorphosis of Gallathea: A Study in Creative Adaption.* University Press of America, 1982.

Sedgwick, Eve Kosofsky. *Tendencies.* Duke University Press, 1994.

Senelick, Laurence. *The Changing Room: Sex, Drag, and Theatre.* Routledge, 2000.

Serano, Julia. *Whipping Girl: A Transsexual Woman on Sexism and the Scapegoating of Femininity.* 2nd ed. Seal Press, 2016.

Shakespeare, William. *Hamlet.* Directed by Federay Holmes and Elle While. Shakespeare's Globe, 2018. Recording available via Globe on Screen, https://player.shakespearesglobe.com/productions/hamlet-2018/.

– *Hamlet.* Edited by Harold Jenkins. The Arden Shakespeare. Routledge, 1990.

– *The Merchant of Venice.* In *The Norton Complete Shakespeare.* 3rd ed. General Editor Stephen Greenblatt, 1327–93. W.W. Norton, 2015.

– *Othello.* Edited by Clare McManus. In *The Norton Complete Shakespeare.* 3rd ed. General Editor Stephen Greenblatt, 2073–2159. W.W. Norton, 2015.

– *Twelfth Night.* Edited by Keir Elam. Arden Shakespeare, 2008.

– *Twelfth Night: A Norton Critical Edition.* Edited by Natasha Korda. W.W. Norton, 2025.

Shakespeare and the Queen's Men (website). https://thequeensmen.ca/history-3/.

Shakespeare's Globe. "Giving Voice to Forgotten Women in History." 28 January 2020. https://www.shakespearesglobe.com/discover/blogs-and -features/2020/01/28/giving-voice-to-forgotten-women-in-history/.

– *Notes to the Forgotten She-Wolves.* 2020. https://www.shakespearesglobe.com /whats-on/forgotten-she-wolves/.

Shapiro, Michael. *Gender in Play on the Shakespearean Stage: Boy Heroines and Female Pages.* University of Michigan Press, 1994.

Smith, Bruce R. *Homosexual Desire in Renaissance England: A Cultural Poetics.* University of Chicago Press, 1991.

Smith, Justin. *Irrationality: A History of the Dark Side of Reason.* Princeton University Press, 2019.

Solga, Kim. "Gender and the Aesthetics of Occupation: Making Room for Women's Labour at the Theatre." In *Analysing Gender in Performance,* edited by J. Paul Halferty and Cathy Leeney, 193–209. Palgrave Macmillan, 2022. https://doi.org/10.1007/978-3-030-85574-1_13.

– *Women Making Shakespeare in the Twenty-First Century*. Cambridge University Press, 2024.

Solodow, Joseph. *The World of Ovid's* Metamorphoses. University of North Carolina Press, 1988.

Soyer, François. *Ambiguous Gender in Early Modern Spain and Portugal: Inquisitors, Doctors and the Transgression of Gender Norms*. Brill, 2012.

Spiecker, Sven. *The Big Archive: From Art to Bureaucracy*. MIT Press, 2008.

Split Britches, "Public Address Systems." Accessed 8 May 2023. http://www.split -britches.com/public-address-systems.

Spriet, Stella. "Des voix venues d'ailleurs: La scène de Daniel Mesguich." *Parole Rubate* 15 (2017): 105–20. https://hdl.handle.net/1889/5032.

St. Bernard, Donna Michelle. 54ology (website). https://54ology.wordpress.com/.

– ed. *Indian Act: Residential School Plays*. Playwrights Canada Press, 2018. Pressbook description, accessed 1 March 2022, at https://www .playwrightscanada.com/Books/I/Indian-Act.

Staging and Representing the Scottish Renaissance Court (website). http:// stagingthescottishcourt.brunel.ac.uk/index.html.

Stallybrass, Peter. "Transvestism and the 'Body Beneath': Speculating on the Boy Actor." In *Erotic Politics: Desire on the Renaissance Stage*, edited by Susan Zimmerman, 64–83. Routledge, 1992.

Steedman, Carolyn. *Dust*. Manchester University Press, 2001.

Steinberg, Sylvie. *La confusion des sexes: Le travestissement de la Renaissance à la Révolution*. Fayard, 2001.

Stokes, James. "Women and Performance: Evidences of Universal Cultural Suffrage in Medieval and Early Modern Lincolnshire." In *Women Players in England, 1500–1660*, edited by Pamela Allen Brown and Peter Parolin, 25–44. Ashgate, 2005.

Stokes, Will. *The Vaulting-Master, Or, The Art of Vaulting*. London, 1652.

Stratford Festival Laboratory. "About the Lab." https://www.stratfordfestival.ca /AboutUs/TheLab.

Stryker, Susan, and Aren Aizura. "Introduction: Transgender Studies 2.0." *Transgender Studies Reader 2*, edited by Susan Stryker and Aren Aizura, 1–12. Routledge, 2013.

Stubbes, Philip. *Anatomie of Abuses*. London, 1583.

– *The Anatomie of Abuses*. Edited by Margaret Jane Kidnie. Arizona Center for Medieval and Renaissance Text Studies, 2002.

Suckling, Sir John. *The Goblins: A Comedy, in Fragmenta Aurea: A Collection of all the Incomparable Peeces, Written by Sir John Suckling*. London, 1646.

Taylor, Gary, and John Lavagnino, eds. *Thomas Middleton and Early Modern Textual Culture: A Companion to the Collected Works*. Oxford University Press, 2007.

Thomas, Miranda Fay. "A Queer Reading of *Twelfth Night*." British Library, *Discovering Literature*. Accessed 9 August 2020. https://web.archive.org /web/20160516040403/https://www.bl.uk/shakespeare/articles/a-queer -reading-of-twelfth-night.

Thomas, Thomas. *Dictionarium Linguae Latinae et Anglicanae.* London, 1587.

Tillotson, Sophie. "From Gimmick Casting to Standard Practice: Re-gendering Shakespeare in Performance." In *Analysing Gender in Performance,* edited by J. Paul Halferty and Cathy Leeney, 259–74. Palgrave Macmillan, 2022. https:// doi.org/10.1007/978-3-030-85574-1_17.

Tiramani, Jenny. "Audio: Seventeenth-Century Costume." Victoria and Albert Museum. Accessed 5 August 2020. https://web.archive.org/web /20201028083755/http://www.vam.ac.uk/content/articles/a/audio-early -17th-century-costume/.

Todd, Janet, and Elizabeth Spearing, *Counterfeit Ladies: The Life and Death of Mal Cutpurse; The Case of Mary Carleton.* Pickering, 1994.

Tomlinson, Sophie. "The Actress and Baroque Aesthetic Effects in Renaissance Drama." *Shakespeare Bulletin* 33, no. 1 (Spring 2015): 67–82. https://doi .org/10.1353/shb.2015.0007.

– "'My Brain the Stage': Margaret Cavendish and the Fantasy of Female Performance." In *Women, Texts and Histories, 1575–1760,* edited by Clare Brant and Diane Purkiss, 133–61. Routledge, 1992.

Traub, Valerie. Introduction to *Ovidian Transversions: Iphis et Ianthe, 1300–1650,* edited by Valerie Traub, Patricia Badir, and Peggy McCracken, 1–41. Edinburgh University Press, 2019.

– "The Renaissance of Lesbianism in Early Modern England." *GLQ: A Journal of Lesbian and Gay Studies* 7, no. 2 (2001): 245–63. https://muse.jhu.edu /article/12169.

Tribble, Evelyn. *Early Modern Actors and Shakespeare's Theatre: Thinking with the Body.* Bloomsbury, 2017.

– "Marlowe's Boy Actors." *Shakespeare Bulletin* 27, no. 1 (2009): 5–17. https:// doi.org/10.1353/shb.0.0060.

Trimingham, Melissa. "A Methodology for Practice as Research." *Studies in Theatre & Performance* 22, no. 1 (2002): 54–60.

Truth and Reconciliation Commission of Canada. "The Indian Act Said What?" 2018. https://www.nwac.ca/wp-content/uploads/2018/04/The-Indian-Act -Said-WHAT-pdf-1.pdf.

– "Truth and Reconciliation Commission of Canada: Calls to Action." 2015. https://ehprnh2mwo3.exactdn.com/wp-content/uploads/2021/01/Calls _to_Action_English2.pdf.

Turner, Jr., Robert K. "Textual Introduction to *The Maid's Tragedy*." In *The Dramatic Works in the Beaumont and Fletcher Canon,* edited by Fredson Bowers. Vol. 2. Cambridge University Press, 1970.

UK Research and Innovation. "Before Shakespeare: The Beginnings of London Commercial Theatre." https://gtr.ukri.org/projects?ref=AH/N001710/1.

– "Staging the Henrician Court." https://gtr.ukri.org/projects?ref=AH%2FF018290%2F1.

UNESCO. "Head-Smashed-In Buffalo Jump." Accessed 9 September 2021. https://whc.unesco.org/en/list/158/.

Ungerer, Gustav. "Mary Frith, Alias Moll Cutpurse, in Life and Literature." *Shakespeare Studies* 28 (2000): 42–84.

Vallbona, Rima de. *Vida i sucesos de la Monja Alférez.* Center for Latin American Studies, Arizona State University, 1992.

"van Buchel's Copy of de Witt's drawing of the Swan Playhouse." British Library, *Discovering Literature.* https://web.archive.org/web/20201111205709 /https://www.bl.uk/collection-items/van-buchels-copy-of-de-witts-drawing -of-the-swan-playhouse.

van Es, Bart. "Captive Children: John Lyly, *A Midsummer Night's Dream,* and Child Impressment on the Early Modern Stage." *Renaissance Studies* 33, no.2 (2019): 166–84. https://doi.org/10.1111/rest.12389.

Vega García-Luengos, Germán. "Juan Ruiz de Alarcón recupera 'La monja alférez.'" In *Sor Juana Inés de la Cruz y el teatro novohispano,* edited by Rafael González Cañal and Almudena García González, 89–149. Ediciones de la Universidad de Castilla-La Mancha, 2021.

Velasco, Sherry M. "Foreword: Antonio/Catalina de Erauso, *The Lieutenant Nun,* and the Play with Portraits." In *The Lieutenant Nun: Annotated Translation of the Play, Historical Accounts and Documents about Antonio/Catalina de Erauso,* translated and edited by Marta Albalá Pelegrín and Edward McLean Test, 59–77. Routledge, 2025.

– *The Lieutenant Nun: Transgenderism, Lesbian Desire, and Catalina de Erauso.* University of Texas Press, 2000.

Viala, Alain, and Daniel Mesguich. *Le théâtre.* Presses universitaires de France, 2018.

W.S. [attrib.; Thomas Middleton?]. *The Puritane or The Widow of Watling-Streete.* London, 1607.

Walen, Denise A. "Constructions of Female Homoerotics in Early Modern Drama." *Theatre Journal* 54, no. 3 (2002): 411–30. https://www.jstor.org /stable/25069094.

– *Constructions of Female Homoeroticism in Early Modern Drama.* Palgrave MacMillan, 2005.

Ward, Edward. *The London Spy,* 4th ed., 1709. Edited by Paul Hyland. Colleagues Press, 1993.

Webster, John. *The Tragedy of the Dutchesse of Malfy.* London, 1623.

Wiggins, Martin, with Catherine Richardson. *British Drama, 1533–1642: A Catalogue.* Vol. 6. Oxford University Press, 2015.

Williams, Nora J. "Incomplete Dramaturgies." *Shakespeare Bulletin* 40, no. 1 (Spring 2022): 1–22. https://doi.org/10.1353/shb.2022.0000.

Wixson, Christopher. "Cross-Dressing and John Lyly's *Gallathea*." *Studies in English Literature: 1500–1900* 41, no. 2 (2001): 241–56. https://doi.org/10.2307/1556187.

Wofford, Susanne L. "Cross-Dressing and Technologies of Desire and Revenge in Ana Caro, *Valor, agravio y mujer* with a Glance at *Twelfth Night*." *Renaissance Drama* 50, no. 2 (Fall 2022): 245–62. https://doi.org/10.1086/723006.

Wofford, Susanne L., and Jane Tylus. "Introduction: Cross-Dressing Technologies of Mobility, Trauma, and Freedom." *Renaissance Drama* 50, no. 2 (Fall 2022): 189–96. https://doi.org/10.1086/722937.

Wright, James. *Historia Histrionica: An Historical Account of the English Stage.* London, 1699.

Zimmerman, Susan, ed. *Erotic Politics: Desire on the Renaissance Stage.* Routledge, 1992.

Contributors

Carmen Alvis is a Turtle Mountain Michif (Métis) artist based in Tkarón:to with Chippewa, Irish, and English ancestors. She is one of the leaders of lemonTree creations, manidoons collective, and AdHoc Assembly, and is on the board of the Dancers of Damelahamid. Carmen has created and toured queer and Indigenous performances across Turtle Island (North America), including to venues in Coast Salish territory, Mi'kma'ki, and Treaty 1, 3, 6, and 7 territories. In 2021–22, Carmen was artist in residence at McMaster University's School of the Arts, where she co-devised and co-directed (with Peter Cockett) *Kontatewenní:yos ne Tyonathonwí:sen* (*The Women Are Free*). As a guest artist for the 2018 Stratford Festival workshop, Carmen took an important leadership role and also performed the role of Aspatia in scene work on *The Maid's Tragedy*. Next up: Carmen is writing her first full-length play called *And Then They Came* about the role of Two-Spirit people in the early days of the Métis nation.

Roberta Barker is a professor of theatre (cross-appointed to gender and women's studies and early modern studies) in the Fountain School of Performing Arts, Dalhousie University, and author of *Early Modern Tragedy, Gender, and Performance, 1984–2000* (Palgrave Macmillan, 2007) and *Symptoms of the Self: Tuberculosis and the Making of the Modern Stage* (University of Iowa Press, 2022). Her work on early modern boy actresses has appeared in journals such as *Early Theatre, Shakespeare Bulletin*, and *Literature Compass*. A working director of theatre and opera, she has led sessions on theatrical praxis as research at the Canadian Association for Theatre Research and the international conferences "Renaissance Drama in Action" and "Theatre Without Borders."

Peter Cockett teaches acting, devising, and collective creation in the Integrated Arts (iArts) program at McMaster University's School of the

Arts. A leading practitioner of performance as research (PaR) in early modern theatre studies, Peter has organized three major international conferences focused on PaR: Shakespeare and the Queen's Men (2005); Chester 2010: Peril and Danger to Her Majesty; and Performance as Research in Early English Theatre Studies: *The Three Ladies of London* in Context (2015). He has directed ten PaR productions of medieval and early modern plays and organized three intensive PaR workshops for scholars and practitioners. His research on the Queen's Men is published on his *Performing the Queen's Men* website and on Queen's Men Editions, for which he is general editor (Performance). He has published articles on early modern performance practices and the use of performance as a tool for scholarship and research. At McMaster, he has directed numerous productions, including *Henry V* (2005), an adaptation of Shakespeare's *Hamlet* entitled *Hamlet's Dorm* (2011), *A Midsummer Night's Dream* (2014), *Women and Servants* (2018), *Kontatewenni:yos ne Tyonathonwi:sen* (*The Women Are Free*, co-devised and co-directed with volume contributor Carmen Alvis [Métis], 2021), and *The Force of Habit* (2022). Peter is also a professional actor.

Callan Davies is lecturer in seventeenth-century literature and culture at the University of Southampton. He has published widely on entertainment, play, and early modern culture, including a book on playhouses across early modern England, *What is a Playhouse: England at Play, 1520–1620* (2023), a monograph on *Strangeness in Jacobean Drama* (2021), articles for a range of major journals, as well as the introduction for the Oxford World's Classics *The Merry Wives of Windsor* (2024). He has also been part of the Before Shakespeare, Middling Culture, and Box Office Bears projects and a series of work on the Curtain playhouse.

Emma Frankland is an award-winning theatre artist working in the United Kingdom and internationally. Her work often focuses on honesty, action, and a playfully destructive DIY aesthetic using materials with different transformative properties – such as water, clay, earth, salt, and ink – to create strong visual imagery, which is often messy, intense, and celebratory. Over the past decade, Emma's status has been established as a prominent and innovative English theatre artist whose work has often focused on issues around gender identity and politically motivated performances. Her collection of five solo performances are published by Methuen as *None of Us Is Yet a Robot: Five Performances on Gender Identity and the Politics of Transition*. In 2023, she co-adapted John Lyly's classic play *Galatea* as a trans love story. It was performed as part of Brighton Festival and is published by Bloomsbury. Her work has been performed internationally in Indonesia, Brazil, Canada, and across the United Kingdom and Europe, and she was featured in the 2013 British Council Showcase with an anarchic adaptation of *Don Quijote*. In 2019, she created *We Dig*, which physically demolished the iconic Ovalhouse Theatre with a cast of trans femmes from around the world. Emma is an associate artist with Marlborough Productions and has written several episodes for Channel 4's iconic continuing drama *Hollyoaks*. She currently has a full-length play, *TRAP*, in development. Emma trained at the Central School of Speech and Drama in classical acting. She has directed and performed in Globe Theatre Read Not Dead readings and revivals of sixteenth-century plays. As a guest artist for the Engendering the Stage Stratford workshop, Emma took a significant leadership role and performed the role of Moll Frith in scene work on *The Roaring Girl*.

Melinda Gough is professor of English and cultural studies at McMaster University, where she is also cross-appointed to the graduate program in gender and social justice. Her research on transnational early modern women's performance history includes *Dancing Queen: Marie de Médicis' Ballets at the Court of Henri IV* (University of Toronto Press, 2019). Since 2013, Melinda has served as editor of *Early Theatre: A Journal Associated with the Records of Early English Drama*. Currently, she is editing the anonymous seventeenth-century tragicomedy *Swetnam the Woman-Hater Arraigned by Women* for the Revels Plays (Manchester University Press); in September 2018, the Stratford Festival piloted her draft edition as part of its Wordplay series.

SL Grange is a poet, theatre-maker, and queer history researcher. Their Poetry Wales award-winning pamphlet *Bodies and Other Haunted Houses* (2022) is published by Seren Books. Writing for performance includes *A Note to Mary Frith*, commissioned by Shakespeare's Globe for *Notes to the Forgotten She-Wolves*; librettist work includes audio walks *Fleet Footing* and *Wou D'Uelzecht* with composer Catherine Kontz. Chapters co-written with E. Mallin Parry appear in *Socially Engaged Creative Practice: Contemporary Case Studies*, ed. Jess Moriarty and Kate Aughterson (Intellect Books, 2024) and *New and Decolonial Approaches to Gender Nonconformity: Forging a Home for Ourselves*, ed. Kit Heyam and Jon Ward (Bloomsbury, 2025).

Natasha Korda is professor of English and director of the Centre for the Humanities at Wesleyan University. She is the author of *Labors Lost: Women's Work and the Early Modern English Stage* (2011) and *Shakespeare's Domestic Economies: Gender and Property in Early Modern England* (2002); and co-editor of *Working Subjects in Early Modern English Drama* (2011) and *Staged Properties in Early Modern English Drama* (2002). She has served on the editorial boards of *Renaissance Quarterly* and *Early Modern Women: An Interdisciplinary Journal* and the executive boards of the Modern Language Association and the Renaissance Society of America. Dr. Korda is a recent past president of the Shakespeare Association of America and is editor of the Norton Critical Edition of Shakespeare's *Twelfth Night* (2025).

Madeleine Krusto is a teacher and arts administrator based in Hamilton, Ontario. Her current research is focused on game-based learning and the impact of Dungeons and Dragons clubs in secondary schools. She holds a Master of Arts in gender studies and feminist research from McMaster University and a Master of Education from the University of Toronto's Ontario Institute for Studies in Education. Maddie has worked as an equity, diversity, and inclusion consultant for the Tim Hortons Foundation and a leadership coach with BGC Canada, and has led youth mentorship and career development programming with the Hamilton Wentworth District School Board for several years. She was also the research lead and project coordinator with the Safer Spaces Project, creating care-based safer space policies and trainings for artistic institutions in Hamilton. Maddie was an undergraduate student research assistant for the Engendering the Stage Stratford workshop.

Keira Loughran is an award-winning artist with over twenty-five years as a director, writer, dramaturg, producer, and actor. Her first feature documentary, *EXCLUSION: Beyond the Silence*, which explores the intergenerational impacts of the Chinese Exclusion Act, premiered at Toronto's 28th Reel Asian Film Festival. She has taught acting, devised theatre, and playwriting, most recently at York University, and is a collaborator with the SSHRC-funded (Re)Setting the Stage research project. At the Stratford Festival, Keira was the inaugural associate producer for the Forum and the Laboratory. From 2005–07, she was artistic producer of the SummerWorks Festival in Toronto. Her company K'Now Theatre has garnered seven Dora nominations, including two for Loughran for Outstanding New Play (*Little Dragon*) and Outstanding Direction (*Pu-Erh*). Other selected directing credits include *Wendy and Peter Pan*, *The Comedy of Errors*, *The Komagata Maru Incident*, and *The Aeneid* (Stratford Festival), *Deportation Cast* (York University), and *Titus Andronicus* (Canadian Stage). As an actor, Keira has performed in theatres across the country and has appeared in CBS's *Good Sam* and Hallmark's *Good Witch*. Keira took a lead role, with the volume's editors, in planning and facilitating the Engendering the Stage Stratford workshop.

Kitoko Mai is a Black, non-binary, multidisciplinary performance, media, and community artist. They are based in Ontario, Canada, and live in Toronto, Hamilton, in Transition/Transit, Underwater, and in Digital Space. Toronto sits on the traditional territory of the Mississaugas of the Credit, the Anishnaabeg, the Chippewa, the Haudenosaunee, and the Wendat peoples. Kitoko moved to Canada in 2010 from the United States and is originally from Congo and South Africa. Kitoko struggles with their connection to the land but finds that the in-between spaces feel like home. In Transition/Transit, Underwater, and in Digital Space underscores an artistic practice that prioritizes fluidity. Kit is a graduate of theatre and film studies and multimedia at McMaster University (which they both love and regret) as well as the APT program at Generator (currently no regrets). Their work is rooted in social justice, anti-oppression, and the pursuit of messiness. Their personal philosophy is to produce work that aims to destabilize hierarchies of power; embraces the fluidity of content, form, and process; and prioritizes accessibility. At the Engendering the Stage Stratford workshop, Kit performed their spoken word poem "Let Shakespeare Die."

Lily McEvenue is a performing artist from Toronto. Lily began her dance training at the Quinte Ballet School of Canada before moving to Toronto to pursue a professional career. She started out as a corps de ballet member with Opera Atelier for three seasons, including two international tours across Europe and the United States. Lily then landed her first role, playing Victoria in the musical *Cats* with Toronto's NuMu Theatricals. Since then, performing credits include *Anne of Green Gables* at the Charlottetown Festival and with Drayton Entertainment. She has also done three seasons with the Stratford Festival, including *Guys and Dolls, HMS Pinafore, The Music Man*, and for the 2020 season, cancelled due to COVID (*Chicago* and *Frankenstein Revived*). Lily's television credits include the CW Network's *Reign*, Global TV's *Mary Kills People*, and most recently, Netflix's *Tiny Pretty Things*. At the Engendering the Stage Stratford workshop, Lily performed the role of Clara in scene work on *Love's Cure.*

Clare McManus is senior vice-chancellor's fellow and professor of English at Northumbria University, Newcastle. She publishes on early modern women's performance and is the author of *Women on the Renaissance Stage: Anna of Denmark and Female Masquing at the Stuart Court* (Manchester University Press, 2002) and editor of *Women and Culture at the Courts of the Stuart Queens* (Palgrave, 2003). With Lucy Munro (King's College London), she led *Engendering the Stage: The Records of Early Modern Performance* (funded by the Leverhulme Trust), part of the international Engendering the Stage collaboration with Melinda Gough and Peter Cockett. Clare has edited Fletcher's *Island Princess* (Arden Early Modern Drama), Shakespeare's *Othello* (Norton Shakespeare 3), and Shirley's *Bird in a Cage* (Routledge); she is currently editing Shakespeare and Fletcher's *Two Noble Kinsmen* for Arden Shakespeare 4, co-editing Marston's *The Fawn* (Oxford University Press), and completing a book on the effects of early modern women's rope-dancing on the Shakespearean stage.

André Morin is an actor, singer, and composer. He was a member of the Stratford Festival Company for nine seasons and is currently a member of the Shaw Festival ensemble. Recent credits include Parry in Kate Hennig's *The Virgin Trial* (Soulpepper) and Seymour in *Little Shop of Horrors* and Ariel in *The Tempest* (Stratford Festival). At the Engendering the Stage Stratford workshop, André performed the role of Lucio for scene work on *Love's Cure, or the Martial Maid.*

Lucy Munro is professor of Shakespeare and early modern literature at King's College London. She is the author of *Children of the Queen's Revels: A Jacobean Theatre Repertory* (Cambridge University Press, 2005), *Archaic Style in English Literature, 1590–1674* (Cambridge University Press, 2013), and *Shakespeare in the Theatre: The King's Men* (Bloomsbury, 2020); her work as a textual editor includes the Arden Early Modern Drama edition of *The Witch of Edmonton* (2016). With Peter Cockett, Melinda Gough, and Clare McManus, she is a lead investigator of the international Engendering the Stage research project. She is currently writing a new history of the Globe and Blackfriars playhouses that seeks to put theatre history into dialogue with current scholarship on gender, race, and colonization.

Marcus Nance is a singer and actor who has worked on Broadway, at the Shaw and Stratford Festivals, and in many opera, concert, and cabaret venues in North America. He has been a member of the Stratford Festival Company for twelve seasons. Recent credits include *A Strange Loop* (Soulpepper, Crows, Musical Stage, TO Live), *The Little Prince* (Pacific Opera Victoria), *Natasha Pierre* (Crows, Musical Stage), *Cymbeline, Frankenstein Revived* (Stratford Festival). For the 2018 Stratford workshop, he performed the role of Amintor in scene work on *The Maid's Tragedy.*

Denise Oucharek is a director, performer, and educator who has appeared on stages across Canada, including three seasons at the Stratford Festival. Denise received her BMus and BEd from Queen's University and is a proud recipient of a Mississauga Arts Council award. Denise has been a member of the voice faculty at Sheridan College and University of Toronto (theatre and drama studies), has taught vocal improv at Second City, teaches/coaches privately, and has served as artistic director for Theatre Atoms. For the Engendering the Stage workshop at Stratford, she performed the role of Guzmán in scene work on *The Lieutenant Nun*.

E.M. Parry is a trans-disciplinary artist and award-winning designer, working across scenography, performance, drag, and visual art. Design for theatre includes *Richard III, Hamlet, As You Like It* (Shakespeare's Globe); *Translyria* (Sogn og Fjordane Teater, Norway); *Effigies of Wickedness* (Gate Theatre/ENO); *Rotterdam* (Arts Theatre/Trafalgar Studios/Theatre503 – London, 59E59 Theatre – New York, and UK Tour – Olivier Award Winner 2018); *We Dig* (Emma Frankland & Co./Ovalhouse); *An Improbable Musical* (Improbable/Royal & Derngate); *The Tempest* (Regent's Park); and *As You Like It* (Northern Broadsides). Their designs were included in Staging Places: UK Design for Performance (V&A Museum), and they've shown work at Prague Quadrennial, Fix 23 Live Art Festival, Belfast, and Brighton Festival, among other platforms. Their first solo exhibition, *Closet Dramas*, was shown at hARTslane Gallery, London. E.M. Parry trained at Motley and Wimbledon School of Art and completed a PhD at the University of Brighton in 2024, exploring trans and queer history through creative practice.

Jessica Swain is an instructor at Kwantlen Polytechnic University. As a PhD candidate in the English and cultural studies program at McMaster University, her dissertation, "The Performance of Feminine Virtue: Rethinking Miranda's Role in *The Tempest*," examines the production of female chastity through forms of theatricality shared by early modern English gardens and court masques. Jessica was a graduate student research assistant for the Engendering the Stage Stratford workshop.

Edward McLean (Mac) Test is professor in the Department of Theatre, Film, and Creative Writing at Boise State University. He is the author of *Sacred Seeds: New World Plants in English Literature* (University of Nebraska Press, 2019). Dr. Test has published articles on Mesoamerican culture in English literature and is the recipient of grants and fellowships from the Idaho Humanities Council, the NEH Summer Seminar, and the Huntington, Folger Shakespeare, and John Carter Brown libraries. A poet and translator of Spanish, he has published a book of poetry and three books of translated poetry. Dr. Test is editor and translator (with Dr. Marta Albalá Pelegrín, Cal Poly Pomona) of the first annotated English translation of *La monja alférez* (1626), under the title *The Lieutenant Nun:*

Annotated Translation of the Play, Historical Accounts and Documents about Antonio/Catalina de Erauso (Routledge, 2025).

Ellen R. Welch is professor of French at UNC-Chapel Hill. Her research specializes in early modern French literature with a focus on theatre and performance. She has published on plays by Molière, Rotrou, Scudéry, and Tristan l'Hermite, and on casting and costuming in seventeenth-century court ballet. Her most recent book, *A Theatre of Diplomacy: International Relations and the Performing Arts in Early Modern France* (University of Pennsylvania Press, 2017), investigates how multimedia theatrical entertainments mediated France's diplomatic relationships within and beyond Europe from 1565 to 1715.

Index

Figures are indicated by page numbers in *italics*.

[illegible]